Montgomery County Tennessee

COUNTY COURT MINUTES

VOLUME 12

1823–1824

WPA RECORDS

Heritage Books
2024

HERITAGE BOOKS

AN IMPRINT OF HERITAGE BOOKS, INC.

Books, CDs, and more—Worldwide

For our listing of thousands of titles see our website
at
www.HeritageBooks.com

A Facsimile Reprint
Published 2024 by
HERITAGE BOOKS, INC.
Publishing Division
5810 Ruatan Street
Berwyn Heights, MD 20740

Nashville, Tennessee
The Tennessee Historical Records Survey
April 1942

International Standard Book Number
Paperbound: 978-0-7884-9084-2

Note: Page numbers in this index refer to those of the original volume
from which this copy was made. These numbers are carried in the body of
the manuscript within parentheses.

Friday July Term 1822

(p-1) ROBERT VANCE & SAM'L KERCHEVAIL)
                      Vs   ) Case
       SAMUEL CHAPMAN   )

This day came the parties by their attornies & thereupon came a
Jury of good & lawful men towit, William Bryant, John Rudolph, John
Caldwell, Joel Crizzard, David Northington, Joseph Bowers, James Hubbard,
Willie Lynes, Wm L. White, Bazell Nelson, Edward L. Walton, Habca C.
Miller who being duly elected, tried & sworn the truth to speak upon the
issues joined upon their oaths do say, that they find the issues in behalf
of the said plaintiffs and that they assess the plaintiffs damages, by
reason of the nonperformance of the several promises in the said plaintiffs
declaration mentioned to four hundred and fifty five dollars sixty two and
one half cents--It is therefore considered by the Court here that the said
plaintiffs, Robert Vance & Samuel Kerchevail recover of the said Defendant
Samuel Chapman, the aforesaid sum of Four hundred and fifty five dollars
and sixty two & one half cents and the costs in this behalf expended.

Upon the application of John Jones & it appearing to the Court,
that he had become the purchaser from Alfred M. Shelby of an undivided
half of a tract of land, that belonged to John Shelby in his life time
bounded on the north by the Kentucky line on the East by Blakney's trail,
on the South by Blakney's Clarkslo Shelby's & Thomas Shelby's heirs lands,
on the West by Alfred M. Shelby lying between the little West fork of Red
River & the State line in this County and it also appearing that the said
Anthony B. Shelby Guardian of Clark Moller Shelby, who owns the other half
had notice of this application & that he also consents to this application
for a division of the same. It is thereupon ordered by the Court that
Francis Baker, Isaac Garrott Ambrose Davy, Sales Selby, David McMinus,
Eebedee Dennis, Elijah Hancock, Shaderick Trammel, Wm Mann or any five of
them partition said land agreeably to law & make return to the next term
of this Court.

(p-2) JOHN MILLER   )
                      Vs   ) Debt
       DAVID ANDERSON & JAMES SMITH)

This day came plaintiff by his Atto. & the Defendants David Anderson & James Smith being solemnly called to come into Court & plead to the
said plffs. declaration failed so to do. It is therefore considered by
the Court that the Court that the said James Miller recover of the said
David Anderson & James Smith the sum of Three hundred & seventy seven
dollars & fifty cents The Debt in the declaration mentioned and also the
sum of twenty two dollars, damages for the detention of the said Debt and
also the costs in this behalf expended.

HENRY SMALL County Trustee)
    Vs   ) Appeal
HUGH CAMPBELL.)

This day came the parties by their attornies and thereupon came a jury of good & lawful men, toWit, Wm Bryant, John Rudolph, John Caldwell, John Grizzard, David Northington & Joseph Bowers, James Hubbard, William Seagrum, William S. White, Bazell Dolson, Edward L. Walton & Hosea C. Miller who being duly elected, tried and sworn the truth to speak upon the matters in controversy between the said parties upon their oaths do say that they find the Defdt. indebted to the plff. as County Trustee in the sum of Thirty dollars. It is therefore considered by the Court that the said Henry Small County recover of the Defdt. the said sum of Thirty dollars and also the Costs in this behalf expended. From which Judgment the defendant prays an appeal to the Circuit Court of Montgomery County & entered into bond & security satisfactory to the Court the same is allowed.

(p-3)   AMBROSE MADISON)
         Vs   ) Debt
      PHILIP JOHNSON)

And now at this day came the defendants and prayed an appeal to to the Circuit Court of Montgomery County, in the nature of a Writ of Error & having given bond & security satisfactory to the Court the same is allowed.

    Court adjourned untill tomorrow morning to meet at nine O'clock.
                        David Gould
                        Jas. Barret
                        James Dennison

The Worshipful County Court of Montgomery County have met according to adjournment Saturday July 20th 1822
Present
    David Gould)
    James Barret) Esquires
    Isaac Dennison) Justices

JAMES MCCAULEY)
      VS   ) Case
DEMPSEY BULL & PETER P. ROBERTS)

This day came the plaintiff by his attorney & the defendants Dempsey Bull & Peter P. Roberts being solemnly caled to come into Court & prosecute his said suit, came not, but made default. ~~////////////////////////////////~~ but the Court not knowing what damages the plaintiff hath sustained in this case it is ordered that a jury come here at next & enquire of the same. Present David Gould, James Barret, & Colmore Duvall Esqrs. Justices.

JAMES SALMON)
     VS   ) Debt
C. H. P. MARR & CO.)

This day came the plaintiff by attorney & here in Court says he intends no further to prosecute this suit against two of said Def'ts. Peter H. Marr & Isaac Dennison, and thereupon the other defendant Constant (p-4) H. P. Marr comes into Court and freely confesses that he is indebted to said plaintiff the sum of three hundred & sixty five dollars, thirty seven cents. Therefore it is considered by the Court that the pl't'ff. recover against the defendant C. H. P. Marr said sum of three hundred sixty five dollars, thirty seven cents aforesaid confessed & his costs in this behalf expended &.
Execution stayed to first Dec'r. next.

FRANCIS MCMORDIE)
        VS   ) Debt
THOMAS SMITH   )

This day came the plaintiff by his attorney & the defendant being solemnly called came not nor does he defend this suit. Therefore it is considered by the Court that the plaintiff recover against said defendant the sum of one hundred & fifty eight dollars 56 cents Ballance of Debt in the declaration mentioned & the further sum of $1.55 cts. damages sustained by the detention of the debt and also the costs in this behalf expended &.

CHARLES BAILEY   )
        VS   ) Scire Facias
PETER P. ROBERTS)

This day came the plaintiff by his attorney and the said defendant being solemnly called to appear and defend this suit, but comes not but makes default. Therefore it is considered by the Court that the plaintiff recover against the defendant the sum of five hundred and twenty six dollars, twenty six cents the debt in the said writ of Scire Facias specified with interest thereon being the sum of fifteen dollars & fifty eight cents, as also as will the sum of twelve dollars & sixtyfour cents former costs in sd. suit specified as his costs expended in suing out & prosecuting this writ of Sci Fa.

ISAAC BENNIT   )
        VS   ) Debt & Sci Fa
JOHN SMITH & SHADERICK TRAPEL)

This day came into Open Court the plaintiff by his attorney & says he will no further prosecute his said suit against the defendant but dismisses the same, & the defendants here in Open Court assumes the payment of all the (p-5) Costs It is therefore considered by the Court that the plaintiff recover of the defendants the Costs in this behalf expended.

LUCY SMITH   )
        VS   ) Debt
JOHN H. SCRUGGS & SAM'L MCFALL)

This day came the parties by their attornies & thereupon all and singular the matters of law arising on the def'ts demurrer to the plaintiffs declaration being argued and by the Court here understood. Because it seems to the Court that the matters of law arrising on Deft's demurrer are not sufficient, It is considered by the Court that said demurrer be overruled and that the plaintiff recover against said defendants the sum of Eighty one dollars & thirteen cents Ballance of debt & damages in the declaration mentioned, & his costs in this behalf expended &.

STATE OF TENNESSEE)
VS   ) Indict. for an Assault & Battery
JOHN EDMONSON   )

This day came the Solicitor General //////// in behalf of the state as well as the defendant John Edmonson in Custody of the Sheriff of the County & was thereupon arraigned & upon his arraignment pleads not Guilty to the Bill of indictment & for his trial puts himself upon his County as does the Solicitor General likewise & thereupon came a Jury of good & lawful men (towit) John Noblett Jr. Richard Bridgwater, Leroy Kesee, William Brantley, James Trotter, Jacob Welker, Peter Rudolph, Francis Williams, Edward Faulk, James Miller Needham Whitfield & William Haynes who being duly elected, tried & sworn the truth to speak upon the issue of Traverse, the jury coming to the bar & informing the Court, that there was no possibility of their agreeing & thereupon by consent of parties the said Court ordered the said Jury to be discharged for the present term of this Court & that the (p-6), / ////// /// defendant be recognized to appear at the next Term of this Court.

STATE OF TENNESSEE)
VS   ) Indict for an assault & Battery
DAVID VAUGHN   )

This day came into Open Court David Vaughn & acknowledged himself bound & indebted to the State of Tennessee in the penal sum of Five hundred dollars for his personal appearance before the Court here on the first Thursday after the third Monday in October next then & there to answer the State of Tennessee on a Bill of Indictment for an assault & Battery & for his not departing hence without leave of Court & David Davis & John Taggart his securities appeared in Open Court & acknowledged themselves bound & indebted to the State of Tennessee in the penal sum of Two hundred & fifty dollars each for the personal appearance of said David Vaughn to be levied & to be void on condition that he makes his personal appearance before the Court here on the first Thursday after the third Monday in October next, to answer the State of Tennessee on a Bill of Indictment & for his not departing hence without leave of the Court.

VANCE & KERCHEVALL)
VS   ) Case
SAM'L CHAPMAN   )

To the opinion given in the progress of the trial and also for their refusal to charge the Jury in this cause the defendant by his counsel excepts & files his two bills of exceptions which are signed, sealed & made a part of the record in this cause / ////// /// ////

C. H. P. MARR)
  VS) On Execution
THOMAS NAPIER & ALEXANDER MARTIN)

Christopher C. Clements & John C. Collier Executors of of William Clements decd. who were Garnisheed by the plaintiff in this case, having filed their answer which being examined by the Court, & because (p-7) it seems to the Court, by anything contained in said affidavits that said Garnishees are no farther answerable, It is considered by the Court, that they be hence discharged & that the plaintiff pay the Costs in this behalf accrued.

PETER H. COLE)
  VS) Original
JOHN S. BALL) Attachment.

This day came the plaintiff by his attorney & it appearing to the Court, that Constant H. P. Marr from the examination of said Marr & Isaac Dennison, that on the 21st February 1822 & from the note of said Constant H. P. Marr dated 29th January 1822 that the said Marr was indebted to said defendant in the sum of sixty two dollars & ninety one cents by his note due 29th January 1822 for that amount, & it appearing from the examination of Wells Fowler & his note filed in the papers of this Cause, that he was indebted to said defendant in the sum of Twenty two dollars & fifty cents on the 5th January 1822, to be paid in work & it appearing from the affidavit of James Riggs & his note filed in the papers of this cause, that on the 11th January 1822, he was indebted to said defendant in the sum of Five dollars & it appearing Thomas Rivers & William R. Hanner are ////// indebted to the said defendant in the sum of Two dollars and it further appearing to the Court that said plaintiff at the April Term 1822 of this Court obtained each Judg't. against said defendant Ball for the sum of $162.00 & that the same is unpaid. All which having been duly considered by the Court. Because it seems to the Court that said debts due said Def't. Ball are in law liable & ought to be condemned subjected in the hands of sd. Garnishees to the satisfaction of said Judgment as aforesaid rendered in favor of Plaintiff against said Ball & that said Plaintiff have execution against (p-8) C. H. P. Marr for the sum of sixty four dollars & seventy five cents am't. of principal & interest now due on his said note, against Wells Fowler for the sum of twenty dollars & fifty eight cents against James Riggs for the sum of five dollars & fifteen cents princ'l, & Interest on his sd. note against Thomas Rivers for the sum of two dollars, against William R. Hanner for the sum of two dollars, ////////// //////// /.& that the costs of this garnishment be paid by the plaintiff & &.

STATE OF TENNESSEE)
  VS)
DAVID VAUGHN)

This day came said defendant by attorney & James Baker & Rebecca Smith each the sum of one hundred & twenty five dollars unless on or before the next term of this Court, they shew cause to the contrary & that a Scieri Facias issue & &.

STATE OF TENNESSEE)
  VS) Contempt
WILLIAM B. WALL)

It appearing to the Court that heretofore (towit) at the April Term 1822 of our said Court William B. Wall was appointed Overseer of the road leading from John P. Vaughn's mill by Gully Moore's to Palmyra & it appearing to the Court that said William B. Wall has refused to accept of the order appointing him overseer of said road & has not nor would not work on said road but has made contempt of this Court. It is therefore considered by the Court that the defendant be fined the sum of fifty dollars unless he comes forward at the next term of this Court & shew cause to the contrary, & that (p-9) a Scieri facias issue & &.

LABAN HOLT
    VS
WILLIAM WICKHAM &
ANTHONY W. VANLEER & CO } Motion

This day came the plaintiff Laban Holt by his attorney & thereupon it appearing to the Court that Samuel Smith Esqr. had issued an execution in behalf of the plaintiff Laban Holt against said William Wickham & Anthony W. Vanleer & Co directed to any lawful Officer to execute & return directing that of the goods & chattles lands & tenements of said William Wickham & Anthony W. Vanleer & Co. to make the sum of Fifty seven dollars thirty four & a half cents with Interest from the 7th of April 1821 to satisfy a Judgment of said Laban Holt rendered 7th April 1821 before the said Samuel Smith & also the costs of said suit, which said execution was issued on 26th June 1822 & placed in the hands of Brantly Sulivant a constable for said County for collection, upon which the said Brantly Sulivant made return thereon, that he had levied the same on One hundred & Eight Acres of land lying on the east Fork of Yellow Creek for the want of personal property belonging to William Wickham & upon motion of the said Laban Holt by his attorney—It is considered by the Court that a Venditioni Exponas issue to the sheriff of Montgomery County, commanding him to expose to sale the said tract of land, to satisfy the aforesaid Judgment & Costs & also the costs of this motion .

ANTHONY W. VANLEER & CO
    VS
WILLIAM WICKHAM } Motion

This day came the plaintiffs by their attorney William A. Cook Esqrs. & thereupon it appearing to the satisfaction of the Court, that Samuel Smith Esqr. had issued an execution in behalf of the said plaintiff Anthony W. Vanleer & Co against said William Wickham, directed to any lawful Officer to execute & (p-10) return, directing that of the goods, Chattles & lands & tenements of said William Wickham to make the sum of Twenty dollars & fifty cents, with Interest from the 24th of June 1820 to satisfy a Judgment of said Anthony W. Vanleer & Co. rendered 19th March 1822 before the said Samuel Smith Esqr. & also the Costs of said suit, which said execution was issued on the 23rd of March 1822 & placed in the hands of Brantley Sulivant a constable of Montgomery County for County for Collection, upon which said Brantley Sulivant made return, that he had levied the same on One hundred & eight acres of land lying on the east Fork of Yellow Creek for the want of personal property of William Wickham & upon motion of the said plaintiff by his attorney. It is considered by the Court, that a Venditioni Exponas issue to the Sheriff of Montgomery County commanding him to expose to sale said tract of land to satisfy the aforesaid Judgment & Costs & also the Costs of this motion.

ANTHONY W. VANLEER & CO ⎫
        VS   ⎬ Motion
WILLIAM WICKHAM   ⎭

This day came the plaintiffs by his attorney William A. Cook Esqr. & thereupon it appearing to the Court, that Samuel Smith Esqr. had issued an execution in behalf of the said plaintiff Anthony W. Vanleer & Co against the said William Wickham directed to any lawful Officer of Montgomery County, directing that of the goods & chattles, lands & tenements of said defendant to make the sum of Thirty eight dollars with interest from the 24th of June 1820 to satisfy a Judgment of said plaintiff rendered 19th March 1822, before the said Samuel Smith Esquire & also the Costs of said suit which said execution was placed in the hands of Brantley Sulivant a (p-11) constable of said County for collection, upon which he made return, that he had levied the same on, One hundred & eight Acres of land lying on the east Fork of Yellow Creek for the want of personal property of sd. William Wickham & upon motion of the said plaintiff by his attorney—It is Considered by the Court that a Venditioni Exponas issue to the sheriff of Montgomery County to Expose to sale said tract of land to satisfy the aforesaid Judgment & Costs & also the Costs of this motion.

LABON HOLT   ⎫
      VS   ⎪
WILLIAM WICKHAM &   ⎬ Motion
ANTHONY W. VANLEER & CO ⎭

This day came the plaintiff by his attorney William A. Cook Esqr. & thereupon it appearing to the Court, that Samuel Smith esqr. issued an execution in behalf of the said plaintiff Labon Holt against the said William Wickham & Anthony W. Vanleer & Co. directed to any lawful officer to execute & return directing that of the Goods & Chattles, lands & tenements of said defendant to make the sum of Fifty six dollars eighty four & a half cents with Interest thereon from the 7th of May 1821 to satisfy a Judgment of said plaintiff rendered 20th May 1822 & ////// //// //// before the said Samuel Smith esqr. & also the Costs of said suit which said execution was placed in the hands of Bartley Sulivant, a Constable of said County, upon which he made return that he had levied the same on One hundred & Eight Acres of land lying on the East fork of Yellow Creek, for the want of personal property belonging to the said William Wickham & upon Motion of the said plaintiff by his Attorney it is considered by the Court that a Venditioni Exponas issue to the Sheriff of Montgomery County Commanding him to expose to sale said tract of land to satisfy the aforesaid Judgment & Costs, & also the Costs of this Motion.

(p-12)   ANTHONY W. VANLEER & CO ⎫
           VS   ⎬ Motion
        WILLIAM WICKHAM   ⎭

This day came the plaintiff by his attorney & thereupon it appearing to the Court, that Samuel Smith esqr. issued an execution in behalf of said plaintiffs Anthony W. Vanleer & Co, against the said

William Wickham directed to any lawful officer of Montgomery County directing that of the goods & chattles lands & tenements of said defendant to make the sum of sixty six dollars & seventy one cents to satisfy a Judgment of said plaintiffs rendered 19th March 1822 with Interest thereon from the 24th December 1820 & also the Costs of said suit, which said execution was placed in the hands of Bartley Sulivant a constable of said County upon which he made return, that he had levied the same One hundred & eight acres of land lying on Yellow Creek (on the east Fork) for the want of personal property of William Wickham & upon Motion of said plaintiffs by their attorney— It is considered by the court that a Venditioni Expenas issue to the Sheriff of Montgomery County commanding him to Expose to sale said tract of land, to satisfy the aforesaid Judgment & Costs & also the Costs of this motion.

On motion it is ordered by the Court that John Hinton Executor of Kimbrough Hinton Deed. be permitted to return the Inventory of said Estate to the next Term of this Court, which in law should have been returned to the present term.

DAVID ANDERSON
   VS   } Original
JESSE COBB   } Attachment

This day came the plaintiff by his attorney & withdraws his motion, to dismiss the Judgment in this case entered on Wednesday of the present Term.

JOSHUA PIKE
   VS   } Certiorari &
CHRISTOPHER BULL } Superceedias

This day came the plaintiff by his attorney & moves the Court to dismiss the Certiorari & (p-13) superceedias in this cause, & the said plaintiff agrees that said motion shall be overruled.

On motion it is ordered by the Court, that Henry Small the present County Trustee, shall receive of Benjamin King, sheriff certificates for the maintainance of paupers & Jurors Certificates & any other Certificates that the County is liable to pay, in discharge of the County Tax for the year 1821, should such certificates be due & payable in said year.

JOSHUA PIKE
   VS   } Certiorari &
CHRISTOPHER BUTTS } Superceedias

On motion it is ordered by the Court, that a Commission issue to take the depositions of Jesse Cobb & Clark Cobb, who reside in Caldwell County Kentucky to be read in evidence in behalf of the defendant, upon giving the plaintiff Twenty days notice of time & place.

WILLIAM DEAN
   VS   }
RANSON SEXTON & } Case
LUCY SEXTON   }

On motion it is ordered by the Court, that a Commission issue to take the deposition of John Hall on Yellow Creek Dickson County upon giving the defendants Ten days notice of time & place to be read as evidence in behalf of the plaintiff on the trial of this case.

LEMUEL PETERS
VS } Case
CONSTANT H. P. MARR

On motion it is ordered by the Court, that the parties have liberty to take depositions upon giving thirty days notice if out of the State & if in the State Ten days notice.

This day came into Open Court William Trigg & Richard B. Blount two of the Commissioners appointed at the last Term of this Court, to take the privy examination of Anes Hyde the wife of John Hyde, Barbara Barker wife of Charles Barker //// // /////// ////// & Mary Merriwether (p-14) wife of Charles Merriwether concerning the execution of a Deed of Conveyance to Solomon Neville for Two hundred Acres of land & make their report to this Court, that they have examined the said Anna Barbara & Mary, seperate & apart from thier husbands & that they freely acknowledge that they executed the said deed of conveyance of their own free will & accord & without the influence or compulsion of their said husbands & on motion the same is ordered to be certified for Registration.

HENRY SMALL Trustee
VS } Appeal
ASHBEL BRUKIN

This day came the parties by their attornies & thereupon came a jury of good & lawful men (towit) William Bryant, John Rudolph, John Caldwell, Joel Grizard, David Northington, Joseph Bowers, James Hubbard, Willie Lyons, William S. White, Dazel Nelson, Edward S. Walton, Hosea C. Miller, who being duly elected tried & sworn the truth to speak the matters in controversy between the parties, upon their Oath do say that they find the defendant indebted to the plaintiff as County Trustee in the sum of Twenty five dollars. It is therefore considered by the Court that the said Henry Small Trustee recover of the said defendant, the said sum sum of Twenty five dollars & also the costs in this behalf Expended. From which Judgment the defendant prays an appeal to the Circuit Court for Montgomery County & having given bond & security satisfactory to the Court, the same is allowed.

THOMAS MCGWIRE
VS } Appeal
THOMAS TRAVIS

This day came the plaintiff by his attorney & says he will no further prosecute his said suit against the defendant but dismisses the same, & the defendant assumes the (p-15) payment of all the Costs. It is therefore considered by the Court, that the plaintiff recover of the defendant his cost his suit in this behalf Expended.

```
CHARLES BAILEY   )
        VS       )  Sci. Fa.
PETER P. ROBERTS )
```

This day came the defendant Peter P. Roberts & prays an appeal to the Circuit Court of Montgomery County & entered into bond & security satisfactory to the Court, the same is allowed.

Benjamin & James Jones Executors of Thomas Jones decd. came into Court & returned an Inventory of the estate of the said Thomas Jones decd. & qualified agreeable to law, & on motion the same is ordered to be Recorded.

A Deed of Conveyance from Henry H. Bryan, Edward Neblett, John Neblett Jr. & Benjamin Neblett to Eli Lockert for Lott No. seventy three & part of lott No. 75 in the town of Clarksville was duly proven in Open Court by the oath of Edward H. Steele & Peter H. Cole as to the execution of said deed by John Neblett Jr. & proved by the oaths of said Edward H. Steele & Samuel Vance as to execution of said deed by said John Neblett, Edward Neblett & Benjamin Neblett (they being subscribing witnesses thereto) & on motion the same is ordered to be certified.

A Deed of Gift from Thomas Blakeny to Oliver Balkeny son of Harriet Blakeney for four Negroes (names as follows) Chainey, Vina, George, & Ephraim was duly acknowledged in Open Court by the said Thomas Blakeney to be his act & deed for the purposes therein contained, & on motion ordered to be Registered.

A Deed of Gift from Thomas Blakeney to Thomas Blakeney Jr. son of Harrett Blakeney for sundry negroes, was duly acknowledged in Open Court by the said Thomas Blakeney to be his act & deed for the purpose therein contained & on motion ordered to be Registered.

(p-16)   A Deed of gift from Thomas Blakeney to John Blakeney Jr. son of Harriet Blakeney for sundry Negroes was duly acknowledged in Open Court by the said Thomas Blakeney to be his act & deed for the purposes therein contained-& on motion ordered to be Registered.

Philip Johnson appeared in Open Court & with the assent of the Court renewed his Tavern License for the next twelve months which was dated back to April Term last by the order of this Court, & entered into bond & security satisfactory to the Court & qualified agreeable to law.

Jeremiah Brown appeared in Open Court & with the assent of the Court, renewed his tavern license for the next twelve months & entered into bond & security satisfactory to the Court & qualified agreeable to law.

Hiram Cooper, Stephen Mallory & Merida Howard commissioners appointed at the last Term of this Court to lay off a years provision for the widow Apperson, make report to this Court & on motion ordered to be Recorded.

On motion it is ordered by the Court that William B. Nelson overseer of the road from the first Fork beyond the ferry of Red River to Hugh F. Bells & have the following hands to work under him on said road (towit),

Thomas Dunbar's hands, Elisha R. Oldham's hands, James G. Hamilton, John Hamilton, George & French Gray, William & Rich'd Hust, Robert Nelson, Elizabeth Nelson's hands, Christopher Oxon's hands, John Chipman, Asa Walter & Armstrong & all other hands that may move with the bounds of said road & that the former order be repeated.

Amos Hatcher overseer of the road from Thomas Travis's to the line Kiln hollow, have the following hands to work on said road under him (to wit) said Hatcher's own hands, Charles Cherry & Thomas Travis's hands, & that the former order be repeated.

(p-17)   On motion it is ordered by the Court, that Henry W. Merriwether overseer of the road from his ferry to the corner of William S. White's field, have the following hands to work under him on said road (to wit) Henry Merriwether's own hands, Newton Sims, Alexander Sims, Henderson's two hands, Willie Seagraves, Thomas Cherry, Jacob Gordan & hands, Bright Herring's hands, James Herring, Bright Herring Jr., Benja. Herring & hands, Spirus Herring, Mrs. Cherry's hands Elisha Reed, William S. White & hands, Samuel Smith's hands, Joseph Hamelton, William Hamelton & Polly Hatcher's hands, & that the former order be repeated.

On motion it is ordered by the Court, that William Stewart be appointed overseer of the road leading from Weakly's ferry to the Robertson County line in place of Howel U. Atkins who was appointed at the last term of this Court through mistake & that the same hands that worked under the former overseer, Joseph Smith, work under the said William Stewart.

On motion it is ordered by the Court that Alexander Vaughn be appointed overseer of the road from Clarksville to Wyatt's ferry in place of Matthew D. Simmons & that all the hands within the bounds of said road work under him the said overseer.

Ordered by the Court that William Brantley be appointed overseer of the road from Clarksville to Merriwether's ferry over Red River & that the following hands work under him on said road, towit, George Dulin's hands, James Elder's hands, James B. Reynold's (p-18) hands, & the hands of said Brantley.

On motion it is ordered by the Court that Raner an orphan of Lucy Sanders be bound to William J. Lynes as a house servant & the said William J. Lynes entered into bond & security agreeable to law.

On motion it is ordered by the Court that John Comperry be bound to William Curry to learn the trade of a house Carpenter, & the said William Curry entered into bond & security agreeable to law.

On motion it is ordered by the Court, that James Wages be bound to Ch. H. P. Narr to learn the trade of a Brick Mason, & the said C. H. P. Narr ~~// //////// //// ////// // / ///// /////~~. // //// ////// enter'd into bond & security agreeable to law.

On motion it is ordered by the Court that Rufus Comperry an orphan of Francis Comperry, be bound to Matthew D. Simmons to learn the trade of a house Carpenter, & the said Simmons entered into bond & security agreeable to law.

On motion it is ordered by the Court that Robert Comporry an orphan of Francis Comporry be bound to John B. Penrise to learn the trade of a Hatter & the said John B. Penrise enter'd into bond & security agreeable to law.

A Bond from Daniel Durham to Ambrose Davie for the conveyance of one hundred & fifty four acres of land, was duly proven in Open Court by the oath of John Davie a subscribing witness thereto & on motion ordered to be certified for registration.

A Deed of conveyance from William A. Cook to Joel C. Rice for part of a town lott in the town of Clarksville, was duly acknowledged in Open Court by the said William A. Cook to be his act (p-19) A Deed for the purposes therein contained & on motion ordered to be certified for registration.

A Division of sixteen hundred & sixteen acres of land signed by Thomas Watson & John H. Marable was duly proven in Open Court by the Oaths of Nathaniel H. Allen, John Caldwell & James H. Smith the subscribing witnesses thereto, & on motion the same is ordered to be certified for registration.

A Deed of Conveyance from John Linder to Charles Hodges for 25 Acres of land, was duly //////////// proven in Open Court by the Oath of John S. Mosley one of the subscribing witnesses thereto & on motion ordered to be certified.

Samuel Smith, John Henderson & Bright Herring Commissioners appointed appointed to divide a tract of land between Charles Cerry & Jeremiah Cherry make their report to Court accompanied with John Caldwell surveyor & on motion ordered to be Recorded.

A Deed of Mortgage from John H. Scruggs & Thenea Thomas to Samuel McFall & Lewis T. Poindexter for a Town lett in the town of Clarksville was duly acknowledged in Open Court by John H. Scruggs & on motion ordered to be certified.

Valentine Allen Esqr. returns into Court the list of Taxable property taken on Capt. John M. Smith's Company for the present year.

Maurice Morris Administrator of the estate of Thomas Morris decd. returned into Open Court an Inventory of said Estate & qualified agreeable to law, & on motion the same is ordered to be Recorded.

The Court proceeded to appoint Jurors to the next October County Court (towit) Peter Wade, Thomas Brodie, John Worthington, Richard Anderson, John Thompson, Thomas Biggers, John Perdue Junr. John Ogburn, Peter P. Roberts (p-20) John Steele, Capt. William Allen, Daniel Rook, William E. Williams, James Brown (Fidler) Nathaniel D. Terry, James Grant, Robert G. Johnson, James Trice Sr. Robert Nelson, Leigh Trice, Manoah Bostick, Stephen Mallery, George W. Blanks, William Killebrew & John Henderson, John Rook, John S. Mosly & Joseph Barbee.

William B. Dancy & Samuel Croath are appointed constables to attend at the next October County Court.

STATE OF TENNESSEE)
        VS   ) Indict. for
JOHN EDMONSON   ) Lewdness

The defendant John Edmonson by his Counsil, on the trial of this case objected to part of the evidence of Mark Thomason the prosecutor in this case and filed his Bill of exception which is signed, sealed & made a part of the Record in this case.

A Deed of Conveyance from Richard B. Dallam admr. of Richard Dallam decd. & attorney in fact for John J. W. Dallam & William S. Dallam heirs of R. Dallam decd. to Jesse Parker, for 183 Acres of land was duly proven in Open Court by the oath of Herbert Whelis, one of the subscribing witnesses thereto & on motion the same is ordered to be certified.

SAMUEL C. HAWKINS)
        VS   ) Debt
JOSHUA WASHBURN)

This day came the plaintiff by his attorney C. Johnson Esqr. & says he will no further prosecute his said suit against the defendant
         but dismisses the same. It is therefore considered by the Court
Cost   that the defendant Joshua Washburn recover of the plaintiff
pd. in Samuel C. Hawkins, the cost in this behalf Expended.
part

(p-21)   ALEXANDER M. BARKER)
             VS   ) Trespass
        WILLIAM G. GRIGGS) vi et Armis

This day came the plaintiff by his attorney, & says he will no farther prosecute his said suit against the defendant but dismisses the same & the defendant assumes the payment of all the Costs. It is therefore considered by the Court, that said suit stand dismissed & that the plaintiff recover of the defendant his Costs about his suit in this behalf Expended.

FRANCIS MCMORDIE asseo)
        VS   ) Debt
WILLIAM J. LYLES)

This day came the plaintiff by his attorney F. W. Huling esqr. & says he will no further prosecute his said against the defendant but dismisses the same & the Plaintiff here in Open Court assumes the payment of all the Costs except the attornies tax fee, which he releases. It is therefore considered by the Court that said suit stand dismissed, & that the defendant recover of the plaintiff his Costs about his defence in this behalf expended.

Court adjourned untill Monday morning to meet at 9 O'clock.
                    David Gould
                    Thos. Smith
                    James Dennison

The Worshipful County Court of Montgomery County have met according to adjournment Monday July 22nd, 1822

Present David Gould)
         Thomas Smith) Esquires
         Isaac Dennison) Justices

(p-22)   On motion it is ordered by the Court, that the Clerk of this Court, ~~give~~ give up to John S. Ball the following notes, which have not been Garnisheed on (towit) A. Howard's note for $5- John Edmonston's note for $20.75 ¢, James C. Hunt's note for $53.86 cts., Hardy Hollands note for $1.75, Hugh Brantley's note for $2—Roger Shackleford's note for 3.00 Wiley Segraves note for $3.25, which said notes were delivered into Court by Isaac Dennison on a Garnishee at the instance of Samuel Vance against John S. Ball—

     Court adjourned untill tomorrow morning to meet at 9 O'clock.
         David Gould
         Jas. Barret
         James Dennison

The Worshipful County Court of Montgomery have met according to adjournment Tuesday July 23rd 1822.

Present David Gould)
         James Barret) Esquires
         Isaac Dennison) Justices

On motion it is ordered by the Court that Birch Rowland & Richard T. Merriwether Jurors who were summoned to attend at the present Term of the Court have failed so to do. It is therefore considered by the Court that sd. Birch Rowland and Richard T. Merriwether Jurors who were summoned to attend at the present Term of the Court, have failed so to do— It is therefore considered by the Court, that sd. Birch Rowland & Richard T. Merriwether be fined the sum of Five dollars each unless they come here at next Court and show Cause to the contrary & that a Sci Fa issue & &.

     Court adjourned untill Court in Course.
         James Dennison
         Jas. Barret
         David Gould

(p-23)   The Worshipful Court of Montgomery County have met according to adjournment Monday October 21st 1822

Present

Matthew Ryburn   )
Thomas W. Atkinson   )
Sterling Neblett   )   Esquires
Alexander M. Rogers   )   Justices

On motion it is ordered by the Court, that Joseph Woolfolk, James Carr Edward S. Walton & John Nevill or any two of them, be appointed Commissioners to lay off the Dower of Sarah Collier, wife of Daniel Collier & make report to the next Term of this Court.

On motion it is ordered by the Court, that Brice Jackson have a credit of Three dollars for that amount over charged him by the Clerk in the making out the list of Taxable property for 1821 & that he have a credit on his present years tax list for the same.

On motion it is ordered by the Court, that Matthew Ryburn Esqr., Abner Gupton Esqr. & Joseph John Williams, be appointed commissioners to settle with Harbert Ally administrator of Miles Ally decd. & make report to the next term of this Court.

On Motion it is ordered by the Court, that Daniel Morrison be appointed Overseer of the road leading from Levi Smith's old Ferry to William Corlew's spring in place of James H. Roberts & that the same hands that worked under said James H. Roberts, work under the said Daniel Morrison together with the hands of Samuel Roberts, Edward Neblett & Moses Collier's, Whitmill Harper, Thomas Tucker & James H. Roberts & hands.

On motion it is ordered by the Court that Charles Bailey be allowed the sum of three Dollars for serving as a juror in the Circuit Court in the case of the State of Tennessee against Stephen D. B. Stewart as per his certificate filed in Court & that the County Trustee pay the same out of any money not otherwise appropriated.

(p-24)   Andrew Lynn come into Court & give in his resignation to the appointment of constable which is accepted by the Court.

William Neblet Renders into Court a list of his Taxable property for the year 1822 which is ordered to be annexed to the present years tax list.

On motion it is ordered by the Court that Ambrose Davie be appointed overseer of the road from Fletcher's fork to the Kentucky line, in the place of Edwin D. Killebrew, who has resigned & that the following hands work on said road under the said Ambrose Davie (towit) Douglass Merriwether & hands, Zebediah Dennis & hands, Glidwell Killebrew & hands, Francis Baker & hands, Robert Hester & hands Joseph Hewell, Isaac Garrett & hands William C. Scott, William Casey, Thomas Blakeney's hands William Faulkner's hands, Alfred M. Shelby's William Thomas & all others within the bounds of said road.

On motion it is ordered by the Court, that Sanford Wilson have liberty to renew his Tavern license for the next twelve months & the said Sanford Wilson entered into bond & security agreeable to law which was approved of by the Court.

On motion is is ordered by the Court that Thomas Smith & Stephen Cooke Esquires & Joshua P. Vaughn Esqr. be appointed commissioners to settle with Elisha R. Oldham admr. of Moses Oldham decd. & make return to the ////// next term of this Court.

On motion it is ordered by the Court that Lucy Joiner be exonerated from the payment of more than the one half appraised value of a certain stray mare posted on the 8th September 1821 & that the County Trustee shall receive the //// half appraised value in discharge of said stray.

(p-25)   On motion it is ordered by the Court, that Henry Williams, Alexander Hamilton, Hiram Bobo, John Gosset, Vincent Ennis, Joseph Woodson, & James Wilson, be appointed a jury of View to alter the road leading from Port Royal to Mosley's ferry, leaving the road between Reuben Holt's field & David R. Slaughter plantation to intersect with the Springfield road & thence on to Mosley's ferry & make report of the same to the the next Term of this Court.

On motion it is ordered by the Court, that Leroy Kezee, be appointed overseer of the Road leading from Port Royal to Hopkinsville, Ky beginning on the north edge of Red River, thence on the main road four miles, and that said Kezee's hands & that the following hands work on said road (towit) Jesse Barlow, David Holland, William Faulk's hands, Nathaniel McRoyster, Hardy Holland, George Gardner, Moses Grant, William Bryan Vardaman Halsel, Etheldred Hargrove, Young Hargrove, Robert Bryan, James Lester, Thomas Reasons ///// ////// / ///// /// /// //// // /// ///// John S. Williamson & hands & those persons who may live on his lands & all others who may live on his lands & all others who may live within the bounds, work on said Road.

The Jury of View appointed at the last Term of this Court to turn the road leading by John Edmonson's report as follows (towit) Pursuant to an order of Court to us directed, we have this day proceeded to the View the road as as to avoid John Edmonson's mill pond, we all agree & say that the road remain, where it is, as we cannot turn it to an advantage, James Carr, Edward S. Walton, Z. Grant, Felix Allen, Jesse Cooksey & James Grant.

On motion it is ordered by the Court, that Henry McFall Sr., & Henry McFall Jr., be permitted to give in their list of Taxable for the present year & that the same be annexed to the Tax list.

(p-26)   On motion is is ordered by the Court, that Washington Lee, be appointed overseer of the road from the mouth of the West Fork to James Trice's Junr. & that the following hands work on said road under said Washington Lee (towit) Abraham Brantley & hands, Hugh Brantley, James Bird, Lewis Trice, Samuel McNichol & hands, Taylor Chisam & hands & John A. Scott & all others who live within the bounds of said, who have not heretofore been ordered to work on any other road.

On motion it is ordered by the Court that Francis Baker & Robert Hester, be appointed commissioners to settle with Thomas W. Atkinson Administrator of Daniel Bain Decd. & make report to the next term of this Court.

On motion it is ordered by the Court that the Clerk of this Court, issue Certificates to the Jurors and witnesses who attend on behalf the State of Tennessee in the Two Cases of said State of Tennessee against Negro slaves, Travis & Kinchen, the Records of which proceedings are filed in said Clerk's office, & that the County Trustee pay the same out of any monies not otherwise appropriated.

On motion it is ordered by the Court that Thomas Travis be appointed Commissioner & that he be empowered to sell the property which belonged to John Sims Decd. (towit) Peter a negro man, Lucy a negro woman & her five children, to be sold on a credit of nine months for the purpose of making a division among the children of said Sims Decd.---Mary Travis formerly Mary Sims consenting & wishing the same said Travis giving Twenty days notice of time & place.

On motion it is ordered by the Court that James Davis have a License to keep an Ordinary & at his now dwelling house in this County & the said James Davis entered into bond &security agreeable to law, which is approved of by the Court.

(p-27)   On motion it is ordered by the Court, that a Licence issue to Lovet Morris to keep an Ordinary at his dwelling house in this County & the said Lovet Morris entered into bond & security agreeable to law, which is approved of by the Court.

On motion it is ordered by the Court, that Daniel Rook be appointed Overseer of the road leading from Well's Old Ferry to Benjamin Whiteheads, in place of Hayden E. Wells, who has resigned, & that the same hands that were ordered to work under the sd. Hayden E. Wells, work under the said Daniel Rook & all other hands that live within the bounds of said ///// ///// road, who have not heretofore been ordered to work on any other Road.

Howel U. Atkins appeared in Open Court & with the assent of the Court, rendered his Bond as Constable for the next two years & duly qualified as such, which was satisfactory to the Court.

There was present the following Justices (towit) Sterling Neblett, Francis Baker, Charles Bailey, Thomas W. Atkinson Matthew Ryburn, J. P. Vaughn, Stephen Cooke, Abner Gupton, Am M. Rogers & Stephen Pettus.

The Court proceeded to the election of a Constable in place of Andrew Sims who has resigned, & the poles being opened, they proceeded to the election & after the votes being Counted out, there appeared a majority in favour of Jeremiah Brown, who was elected Constable in due form, & the said Jeremiah Brown came into Court & entered into bond & security satisfactory to the Court & qualified accordingly.

On motion it is ordered by the Court that Thomas Walker be appointed Guardian to Nancy Bridges & Elizabeth Bridges, & the said Thomas Walker appeared in Open Court & entered & entered into bond & security satisfactory to the Court & qualified agreeable to law.

(p-28)   On motion it is ordered by the Court, that letters of Administration be granted to Thomas Williams on the Estate of William McCauley decd. & the said Thomas Williams entered into bond & security satisfactory to the Court & qualified agreeable to law.

On motion it is ordered by the Court, that letters of Administration be granted to Robert G. Johnson & Abner V. Hampton, on the Estate of Philip Johnson decd. & the said Robert G. Johnson & Abner V. Hampton on the Estate of Philip Johnson decd. & the said Robert G. Johnson & Abner V. Hampton entered bond & security satisfactory to the Court & qualified agreeable to Law.

On motion it is ordered by the Court that Warren Bryan be bound to Hardy Bryan, to learn the art or Mistery of farming untill he attains to the age of Twenty one years, & the said Hardy Bryan came into Court & entered into articles of agreement agreeable to law.

On motion it is ordered by the Court that Edward Trice be appointed first Inspector of Tobacco at ~~////~~ Cheatham & Trice's ware house at the mouth of Red River & also at Thomas W. Atkinson's warehouse on the north side of Cumberland River & the said Edward Trice entered into bond & security satisfactory to the Court & qualified agreeable to law.

On motion it is ordered by the Court that Nace F. Trice, be appointed second Inspector of Tobacco at Cheatham & Trice's warehouse at the mouth of the Red River & also at Thomas W. Atkinson's ware house on the north side of Cumberland River & the said Nace F. Trice entered into bond & security satisfactory to the Court & qualified agreeable to law.

On motion it is ordered by the Court, that John Dunn, an orphan of Benjamin ~~// ////////~~ Dunn be bound to Samuel Grant to learn the BlackSmith's Trade & the said Samuel Grant came into Court & entered into articles of agreement agreeable to law.

(p-29)   Alexander M. Rogers & Sterling Noblett, commissioners appointed at the last Term of this Court to settle with John Wyatt Guardian of Sally Ussory, make their report to this Court & on motion ordered to be Recorded.

A Deed of conveyance from Robert Sawers to Robert Hester for 24 Acres of land was produced in Open Court, & the execution thereof was duly acknowledged in Open Court by the said Robert Sawers to be his act & deed for the purposes therein contained & on motion ordered to be Certified for Registration.

A Deed of Conveyance from Richard B. Blount to Solomon Nevill Sr., was duly acknowledged in Open Court by the said Richard B. Blount to be his act & deed for the purposes therein contained & on motion ordered to be Registered for 100 Acres of land.

A Deed of Conveyance from Booth Malone to Hanoah Taylor for 104 acres of land, was duly proven in Open Court by the oaths of Needham Whitfield & Bryan Whitfield, two of the subscribing witnesses thereto, & on motion ordered to be certified for registration.

A Deed of Conveyance from James Adams to John Adams for 50 Acres of land was duly acknowledged in Open Court by the said James Adams to be his act & Deed for the purposes therein contained & on motion ordered to be Certified for Registration.

A Deed of Conveyance from William Fortson to John S. Johnson for 333 Acres of land, was duly acknowledged in Open Court by the said William Fortson to be his act & Deed for the purposes therein contained & on motion ordered to be certified for Registration.

A Deed Conveyance from John S. Johnson to William Fortson for 333 Acres of land was duly acknowledged in Open Court by the said John S. Johnson to be his act & deed for the purposes therein contained & on motion ordered to be certified for registration.

(p-30) A Deed of conveyance from James Easly to Richard Daly for 60 acres of land, was duly acknowledged in Open Court by the said James Easly to be his act & deed for the purposes therein contained & on motion ordered to be certified for Registration.

A Deed for conveyance from Isaac Garrot to Ambrose Davie for 2 Acres of land was duly proven in Open Court by the oaths of Jacob Garrot & Jones Davie two of the subscribing witnesses thereto & on motion ordered to be certified for Registration.

A Deed of conveyance from Christopher C. Clements & John C. Collier Executors of the last will & Testament of William Clements Decd. to Mary Jordan an infant daughter of Seth B. Jordon's for 320 Acres of land was produced in Open Court & the execution thereof was duly proven by the oath of William Thornton a subscribing witness thereto & on motion ordered to be Certified.

A Bill of Sale from Samuel Daniel to Elizabeth Davis for a Negroe Girl named Caroline was produced in Open Court & the execution thereof was duly proven by the Oaths of William Mayes & John Brigs the subscribing witnesses, thereto, & on motion ordered to be Recorded.

A Deed of Trust from Daniel Kyle to John W. Barker, was produced in Open Court & the execution was duly proven by the Oath of Bryan Whitfield one of the subscribing witnesses thereto & on motion ordered to be Certified accordingly.

A Power of Attorney from Robert Armisted to George E. Spruce was produced in Open (p-31) Court & the execution thereof duly acknowledged in Open Court, by the sd. Robert Armisted to be his act & deed for the purposes therein contained & on motion ordered to be Certified.

A Deed of Conveyance from Thomas Walker & Elizabeth Walker his wife, to Alsa Jones for 60 acres of land, was produced in Open Court & the execution thereof was duly acknowledged in Open Court by the said Thomas Walker being present & examined in Open Court by the said court, seperate & apart from her husband and in the absence of the said husband acknowledges she executed the said Deed of Conveyance, freely, voluntarily of her own accord & without the constraint or compulsion of her said Husband & on motion the same is ordered to be Certified.

A Deed of Conveyance from Abraham Brantley, Lydia Bennitt, Lydia

Brantley & sd. Abraham Brantly as Guardian to George & Elisha Bennitt, to
Archibald D. Murphey for certain lands belonging to the estate of John Rice
Decd. was produced in Open Court & Abraham Brantley & Lydia Bennitt personally appeared in Open Court and acknowledged the execution of said deed
for the purpose therein mentioned & that they had seperately affixed their
hands & seal thereto and at the same time appeared in Open Court, Lydia
Brantley wife of the said Abraham Brantley & acknowledged the execution
of said deed & that she had affixed her hand & seal thereto, and the said
Lydia Brantley by her said acknowledgement was privily examined by the
said Court seperate & apart from her said husband, & on said examination
she stated that she had executed said Deed freely & Voluntarily, without
any fear or compulsion from her said husband, wherefore said acknowledgement was reviewed of said Deed, that the same might be Registered.

(p-32)   Edward Noblett & Peter P. Roberts produced in Open Court the
last will & Testament of Samuel Roberts Decd. & offered it for probate
which was duly proven in Open Court by the Oaths of Richard H. Adams &
Stephen Noblett two of the subscribing witnesses thereto to be the last
will & testament of Samuel Roberts Decd., who deposed that they became
subscribing witnesses to said Will at the request of the said deceased &
that he was in his perfect mind & memory & on motion the same is ordered
to be recorded, & the said Peter P. Roberts & Edward Noblett two of the
executors named in said will appeared in Open Court having given bond &
security satisfactory to the Court & taken the oath of executors, took
upon themselves the execution of said last will & testament, therefore it
is considered by the Court that letters Testamentary issue to the said
Edwin Noblett & Peter P. Roberts upon the estate of the said deceased.

The pursuance of the order of the County Court of Montgomery,
deposition as produced to the Court of Abram Ferguson, John Ferguson &
George Ware, citizens resident of Kentucky & they having been duly
examined relative to the last Will & testament of Mildred Fortson they
being the subscribing witnesses thereto & upon their examination in
pursuance of the order of this Court of the order of this Court, prove the
execution thereof by the said Mildred & it is thereupon ordered that the
said Will be admitted to Record together with the Deposition annexed thereto, and thereupon administration with the Will annexed is granted to
Richard Fortson who enters into Bond & security & is qualified agreeably
to law.   It is therefore considered by the Court that letters of administration issue to the said William Fortson on the estate of the said Mildred
Fortson.

(p-53)   The last Will & Testament of David Harrison which was heretofore
contested in this Court & a jury having passed thereon & found the same
to be the last Will & testament of David Harrison decd. from which an
appeal was prayed to the Circuit Courts & the said Stephen Noblett & wife
having agreed & admitted in the presence of the Court, that the said
paper is the last Will & Testament of the said David Harrison & that there
will not be any future contest relative thereto & the said Will having
proven heretofore in presence of this Court, by Thomas Wyatt & Priscilla
Wyatt the subscribing witnesses thereto.   It is thereupon ordered by the
Court that the same be recorded and Sterling Noblett one of the executors
appointed in said Will, was duly quallified as executor to the said Will
& entered into bond & security satisfactory to the Court, it is therefore
ordered by the Court that letters Testamentary issue to the said Sterling
Noblett upon the estate of said David Harrison decd.

This day was produced in Open Court the nuncupative Will of Benjamin Dunn deceased and was proven by the oath of Stephen H. Carney who proved he was called on by said Dunn in his last illness at the house of sd. Dunn to witness his sd. will, that it was told over to sd. Carney & Richard Bradshaw sd. by them reduced it to writing two days after his death, Richard Bradshaw proves the sd. Will as afore reduced to writing with the exception annexed to sd. written nucupative will produced in Court and on motion the same is ordered to be recorded.

(p-34)   Upon the petition of Stephen Noblett and Sally his wife Thomas Organ and Martha his wife and Nancy Harrison, it is ordered by the Court that John S. Mosely, Alexander M. Rogers, John Wyatt, Thomas Batson and John Rook, or any three of them do divide the land and slaves of David Harrison in the following manner to wit, one third of the said land and slaves to be allotted to Mary Harrison widow of said David Harrison deceased that they then proceed to divide the remaining two thirds of said land and slaves into eight equal parts and allot one equal eighth part to each of the Petitioners, that is to say one equal eighth part to Stephen Noblett & Sally his wife one equal eighth part to Thomas Organ and Martha his wife and one equal eighth part to Nancy Harrison and make report thereof to the next Term of this Court.

This day was produced in Open Court the nuncuperative will of Samuel Hawkins deceased & was proven by the oaths of Cordall Norfleet & George B. Hopson two of the subscribing witnesses thereto who proved that they were caled on by said Samuel Hawkins in his last illness at the house of said Hawkins to witness his said Will, that it was told over to them & by them reduced to writing & he the said Hawkins was in his perfect mind & memory & the same was reduced to writing within fourteen days after the death of said Hawkins or less & thereupon the same is ordered to be Recorded & the Court ordered that administration be granted to Joel Grizard with the Will annexed & the said Joel Grizard entered into bond & security satisfactory to the Court & qualified agreeable to law, therefore it is ordered by the Court that letters of administration issue to said Joel Grizard on the estate of the said deceased.

(p-35)   Joel Grizard Admr. of Samuel Hawkins decd. rendered into Court an Inventory of the estate of sd. Samuel Hawkins decd. & qualified agreeable to law & on motion ordered to be recorded.

On motion it is ordered by the Court that Joel Grizard admr. of Samuel Hawkins decd. be permited to sell a sufficient portion of the perishable property of said Samuel Hawkins decd. to pay his debts.

A deed of conveyance from James B. Bowlin to William A. Cook for the half of Lott No 86 in the town of Clarksville was proven in Open Court by the Oaths of Thomas King, & Thornton K. Cook subscribing witnesses thereto and on motion it is ordered to be registered.

Court adjourned untill tomorrow morning to meet at nine O'clock.

A. M. Rogers
Stephen Cooke
F. Carter
Thos. Smith

The Worshipful Court of Montgomery County have met according to adjournment Tuesday October 22nd 1822.

Present   Alexander M. Rogers)
           Stephen Cocke   )
           Francis Carter   ) Esquires
           Thomas Smith   ) Justices

The following Persons were duly elected, empaneled & sworn as a Grand Jury to enquire for the body of the County towit (p-36) William E. Williams Foreman Daniel Rook, John Henderson, Joseph Barbee., George W. Blanks, John Rook, Robert Nelson, John Northington, John Thompson, Peter F. Roberts, Nathaniel D. Terry, Thomas Diggers, & John Perdue Jr., having received their charge retired to consider of presents. William E. Dancy was sworn as a constable to attend the Grand Jury during this Court.

Upon the affidavit of William Allen it is ordered by the court that he be discharged from any further attendance as a juror at the present term of this Court.

On motion it is ordered by the Court that Robert G. Johnson be discharged from any further attendance as a juror at the present term of this Court in consequence of his being an overseer of a road

On motion it is ordered by the Court that John S. Mosley be exonerated from any further attendance as a juror at this Court, in consequence of his being an overseer of a road

On motion it is ordered by the Court that James Grant be exonerated from any further attendance as a juror at this Court in consequence of him being an overseer of a road.

On motion it is ordered by the Court that Robert Searcy, Richard Overton, Samuel Haggard, Joseph Shamel, Edward A. Lucy, Zenos Bush or
this order was   /// /// any four of them be appointed Commissioners to
rescinded   settle with Francis Baker, Guardian of the children of
                      William Cooper & make report to the present term of
                      this Court.

(p-37)   On motion it is ordered by the Court, that Robert G. Johnson & Abner V. Hampton administrators of Philip Johnson decd. be permitted to expose to sale all the Personal & perishable property of the said Philip Johnson decd. & also Four Negroes named Moses, John Bob & Betty upon giving Twenty days public notice of time & place.

On motion it is ordered by the Court, that John Blackwell by his agent James Blackwell, be permitted to give in his list of Taxable property for 1822 & that it be annexed to the present years tax list.

A Bill of Sale from George W. Rogers to John H. Marable for a negro man named Shade, was produced in Open Court & the execution thereof duly acknowledged by the said George W. Rogers to be his act & deed for the purposes contained therein & on motion ordered to be /////// Recorded.

On motion it is ordered by the Court that Dorrell Young be permitted to give in his list of Taxable property for 1822 & that it be annexed to the present years tax list.

On motion it is ordered by the Court that John Steele admr. of John Steele Decd. be permitted to give in his list of Taxable property for 1822 & that it be annexed to the present years tax list.

Richard B. Blount & James Carr commissioners appointed at the last Term of this Court to attend at the beginning corner of Edward S. Walton's tract of land & established the boundaries or any special corner called for on said tract of land & to take the examination of witnesses concerning said boundaries, make their report with said (p-58) depositions to this Court & on motion the same is ordered to be Recorded.

The Commissioners appointed at the last Term of this Court to settle with Edward S. Walton administrator of Edward Walton Decd. make their report to this Court & on motion the same is ordered to be Recorded.

On motion it is ordered by the Court that the following hands work under Jeffry Sims overseer of the road from the mouth of the West Fork to Thomas Chenys, to wit, Willie Segraves Barnet Sims, Mrs. Elizabeth Roberts hands, Thomas Cherry & hands, Daniel Henderson & hands & Jacob Cordan.

ELISHA MAGEHEE)
VS) Motion
JESSE CULBERTSON & PYRANT MEGEHEE)

This day came the plaintiff Elisha Megehee by his attorneys Huling & Turley & thereupon it appearing to the Court, that John Kercheval Esquire had issued an execution in behalf of Elisha Megehee against Jesse Culbertson & Pyrant Megehee directed to any lawful officer of said County directing that of the goods and chattles, lands & Tennements of Jesse Culbertson & Pyrant McGehee to make the sum of Eighty three dollars & fifty cents with Interest thereon from the first day of October 1818 to satisfy a judgment of the sd. Elisha Megehee rendered against the said Jesse Culbertson & Pyrant Megehee on the 11th November 1818 before the said John Kercheval esquire & also the Costs of said suit, which said execution was issued on the 2nd September 1822 & placed in the hands of John Bowers a constable of said County for collection, upon which the said John Bowers made return that he had levied (p-59) the same on sixty two & a half acres of land belonging to sd. Jesse Culbertson, whereon he now lives no personal property formed of principal & upon motion of the said Elisha Megehe. It is considered by the Court that a Venditioni Exponas issue directed to the sheriff of Montgomery County commanding him to expose to sale, said tract of land to satisfy the aforesaid Judgment & Costs & also the costs of this motion.

ISRAEL MCLAUGHLIN)
VS) Case
ISAAC W. VANLEER)

This day came the parties by their attornies & it is suggested to the Court here that since last continuance of this cause, the defendant departed this life & the same is not denied.

WILLIAM NEWEL)
VS) Debt
SAMUEL McFALL & FRANCIS PENRICE)

This day came the parties by their attornies & thereupon came a jury of good & lawful men (to wit) Lee Trice, William Killebrew, James Reeves, Abner V. Hampton, John Ogburn, John Steele, John Cooke, David Davis, Ambrose Davis, John S. Gainer, William S. White & Amos Hatcher who being duly elected tried & sworn, the truth to speak upon the issues joined upon their Oaths do say, that they find the issues in favour of the plaintiff, that the //////// Defendants doth owe to the plaintiff the sum of Three hundred Dollars the debt in the declaration mentioned & do assess his damages to thirteen dollars, by reason of the detention of said debt besides Costs.

Therefore it is considered by the Court, that the plaintiff William Newel recover of the Defendants Samuel McFall & Francis Penrice, the sum of Three hundred & thirteen dollars the debt & damages by the jury aforesaid in form aforesaid assessed together with his costs about his suit in this behalf Expended.

(p-40) JOHN DEMLESSEE of ISRAEL ROBINSON) Trespass
VS) with force &
DANIEL ROOK) Arms.

This day came the plaintiff by his attorney C. Johnson esquire & says he will no further prosecute his said suit against the defendant but dismisses the——— It is therefore Considered by the Court that the defendant Daniel Rook go hence without day & recover of the plaintiffs, his Costs by him about his defence in this behalf Expended.

LUCY PEGRAM EXECUTRIX OF DANIEL PEGRAM)
Decd. benefit of LEWIS PIKE)
VS) Debt
CLAIBORNE HARRIS)

This day came the plaintiff by her attorney C. Johnson esquire & says he will no further prosecute her said suit against the defendant, but dismisses the same.

It is therefore considered by the Court that the plaintiff Lucy Pegram Executrix of Daniel Pegram Decd. recover of the defendant Claiborne Harris, her costs by her about her suit in this behalf Expended.

A. B. SHELBY admr.) It appearing to the Court
VS) that William C. Jamison one of the admrs. of
CRAFT & WILLIS) Sally Shelby Decd. hath departed this life.

It is ordered that A. B. Shelby the other admr. be permitted to prosecute this suit in his own name as the surviving administrator.

(p-41) JOHN H. MARABLE)
VS) Case
GEORGE H. ROGERS)

This day came the plaintiff in proper person & says he will no
further prosecute his said suit against the defendant but dismisses the
same. It is therefore considered by the Court, that the defendant George
M. Rogers go hence without day & recover of the plaintiff John H. Marable
his costs by him about his defence in this behalf Expended.

JAMES SMITH)
VS)
JOSEPH NORVELL) Debt
JACOB McGAVOCK)
HENRY H. BRYAN)

This day came the parties by their attornies & thereupon came a
jury of good and lawful men to wit, Leigh Trice, William Killebrew
James Rieves, Abner V. Hampton, John Ogburn, John Steele, John Cocke,
David Davis, John S. Gainer, William S. White and Amos Hatcher, Ambrose
Davie, who being duly elected, tried & sworn the truth to speak upon
the issues joined upon their oaths do say that they find that the
Defendants Norvell & McGavock have not paid the said Debt in the Declaration mentioned as in pleading they have alledged & they also find the
said ~~/// ///// //~~ issue joined between the said Henry H. Bryan & the said
plaintiffs in behalf of the said plaintiffs against the said Henry H.
Bryan & they also find for the plaintiff his Debt in the Declaration
mentioned amounting to the sum of five hundred dollars & they assess the
the plaintiffs damage for the detention of the said Debt to the sum of
~~////~~ Thirty two dollars and fifty cents. It is therefore considered by the
Court that the said plaintiff James Smith recover of the said Joseph
Norvell Jacob McGavock & Henry H. Bryan the aforesaid sum of Five hundred
& Thirty two dollars & fifty cents the Debt & damages aforesaid and also
the costs in this behalf expended.

(p-42) ANTHONY B. SHELBY admr. of)
SALLY SHELBY Decd.)
VS) Debt
ELISHA WILLS & SAMUEL CRAFT)

This day came the parties by their attornies and thereupon came
a jury of good & lawful men, to wit, Leigh Trice, William Killebrew,
James Reeves, Abner V. Hampton, John Ogburn, John Steel, John Cooke,
David Davis, Ambrose Davie, John S. Gainer, William S. White & Amos
Hatcher, who being duly elected tried & sworn the truth to speak upon
the issue joined upon their oaths do say that they find that the defendant
hath not paid the debt in the Declaration mentioned of Eleven hundred &
forty Dollars and that they assess the plaintiffs damages by reason of
the non payment thereof to Forty five dollars & Fifty cents.
It is therefore considered by the Court that the said A. B. Shelby Admr.
as aforesaid recover of the said Elisha Willis & Sam'l Craft the sum of
Eleven hundred & forty dollars, the Debt in the Declaration mentioned
and also the sum of Forty five dollars & fifty cents the damages as
aforesaid and also the costs in this behalf expended.

SAMUEL KERCHIVAL &)
JOHN KERCHIVAL)
VS) Debt
ELLINOR SHELBY)

This day came the parties by their attornies & thereupon came a jury of good & lawful men (towit) Lee Trice, William Killebrew James Reeves, Abner V. Hampton, John Ogburn, John Steele, John Cooke, David Davis, Ambrose Davis, John S. Gainer, William S. White & Amos Hatcher who being duly elected, tried & sworn, the truth to speak upon the issues joined their Oaths do say that they find the issues in favour (p-43) of the plaintiffs, that the defendant doth owe to the plaintiffs the sum of Two hundred & forty four Dollars & fifty five cents, the debt in the declaration mentioned & do assess the plaintiffs Damages to Eleven dollars & forty five cents by reason of the detention of said Debt, besides Costs. Therefore it is considered by the Court that the plaintiffs Samuel Korcheval & John Kerchival recover of the Defendant Ellinor Shelby the sum of Two hundred and fifty six Dollars, the debt & damages so assessed by the jury aforesaid in form aforesaid assessed together with their Costs by them about their suit in this behalf Expended.

```
JACOB H. FORT   )
    VS          )  Debt
PETER H. COLE   )
```

This day came the parties by their attornies & thereupon came a jury of good & lawful men towit, Lee Trice, William Killebrew, James Reeves, Abner V. Hampton, John Ogburn, John Steele, John Cooke, David Davis, Ambrose David, John S. Gainer, William S. White, Amos Hatcher, who being duly elected, tried & sworn the truth to speak on the Issues Joined on their Oath do say that the defendant hath an offset to the amount of one hundred & fifty two dollars 97 cents but that he doth owe the plaintiff of Ballance of debt & damages the sum of forty nine dollars thirty seven cents. Therefore it is considered by the Court that the plaintiff recover against said defendant forty nine dollars 37 cents Ballance of Debt & damages aforesaid by the Jury, found & his Cost by him about his suit in this behalf expended & &.

(p-44) 〜〜〜〜〜〜〜〜〜 Court adjourned to meet tomorrow morning at nine O'clock.

> Stephen Cooke
> Samuel Smith
> F. Carter

The Worshipful Court of Montgomery County have met according to adjournment, Wednesday October 23rd 1822.

```
Present   Stephen Cooke  )
          Samuel Smith   )  Esquires
          Francis Carter )  Justices
```

```
DIXON GIVEN, ARCHIBALD          )
MCALISTER & JOSEPH GIVEN        )
        VS                      )  Covenant
JOHN MCCAULEY & JAMES MCCAULEY  )  Broken
```

This day came the parties by their attornies & thereupon came a jury of good & lawful men, to wit, Lee Trice, John Ogburn, John Steele, William O. Robins, Joshua Pike, Jourden Lisle, David Council, Joseph Bogard, John Luke, George McCauley, Nathan Sulivant & Joseph Bosley, who being duly elected tried & sworn the truth to speak upon the issues joined, upon their Oaths do say, that they find the issues in favour of the plaintiffs & do assess their damages to seven hundred & fifty seven dollars & sixty two cents by reason of the several promises & undertakings in the plaintiff's declaration mentioned, besides Costs. Therefore it is considered by the Court that the plaintiffs Dixon Given, Archibald McAlister & Joseph Given recover of the defendants John McCauley & James McCauley the sum of seven hundred (p-45) & fifty seven dollars & sixty two cents, the damages so assessed by the jury aforesaid in form aforesaid assessed together with their costs by them about their suit in this behalf Expended.

```
GIVEN MCALLISTER & GIVEN )
          VS             )  Covenant
JAMES & JOHN MCCAULEY    )  Broken
```

And now at this day came the Defendant W & prays an appeal to the Circuit Court of Montgomery County, in the nature of a writ of Error & having given bond & security satisfactory to the Court, the same is allowed.

```
ANTHONY B. SHELBY admr.         )
          VS                    )
SAMUEL CRAFT, JOHN H. MARABLE   )  Debt
& ELISHA WILLIS                 )
```

It appearing to the Court, that William C. Jamison, one of the administrators of Sally Shelby decd. hath departed this life. It is ordered that Anthony B. Shelby the other administrator be permitted to prosecute this suit, in his own name as the surviving administrator.

```
ANTHONY B. SHELBY surviving    )
Admr. of SALLY SHELBY decd.    )
          VS                   )  Debt
SAMUEL CRAFT, ELISHA WILLIS&   )
JOHN H. MARABLE                )
```

This day came the parties by their attornies & thereupon came a jury of good & lawful men to wit, Lee Trice, John Ogburn, John Steele, William O. Robins, Joshua Pike, Jourdan Lester, David Council, Joseph Bogard, John Luke, George McCauley, Nathan Sulivant & Joseph Bosley, who being duly elected, tried & sworn the truth to speak upon the issue joined, upon their Oaths do say that they find the issue in favour of the plaintiff & that the defendants doth owe to the plaintiff the sum of one thousand and one dollars the debt in the declaration mentioned & do assess the plaintiffs damages to forty dollars, by reason of the detention of said debt besides Costs.
(p-46)   Therefore it is considered by the Court that the plaintiff Anthony B. Shelby Administrator as aforesaid, recover of the defendants Samuel Craft, Elisha Willis & John H. Marable the sum of Ten hundred & forty one dollars, the debt & damages by the jury aforesaid, in form aforesaid, assessed, together with his Costs by him about his suit in this behalf Expended.

GEORGE HUMPHREYS assee)
of WILLIAM L. BROWN &)
F. W. HULING) Debt
VS)
SAMUEL VANCE)

This day came the plaintiffs by his attorney & the defendant in
proper person, & thereupon came a Jury of good & lawful men towit,
Lee Trice, John Ogburn, John Steele, William O. Robbins, Joshua Pike,
Jourdan Lisles, David Council, Joseph Bogard, John Luke, George McCauley,
Nathan Sulivant, & Joseph Bosley, who being duly elected tried & sworn
the truth to speak upon the issues joined, upon their Oaths do say, that
they find the issues in favour of the plaintiff & that the defendant
doth owe to the plaintiff the sum of sixteen hundred & sixty six dollars
& sixty six cents the debt in the declaration mentioned & do assess the
plaintiff's damages to Eighty three dollars & thirty cents by reason of
the detention of said debt, besides Costs.   Therefore it is considered
by the Court that the plaintiff, George Humphreys assignee as aforesaid,
recover of the defendant Samuel Vance, the sum of seventeen hundred &
forty nine dollars & ninety cents, the debt & damages by the jury
aforesaid in form aforesaid assessed together with his Costs by him
about his suit in this behalf Expended.

(p-47)   JESSE BECK)
VS) Debt
JAMES DAVIS)

This day came the parties, by their attornies & thereupon came
a jury of good & lawful men to wit, Lee Trice, John Ogburn, John Steele,
William O. Robbins, Joshua Pike Jourdan Lisles, David Council, Joseph
Bogard, John Luke, George McCauley, Nathan Sulivant & Joseph Bosley who
being duly elected tried & sworn the truth to speak upon the issue
joined, upon their Oaths do say that they find the issue in favour of
the plaintiff & that the defendant doth owe to the plaintiff the sum of
one hundred & fifty one dollars & eighty cents, the debt in the declaration mentioned, & do assess the plaintiffs damages to seven dollars by
reason of the detention of said debt, besides Costs.

Therefore is is considered by the Court that the plaintiff Jesse
Beck recover of the defendant James Davis the sum of one hundred & fifty
///// eight dollars & eight cents the debt & damages so assessed by the
jury in form aforesaid, together with his costs by him about his suit in
this behalf Expended.

JAMES ELDER)
VS) Debt
ASHBEL BRUNSON) On writ of Enquiry

This day came the parties by their attornies & thereupon came a
jury of good & lawful men to wit, Lee Trice, John Ogburn, John Steele,
William O. Robbins, Joshua Pike, Jourdan Lisles, David Council, Joseph
Bogard, John Luke, George McCauley, Nathan Sulivant & Joseph Bosly who
being duly elected tried & sworn the truth to speak ///// & well & truly
to enquire & assess the plaintiff's damages in this case, upon their

oaths do say that the plaintiff hath sustained damages to the amount of three hundred & seventy eight (p-48) dollars besides costs. Therefore it is considered by the Court that the plaintiff James Elder, recover of the defendant Ashbel Brunson the aforesaid sum of Three hundred & seventy eight dollars, the damages by the jury aforesaid in form aforesaid assessed together with his Costs by him about his suit in this behalf Expended.

WILLIAM DEAN
VS   } Case
RANSOM SEXTON

This day appeared in Open Court, the defendant by his attorney Richard Daly Esquire & the plaintiff being solemnly called to come into Court & prosecute his suit, came not, nor does he prosecute the same. Therefore it is considered by the Court that said suit be dismissed & that the defendant Ransom Sexton recover of the plaintiff William Dean his Costs by him about his defense in this behalf Expended.

WILLIAM DEAN
VS   } Case
LUCY SEXTON

This day appeared in Open Court the defendant by his attorney Richard Daly esquire and the plaintiff being solemnly called to come into Court & prosecute his said suit came not nor does he prosecute the same. Therefore it is considered by the Court that said suit stand dismissed & that the defendant Lucy Sexton recover of the plaintiff William Dean, her costs by her in this behalf Expended.

ELDRIDGE B. ROBERTSON
VS   } Case
JOHN ROACH

This day came the plaintiff by his attorney C. Johnson esquire & says he will no further prosecute his said suit against the (p-49) defendant, but dismisses the same.
It is therefore considered by the Court, that the defendant John Roach recover of the plaintiff Eldridge B. Robertson the Costs in this behalf Expended.

ROBERT VANCE
VS   } Case
SAMUEL CHAPMAN

This day came the plaintiff in proper person & says he will no further prosecute his said suit against the defendant but dismisses the same.
It is therefore considered by the Court that said suit stand dismissed & that the defendant Samuel Chapman, go hence without day & recover of the plaintiff Robert Vance the Costs in this behalf Expended.

WILLIAM PORTER
VS   } Motion
WILLIAM THOMPSON

////// // // ////// // // ////// ////// William Thompson a witness summoned in the case of Jesse Sulivant Guardian of William Sulivant Sr. against William Porter & others to appear at the present term of this Court to testify on behalf of said William Porter & others being solemnly called to come into Court & testify on behalf of said William Porter & others as he was bound to do Came not but made default, whereupon it is Considered by the Court that said William Porter recover of the said William Thompson the sum of one hundred & twenty five dollars unless on or before the next term of this Court he can shew sufficient cause to the contrary & that a Scieri Facias issue & &.

EPHRAIM H. FOSTER assee)
of NEEDHAM WHITFIELD)
　　　　VS　　　　　　　　) Debt
WILLIAM O. ROBBINS &)
NEEDHAM WHITFIELD)

This day came the plaintiff by his attorney's & here in Open Court says he intends no further　(p-50) to prosecute his said suit against one of the defendants Needham Whitfield, & thereupon the other defendant William O. Robbins, comes into Court and freely confesses , that he is indebted to said plaintiff in the sum of three hundred & fifty dollars the principal of said debt & also the further sum of Thirty eight dollars & fifty cents the Interest due thereon.
Therefore it is considered by the Court that the plaintiff Ephraim H. Foster assee as aforesaid recover of the defendant William O. Robbins said sum of Three hundred & fifty dollars the debt & said sum of Thirty eight dollars interest thereon, so as aforesaid confessed together with his Costs in this behalf Expended.

ALEXANDER McCLURE)
　　　VS　　　　　　) Debt
ELLINOR SHELBY)

This day came the parties by their attornies & thereupon, came a Jury of good & lawful men to wit Lee Trice, John Ogburn, John Steele, William O. Robbins, Joshua Pike, Jourdan Isles, David Council, Joseph Bogard, John Luke, George McCauley, Nathan Sulivant & Joseph Beasley, who being duly elected, tried & sworn the truth to speak upon the issues joined upon their Oaths do say that they find the issue in favour of the plaintiff & that the defendant doth owe to the plaintiff the sum of Two hundred Dollars the debt in the declaration mentioned & do assess the plaintiffs damages to Twenty six Dollars by reason of the detention of said debt besides Costs.
Therefore it is considered by the Court that the plaintiff Alexander McClure recover of the defendant Ellinor Shelby the sum of Two hundred & twenty six dollars the debt & damages by the jury aforesaid in form aforesaid assessed, together with his Costs by him about his suit in this behalf Expended.

(p-51)　　JOHN H. MARABLE)
　　　　　　 VS　　　　　) Case
　　　　JOHN PEYTON)

This day came the plaintiff by his attorney C. Johnson esquire & says he will no further prosecute his said suit against the defendant but dismisses the same.

It is therefore considered by the Court that said suit stand dismissed & that the defendant John Peyton, recover of the plaintiff John H. Marable the Costs in this behalf Expended.

The Grand Jury appeared in Open Court & returned the following presentments, to wit, State Vs William B. Nelson as an overseer of a road State against James Waller for an assault & Battery, State against James Waller for the same, State against Andrew Peterson for Open & notorious Lewdness.

> HAMBLIN MANLY
> VS } Debt
> ROBERT SEARCY

This day came the parties by their attornies & thereupon came a jury of good & lawful men, to wit, Lee Trice, John Ogburn, John Steele, William O. Robbins, Joshua Pike, Jourdan Isles, David Council Joseph Bogard, John Luke, George McCauley, Nathan Sulivant & Joseph Bosley, who being duly elected, tried & sworn the truth to speak, upon the issues joined, upon their Oaths do say, that they find the issues in favour of the, of the plaintiff & that the defendant doth owe to the plaintiff the sum of One hundred & twelve dollars the debt in the declaration mentioned & do assess the plaintiffs damages to Fourteen dollars & forty cents, by reason of the detention of said debt besides his Costs. Therefore it is considered by the Court, that the plaintiff Hamblin Manly, recover of the defendant Robert Searcy, the sum of One hundred & twenty six dollars & forty cents the debt & damages by the jury aforesaid, in form aforesaid assessed together with his Costs by him about his suit in this behalf Expended.

(p-52)   Court adjourned untill tomorrow morning to meet at nine O'clock.

> Samuel Smith
> T. W. Atkinson
> Stephen Cooke

The Worshipful Court of Montgomery County have met according to adjournment Thursday October 24th 1822

Present

> Samuel Smith)
> Thomas W. Atkinson) Esquires
> & Stephen Cooke) Justices

> JESSE SULIVANT GUARDIAN
> of WILLIAM SULIVANT SR.)
> VS)
> WILLIAM PORTER, SAMUEL SMITH) Case
> WILLIAM SULIVANT JR., WILSON)
> SULIVANT & BALEM BULL)

William Sulivant Jr. one of the defendants in this case, being solemnly called to come into Court & plead to the plaintiffs declaration in this case, came not, but made default, but because the Court does not

know what damages the plaintiff hath sustained in this behalf.
It is therefore considered by the Court that a writ of Enquiry be awarded
returnable to the next Term of this Court to enquire what damages the
plaintiff hath sustaind in this case.

JESSE SULIVANT GUARDIAN of
WILLIAM SULIVANT SR.
      VS
WILLIAM PORTER, SAMUEL SMITH   } Case
WILLIAM SULIVANT JR. WILSON SULIVANT &
BALUM HULL.

William Sulivant Jr., one of the defendants in this case being
solemnly caled to come into Court & plead to the plaintiffs declaration
in this case failed so to do, but because the said Court does not know
what damages the plaintiff hath sustained in this behalf. It is therefore
considered by the Court, that a Writ of Enquiry be awarded (p-53)
returnable to the next term of this Court, to enquire what damages the
plaintiff hath sustained in this behalf.

MATTHEW RYBURN GUARDIAN
of HARMON JENKINS & PATSEY M. JENKINS }
      VS   } Petition
JOSHUA P. VAUGHN Guardian

This day came the parties // ////// in proper person & it is agreed
by & between the said parties to refer all matters in dispute in this
cause to the arbitration of Frederick W. Huling & William A. Cook & in
case of their disagreement to choose an umpire & their award to be the
final Judgment of this Court & to be returned to this Term of the Court
if practicable

On motion it is ordered by the Court that the Clerk of this Court
issue a notice to John B. Persise to appear before this Court on Saturday
next & bring with him Robert Comperry an orphan of Francis Comperry &
show sufficient cause why, said Francis Comperry should not have the said
apprentice back, as she has sufficient property to maintain said orphan.

JESSE BECK   }
   VS   } Debt
JAMES DAVIS }

This day came the defendant into Open Court & prays an appeal to
the Circuit Court of Montgomery County, & having given bond & Security
satisfactory to the Court, the same is allowed.

CHARLES ////// BAILEY }
      VS   } Certiorari & Supercoedias
PETER HOLT J.,

This day came the plaintiff in proper person & says he will no
further prosecute his said suit against the defendant but dismisses the
same, & the defendant in proper person assumes the payment of all the
Costs. Therefore it is considered by the Court, that (p-54) the
plaintiff Charles Bailey recover of the defendant Peter Holt & on motion
against Peter Holt Sr. the Security for the Costs in this behalf Expended.

```
PHILIP JOHNSON  )
       VS        )   Appeal
AMBROSE MADISON  )
```

It appearing to the Court that Philip Johnson the plaintiff in this Case hath departed this life, which is not denied, It is therefore considered by the Court that Robert G. Johnson & Abner V. Hampton his administrator be permitted to prosecute this suit.

```
STATE             )
       VS          )
JOSHUA P. VAUGHN   )
```

On motion it is ordered by the Court, that Joshua P. Vaughn be fined the sum of Five dollars for a Contempt of this Court & that a Fieri Facias issue for said fine & Costs.

```
STATE         )
      VS       )
THOMAS JOLLY   )
```

On motion it is ordered by the Court that Thomas Jolly be fined the sum of Two dollars & fifty cents for a Contempt of this Court & that a Fieri Facias issue for said fine & Costs.

On motion it is ordered by the Court, that a subpoena issue directed to the sheriff to summon John B. Persise to appear before the Court here, on Saturday next, & shew Cause why he should not deliver Robert Comperry a minor of Francis Comperry, who was bound to said Persise by order of the last Term of this Court to the said Francis Comperry his Father who claims him under his protection.

On motion it is ordered by the Court that James Carr esquire, William McGowan & Meridith Williams be appointed Commissioners, to settle with Sarah Shaw Guardian to the minor heirs of Henry Shaw decd. & make report to the next Term of this Court.

A Power of attorney from Amos Hatcher to Lemuel Barnes was proven in Open Court, by the Oaths of Mortimer A. Martin & John F. Forest, the subscribing witnesses thereto & on motion ordered to be Certified.

```
(p-55)  JESSE SULIVANT Guardian     )
        OF WILLIAM SULIVANT SR.      )
                VS                    )
        WILLIAM PORTER, SAMUEL SMITH  )  Case
        WILLIAM SULIVANT JR., WILSON SULIVANT )
        and BALUM BULL                )
```

This day came the parties by their attornies & thereupon came a jury of good and lawful men towit, Daniel Rook, John Henderson, William E. Williams, Joseph Barbee, John Rook, Robert Nelson, John Worthington, John Thompson, Peter P. Roberts Thomas Biggers & John Perdue Jr. & George W. Blanks, who being duly elected, tried & sworn the truth to speak upon the issues joined between the plaintiff & William Porter one of the said defendants, upon their oaths do say that they find the issues in behalf of said defendant William Porter.

Therefore it is considered by the Court that the said defendant William Porter, recover of the plaintiff Jesse Sulivant, Guardian of William Sulivant Sr. the costs in this behalf Expended.

Court adjourned untill tomorrow morning to meet at Nine O'clock.
                                    Jas. Barret
                                    S. Thomas
                                    Stephen Cooke

The Worshipful Court of Montgomery County have met according according to adjournment Friday October 25th 1822.
Present

        James Barret   )
        Stephen Thomas) Justices
        Stephen Cooke) Esquires

        STATE OF TENNESSEE)
             VS   ) Contempt
        THOMAS JOLLY   )

On motion it is ordered by the Court that the fine assessed against Thomas Jolly for a Contempt of this Court, on yesterday (p-56) be remitted, & that the state of Tennessee only recover of the defendant Thomas Jolly, the Costs in this behalf Expended.

        STATE OF TENNESSEE)
             VS   ) Riot
        DEMPSEY BULL   )

The defendant Dempsey Bull came into Court & acknowledged himself bound & indebted to the State of Tennessee in the penal sum of Five hundred Dollars, to be levied of his goods & chattels, lands & Tenements to be void on condition, that he doth make his personal appearance before the justices of the County Court of pleas & quarter sessions, at the Court house in the town of Clarksville, on the first Thursday after the third Monday in January next, then & there to answer the charge of said state of Tennessee exhibited against him upon an Indictment for a Riot & not to depart without leave of the Court.

William Posy & Labon Holt the securities of said Dempsey Bull came into Court & acknowledged themselves indebted to the State of Tennessee in the penal sum of Two hundred & fifty Dollars, each, to be levied of their proper goods & chattles, lands & tenements to be void on condition that sd. Dempsey Bull doth make his personal appearance before the justices of the County Court of pleas & quarter sessions, at the Court house in the town of Clarksville on the first Thursday after the third Monday in January next then & there to answer said State on a Bill of Indictmt. & not to depart without leave of Court.

        STATE OF TENNESSEE)
             VS   ) Indictment
        HEZEKIAH DAVIS   ) for a Riot

This day came the Solicitor General in behalf of the State as well as the defendant Hezekiah Davis in Custody of the Sheriff of the

County & was thereupon arraigned & upon his (p-57) arraignment pleads
not Guilty to the Bill of Indictment & for his trial puts himself upon
his County, as does the Solicitor General likewise , & thereupon came a
jury of good & lawful men (to wit) Lee Trice, John Ogburn, John Steele,
Jesse Sulivant, Labon Holt, James Baker, Cyprus Hensly, Septimus Williams,
John Hust, John Edmonson, Jourdan Lisles & John Bell, who being duly
Elected tried & sworn, the truth to speak upon the issue of Traverse upon
their Oaths do say, that the defendant Hezekiah Davis is Guilty of a Riot
as charged in the Bill of Indictment.
Therefore it is considered by the Court that the defendant Hezekiah Davis
be fined the sum of Ten Dollars & that he pay the Costs of this prosecution.
the said defendant Hezekiah Davis being dissatisfied with the verdict in
this case, prays an appeal to the Circuit Court of Montgomery County, &
the said Hezekiah Davis, came into Court & acknowledged himself bound &
indebted to the State of Tennessee in the penal sum of five hundred Dollars
to be levied off his proper Goods & Chattles, lands & tenements to be void
on condition, that he doth make his personal appearance before the Judge
of the Circuit Court in the town of Clarksville on the //X/X/ first Monday
after the third Monday in February next, then & there & there to answer the
State of Tennessee on a Bill of Indictment against him for a Riot & not to
depart without leave of the Court, & David Davis & Samuel C. Hawkins his
Securities came into Court & acknowledged themselves indebted to the State
of Tennessee in the penal sum of Two hundred & fifty dollars each, to be
levied of their proper goods & chattles, lands & tenements, to be void
on condition that Hezekiah Davis doth make his personal appearance before
the Judge of the Circuit Courts in the town of Clarksville on the first
Monday after the third Monday in February next to answer the State of
Tennessee on a Bill of Indictment for a Riot, & for his not departing
without leave of Court.

(p-58) WILLIAM HENEL
              VS
        SAMUEL INFALL & FRANCIS   } Debt
        PENRICE

       And now at this day came the defendants & prayed an appeal to
the Circuit Court of Montgomery County, & having given bond & security
satisfactory to the Court the same is allowed.

        JAMES ELDER
             VS   } Covenant
        ASHBEL BRUNSON   } Broken

       And now at this day came the defendant & prayed an appeal to the
Circuit Court of Montgomery County, & having given bond & security,
satisfactory to the Court the same is allowed.

       Upon the petition of Robert A. Paine, Mildred W. Paine & Sally W.
Paine, by their Guardian Richard Taylor against Gerard Van Buren & Mary
his wife, it is ordered that Howel Taylor, John Y. Taylor, John Williams,
William Daniel & Elijah Hancock be appointed Commissioners to divide the
personal estate of James Paine Decd. of which he died intestate between
the Petitioners & Gerard Van Buren & wife according to law & make report
to the next term of this Court.

The last Will & Testament of James Paine decd. was produced in Open Court, certified by the Clerk of Robertson County Court, & on motion ordered to be Recorded & Gerard Van Buren appeared in Open Court & qualified agreeable to law.

(p-59)   On motion it is ordered by the Court, that a License issue to Mace F. Trice to keep & ordinary in the town of Cumberland, & that said Mace F. Trice entered into bond & security satisfactory to the Court & qualified agreeable to law.

On motion it is ordered by the Court, that William Waters be permitted to give in his list of Taxable property, & that it be annexed to the present year tax list—(list for 1822)

The Grand Jury appeared in Open Court & returned the following Bills of Indictment & Presentments (to wit) State Vs Obediah Broomfield for an assault & Battery, a true Bill, State against Henry W. Merriwether for obstructing the public Road a true Bill, State against William Brantley, Presentments—

A Deed of Conveyance from Israel Head to Lebon Holt for 22 acres of land, was produced in Open Court, & the execution thereof duly proven by the Oaths of James McCauley & William McCauley, the subscribing witnesses thereto, & on motion ordered to be Certified for Registration.

A Deed of Conveyance from Frederick W. Huling to Sarah Lockert for 155 acres of land was produced in Open Court, & the execution thereof, duly ////// acknowledged by the said Frederick W. Huling to be his act & deed for the purposes therein contained & on motion ordered to be certified for Registration.

A Deed of Conveyance from Cornelius Crusman sheriff of Montgomery County to William Peay /// for 3840 acres of land, was produced in Open Court, & the execution thereof, duly acknowledged by the said Cornelius Crusman to be his act & Deed for the purposes therein contained, & on motion ordered to be certified for Registration.

(p-60)   VANCE & BAILEY   )
                VS   ) On Motion
       WILLIAM HAWKINS Constable)

This day came said plaintiffs by attorney and it appearing to the satisfaction of the Court that heretofore to wit, on the 13th day of October 1822 a Capias ad satisfaciendum Issued from Stephen Thomas a justice of the Peace for said County which came to the hands of William Hawkins a constable for Montgomery County against William Davis for the sum of $28. 58 cents with interest from 20th May 1820 & Eighty seven ½ cents Cost by virtue of which case the said Hawkins arrested said Davis & let him go at large contrary to law. On motion therefore of said plaintiffs by attorney
It is considered by the court, that the plaintiff recover against said defendant said sum of twenty eight dollars & fifty eight cents with interest thereon from the 20th day of May 1820 and also 87½ cents costs aforesaid & their costs by them in this behalf expended & &.

STATE OF TENNESSEE) Indictment and
VS) assault & Battery
DAVID VAUGHN) *// & 7///*

This day came the solicitor General in behalf of the State as well
as the defendant David Vaughn in Custody of the Sheriff of the County &
was thereupon arraigned and upon his arraignment pleads not Guilty to the
Bill of Indictment & for his trial puts himself upon his Country as does
the Soliciter General likewise & thereupon came a jury of good & lawful
men, to wit, Lee Trice, John Ogburn, John Steele, Ambrose Madison,
William Nelson Sr., William B. Wall, John Edmonson, Hayden E. Wells, Charles
D. McLean, John Bell, Curl Tucker & Jesse Cooksey, who being duly Elected
tried & sworn the truth to speak upon the issue of Traverse, upon their
Oaths do say that the defendant David Vaughn, is Guilty of an assault &
Battery in manner & form as charged in the Bill of Indictment.
(p-61)   Therefore it is considered by the Court that the defendant David
Vaughan be fined the sum of Five dollars & that he pay the Costs of this
prosecution.

STATE OF TENNESSEE)
VS) Indictment for an Assault & Battery
DAVID VAUGHAN)

This day came the Soliciter General in behalf of the State & says
he intends no further to prosecute this suit against the Defendant, David
Vaughan, but dismisses the same--& the said defendant, David Vaughan,
David Davis & Michael Vaughan came into Court in proper person & assumes
the payment of all the Cost which has accrued on said prosecution.
Therefore it is considered by the Court that the State of Tennessee recover
of the of the said defendant David Vaughan, David Davis & Michal Vaughan
the costs of this prosecution.

DIXON GIVEN, ARCHIBALD)
MCALLISTER & JOSEPH GIVEN)
VS) Debt
WILLIS LYONS & GUTHRIDGE LYONS)

This day came the plaintiffs by their attornies & the defendant
Willie Lyons in proper person & as attorney in fact for the other defendant
Guthridge Lyons & freely confesses in his own name & as the attorney in
fact for the said Guthridge Lyons, that they are indebted to the said
plaintiffs in the sum of one hundred & sixty two Dollars & eighty seven
cents Balance of debt & interest thereon up to this date besides their
Costs.
Therefore it is considered by the Court, that the plaintiff Joseph Given
Archibald McAllister & Dixon Given recover of the defendants, Willie Lyons
& Gutheridge Lyons, the aforesaid sum of one hundred and sixty two dollars
& eighty seven cents so confessed by the defendants aforesaid, together
with their costs by them about their suit in this behalf Expended & the
plaintiffs agree to stay Execution untill the first of May next.

(p-62)   JOSEPH GIVEN, ARCHIBALD)
MCALLISTER & DIXON GIVEN)
Assee of GULLY MOORE) Debt
VS)
WILLIAM LYONS & GUTHRIDGE LYONS)

This day came the plaintiffs by their attornies, & the defendant
William Lyons in proper person & Willie Lyons attorney in fact for the
other defendant Cuthridge & freely confesses that they are indebted to
the said plaintiffs the sum of one hundred & fourteen Dollars, forty
three & a half cents Balance of debt & interest thereon up to this date
besides their costs.

Therefore it is considered by the Court that the plaintiffs Joseph Given,
Archibald McAllister & Dixon Given recover of the defendant the aforesaid
sum of One hundred & fourteen dollars & forty three & a half cents, so
confessed by the defendants aforesaid together with the Costs in this
behalf Expended & the plaintiffs agree to stay execution untill the first
of May next.

Court adjourned untill tomorrow morning to meet at nine O'clock.

Stephen Cooke
John McCauley
Samuel Smith

The Worshipful Court of Montgomery County have met according to
adjournment Saturday October 26th 1822

Present Stephen Cooke)
John McCauley &) Esquires
Samuel Smith) Justices

(p-63) SAMUEL VANCE assee)
vs) Upon the
WILLIAM WEST) application of William West

It is ordered by the Court that a supersedias issue agreeably to
the prayer of the petition upon Bond & Security being given agreeably
to law.

WILLIAM S. WHITE)
VS)
JAMES MALLORY former Shff. of Stewart County)
HOSEA H. SEAGER) HIS SECURITIES
THOMAS ROBERTS) IN OFFICE
WILLIAM KING)

This day came the plaintiff by his atto. & moves the Court for a
judgment against James Mallory former Sheriff of Stewart County and also
against Hosea H. Seager, Thomas Roberts & William King his securities
in office & it appearing to the Court that the said James Mallory had
collected the sum of Fifty dollars on a judgment in behalf of William
S. White against Jesse A. Brunson by virtue of an execution from this
Court in this Court six months ago & that he had failed to //////// pay
the same to the plaintiff the same & that the said Sheriff had a notice
of this motion more than Ten days before this Court. It is thereupon
considered by the Court that the said William S. White recover of the
said James Mallory & the said Hosea H. Seager, Thomas Roberts & William
King the aforesaid sum of Fifty dollars and also the sum of twelve &
one half flentum damages thereon, being the sum of six dollars & twenty
five cents & also the costs in this behalf expended.

(p-04) JACOB B. FORT)
        VS   } Debt
        PETER B. COLE)

And now at this day came the plaintiff, being dissatisfied with the judgment rendered against him in this case & prays an appeal to the Circuit Court of Montgomery County & having given bond & security satisfactory to the Court the same is allowed.

        JAMES SMITH   )
        VS   )
        HENRY H. BRYAN,   } Debt
        JACOB McGAVOCK &)
        JOSEPH NORVELL   )

And now at this day came the defendants by attorney, & prays an appeal to the Circuit Court for Montgomery County in the nature of a writ of Error, & having given bond & security satisfactory to the Court, the same is allowed.

        ANTHONY B. SHELBY admr.,)
        of SALLY SHELBY DECD.   )
        VS   } Debt
        ELISHA WILLIS &   )
        SAMUEL CRAFT   )

And now at this day came one of the defendants Elisha Willis & prays an appeal to the Circuit Court of Montgomery County, & having given bond & security satisfactory to the Court, the same is allowed.

        ANTHONY B. SHELBY Admr.)
        of SALLY SHELBY decd.   )
        VS   } Debt
        SAMUEL CRAFT, JOHN H.   )
        MARABLE & ELISHA WILLIS)

And now at this day came one of the defendants, Elisha Willis, & prayed an appeal to the Circuit Court of Montgomery County, & having given bond & security, satisfactory to the Court, the same is allowed.

        JESSE SULIVANT Guardian   )
        of WILLIAM SULIVANT SR.   )
        VS   )
        WILLIAM PORTER, SAMUEL SMITH} Case
        WILLIAM SULIVANT JR., WILSON)
        SULIVANT & BALUM BULL   )

(p-05) This day came William Sulivant Jr., & Wilson Sulivant, two of the defendants by attorney & enters a motion to shew cause why the Judgment taken by default against them at this Term of the Court, should not be dismissed & have filed their affidavits relative to the same, to be argued at the next Term of the Court.

        ELIJAH HUGHES   )
        VS   )
        WILLIAM H. BELL &} Debt
        JAMES GORDEN   )

This day came the plaintiff by his attorney William A. Cook esquire & says he will no further prosecute his said suit against the defendants, but dismisses the same. It is therefore considered by the Court, that said suit stand dismissed, & that the defendants William M. Bell & James Gordon recover of the plaintiff Elijah Hughes the Costs in this behalf Expended.

WILLIAM BARNETT)
    VS   ) Debt
VALENTINE ALLEN)

This day came the parties by their attornies & thereupon came a Jury of good & lawful men (towit) Leo Trice, John Ogburn, John Steele, William O. Robbins, Joshua Pike, Jourdan Lisles, David Council, Joseph Bogard, John Luke, George McCauley, Nathan Sulivant, & Joseph Bosley, who being duly Elected, tried & sworn the truth to speak upon the issues joined, upon their Oaths do say that they find the issues in behalf of the plaintiff & that the defendant doth owe to the plaintiff the sum of One hundred & forty six dollars & seventy five Cents, Balance of Debt in the declaration mentioned & do assess the plaintiffs damages to nine dollars & fifty five cents, by reason of the detention of said debt besides Costs.
Therefore it is considered by the Court, that the plaintiff William Barnett recover of the defendant Valentine Allen the sum of One hundred & fifty six dollars & thirty cents, Balance of debt & damages (p-66) by the Jury aforesaid, in form aforesaid assessed together with his Costs by him about his suit in this behalf Expended. From which Judgment the defendant being dissatisfied prays an appeal to the Circuit Court of Montgomery County, & having given bond & Security satisfactory to the Court, the same is allowed.

FRANCIS McWORDIE assee)
of WILLIAM S. WHITE   )
    VS   ) Debt
WILLIAM B. NELSON)

This day came the plaintiff by his attornies & the defendant William B. Nelson being solemnly called to come into Court & plead to the said plaintiffs declaration failed so to do but made default.
It is therefore considered by the Court, that the plaintiff Francis McWordie assignee of William S. White recover of the defendant William B. Nelson, the sum of one hundred & twelve dollars the debt in the declaration mentioned & the further sum of Five dollars & fifty cents the damages thereon together with the Costs in this behalf Expended.

JOHN F. VAUGHAN)
    VS   ) Appeal from a
ABSALOM BURRUS) Justices Court

This day came the defendant Absalom Burrus by attorney, & the plaintiff John F. Vaughan being solemnly called, to come into Court & prosecute his said suit came not, nor does he prosecute the same. It is therefore considered by the Court that the Defendant Absalom Burrus go hence without day & recover of the plaintiff John F. Vaughan, the Costs in this behalf Expended.

SAMUEL YOUNG)
VS) Appeal from a Justices Court
WILLIAM BROWN)

This day came the parties by their attornies & it is ordered by the Court, that unless the /////// defendant comes in & gives bond & security (p-67) for the prosecution of said appeal on or before the second day of the next Court, that the same be dismissed & it is further ordered by the said Court, that the plaintiff Samuel Young come in & give bond & security for the Costs of said suit.

WILLIAM WEST)
VS) Certiorari &
SAMUEL CRAFT) supersedias

This day came the plaintiff by his attorney C. Johnson esquire & says he will no further prosecute his said suit against the defendant but dismisses the same & the said William West & Samuel Craft, came into Court in proper person & each assumes the payment of half the Costs. It is therefore considered by the Court, that said suit stand dismissed, & that the parties aforesaid recover of each other the Costs agreeable to the aforesaid agreement, (in this behalf Expended)

PHILIP JOHNSON for the use of)
JOHN COCKE)
VS) Debt
WILLIAM BISHOP)

It appearing to the Court that the plaintiff Philip Johnson hath departed this life, which is not denied, it is therefore ordered by the Court that Robert C. Johnson & Abner V. Hampton his administrator be permitted to prosecute this suit.

GIVEN McALLISTER & GIVEN)
VS) Debt
JOHN NEBLETT JR.)

This day came the plaintiffs by their attornies Huling & Turley esquires & say they will no further prosecute their said suit against the defendant, but dismisses the same & the defendant John Neblett Jr. assumes the payment of all the Costs.
Therefore it is considered by the Court that the plaintiffs Given, McAllister & Given recover of the defendant John Neblett Jr., the Costs in this behalf Expended.

(p-68) A Deed of Conveyance from William Campbell to Peter Teasley for 71 Acres of land, was produced in Open Court, & the execution thereof duly proven by the Oath of Adam Brown, one of the subscribing witnesses thereto & Edmund Tunstall a subscribing witness thereto having departed this life, his hand writing was duly proven in Open Court by the oath of Cave Johnson & Charles D. McLean, who deposed that they believe the same to be his proper hand writing & on motion ordered to be certified for registration.

Present, John McCauley, Sam'l Smith & A. M. Rogers Esqr. Justices.

On motion it is ordered by the Court that Charles Hutchison be appointed administrator of the Goods & chattles rights & credits of John Hutchison, decd. & the said Charles Hutchison came into Court & entered into bond & Security satisfactory to the Court & took the Oath prescribed by law.   Same Justices present.

On motion it is ordered by the Court that Charles A. Hutchison, one of the Executors named in the last will & Testament of Repps Barnes decd. came into Court & quallify agreeable to law & the said Charles A. Hutchison came into Court & entered into bond & security satisfactory to the Court & took the Oath prescribed by law.

Present Isaac Donnison, John McCauley, & Sam'l Smith esquires Justices- On motion it is ordered by the Court that Alexander M. Rogers, be appointed Guardian to John F. Barnes, Thomas H. Barnes, Sally A. A. Barnes decd. & the said Alexander M. Rogers came into Court & qualified agreeable to law.
                                    Present,

                    Stephen Cocke,   )
                    Samuel Smith, &   ) esquires
                    Alexander M. Rogers   ) Justices.

On motion it is ordered by the Court that Samuel Vance be appointed Guardian to Thomas G. Hutchison minor heir of John Hutchison decd. & the said Samuel Vance came into Court & entered into bond (p-69) & security, satisfactory to the Court & qualified agreeable to law.

On motion it is ordered by the Court, that Robert Comperry, who was bound to John B. Persise at the last Term of this Court, be delivered to Francis Comperry & the said Francis Comperry came into Court & entered into bond & Security in the sum of Five hundred Dollars to maintain said Robert Comperry & keep him from the house of John Edmonson's which was approved of by the Court.

On motion it is ordered by the Court that Charles A. Hutcheson who qualified as administrator of John Hutchison decd. at this Term, be permitted to expose to sale all the perishable property of John Hutchison decd. & after advertising the same at least twenty days make return of the same to the next Term of this Court.

On motion it is ordered by the Court that Sterling Neblett, Richard Adams, & John Martin, be appointed commissioners to settle with William E. Williams administrator of Burrel H. Peeples decd. & also to settle with said William E. Williams Guardian of Elizabeth Peeples & make report of the same to the next Term of this Court.

On motion it is ordered by the Court, that the Sheriff of Montgomery County summon twelve free holders of said County to lay off the dower of Sarah Hutchison relict of John Hutchison decd. & make report of the same to the next Term of this Court.

On Braxton Wall administrator of Johnson Wall decd. returns into Court an Inventory of the estate of sd. Johnson Wall decd. also an a/c sales & qualified to the same agreeable to law, & on motion ordered to be Recorded.

On motion it is ordered by the Court, that the following hands work under Bace F. Trice overseer of the road from the mouth of Red River leading to Hopkinsville as far as Hugh McClures (to wit) (p-70) Hugh McClure's hands, James Trice Sr. hands, James Trice Jnr., Thomas Mallory, Mordica Redd, Edward Garrett, Leigh Trice, Thomas A. Trice, Joshua Pike, Thomas A. Trice, Joshua Pike, Thomas W. Atkinson, & hands, Dennis Dougherty, John Bowers, John Trice & hands, Edward Dikds, John Riggins, Noble Osborn, & hands, Shephard Trice & hands, Morris Pearson, Joseph Riggins, James Riggins, James Davis & hands, William Riggins, & Quintas Atkinson, who shall compose the number of hands to work on said Road.

On motion it is ordered by the Court, that the order appointing Commissioners to settle with Sam'l Craft & Henry D. Jamison, administrator of Nathan Peeples decd. at the last Term of this Court, be continued & that the same Commissioners settle with the sd. Samuel Craft & Henry D. Jamison administrators as aforesaid & make report of the same to the next Term of this Court.

On motion it is ordered by the Court, that Robert Searcy, Richard Overton, Samuel Haggard, Joseph Sherwell & Edward A. Lucy or any three of them be appointed to settle with William Cooper administrator of Charles Wall decd. & make report of the same to the next Term of this Court.

This day appeared in Open Court, Francis Comperry the Father of John Comperry who was bound to William Curry by order of this Court, at their July Term 1822 & confirmed the binding of said Court to be as valid as if it had been done by himself (to all intent & purposes)

On motion it is ordered by the Court, that the order appointing commissioners to settle with Elisha R. Oldham administrator of the Estate of Moses Oldham decd. be continued & that the same Commissioners, that were appointed in the former order settle with the said Elisha R. Oldham Administrator as (p-71) aforesaid & make report of the same to the next Term of this Court.

Court adjourned untill Monday morning to meet at nine O'clock.
James Dennison
Jas. Barret
Stephen Cocke

The Worshipful Court of Montgomery County have met according to adjournment, Monday October 28th 1822

Present   Isaac Dennison)
James Barret) Esquires
Stephen Cocke) Justices

JESSE SULIVANT Guardian)
VS   } Case
WILLIAM PORTER & others)

It is ordered by the Court that a Commission issue to the plaintiff to take the deposition of Thomas Johnson, Henry Fry & George Murphey & Thomas Martin of Robertson County. Robert Jarman, John Massey, Lewis Powers & Thomas Hutchison esquires of Humphreys County & Oney Harvey of

Dickson County upon giving the adverse party twenty days notice of time & place.

JESSE SULIVANT Guardian ⎫
VS ⎪
WILLIAM PORTER, SAM'L SMITH ⎬ Case
WILLIAM SULIVANT JR. & ⎪
WILSON SULIVANT & DALEM BULL ⎭

It is ordered by the Court that the Judgment taken by default against William Sulivant Jr. & Wilson Sulivant two of the defendants in this case, but set aside upon their paying the Cost which has accrued against them at this Time. It is therefore (p-72) Considered by the Court, that the plaintiff Jesse Sulivant Guardian recover against the said William Sulivant Jr. & Wilson Sulivant the Cost as aforesaid & the Cost in this behalf Expended.

JOHN COOKE Guardian ⎫
VS ⎬ Petition
EDWARD NEBLETT Guardian ⎭

It is ordered by the Court that the ######## parties have liberty to take Deposition of Sundry persons, upon giving Ten days notice of time & place

On motion it is ordered by the Court, that Martin Thomas have a Licence for retailing spiritous Liquors at his Grocery in the Town of Clarksville & the said Martin Thomas came into Court & entered into bond & security satisfactory to the Court.

A Deed of Conveyance from John Noblett Sr., to John Noblett Jr. for 100 Acres of land, was produced in Open Court & the execution thereof duly acknowledged by the said John Noblett Sr., to be his act & deed for the purposes therein contained & on motion ordered to be certified for registration.

Upon the petition of Jesse A. Brunson & wife Levisa Brunson, it is ordered by the Court, that Burroll Bayliss, Matthew Ogburn, Joseph Horn, John Blair, James Smith, Joseph Bowers, George Nixon, Dawson Bayless, & Tyrant McGehee or any five of them together with John Caldwell the County surveyor, be appointed Commissioners to make partition of the following tract of land between ## /// the petitioners ///// Jesse A. Brunson & Levisa Brunson (his wife), Clark Morton, Shelby & Alfred M. Shelby heirs of John Shelby decd. of the following Tracts of land (to wit) 750 Acres of land on Conrad's Creek, one other tract on the Blooming Grove of about 600 Acres , one other tract of about 150 Acres on Bud's Creek & one (p-73) other tract of 50 Acres on Cumberland River below Conrad's Creek & part of a lott in Clarksville near Foston' store.

Anthony B. Shelby the Guardian of Clark Moulton Shelby & Alfred M. Shelby has had notice more than Ten days previous to this motion & it is ordered by the Court that said Commissioners together together with said John Caldwell, surveyor, make return of said Partition to the next Term of this Court, with a distinct platt of the said tract of land & the several portions, & setting forth & shewing the division thereof & the respective portion of the said heirs at law.

The Court proceeded to appoint Jurors to the next January County Court, who are as follows to wit, William Stewart Sr., Philmer Whitworth, John B. Wilcox Alexander Barker, Edward Trice, James Trice Sr., William Henderson, Charles Cherry, John Russel, Robert Noland, James Allen, John P. Epps, Samuel Kercheval, Guthridge Lyons, Needham Whitfield Stephen Mallory, Edward S. Walton, Pray H. Whipple, John Wyatt, Capt. William Porter, Samuel White, Richard Taylor, Burwell Bayless, William Blair, Matthew Ogburn, & Henry Weeks.

The Court proceeded to appoint Jurors to the next February Circuit Court, who are as follows to wit, Joseph J. Williams, Matthew Ryburn, James Brown, Richard Cooke, Leigh Trice, Stephen Cooke, Edward Trice, Thomas Cherry, William Howel, Francis Carter, Capt. William Allen, Elias F. Pope, Robert Vance, Samuel C. Hawkins, Reuben Pollard, Bryant Whitfield, Thomas L. Carney, Hiram Bobo, William Noblett, Simon Holmes, Lewis C. Taylor, Francis Baker, John Kirchival, James Bowers, Valentine Allen & John Smith.

(p-74) STATE OF TENNESSEE)
VS) Sci Fa
BIRCH ROWLAND)

Upon the affidavit of Birch Rowland it is considered by the Court that said Sci Fa be dismissed & that the County of Montgomery pay the Costs in this behalf Expended.

The jury who were summoned by the Sheriff to lay off the dower of Frances Mallory late widow of Thomas Mallory decd. now Frances McCarroll & to make division of the balance of the land of Thomas Mallory decd. among the children of said Thomas Mallory decd. make their report to this Court & on motion ordered to be Recorded.

STATE OF TENNESSEE)
VS)
RICHARD ANDERSON)

On motion it is ordered by the Court, that Richard Anderson a juror summoned to appear at this Court be fined the sum of Ten Dollars for his non attendance unless he can show sufficient cause at the next term of this Court to the Contrary & that a Sci Fa issue & &.

On motion it is ordered by the Court that James Donalson be appointed overseer of the road from the State line to River's Mill & that the following hands work under the said James Donalson (to wit) Thomas Rivers hands, Samuel Dabney's Douglass Merriwether's, William Waters, John Gaines, hands Barett Gaines & William Donalson.

On motion it is ordered by the Court that Robert Sawer be appointed overseer of the (p-75) Road from Hugh McClure's to River's Mill & that the following hands work under him to wit, Robert Sawer's hands Edwin Killebrew & hands, Thomas Carraway & hands, Hugh Campbell & hands, Hanoah Bostick & hands, Benjamin Lee, William Terroll, Mirida Howard & all other hands within the bounds of said road.

Court adjourned untill Court in Course

James Dennison

Jas. Barret

Stephen Cooke

The Worshipful Court of Montgomery County have met according to adjournment Monday January 20th 1823.

Present   Matthew Ryburn   )

Isaac Dennison &) Esquires

Sterling Neblett) Justices

On motion ordered by the Court that Benjamin Orgain, Edward Neblett & Alexander M. Rogers, be appointed commissioners to settle with Elias F. Pope Guardian of Drewry Smith & make report to the next Term of this Court.

On motion ordered by the Court, that William Dicks Jr., be appointed overseer of the road from Clarksville to Henry & Valentine W. Merriwether's ferry on Red River & that he open the same as viewed & reported to the last term of this Court & that he have the following hands to work under him on said Road (towit) William Brantly, & hands, James B. Reynolds, hands & the hands of John H. Poston ~~his hands~~ at his farm.

On motion ordered by the Court, that Alexander M. Rogers & Stephen Cooke be appointed commissioners to settle with Isham Trotter, Guardian of Abraham Cooke's heirs & make report to the next Term of this Court.

(p-76)   On motion ordered by the Court, that Manoah Bostick & James Barret esquire be appointed to settle with John Long & James Trice Jr. administrators of Dolphy Mitchell decd. & make report to the next term of this Court.

On motion ordered by the Court that Sterling Neblett administrator of Dolphy Mitchell decd. & make report to the next term of this Court.

On motion it is ordered by the Court that Simon Holmes, William Corban & Stephen Cooke esquire be appointed commissioners to lay off a years provision to Elizabeth Vick widow of the late Rowland Vick deceased and make report to the next Term of this Court.

On motion ordered by the Court, that Francis Baker, Nathan Nestor & Samuel Haggart be appointed commissioners to settle with Robert Wade administrator of William Faulkner decd. & make report to the next Term of this Court.

On motion ordered by the Court that Matthew Ryburn esqr. Abner Gupton esquire & William McDaniel, be appointed commissioners to settle with Thomas Williams admr. of the estate of John Everit decd. & make report to next Court.

This order is void   On motion of Thomas Williams, it is ordered by the Court, that the Sheriff of Montgomery County, summon twelve lawful men of said County to lay off & Allot to Sally Wilson now Sally Woodson her dower in the estate, of Sanford Wilson decd. & put her in possession of the same & make return to our next Court.

On motion ordered by the Court that Stephen Cooke & Thomas Smith esquires be appointed to settle with John Duke ///////// Admr. of John Duke decd. & make report to the present Term of this Court.

(p-77)   On motion ordered by the Court, that Thomas Williams administrator of William McCauley decd. be permitted to sell a tract of land containing thirty one & a half acres for the purpose of paying the debts against the estate of the said deceased, there not being personal property sufficient to satisfy the same, the said Thomas Williams is permitted to sell said tract of land on a credit of Nine months after advertising the same agreeable to law.

Ordered by the Court that the State & County Tax be the same as last year, & that the jurors shall be entitled to receive as compensation for their services the sum of one dollar for each & every day they may serve to be paid out of the County levy.

On motion ordered by the Court that Daniel Tolson & Stephen Neblett be appointed first & second Inspectors of Tobacco at the ware house of Robert Vance in the Town of Palmyra, & the said Daniel Tolson & Stephen Neblett entered into bond & security & qualified agreeable to law.

Isaac Dennison & James Carr Commissioner appointed at the last Term of this Court to settle with Matthew Ryburn Guardian of Harmon R. Jenkins, & make report to the present term of the Court as above.

On motion ordered by the Court that William B. Wall, be appointed Constable in Capt. Epp's company, & the said William B. Wall entered into bond & security in the penal sum of six hundred & forty dollars conditioned as the law directs & took the oath prescribed by law.

(p-78)   The Commissioners appointed at the last term of this Court to settle with William E. Williams Administrator of Burrell H. Peeples decd. make their report to this Court, & on motion ordered to be recorded.

Thomas Williams administrator of William McCauley decd. returns into Court an Inventory & account of Sales of the estate of the said deceased & quallified agreeable to law & on motion the same is ordered to be Recorded.

John Hinton Executor of Kimbrough Hinton decd. returned into Court, an Inventory of the goods & chattles, rights & credits of the said decd. & quallified agreeable to law, & on motion the same is ordered to be Recorded.

On motion ordered by the Court, that Richd. B. Blount and Joseph Woolfolk esquires, be appointed Commissioners to settle with William Trigg admr. of the estate of Daniel Collier decd. & make report to the next term of this Court.

On motion it is ordered by the Court, that Wyatt Epps be appointed Guardian to Thomas Epps & the said Wyatt Epps entered into bond & security in the sum of Two thousand dollars conditioned as the law directs & quallified agreeable to law.

James Carr & Mathew Ryburn Commissioners appointed at the last term of this Court to settle with Cordall Norfleet Guardian to Philips Ford (minor) make their report to this Court & on motion ordered to be Recorded.

William McGowan, Merideth Williams & James Carr esquires Commissioners appointed at the last Term of this Court, to settle with Sarah Shaw Guardian to the minor heirs of Henry Shaw decd. make their report & on motion ordered to be Recorded.

Matthew Ryburn & Abner Gupton esquires, commissioners appointed at the last Term of this Court to settle with Herbert Ally, administrator (p-79) of Miles Ally decd. make their report, & on motion ordered to be Recorded.

On motion, ordered by the Court, that Randolph Raimey be discontinued as ferry keeper at the ferry on Cumberland River commonly called Noll's ferry.

This day was produced in Open Court, the last will & Testament of Rowland Vick decd. and the execution thereof duly proven by the oaths of Henry Small & Nathan Vick, two of the subscribing witnesses thereto, to be the last will & Testament of the said Rowland Vick decd & thereupon Daniel & John Rook, the executors therein named appeared in Open Court & entered into bond & security in the penalty of Three thousand dollars & quallified agreeable to law therefore it is ordered by the Court that letters Testamentary issue to the said Daniel Rook & John Rook upon the estate of the said decd.

William E. Williams, administrator of Burrell H. Peeples decd. returned to Court an Inventory of the Book account of the said deceased & on motion ordered to be Recorded.

The Commissioners appointed at the last Term of this Court to divide the personal estate of James Paine decd. between Gerard Van Buren & the heirs of said Paine, make their report with the a/c of sales to this Court & on motion ordered to be Recorded.

On motion ordered by the Court, that Henry W. Merriwether be appointed their Inspector of Tobacco at the ware house of Henry W. & Valentine Merriwether's on Red River, & the said Henry W. Merriwether entered into bond & security in the penal sum of Three thousand dollars & quallified agreeable to law.

On motion ordered by the Court, that William Trigg & Richard B. Blount esqrs. be appointed commissioners to settle with James Adams admr. of Daniel Venable decd. & make report to next Court.

(p-80) On motion ordered by the Court, that Lewis Terrell, Richard B. Blount & James Carney be appointed Commissioner to divide the Estate of William Fortson & Mildred Fortson that was left them by Elizabeth Johnson & after the death of Mildred to the heirs of the said Elizabeth, William, & Mildred in pursuance of the deed of Gift, from the said Elizabeth Johnson, & that the said Commissioners set out & shew particularly what amount is due each of the said distributees & make return to next Court.

On motion ordered by the Court, that Daniel Rook be appointed Guardian to John Vick a minor heir of the late Rowland Vick decd. & the said Daniel Rook entered into bond & security satisfactory to the Court & took the oath prescribed by law.

On motion ordered by the Court, that John Rook, be appointed Guardian to Drucilla Vick, minor heir of Rowland Vick lately decd. — & the said John Rook entered into bond and security satisfactory to the Court & took the oath prescribed by law.

On motion, ordered by the Court, that John Mallory, be appointed Guardian, to Thomas Mallory, his Brother, & the said John Mallory entered into bond & security satisfactory to the Court & quallified agreeable to law.

On motion ordered by the Court, that John Mallory, be appointed administrator of Frances Mallory decd. & the said John Mallory entered into bond & security ///////// satisfactory to the Court & took the oath prescribed by law, therefore it is ordered by the Court, that letters of administration issue to the said John Mallory on the estate of the said decd.

On motion ordered by the Court that Matthew Ryburn & James Carr esquires be appointed a committee to settle with Cordall Norfleet, Guardian to Philip Ford, minor, & make report to next Court.

(p-81)   The jury summoned by the Sheriff by order of last Court, to lay off the dower of Sarah Hutcheson, widow of John Hutcheson decd. make their report to this Court & on motion ordered to be Recorded.

On motion ordered by the Court, that William Trigg & Richard B. Blount Esqrs. be appointed commissioners to settle with Richard Fortson his administration on the estate of Mildred Fortson decd. & report to the next Term of this Court.

Sterling Noblett esquire , Richard H. Adams, & John Martin, commissioners appointed at the last Term of this Court to settle with William E. Williams Guardian to Elizabeth Peoples, make their report & on motion ordered to be Recorded.

On motion ordered by the Court, that Douglass Merriwether be appointed overseer of the road leading from the state line of Kentucky, to Capt. Thomas River's Mill in place of James Donnollson & that the following hands work on said road, to wit, said Capt. Thomas Rivers hands, Samuel Dabney's hands, sd. Douglass Merriwether's hands, William Walter's & hands, John Gaines' hands, Parret Gaines & William Donnalson.

On motion ordered by the Court, that the following hands, work under William Hubbard overseer of the road leading up Dud's Creek in place of Thomas Wyatt (to wit) Tristam Hubbard, Philip Hubbard, James Mickle, James Hubbard, George Mickle, Absalom Williams, Edwin Williams, John Noblett Sr. hands, Thomas Wyatt & hands, Samuel Wilkerson, John Wilkerson, Sterling Noblett's hands, John Martin, Robert Dumpass, Richard H. Adams & hands, Eaton Powel, Samuel Caldwell, & hands, Robert Mickle & John Mickle, who shall compose the number of hands to work on said Road.

(p-82)   On motion ordered by the Court that William Broom be appointed overseer of the road leading from Charnal Corbins' to Samuel C. Hawkin's place in place of William McClure who has resigned, & that the following hands work on said road (to wit) Absalom Rye, Thomas Rye, Charnall Corbin's hands, J. Bond's hands & W. Gibson & all others within the bounds of said road, who have not heretofore been ordered to work on any other road.

On motion ordered by the Court, that William Rye be appointed Overseer of the road in place of Samuel Hire, who has resigned, & that the following hands who worked under the former Overseer, work under the said William Rye, to wit, Elijah Lewis, John Little, James Smith Jr., Aaron Rainwaters, Washington Baird Abraham Baggot & John Yarbrough & all others in the bounds of said road, who have not heretofore been ordered to work on any other road.

On motion ordered by the Court, that Joel Bayliss be appointed Overseer of the road, leading from Majr. Frosts toward Hopkinsville, as far as Fletcher's fork & that the following hands work on said road, to wit, Widdow Bayliss' hands, the hands of said Joel Bayliss, John Mitchel, Durrell Bayliss Jr., D. Frost & hands, W. Haney, William Jeffries, Thomas Jeffries, Robert White & hands, Vinson Cooper & hands, John Stagney & Samuel White & hands, & all others who live within the bounds of said road, who have not heretofore been ordered to work on any other road.

On motion ordered by the Court, that Peter Holt Sr., be appointed Overseer of the road leading from Clarksville to said Peter Holt's ferry & that the following hands work on said road, to wit, Joshua P. Vaughan's hands, Mark Booths' hands, Uriah Humphreys & hands to wit, his sons & the hands of Mary Duff compose the number of hands to work on said road.

(p-83)   On motion ordered by the Court, that Wilson Vick be appointed overseer of the road from ////////////// // //// Vick's ferry to where it intersects the road leading to Holt's ferry it being /// the road leading to Charlotte, & that the following hands work on said road, to wit, Norfleet Smith, William L. Brown's hands, who reside on his farm & Major Henry Small's hands, compose the number of hands to work on said road. On motion Ordered by the Court, that John W. Barker be appointed Overseer of the road, in the place of Thomas Merriwether, & that the same hands that were ordered to work under the said Merriwether, work under the said John W. Barker.

On motion ordered by the Court, that David Northington, be appointed Overseer of the road in place of James Grant, who has resigned & that the following hands work on said road, to wit, Samuel Northington & hands, Henry Northington & hands, Joel Grizard & hands, John Edmonson, & hands, sd. David Northington's hands & the hands of John Northington, & all other hands within the bounds of said road, who have not heretofore been ordered to work on any other road.

Thomas Williams administrator of Benjamin Wilson decd. returned into Court, an account of the hire of the Negroes belonging to said estate for the year 1823 & quallified to the same agreeable to law & on motion ordered to be Recorded.

A Power of Attorney from James McDaniel & Joel McDaniel to Major Price, was duly proven in Open Court, by Cave Johnson & William G. McClure subscribing witnesses thereto, & the same is ordered to be Certified.

A Deed of Conveyance from Darnall Campbell to William McCauley for 31½ Acres of land, was produced in Open Court & the execution thereof duly proven, by the oaths of Willis Harris & Thomas Williams two of the subscribing witnesses thereto & on motion ordered to be Certified for registration.

(p-84)   A Deed of Conveyance from Sampson Moore to Thomas Moore for 228 Acres of land, was produced in Open Court & the execution thereof was duly proven by the Oath of Solathiel Sherrod, one of the subscribing witnesses thereto to be the act & Deed of the said Sampson Moore & the said Solathiel Sherrod also proved the hand writing of Benjamin A. Yeargin the other subscribing witnesses thereto, to be in the proper handwriting of the said Benjamin A. Yeargin & that he subscribed his name thereto in his presence & on motion the same is ordered to be certified for registration.

This day came into Open Court Rebecca Stewart, and moved the Court for an allowance to be made her out of the estate of Robert W. Stewart and it appearing to the Court that sd. Rebecca Stewart is the administrator of of the estate of said Robert Stewart, and that she has been at great expence and trouble in and about the management & settlement of the same, It is therefore the opinion of the Court that she is entitled to the sum of one hundred dollars for her trouble and personal expences and the same is to her accordingly adjudged.

This day came into Open Court Rebecca Stewart widow of Robert W. Stewart decd. and moved the Court to appoint commissioners to ////// /////// /////////////// lay off her years provision, and it is ordered by the Court that William Morrow, Drewry Bagwell & Abner Harris, be appointed for the purpose aforesaid & that they make return to the next term of this Court.

(p-85)   A Deed of Conveyance from Thomas A. Morris to Robert L. Lawrason for 140 acres of land in two tracts was produced in Open Court & the execution thereof was duly ////// acknowledged, by the said Thomas A. Morris to be his act & Deed for the purposes therein contained & on motion ordered to be Certified for registration.

A Deed of Conveyance from John Noblett Jr., to Ambrose Martin was produced in Open Court & the execution thereof was duly acknowledged by the said John Noblett Jr., to be his act & Deed for the purposes therein mentioned & on motion ordered to be Certified for registration.

An order of the Louisa County Court State of Virginia appointing /////// /.//////// Forest Hunter Guardian to Eliza Hudson Mitchel, Martha Ann Mitchel and Mardinia C. Mitchel orphans of William S. Mitchell decd. Certified by the Clerk of said County was produced in Court & ordered to be Recorded.

A Deed of Conveyance from Warren Sikes to James Miller for 35½ acres of land, was produced in Open Court & the execution thereof duly acknowledged by the said Warren Sikes to be his act & Deed for the purposes therein contained & on motion ordered to be Certified for registration.

A Deed of Conveyance from James H. Brigham to Thomas Williford for 100 acres of land, was produced in Open Court & the execution thereof was duly proven by the Oaths of John Williford & Edward Dicas, the subscribing witnesses thereto & on motion ordered to be Certified for registration.

A Bill of Sale from Benjamin King Sheriff of Montgomery County to Stephen Cantrell for certain negro slaves therein mentioned, was produced in Open Court & the execution thereof was duly proven by the oaths of Andrew Vance & Peter H. Marr the subscribing witnesses thereto & on motion ordered to be Recorded.

(p-86) A Deed of Conveyance from F. W. Huling to John Rudolph for 20 Acres of land, was produced in Open Court & the execution thereof, was duly acknowledged by the said F. W. Huling to be his act & Deed for the purposes therein contained, & on motion ordered to be certified for registration.

A Deed of Conveyance from C. Crusman sheriff of Montgomery County to F. W. Huling for 180 acres of land, was produced in Open Court & the execution thereof, was duly acknowledged by the said C. Crusman sheriff of Montgomery County to F. W. Huling for 180 acres of land, was produced in Open Court & the execution thereof, was duly acknowledged by the said C. Crusman, to be his act & deed for the purposes therein contained, & on motion ordered to be Certified for registration.

A Deed of Conveyance from James Loggins to Henry Neblett & Benjamin Neblett for 250 acres of land, was produced in Open Court & the execution thereof was duly proven by the Oaths of John Wyatt & John S. Mosley the subscribing witnesses thereto & on motion ordered to be certified for registration.

A Deed of Conveyance from John Emberson to James Loggins, for 250 Acres of land, was produced in Open Court, & the execution thereof was duly proven by the oaths of John Wyatt & John S. Mosley two of the subscribing witnesses thereto & on motion ordered to be certified for registration.

Court adjourned untill tomorrow morning to meet at nine O'clock.
Stephen Cocke
Thos. Smith
James Carr

The Worshipful Court of Montgomery County have met according to adjournment Tuesday January 21st 1823.

Stephen Cocke)
Thomas Smith &) Esqrs.
James Carr) Justices

(p-87) The following persons were duly elected empannelled, sworn & charged as a grand jury to enquire for the body of the County (to wit) Edward S. Walton foreman, Samuel Kerchival, Stephen Mallory, John P. Epps, Philmer Whitworth, Needham Whitfield, William Stewart Sr., Samuel White, Pray H. Whipple, James Trice Sr., William Porter, Burrell Bayliss, & Matthew Ogburn, having received their charge retired to consider of their presentments.

On motion ordered by the Court, that James Fentress, Francis Carter, & Robert Vance esquires be appointed to lay off ~~the~~ ~~off~~ a years provision to Elizabeth Corbin widow of Charnall Corbin decd. & make report to the next Term of this Court.

On motion and for reasons appearing satisfactory to the Court from the affidavit of James McClure that Thomas Hester be exhonerated from the payment of the whole appraised value of some hogs Posted by him in this County in the year 1822, & that the County Trustee receive of the said Thomas Hester half the appraised value & receipt in same manner as if paid before the legal Term of payment had elapsed.

The Court proceeded to the classification of the justices of the peace, to hold the Court of pleas & quarter sessions of Montgomery County & thereupon the following Class were elected in the first Class to hold the Court at this Term, to wit, Alexander M. Rogers, Stephen Pettus, Thomas Smith, Abner Gupton, John Korohival, Sterling Noblett, John McCauley, & William R. Gibson & the following justices were elected in the second class to hold the Court at April Term (to wit) James Carr, Francis Baker, Richard B. Blount Isaac Dennison, Bryan Whitfield, & Stephen Cooke & Henry H. Bryan & Charles Bailey & the following justices were elected in the third class to hold the (p-88) Court at July Term 1823 to wit, Thomas W. Atkinson Samuel Smith, James Barret, William McDaniel, Valentine Allen, Joseph Woolfolk & Lewis C. Taylor, & the following justices were elected ~~//~~ ~~////~~ in the fourth class to hold the Court at October Term (to wit) Abner Harris Robert Vance, Matthew Ryburn, ~~//////~~ John Wickham, William Trigg, Joshua P. Vaughan, James Bowers & Francis Carter.

On motion ordered by the Court, that Sandy Barker be permitted to give in his list of Taxable property for the year 1822 & that the same be annexed to said years tax list.

Stephen Thomas esquire hands into Court, his resignation as a justice of the peace & the same is received by the Court.

From the affidavit of James Allen, it is ordered by the Court, that he be exonerated from serving as a juror at the present term of the Court.

On motion ordered by the Court, that Ellinor Adams, John & William Hust, Joseph Barbee, Thomas Carraway & Jesse Smith, be ~~////////~~ permitted to give in their list of Taxable property for the year 1822, & that the same be annexed to the tax list of said year.

On motion ordered by the Court, that, William Mamy, W. H. Murfee, & the heirs of H. Murfee, by their agent Benjamin Orgain be permitted to give in their list of Taxable property for 1822 & that the same be annexed to said years Tax list.

On motion ordered by the Court that Nathaniel H. Allen be permitted to give in his list of Taxable property for 1822 & that it be annexed to said years Tax list.

(p-89) The Grand Jury appeared in Open Court & returned a Bill of Indictment the state against Joseph Woolfolk a True Bill.

Richard Fortson administrator of Mildred Fortson decd. returned into Court an Inventory of ~~////~~ the estate of said decd. & quallified agreeable to law & on motion the same is ordered to be recorded.

Charles A. Hutcheson, administrator of John Hutcheson decd. returned into Court, an Inventory & account of Sales of the estate of said decd. & Quallified to the same agreeable to law & on motion ordered to be Recorded.

On motion ordered by the Court, that Sterling Noblett be appointed administrator of Charnall Corbin decd. whereupon the said Sterling Noblett entered into bond & security satisfactory to the Court & quallified agreeable to law & it is ordered that the same be made as of yesterday.

A Deed of Conveyance from ~~//////// //.//////~~ James Johnson to William B. Pansy for 200 acres of land, was produced in Open Court & the execution thereof was duly proven by the Oath of John Noville one of the subscribing witnesses thereto & on motion ordered to be Certified accordingly.

A Deed of Conveyance from William Whitehead & Benjamin Whitehead Jr., to John Noblett Junr., was produced in Open Court & the execution thereof was duly proven by the Oath of John Caldwell one of the subscribing witnesses thereto, & on motion ordered to be certified.

A Conveyance from David Outlaw to William Haynes for three negroes named, Tom, Hannah, & Silas, was produced in Open Court & the execution thereof, was duly proven by the Oath of Daniel Tolson, one of the subscribing witnesses thereto & on motion ordered to be Certified accordingly.

(p-90) A Power of Attorney from Leroy Ellis and Harriet Dabney Ellis his wife & Catherine Suelson Mitchel to Forest Hunter of the state of Virginia, certified by the Clerk of Louisa County state aforesaid, was reviewed by the Court & on motion ordered to be Recorded.

A Deed of Conveyance from John Ellis to Richard K. Tyler for 320 acres of land was produced in Open Court & the execution thereof was duly proven by the Oaths of Richard B. Blount & John Hampton the subscribing witnesses thereto & on motion ordered to be certified for registration.

A Deed of Conveyance from Christopher Mulcaster to Thomas McGill for 160 acres of land in the Arkansas Teritory, was produced in Open Court, & the execution thereof, was duly acknowledged by the said Christopher Mulcaster to be his act and deed for the purposes therein mentioned, & on motion ordered to be Certified.

A Deed of conveyance from William Jones to Benjamin Jones for 30 acres of land was produced in Open Court, & the execution thereof was duly proven by the Oaths of William M. Williams & John S. Carroll, the subscribing witnesses thereto & on motion ordered to be certified for registration.

A Deed of Conveyance from David Outlaw to William Haynes for 260 Acres of land & Sundry other property, was produced in Open Court & the execution thereof was duly proven by the oath of Jesse Craft, one of the subscribing witnesses thereto, & on motion ordered to be certified.

A Deed of Conveyance from Joseph Bogard & Charles Bogard to Frederick W. Huling for 326 acres of land was produced in Open Court & the execution thereof was duly acknowledged (p-91) by the said Joseph Bogard & Charles Bogard, to be their act & deed for the purposes therein mentioned & on motion Ordered to be Certified for registration.

A Deed of Conveyance from Thomas C. Carney, David Wilson, & William S. Wilson of the state of North Carolina Cunituck County to William Sanderline of the County of Camden & state aforesaid, for the one half of 3840 Acres of land, certified by the Clerk & presiding Magistrate of the County of Cunituck & State of North Carolina aforesaid, after being examined by the Court, the same was ordered to be Registered.

Present Alexander M. Rogers, James Carr & Richard B. Blount esquires justices.

WILSON GILBERT)
    vs   ) Debt
JESSE CRAFT   )

This day came the parties by their attornies & thereupon came a jury of good & lawful men, to wit, Edward Trice, Henry Weeks, John Hust, William B. Nelson, Matthew D. Simmons, John Gainer, Dennis Doherty, Daniel Kyle, Wilson Gibson, John Hampton, Peter P. Roberts & Jourdan Lisles, who being duly elected tried & sworn the truth to speak upon the issue joined upon their Oaths do say, that they find the issue in favour of the Plaintiff & that the defendant doth owe to the plaintiff the sum of one hundred & fifty dollars, the debt do assess his damages by reason of the detention of said debt to seven dollars eighty seven & ½ Cents besides Costs.
Therefore it is considered by the Court that the plaintiff, Wilson Gilbert recover of the defendant Jesse Craft, the sum of One hundred and fifty seven dollars eighty seven & half Cents, the debt & damages so assessed by the jury in form aforesaid, together with his cost by him about his suit in this behalf Expended.

(p-92)   A Deed of Conveyance from Dempsey Creekmour & wife Elizabeth of the County of Cunituck & state of North Carolina to Thomas C. Cassey of the County & state aforesaid for one fourth part of 3840 Acres of land in the County of Montgomery & State of Tennessee, was produced in Open Court, Certified by the Clerk & presiding Magistrate of the County of Cunituck & State of North Carolina aforesaid, whereupon the same was ordered to be Registered.

This day was produced in Open Court A Deed of Conveyance from Joseph White, Oney Bailey, Margaret Bailey & Sarah Elliott heirs at law of Benjamin & Joseph Bailey decd. to Wilson Sanderline of the State of North Carolina & County of Camden for 3840 Acres of land Certified by the Clerk & presiding magistrate of the County of Pasquotank & state aforesaid, whereupon the same was ordered to be Registered.

This day was produced in Open Court a Deed of Conveyance from Eldridge D. Robertson for himself & attorney in fact for Sterling C. Robertson & Elizabeth Childress, to Abner Gupton for 640 Acres of land Certified by the Clerk of Davidson County, whereupon the same is Ordered to be Registered.

This day was produced in Open Court A Deed of Conveyance from Samuel Woods of North Carolina & County of Orange to John A. Woods of the State of Kentucky, & County of Henderson for 333 3/4 Acres & twenty five poles of land Certified by the Clerk & presiding Magistrate of the County of Orange, State of North Carolina aforesaid, whereupon the same is Ordered to be Registered.

A Deed of release from James W. Carney to Polly Carney his wife, to Kenchen Taylor of Martin County state of North Carolina, was produced in Open Court & the execution thereof duly acknowledged by the said James W. Carney to be his act & deed for the purposes therein mentioned & the said Polly Carney being examined by the Court, privily & apart from her (p-93) said husband, freely confesses that she executed the said deed freely of her own accord, and without the compulsion or restraint of her said husband, and on motion the same is ordered to be certified.

            SAMUEL DABNEY   )
                 VS   ) Debt
        THOMAS BATSON & STEPHEN PETTUS   )

This day came the said plaintiff by his attorney & said defendant, being called came not but made default. Therefore it is considered by the Court that said plaintiff recover against said defendants the sum of one thousand dollars, the debt in the declaration mentioned & the further sum of $65.00 damages by the plaintiff sustained by reason of t the detention of the debt aforesaid & his Costs in this behalf expended & &.
The plaintiff by his attorney here in Court releases of the above Judgt. the sum of three hundred & twenty five dollars.

            CHARLOTTE OLDHAM Guardian   )
                 VS   ) Debt
        JOHN BRODIE & LODWICK BRODIE   )

This day came the said plaintiff by his attornies & said defendants being solemnly caled, came not, came not but made default. Therefore it is considered by the Court that the said plaintiff, Charlotte Oldham Guardian as aforesaid recover of the said defendants, John Brodie & Lodwick Brodie, the sum of Four hundred & sixty dollars, the debt in the declaration mentioned α the further sum of forty eight dollars & thirty cents, damages, by the plaintiff sustained by reason of the detention of the debt aforesaid & her costs in this behalf Expended & &.

        Court adjourned untill tomorrow morning to meet at nine O'clock.
                                    Stephen Cocke
                                    J. P. Vaughan
                                    Thos. Smith

(p-94)   The Worshipful Court of Montgomery County have met according to adjournment Wednes day January 22nd 1823.
                    Present

                            Stephen Cocke   )
                            Joshua P. Vaughan   ) Esquires
                            & Thomas Smith   ) Justices

On motion ordered by the Court, that Henry Williams be permitted to give in his list of Taxable property for the year 1822 & that the same be annexed to said years tax list.

On motion Ordered by the Court that the ferry on Cumberland River formerly kept by James Good be discontinued, & that said James Good be exonerated from any further responsibility relative to said ferry.

Joshua P. Vaughan, Thomas Smith & Stephen Cooke, Esquires Commissioners Appointed at the last term of this Court to settle with Elisha R. Oldham administrator of Moses Oldham decd. make their report & on motion ordered to be Recorded.

THOMAS JOHNSON
    VS   } Debt
SAMUEL CRAFT

This day came the parties by their attornies & thereupon came a jury of good & lawful men (to wit) Edward S. Walton, Samuel Korchival, Stephen Mallory, John P. Epps Philmor Whitworth, Needham Whitfield, William Stewart Sr., Samuel White, Frey H. Whipple, James Trice Sr., Burrell Bayliss & Matthew Ogburn, who being duly elected tried & sworn the truth to speak upon the issues joined upon their oaths do say that they find the issues in favour of the plaintiff, & that the defendant doth owe to the plaintiff the sum of One hundred & **five dollars** Debt, & do assess the plaintiffs damages to Twenty four dollars & fifteen cents, by reason of the detention of said debt besides his Cost.

(p-95) Therefore it is considered by the Court, that the plaintiff Thomas Johnson, recover of the defendant Samuel Craft, the sum of One hundred and twenty nine dollars & fifteen cents, the debt & damages so assessed by the jury aforesaid, together with his Costs by him about his suit in this behalf Expended.

WILLIAM B. NELSON
    VS   } Debt
HUGH F. BELL

This day came the parties by their attornies & thereupon came a jury of good & lawful men to wit, Edward S. Walton, Samuel Korchival, Stephen Mallory, John P. Epps, Philmer Whitworth, Needham Whitfield, William Stewart Sr., Samuel White, Frey H. Whipple, James Trice Sr., Burrell Bayliss, & Matthew Ogburn, who being duly elected tried & sworn, the truth to speak upon the issues joined upon their Oaths do say, that they find the issues in favour of the plaintiff, & that the defendant, doth owe to the plaintiff the sum of Two thousand dollars, Debt, & do assess the plaintiffs damages to Four hundred and ten dollars by reason of the detention of said debt, besides his Cost.
Therefore it is considered by the Court that the plaintiff William B. Nelson, recover of the defendant Hugh F. Bell the sum of Two thousand four hundred and ten dollars, the debt and damages so assessed by the jury in form aforesaid together with the Costs in this behalf Expended.

WILLIAM B. NELSON)
VS   ) Debt
HUGH P. BELL   )

This day came the parties by their attornies & thereupon came a
jury of good & lawful men to wit, Edward S. Walton, Samuel Kerchival,
John P. Epps, Philmer Whitworth, Needham Whitfield, William Stewart
Jr., Samuel White, Pray H. Whipple, James Trice Sr., //////// ///////
(p-93) Durrell Bayliss, & Matthew Ogburn & Stephen Mallory, who being
duly elected, tried & sworn, the truth to speak upon the issues joined
upon their Oaths do say, that they find the issues in favour of the
plaintiff that the defendant doth owe the plaintiff the sum of Two
thousand dollars Debt and do assess the plaintiffs damages to Two hundred
and ninety dollars by reason of the detention of said debt besides his
Cost.
Therefore it is considered by the Court that the plaintiff William B.
Nelson, recover of the defendant Hugh P. Bell the sum of Two thousand
two hundred & ninety dollars, the debt & damages so assessed by the jury
in form aforesaid together, with the Costs in this behalf Expended.

JOHN BRODIE assignee)
of ROBERT SEARCY   )
VS   ) Debt
PATRICK H. DARBY   )

This day came the parties by their attornies & thereupon came a
jury of good & lawful men (to wit) Edward S. Walton, Samuel Kerchival,
Stephen Mallory, John P. Epps, Philip Whitworth, Needham Whitfield,
William Stewart Sr., Samuel White, Pray H. Whipple, James Trice Sr.,
Durrell Bayliss & Matthew Ogburn, who being duly elected, tried & sworn
the truth to speak upon the issues joined upon their Oaths do say that
they find the issues in favour of the plaintiff & that the defendant
doth owe to the plaintiff the sum of Three hundred dollars, the debt in
the declaration mentioned, & do assess the plaintiffs damages to fifty
two dollars, by reason of the detention of said debt, besides his Costs.
Therefore it is considered by the Court that the plaintiff John Brodie
assignee as aforesaid recover of the defendant, Patrick H. Darby, the
sum of Three hundred & fifty two dollars (p-97) the debt & damages,
so assessed by the jury aforesaid together with the Costs in this behalf
Expended.

JAMES B. BOWLEN)
VS   ) Debt
PATRICK DAWSON)

This day came the parties by their attornies & thereupon came a
jury of good & lawful men (to wit) Edward S. Walton, Samuel Kerchival,
Stephen Mallory, John P. Epps, Philmer Whitworth, Needham Whitfield,
William Stewart Sr. Samuel White, Pray H. Whipple, James Trice Sr.,
//////// /////// Durrell Bayliss, & Matthew Ogburn, who being duly elected
tried & sworn the truth to speak upon the issues joined upon their oaths,
do say, that they find the issues in favour of the plaintiff, & that the
defendant doth owe to the plaintiff the sum of one hundred & fifty dollars
Debt, & do assess his damages to Eight dollars and twenty five cents, by
reason of the detention of said debt besides his Costs.

Therefore it is considered by the Court that the plaintiff James B. Bowlin, recover of the defendant Patrick Dawson, the sum of One hundred & fifty eight dollars & twenty five cents, the debt and damages so assessed by the jury in form aforesaid, together with the Costs in this behalf Expended.

EPHRAIM H. FOSTER assee)
of JOHN H. POSTON)
VS) Debt
CHARLES BAILEY)

This day came said plaintiff by his attornies, & the defendant being solemnly called, came not, but made default.
Therefore it is considered by the Court, that the plaintiff Ephraim H. Foster assignee as aforesaid, recover of the defendant Charles Bailey, the sum of Two hundred & twenty three dollars & thirty nine cents, the debt in the declaration mentioned, & the further sum of twenty five dollars & sixty two cents damages sustained by the detention of said debt & also the Cost in this behalf Expended.

(p-93) EPHRAIM H. FOSTER assee)
VS) Debt
ROWLAND VICK)

It appearing to the Court, that Rowland Vick, the defendant in this case hath departed this life, whereupon it is ordered that a Scieri Facias issue against the Executors to revive said suit.

ZACHARIAH GRANT)
VS)
RICHARD BROWN &) Debt
JACOB FOUST)

This day came the parties by their attornies & thereupon came a jury of good & lawful men, to wit, Edward S. Walton, Samuel Kerchival, Stephen Mallory, John P. Epps, Philmer Whitworth, Needham Whitfield, Pray H. Whipple, James Trice Sr., Burrell Bayliss & Matthew Ogburn, William Stewart Sr., & Samuel White, who being duly elected, tried & sworn, the truth to speak upon the issues joined, upon their Oaths do say that they find the issues in favour of the plaintiff, & that the defendant doth owe to the plaintiff the sum of Three hundred and seventy five dollars, Debt & do assess his damages to nine dollars and seventy five cents by reason of the detention of said debt besides his Costs. Therefore it is considered by the Court, that the plaintiff Zachariah Grant recover of the defendant, Richard Brown & Jacob Foust, the sum of Three hundred & eighty four dollars & seventy five cents the debt & damages so assessed by the jury in form aforesaid together with the Cost in this behalf Expended.

THOMAS RIVERS)
VS) Debt
MERRIDA HOWARD)

This day came the parties by their attornies & thereupon came a jury of good & lawful men, to wit, Edward S. Walton Samuel Kerchival, Stephen Mallory, John P. Epps, Philmer Whitworth, Needham Whitfield,

William Stewart, Sr., Samuel White, Pray H. Whipple, James Trice Sr.,
(p-99) Burrell Bayliss & Matthew Ogburn, who being duly elected, tried
& sworn, the truth to speak upon the issues joined, upon their Oaths do
say, that they find the issues in favour of the plaintiff, & that the
defendant doth owe to the plaintiff the sum of seven hundred & twenty
one dollars and ninety four cents, ballance of Debt & do assess the
plaintiffs damages to Forty two dollars & seventy five cents, by reason
of the detention of said debt, besides his Costs.
Therefore it is considered by the Court, that the plaintiff Thomas Rivers,
recover of the defendant Nerida Howard the sum of seven hundred and sixty
four dollars and sixty nine cents, the balance of the debt and damages
so assessed by the jury in form aforesaid, together with the Costs in
this behalf Expended.

```
HUGH McCLURE assee   )
        VS           )  Debt
WILLIAM HAYNES &     )
WILLIAM E. WILLIAMS  )
```

This day came the parties by their attornies & thereupon came a
jury of good & lawful men, to wit, Edward S. Walton, Samuel Kerchival,
Stephen Mallory, John P. Epps, Philmer Whitworth, Needham Whitfield
William Stewart Sr., Samuel White, Pray H. Whipple, James Trice Sr.,
Burrell Bayless & Matthew Ogburn, who being duly elected, tried & sworn
the truth to speak upon the issue joined, upon their Oaths do say that
they find the issue in favour of the plaintiff; & that the defendant doth
owe to the plaintiff the sum of one hundred & fifty dollars Debt & do
assess his damages to nine dollars by reason of the detention of the said
debt besides his Cost.
Therefore it is considered by the Court, that the plaintiff Hugh McClure
assignee as aforesaid recover of the defendants, William Haynes & William
E. Williams, the sum of One hundred and fifty nine dollars, the debt &
damages so assessed by the jury in form aforesaid, together with the
Costs in this behalf Expended.

```
(p-100)   SAMUEL VANCE     )
             VS            )  Debt
          CHARLES BAILEY   )
```

This day came the parties by their attornies & there upon came
a jury of good & lawful men, to wit, Edward S. Walton, Samuel Kerchival,
Stephen Mallory, John P. Epps, Philmer Whitworth, Needham Whitfield,
William Stewart Sr., Samuel White, Pray H. Whipple, James Trice Sr.,
Burrell Bayliss, & Matthew Ogburn, who being duly elected, tried & sworn
the truth to speak upon the issues joined upon their Oaths do say that
they find the issues in favour of the plaintiff & that the defendant doth
owe to the plaintiff the sum of One hundred and forty two dollars & seventy
five cents the debt in the declaration mentioned & do assess the plaintiffs
damages to twenty two dollars & Eighty seven & half cents by reason of the
detention of said debt besides his costs.
Therefore it is considered by the Court that, the plaintiff Samuel Vance
recover of the defendant Charles Bailey, the sum of One hundred and sixty
five dollars, sixty two & a half cents, the debt & damages so assessed by
the jury in form aforesaid, together with the costs in this behalf
Expended.

STEPHEN CANTRELL)
    VS)
CHARLES D. MCLEAN,) Case
WILLIAM GRAY &)
MARY his wife admrs.)

This day came the parties by their attornies & thereupon came a
jury of good & lawful men (to wit) Edward S. Walton, Samuel Kerchival,
Stephen Mallory, John P. Epps, Philmer Whitworth, Needham Whitfield,
William Stewart Sr., Samuel White, Tray H. Whipple, James Trice Sr.,
Burrell Bayliss, & Matthew Ogburn, who being duly elected, tried & sworn
the truth to speak, upon their Oaths do say that the defendants have not
paid the debt in the declaration mentioned, nor have they any asset and
and they also find that the said defendants have fully administered all
& singular the goods & chattles, rights (p-101) & ~~~~~ Credits of
Bennit Searcy decd. that have come to their hands to be administered &
they find for the plaintiff the sum of Fifty six dollars twelve & a half
cents the balance of the debt in the pltfs. declaration mentioned.
It is therefore considered by the Court, that said plaintiff recover of
the said defendants the aforesaid sum of Fifty six dollars twelve & a
half cents, the debt aforesaid assessed by the jury aforesaid to be
levied of the goods & chattles of Bennit Searcy decd. that may hereafter
come to the hands of the said administrator to be administered, & the
Costs to be levied of the proper goods & chattles of the said administrators,
& the said plaintiff suggesting to the Court here that real estate hath
descended to the heirs of the said Bennit Searcy decd. it is ordered
that a Sciari Facias issue against said heirs returnable & &.

HENRY H. BRYAN Admr.)
of DREW S. WHITMILL)
    VS) Case
MORGAN BROWN)

This day came the parties by their attornies & thereupon came a
jury of good & lawful men (to wit) Edward S. Walton, Samuel Kerchival,
Stephen Mallory, John P. Epps, Philmer Whitworth, Needham Whitfield,
William Stewart Sr., Samuel White, Tray H. Whipple, James Trice Sr.,
Burrell Bayliss & Matthew Ogburn, who being duly elected, tried & sworn
the truth to speak upon the issues joined between the parties, upon their
Oaths do say that they find the issue in behalf of the said defendant.
Therefore it is considered by the Court that the defendant Morgan Brown
recover of the plaintiff Henry H. Bryan administrator as aforesaid, the
Costs in this behalf Expended, to be levied of the goods & Chattles,
rights & Credits, which were of Drew S. Whitmill at the time of his
death & which have come to the hands of the said Henry H. Bryan his
administrator to be administered if so much he has, if not (p-102)
to be levied of the proper goods & chattles lands & tenements of the said
Henry H. Bryan.

SAMUEL VANCE)
    VS) Debt
AMBROSE MADISON)

This day came the parties by their attornies & thereupon came a
jury of good & lawful men (to wit) Edward S. Walton, Samuel Kerchival,

Stephen Mallory, John F. Epps, Philmer Whitworth Needham Whitfield, William Stewart Sr., Samuel White, Fray H. Whipple, James Trice Sr., Durrell Bayliss & Matthew Ogburn, who being duly elected, tried & sworn the truth to speak upon the issues joined, upon their Oaths, do say, that they find the issues in favour of the plaintiff & that the defendant doth owe to the plaintiff the sum of Two hundred and sixty eight dollars, twelve & a half cents & do assess the plaintiffs damages to seven dollars & twenty cents by reason of the detention of said debt, besides his Costs. Therefore it is considered by the Court that the plaintiff Samuel Vance, recover of the defendant Ambrose Madison the sum of Two hundred and seventy five dollars, thirty two & a ½ cents, the debt & damages so assessed by the jury in form aforesaid, together with the Costs in this behalf Expended.

CONSTANT H. F. BARR & CO.)
VS) Debt
JOSIAH S. ELLIS)

This day came into Court Cave Johnson Esqr. attorney in fact for said Josiah S. Ellis & produced to the Court a power of attorney & in conformity with the direction of the same confesses Judgt. in favor of the plaintiff for the sum of one hundred & ninety dollars & fifty cents besides cost.
Therefore it is considered by the Court that the plaintiff recover against said defendant, said sum of $190. 50 aforesaid confessed & his costs in this behalf expended. & &.

(p-103)   Court adjourned untill tomorrow morning to meet at nine O'clock.
                                        Thos. Smith
                                        Stephen Cooke
                                        Sterling Neblett

The Worshipful Court of Montgomery County have met according to adjournment, Thursday morning January 23rd 1823.

                    Present   Thomas Smith   )
                               Stephen Cooke   ) Esquires
                               Sterling Neblett) Justices

This day was produced in Open Court, a Power of Attorney from John G. Fletcher & Samuel Mitchell of Lawrence County State of Missouri, to James Fletcher of the County of Stewart & state of Tennessee—Certified by the Clerk of the state of Missouri & County of Lawrence aforesaid—and after being examined by the Court was ordered to be Registered.

REUBEN POLLARD)
VS) Debt
WILLIAM L. WILLIAMS)

This day came the parties by their attornies & thereupon came a jury of good & lawful men, to wit, Edward S. Walton, Samuel Kerchival, Stephen Mallory, John F. Epps, Philmer Whitworth, Needham Whitfield, William Stewart Sr., Samuel White, Fray H. Whipple, James Trice Sr., Durrell Bayliss & Matthew Ogburn, who being duly elected tried & sworn the truth to speak upon the issues joined upon their Oaths do say, that they find the issues in favour of the plaintiff, & that the defendant

doth owe to the plaintiff //// ///the sum of seven hundred dollars, the debt in the declaration mentioned & do assess the plaintiffs damages to seventy four dollars & sixty five Cents by reason of the detention of said debt besides his costs.
Therefore it is considered by the Court that the plaintiff Reuben Pollard, recover of the defendant (p-104) William L. Williams, the sum of seven Hundred & seventy four dollars & sixty five cents, the debt and damages so assessed by the jury in form aforesaid together with the Costs in this behalf Expended.

```
REUBEN POLLARD   )
       VS        ) Debt
WILLIAM L. WILLIAMS )
```

This day came the parties by their attornies & thereupon came a jury of good & lawful men to wit, Edward S. Walton, Samuel Korchival, Stephen Mallory, John P. Epps, Philmer Whitworth, Needham Whitfield, William Stewart Sr., Samuel White, Fray H. Whipple, James Trice Sr., Burrell Bayliss & Matthew Ogburn, who being duly elected tried & sworn the truth to speak upon the issues joined upon their Oaths do say that they find the issues in favour of the plaintiff, that the defendant doth owe to the plaintiff the sum of one hundred and one dollars fifty one & a fourth cents the debt in the declaration mentioned and do assess the plaintiffs damages to three dollars and twenty nine cents, by reason of the detention of said debt, besides his costs.
Therefore it is considered by the Court, that the plaintiff Reuben Pollard, recover of the defendant William L. Williams the sum of One hundred and four dollars, eighty & ¼ cents, the debt and damages so assessed by the jury in form aforesaid, together with the Costs in this behalf Expended.

```
ANTHONY B. SHELBY )
       VS         )
SAMUEL CRAFT,     ) Debt
JOHN H. MARABLE   )
& ELISHA WILLIS   )
```

This day came the parties by their attornies & thereupon came a jury of good & lawful men (to wit) Edward S. Walton, Samuel Korchival, Stephen Mallory, John P. Epps, Philmer Whitworth, Needham Whitfield, William Stewart Sr., Samuel White, Fray H. Whipple, James Trice Sr., Burrell Bayliss & Matthew Ogburn, who being duly elected, tried & sworn the truth to speak upon the issues joined upon (p-105) their Oaths do say, that they find the issues in favour of the plaintiff, & that the defendants doth owe to the plaintiff / //// //// sum of one hundred & ninety nine dollars the debt in the declaration mentioned & do assess his damages to Ten dollars & ninety five cents, by reason of the detention of said debt, besides his Costs.
Therefore it is considered by the Court, that the plaintiff Anthony B. Shelby, recover of the defendants Samuel Craft, John H. Marable & Elisha Willis, the sum of Two hundred & nine dollars & ninety five cents, the debt & damages, so assessed by the jury in form aforesaid, together with the costs in this behalf Expended.

BENJAMIN WILLIAMS ⎫
      VS   ⎬ Debt
WILLIAM L. WILLIAMS ⎭

    This day came the parties by their attornies & thereupon came a jury of good & lawful men (to wit) Edward S. Walton, Samuel Kerchival, Stephen Mallory, John P. Epps, Philmer Whitworth, Needham Whitfield, William Stewart Sr., Samuel White, Pray H. Whipple, James Trice Sr., Burrell Bayliss & Matthew Ogburn, who being duly elected, tried & sworn, the truth to speak upon the issues joined upon their Oaths do say that they find the issues in favour of the plaintiff & that the defendant doth owe to the plaintiff the sum of One hundred & sixty three dollars, the debt in the declaration mentioned & do assess his damages to fourteen dollars & seventy six cents, by reason of the detention of said debt, besides his Costs.
Therefore it is considered by the Court, that the plaintiff Benjamin Williams recover of the defendant William L. Williams, the sum of One hundred & seventy seven dollars & seventy six cents, the debt & damages so assessed by the jury in form aforesaid, together with the Costs in this behalf Expended.

WOOLFOLK & GOULD for the ⎫
benefit of MATTHEW WATSON ⎬
      VS   ⎬ Debt
WILLIE BLOUNT ⎭

    This day came the parties by their attornies & thereupon (p-106) Came a jury of good & lawful men, to wit, Edward S. Walton, Samuel Kerchival, Stephen Mallory, John P. Epps, Philmer Whitworth, Needham Whitfield, William Stewart Sr., Samuel White, James Trice Sr., Burrell Bayliss, Matthew Ogburn, & Pray H. Whipple, who being duly elected, tried & sworn the truth to speak, upon the issues joined upon their Oaths do say that they find the issues in favour of the plaintiffs & that the defendant doth owe to the plaintiffs the sum of Five hundred and ninety three dollars the debt in the declaration mentioned & do assess their damages to Thirty five dollars & fifty cents, by reason of the detention of said debt besides their costs.
Therefore it is considered by the Court that the plaintiffs Woolfolk & Gould (for the benefit of Matthew Watson) recover of the defendant, Willie Blount, the sum of six hundred and twenty eight dollars & fifty cents, the debt & damages aforesaid by the jury in form aforesaid, assessed together with their costs by them about their suit in this behalf Expended.

WOOLFOLK & GOULD for the ⎫
benefit of MATTHEW WATSON ⎬
      VS   ⎬ Debt
WILLIE BLOUNT ⎭

    This day came the parties by their attornies, & thereupon came a jury of good & lawful men (to wit) Edward S. Walton, Samuel Kerchival, Stephen Mallory, John P. Epps, Philmer Whitworth, Needham Whitfield, William Stewart Sr., Samuel White, Pray H. Whipple, James Trice Sr., Burrell Bayliss & Matthew Ogburn who being duly elected, tried & sworn the truth to speak upon the issues joined, upon their Oaths do say that they find the issues in favour of the plaintiffs & find that the defendant doth owe to the plaintiffs the sum of six hundred & sixty two dollars & seventy nine cents, the debt in the declaration mentioned & do assess their damages to One hundred and twenty dollars & fifty cents, by reason of the detention of said (p-107) debt besides their cost.

Therefore it is considered by the Court, that the plaintiffs Woolfolk & Gould (for the benefit of Matthew Watson) recover of the defendant Willie Blount the sum of seven hundred & eighty three dollars, twenty nine cents, the debt and damages aforesaid, together with their costs by them about their suit in this behalf expended.

```
STATE OF TENNESSEE )
          VS       ) Presentment
JAMES WALLER       )
```

This day came the Solicitor General in behalf of the State, as well as the defendant James Waller in proper person, & was thereon arraigned, & upon his arraignment pleads Guilty to the Bill of presentment--whereupon the evidence being heard, It is considered by the Court, that the defendant be fined the sum of one dollar, & that he pay the Costs of this prosecution.

```
STATE OF TENNESSEE )
          VS       ) Presentment
JAMES WALLER       )
```

This day came the Solicitor General in behalf of the state as well as the defendant James Waller in proper person, & was thereupon arraigned and upon his arraignment pleads guilty to the bill of presentment whereupon the evidence being heard, It is considered by the Court, that the defendant be fined the sum of one dollar & that he pay the Costs of this Prosecution.

```
STATE OF TENNESSEE )
          VS       ) Indictment
DEMPSEY BULL       )
```

This day came the Solicitor General in behalf of the State, as well as the defendant Dempsey Bull in Custody of the Sheriff, & was thereupon arraigned & upon his arraignment pleads not Guilty to the Bill, of Indictment, & for his trial puts himself upon his Country as does the Solicitor General likewise, & thereupon came a jury of good & lawful men, to wit, Henry W. Merriwether, Edward Trice, Henry Weeks, John Bell, Benjamin Herring, Asa W. Hooper, Reuben Pollard, John Frazier, John Edmonson, Vincent Cooper, Isaac (p-108) Humphreys, & Daniel Taylor, who being duly elected, tried & sworn the truth to speak upon the issue of Traverse & the said jury coming to the bar and informing the Court, that there was no possibility of their agreeing, Henry W. Merriwether one of the jurors is withdrawn and the rest of the jurors respited from rendering their verdict, whereupon by consent of the said parties & with the assent of the Court, a mistrial is entered & said cause continued untill the next term of this Court.

```
STATE OF TENNESSEE )
          VS       ) Indictment
DAVID COOPER       )
```

The defendant David Cooper came into Court & acknowledged himself indebted to the State of Tennessee in the sum of Two hundred & fifty dollars to be levied of his proper goods & chattles, lands & tenements to be void on condition, that he doth make his personal appearance at the Courthouse in the town of Clarksville on the first Thursday after the third Monday in April next, to answer the state on an Indictment against him for an assault & Battery & not to depart without leave of Court, & Vincent Cooper his security came into Court & acknowledged himself indebted to the state of Tennessee in the sum of Two hundred & fifty dollars to be levied of his proper goods & chattles, lands & Tenements to be levied of his proper goods & chattles, lands & Tenements to be void on condition, that the said David Cooper doth make his personal appearance before the Courthouse on the first Thursday after the third Monday in April next, to answer the State of Tennessee on a Bill of Indictment, for an assault & Battery & not to depart without leave of Court.

STATE OF TENNESSEE)
      VS   } Indictment
JOHN COOPER   )

The defendant John Cooper came into Court, & acknowledged himself indebted to the State of Tennessee in the sum of Two hundred & fifty dollars & Vincent Cooper his security acknowledged himself indebted to state of Tennessee in the sum of Two hundred & fifty dollars, to be levied of their proper goods & chattles, lands & Tenements to be void on condition that the said David Cooper doth make his personal appearance before the Court here on the first Thursday after the third Monday in April next to answer the State of Tennessee on a Bill of Indictment for an assault & Battery & not to depart without leave of Court.

STATE OF TENNESSEE)
      VS   } Indictment
JOHN COOPER   )

The defendant John Cooper came into Court & acknowledged himself indebted to the State of Tennessee in the sum of Two hundred & fifty dollars & Vincent Cooper his security acknowledged himself indebted to the State of Tennessee in the sum of Two hundred & fifty dollars, to be levied of their proper goods & Chattles, lands & tenements, to be void on (p-109) on Condition that said John Cooper, doth make his personal appearance before the Court here, on the first Thursday after the third Monday in April next, then & there to answer the state of Tennessee on a Bill of Indictment against him for an assault & Battery & not depart without leave of Court.

STATE OF TENNESSEE   )
      VS   )
MOSES OLDHAM, CAP'T. WILLIAM)
ALLEN & WILLIS SEGRAVES   )

It appearing to the Court that said defendants were summoned by the sheriff as talesman jurors & after being solemnly caled failed to appear. It is therefore considered by the Court, that said defendant be fined each the sum of Two dollars & fifty cents each unless they come here at the next term of the Court & show sufficient Cause to the contrary, & that a Scieri Facias issue & &.

JESSE SULIVANT Guardian
of WILLIAM SULIVANT SR.,   )
            VS   )   Case
SAMUEL SMITH, WILLIAM SULIVANT   )

This day came the parties by their attornies & thereupon came a
jury of good & lawful men (to wit) Edward S. Walton, Samuel Perchival,
Stephen Mallory, John P. Epps, Philmer Whitworth, William Stewart Sr.,
Samuel White, Pray H. Whipple, Burrell Bayliss, & Matthew Ogburn,
Needham Whitfield & James Trice, who being duly elected, tried & sworn, the
truth to speak upon the issue joined between the plaintiff & one of the
defendants, to wit, Samuel Smith, upon their Oaths do say, that they
find the issue, between said plaintiff & defendant in favour, of the
plaintiff & do assess his damages to One Dollar, besides his Costs,——
Therefore it is considered by the Court that the plaintiff Jesse Sulivant
Guardian as aforesaid recover of the said defendant Samuel Smith, the
aforesaid sum of one dollar, the damages, so assessed by the jury in form
aforesaid, together with his Costs by him about his suit in this behalf
Expended.

(p-110)   REUBEN N. BULLARD)
                   VS   )   Motion
               LEWIS THOMAS   )

This day came said Reuben N. Bullard into Open Court & moves
the Court for a judgment against Lewis Thomas on a note of hand executed
the 1st January 1820, by Lewis Thomas & said Reuben N. Bullard, payable
to Thomas M. Smith Guardian for the heirs of Polly Smith, for the sum of
One hundred thirty seven dollars sixty two & a half Cents on or before the
first day of January 1821, for the hire of a negroe named Buck in which
said note the said Reuben Bullard alledges, he was only the security of
the said Lewis Thomas & because it does not appear to the Court, from
the face of said note, whether the said Reuben was security for the said
Lewis,——Therefore there came a jury of good & lawful men (to wit) Henry
McFall Sr. Edward Trice, Henry Weeks, John Bell, William B. Nelson, Asa W.
Hooper, William Lee, Reuben Pollard, John Frazier, Aquilla Whalis, Vincent
Cooper, & Pleasant Taylor, who being duly elected, tried & sworn, the
truth to speak, whether the said Reuben N. Bullard was security in the
note aforesaid (& whether the said Lewis Thomas was the principle in said
note) upon their oaths do say, that the said Reuben, was the security for
the said Lewis, in the said note, and it further appearing to the said
Court that a suit had been instituted by George W. L. Marr assignee of
the said Thomas M. Smith, against the said Reuben N. Bullard, & the said
Lewis Thomas & a judgment recovered against them for the principle &
interest of the said note, at the July Term 1821 of the County Court of
Montgomery for the sum of One hundred & forty two dollars besides the Costs
of said suit in that behalf Expended.
It is therefore considered by the Court that the said Reuben N. Bullard
recover of the said Lewis Thomas the said sum of One hundred & forty two
dollars, the amount of the judgment aforesaid, & the further sum of Twelve
(p-111) dollars & seventeen cents interest from the date of sd. judgment
up to this time, & also the Costs of the former suit, as well as the Costs
in this behalf Expended.

On motion ordered by the Court, that Charles Bailey, be permitted to take out Tavern Licence for the next twelve months, whereupon the said Charles Bailey came into Court & entered into bond & security & took the oath prescribed by law.

Court adjourned untill tomorrow morning to meet at nine O'clock.

Thos. Smith
Sterling Neblett
James Carr

The Worshipful Court of Montgomery County have met according to adjournment Friday January 24th 1823.

Present   Thomas Smith   )
               Sterling Neblett   ) Esquires
               James Carr   ) Justices

JAMES STEWART   )
      V S   ) Debt
JOHN NEBLETT JR.   )

This day came the parties by their attornies & thereupon came a jury of good & lawful men (to wit) Edward S. Walton, Samuel Kerchival, Stephen Mallory, John P. Epps Philmer Whitworth, Needham Whitfield, William Stewart Sr., Samuel White, Pray H. Whipple, James Trice, Sr., Burrell Bayliss, & Matthew Ogburn who being duly elected, tried & sworn the truth to speak upon the issues joined, upon their Oaths do say, that they find the issues in favour of the plaintiff & find that the defendant doth owe to the plaintiff the sum of Four hundred & fifty dollars, the debt in the declaration mentioned & do assess his damages to Twenty four dollars & seventy cents, by reason of the detention of said debt besides his Costs.

Therefore it is considered by the Court, that the plaintiff James Stewart Sr., recover of the defendant John Neblett Jr., the sum of Four hundred & seventy (p-112) four dollars and seventy cents, the debt and damages aforesaid so assessed by the jury in form aforesaid together with his Costs by him about his suit in this behalf Expended. From which judgment the defendant prayed an appeal to the Circuit Court for Montgomery, & entered into bond & security satisfactory to the Court, & the same is allowed.

WILLIAM KILLEBREW assee   )
of CHARLES BAKER   )
      VS   ) Debt
THOMAS WATSON & JOHN STEELE Admr.)
of JOHN STEELE decd.   )

This day came the parties by their attorney & thereupon came a jury of good & lawful men to wit, Edward S. Walton, Samuel Kerchival, Stephen Mallory, John P. Epps, Philmer Whitworth, Needham Whitfield, William Stewart Sr., Samuel White, Pray H. Whipple, James Trice Sr., Burrell Bayliss & Matthew Ogburn, who being elected, duly tried & sworn the truth to speak upon the issues joined between the parties upon their oaths do say, that they find the issues in favour of the plaintiff & find that the defendants do owe to the plaintiff, the sum of Four hundred and ninety nine dollars, & seventy five cents, balance of debt in the declaration mentioned as also the sum of Forty two dollars & fifty seven cents the damages sustained by reason of the detention of said debt, besides his Costs.

Therefore it is considered by the Court, that the plaintiff William Kille-brew assignee as aforesaid, recover of the defendants Thomas Watson, & John Steele admr. said sum of four hundred & ninety nine dollars & seventy five cents balance of debt as aforesaid as also the sum of forty two dollars & fifty seven cents damages aforesaid in form aforesaid assessed and his Costs by him about his suit in this behalf expended & &. To be levied of the goods & chattles lands & tenements of said Thomas Watson, and of the goods and Chattles, rights & credits, which were of said John Steele at the time of his death & which have come to the hands of said defendant John Steele as administrator to be administered & &.

(p-113)   STATE OF TENNESSEE)
                  VS   ) Indictment
           JOHN EDMENSON   )

        This day came the Solicitor General in behalf of the state & the defendant John Edmonson in custody of the sheriff & was thereupon arraigned and upon his arraignment pleads not guilty to the bill of Indictment, & for his trial puts himself upon his Country as does the Solicitor General likewise, & thereupon came a jury of good & lawful men, to wit, Edward Trice, Henry Weeks, William B. Wall, Joseph Heathman, Rowland Peterson, Isaac Humphreys, Pleasant Taylor, John Rinehart, Lemuel Barton, Spirus Herring, James Herring & John Steele Jr., who being duly elected, tried & sworn the truth to speak upon the issue of Traverse upon their oaths do say that the defendant is not guilty of an assault & Battery as charged in the bill of Indictment—it is therefore considered by the Court, that the defendant be hence discharged & because it seems to the Court, that said prosecution is frivolous & without any just grounds. It is therefore considered by the Court that Mark Thomason the prosecution in this Case be taxed with the Costs of this prosecution in this Case be taxed with the Costs of this prosecution & that a Fi. Fa. issue & &.

STATE OF TENNESSEE)
        VS   ) Indictm't. for ass'lt
MOSES YARBOROUGH   )

        This day came the Soliciter General in behalf of the state, & the defendant Moses Yarborough in proper person & by permission of the Court, enters a Nolle prosique, & the said defendant Moses Yarborough in proper person assumes the payment of all the costs. It is therefore considered by the Court, that the said state of Tennessee recover of the said defendant Moses Yarbrough, the costs in this behalf Expended.

STATE OF TENNESSEE)
        VS   ) Indictment for
ANDREW PETERSON   ) Lewdness

        This day came the Soliciter General in behalf of the state, & the defendant Andrew Peterson in Custody of the sheriff, & was thereupon arraigned & upon his arraignment pleads not Guilty, to the Bill of Indictment & for his trial puts himself upon his Country, as does the   (p-114) Solicitor General likewise, & thereupon came a jury of good & lawful men, to wit, Edward Trice, Henry Week, William B. Wall, Joseph Heathman, Jesse Oldham, Isaac Humphreys, Pleasant Taylor, John Rinehart, Bright Herring Sr., Spirus Herring, James Herring, & John Steel, who being duly elected; tried & sworn the truth to speak upon the issue of Traverse, upon their

Oaths do say, that the defendant is not Guilty as charged in the bill of Indictment.

It is therefore considered by the Court that the said defendant, be hence discharged, & that the County of Montgomery pay the Costs of this prosecution.

```
STATE OF TENNESSEE )
        VS          ) Indict. for
OBEDIAH BROOMFIELD ) an ass't. & Battery
```

This day came the defendant Obediah Broomfield, into Open Court & acknowledged himself indebted to the State of Tennessee in the sum of Five hundred dollars, & his security Rowland Peterson came into Court & acknowledged himself indebted to the state of Tennessee in the sum of Two hundred & fifty dollars to be levied of their proper goods & chattles, lands & Tenements conditioned for the personal appearance of the said Obediah Broomfield, before the Court here on the first Thursday after the third Monday in April next, then and there to answer the state of Tennessee in a Bill of Indictment against him for an assault & Battery, & not depart without leave of Court.

The Grand Jury appeared in Open Court & returned the following Bills of Indictment, to wit, State against David Laird for an assault & Battery a true Bill .
State against, James Hollis, John Hollis, William Hollis, & Henry Hollis for a Riot a true Bill.

```
STATE OF TENNESSEE )
        VS          ) Indict. for
JAMES HOLLIS        ) a Riot
```

This day came the Solicitor General in behalf of the State, & the defendant James Hollis in proper person, & was thereupon arraigned & upon his (p-115) arraignment, pleads guilty to the Bill of Indictment whereupon the evidence being heard, it is considered by the Court, that the defendant James Hollis, be fined the sum of Ten dollars, & that he pay the Costs of this prosecution.

```
STATE OF TENNESSEE )
        VS          ) Indict. for
WILLIAM HOLLIS      ) a Riot
```

This day came the Solicitor General in behalf of the State & the defendant William Hollis in proper person, & was thereupon arraigned & upon his arraignment, pleads Guilty to the bill of Indictment & submits his case to the Court, whereupon the evidence being heard, it is considered by the Court, that said defendant, be fined the sum of Five dollars, & that he pay the costs of this prosecution.

```
JOSIAH PUCKET & WIFE MARTHA )
            VS               ) Debt
WILLIAM T. COOLEY            )
```

This day came the said plaintiffs, by their attorney James B. Reynolds esquire & says he will no further prosecute, their said suit against the defendant but dismisses the same, & the said defendant, William T. Cooly assumes the payment of all the Costs.

It is therefore considered by the Court, that the plaintiffs Josiah Lucket & wife Martha recover of said defendant William T. Cooly, the Costs in this behalf Expended.

SAMUEL VANCE   )
    VS   ) Debt
AMBROSE MADISON)

And now at this day came the defendant & prayed an appeal to the Circuit Court of Montgomery County & having given bond & security satisfactory to the Court, the same is allowed.

A Bill of Sale from Obediah Woodson to Elizabeth West, for Five negroes & certain other property therein mentioned, was produced in Open Court & the execution thereof duly acknowledged in Open Court by the said Obediah Woodson to be his act & Deed for the purposes therein mentioned, & the condition to said Bill of sale was duly acknowledged by said Obediah Woodson, to be his act & Deed for the purposes therein mentioned & the execution of the same by ///////// (p-116) Richard V. Woodson, agent for Elizabeth A. West was duly proven by the Oath of George West a subscribing witness thereto, & on motion the same is ordered to be Recorded.

Thomas Smith & Stephen Cocke Commissioners appointed by order of this Court, to settle with John Duke administrator of John Duke decd. make their report to this Court & on motion ordered to be Recorded.

A Deed of Trust from Daniel Kyle to John W. Barker on a Negro Girl named Nancy, was produced in Open Court & the execution, thereof duly proven by the Oath of Henry W. Merriwether a subscribing witness thereto & on motion ordered to be Recorded.

On motion ordered by the Court, that William McDaniel esquire, James Wilson & Thomas Hunter, be appointed Commissioners to settle with Britian Nicholson & Dempsey Hunter Executors of Allen Hunter decd. & make report to the next term of this Court.

On motion ordered by the Court, that Isaac Dennison esqrs. James McClure & John Foston, be appointed, commissioners to settle with William O. Robins, & Nancy Harelson administrators of Burgess Harelson decd. & make report to the next term of this Court.

STATE OF TENNESSEE)
       VS   ) Sci Fa
WILLIAM B. WALL   )

This day came the Soliciter General in behalf of the state & the defendant William B. Wall in proper person, & by his Counsil & moves the Court to sett aside the judgment nisi rendered against the said William B. Wall at the last term of this Court & after the evidence being heard & //// /// it is considered by the Court, that said judgment as mentioned in the Sciori Facias be made final & upon the affidavit of the said William B. Wall it is further considered by the Court that he be released from said fine.

(p-117)   STATE OF TENNESSEE)
              VS   ) Sciori Facias
           WILL B. WALL   )

This day came as will the Solicitor General on the part of the state as the defendant in proper person and all & singular the matters and things arising upon said scieri facias being inspected and by the Court here fully understood because it appears to the satisfaction of the Court by Testimony that defendant Will B. Wall has been guilty of a contempt of Court in refusing to accept the appointment of an overseer of road to which he had heretofore been appointed by said Court it is therefore ordered by the Court that said defendant Will B. Wall be fined one dollar & the balance of the fine nisi rendered at last Term be remitted & that defendant pay all costs arising as will upon the Judgment nisi as this scire Facias.

BRITTAIN NICHOLSON
VS
WILLIAM M. BELL & CO

This day came the parties into Open Court by three attornies & the plaintiff recover the Court for leave to file two additional counts to his declaration which is allowed by the court upon the payment of the costs of this term & it is further ordered by the Court that the defendants plead to sd. counts & that this case shall stand for trial at the next term of this court & it is ordered that execution issue for sd costs.

JAMES H. BRYAN
VS   } Debt
WILLIAM M. WELL & CO

This day came the parties by their attornies into Open Court & the plaintiff moved the Court for leave to file two additional counts to his declaration, which is allowed by the Court upon the payment of the costs of this term & it is further ordered by the Court, that the defendants plead to said Counts & that this case shall stand for trial at the (p-118) next term of this Court, & it is also ordered that execution issue for said Costs.
Court adjourned untill tomorrow morning to meet at nine O'clock.

Sterling Noblett
John McCauley J. P.
Jas. Barrett

THOMAS RIVERS
VS   } Debt
MARIDA HOWARD

The worshipful Court of Montgomery County have met according to adjournment Saturday Janury 25th 1825. Present Sterling Noblett, John McCauley & James Barret Esqrs justices.
This day came into Open Court Marida Howard by attorney and prayed an appeal in the nature of a writ of Error to the Circuit Court and having entered into bond and security the same is allowed.

WILLIAM KILLEBREW assee
VS   } Debt.
THOMAS WATSON & JOHN STEELE Admr.

And now at this day came the defendants & prayed an appeal to the Circuit Court of Montgomery County, & having given bond & security, satisfactory to the Court the same is allowed.

STATE OF TENNESSEE)
VS) Indict. for
//////NANCY YARBROUGH) an asst. & Battery

This day came the Solicitor General in behalf of the state & the
defendant Nancy Yarbrough in proper person & by permission of the Court
enters a Nolli prosequi, & Moses Yarbrough came into Court & assumes the
payment of all the Costs.
It is therefore considered by the Court, that the state of Tennessee,
recover of the said Moses Yarborough, the Costs of this prosecution &
that Fi Fa issue & &.

STATE OF TENNESSEE)
VS) Indict. for an
DAVID LAIRD) asst. & Battery

This day came the Solicitor General in behalf of the state & the
Solicitor General in behalf of the state & the defendant David Laird in
proper person & by permission of the Court enters a Nolli prosequi,
(p-119) and the said defendant David Laird assumes the payment of all
the Costs,—
It is therefore considered by the Court that the State of Tennessee
recover of the said defendant David Laird the costs of this prosecution
& that a Fi Fa issue & &"

ABRAHAM BRANTLY)
VS) Appeal
DANIEL KYLE)

On motion leave is granted to the defendant Daniel Kyle, to take
the deposition of Robert Kyle, who resides in the state of Kentucky
Christian County upon giving the plaintiff twenty days notice of time &
place.

JOHN MCNAIRY)
VS) Debt
CHARLES D. MCLEAN)

This day came into Court, the plaintiff by his attorney & produced
here to the Court, the writing obligatory or Bill single of said defendant,
for the sum of Two hundred dollars, dated 31st December 1819 & due thirty
days after date payable at the Nashville Bank & the said defendant Charles
D. McLean, appeared in Open Court & fully confesses that he doth owe the
plaintiff, said sum of Two hundred dollars, the debt aforesaid, & the
further sum of Eighteen dollars, damages sustained by the detention of
said debt.
Therefore it is considered by the Court, that the plaintiff John McNairy,
recover of the defendant Charles D. McLean the sum of Two hundred and
eighteen dollars, the debt and damages aforesaid, confessed, together with
the Costs by him about his suit in this behalf Expended.

On motion ordered by the Court, that Alexander M. Rogers, William E.
Williams & Thomas Wyatt, be appointed commissioners to settle with,
Elijah Martin & John Martin, Executors of Jesse Martin decd. & make report
to the next term of this Court.

On motion ordered by the Court, that Stephen Cooke, John McCauley, & Joshua P. Vaughn, be appointed Commissioner to settle with Jesse Sulivant Guardian of William Sulivant Sr., & make report to this Court if practicable (if not) to the next term of this Court. (p-120) There was present the following justices (to wit) Sterling Neblett, Stephen Cooke, John McCauley, Thomas Smith, Thomas W. Atkinson, Francis Baker, Samuel Smith, James Barrett & Isaac Dennison.

On motion ordered by the Court, that Daniel Taylor & Eaton Tatum, be allowed to establish a ferry across Cumberland River, immediately below Davidson's old ferry on said Cumberland River upon giving bond & security agreeable to law—Same justices present.

On motion ordered by the Court, that Andrew Vance, Clerk, be allowed Forty dollars for his Exofficio Services from first October 1821 to first October 1822, & that the County Trustee pay the same out of any money not otherwise appropriated—Same justices present.

On motion ordered by the Court that the Commissioners report of settlement with William Allen Guardian of Thomas Epps return'd at January Term 1823 be not admitted to record, because it appears to the Court, that said settlement is not made agreeable to law.

On motion ordered by the Court, that the witnesses who attended in behalf of the State, in the Case of the sd. State against George Nixon in the Circuit Court of this County, be allowed agreeable to their certificates from the Clerk of said Circuit Court & that the County Trustee pay the same out of any money in the Treasury not otherwise appropriated.

(p-121) A Deed of Conveyance from Richard B. Dollan admr. of Richard Dollan decd. & the attorney in fact for John J. M. Dallam & William S. Dallam heirs of the said Richard Dallam decd. of the County of Butler and State of Kentucky to John Parker of Montgomery County state of Tennessee for 183 Acres of land, was produced in Open Court & the execution thereof duly proven in Open Court, by the oath of Thomas Williams, one of the subscribing witnesses thereto, & on motion ordered to be certified for registration.

On motion ordered by the Court, that John R. Dougherty be appointed Guardian to Nancy R. Dougherty, whereupon the said John R. Dougherty came into Open Court & entered into bond & security satisfactory to the Court, & took the Oath prescribed by law, & it is further ordered by the Court that Josiah G. Duke & George Dulin, the former securities be released from any further responsibility on their bond as security for the said John R. Dougherty aforesaid.

On motion ordered, by the Court, that Francis Baker be appointed Guardian to Ezekial Herrelson—whereupon the said Francis Baker came into Open Court & entered into bond & security satisfactory to the Court & qualified agreeable to law.

```
STATE OF TENNESSEE )
        VS           )
WILLIAM ALLEN        )
```

On motion of defendant & for reasons appearing satisfactory to the Court, it is ordered that the fine assessed against said defendant on Thursday of the present term, for not attending as a juror, be set aside, & that said defendant pay the Costs in this behalf Expended.

Francis Baker & Robert Hester Commissioners appointed at the last Term of this Court, to settle with Thomas W. Atkinson administrator of Daniel Bain decd. make their report to this Court & on motion ordered to be Recorded.

(p-122) On motion ordered by the Court that Thomas W. Atkinson & Francis Baker esquires, be appointed commissioners to settle with John B. French Guardian to the children of Aquilla Tubbs decd. & make report to the next Term of this Court.

On motion ordered by the Court, that Thomas W. Atkinson, Robert Hester & John B. French, be appointed commissioners to settle with Francis Baker Guardian of Mary Davis & make report to the next term of this Court.

On motion ordered by the Court, that Thomas W. Atkinson, Robert Hester & John B. French be appointed commissioners to settle with Francis Baker Guardian of the heirs of Charles Wall decd. & make report to the next term of this Court.

On motion Ordered by the Court, that William R. Gibson, William Trigg & Richard B. Blount esqrs. be appointed Commissioners to ////// divide the property left to Frances Isbel & Patsey Isbell, by the will of George Hunt decd. between the said Frances & her husband, & the said Patsey & her husband & make report t o the next term of this Court.

On motion ordered by the Court, that Thomas Carraway, be appointed overseer of the road leading to Hopkinsville from Hugh McClures, to Cap't. Thomas River's mill in place of Robert Sawers & that the same hands that worked under sd. Sawers, work under the sd. Thomas Carraway, who are as follows, to wit, sd. Robert Sawers & hands, Edwin Killebrew & hands, said Thomas Carraway's hands, Hugh Campbell & hands, Manoah Bostick & hands, Benjamin Lee, William Terrell & Merrida Howard & all other hands, within the bounds of said road, who have not heretofore been ordered to work on any other road.

On motion ordered by the Court that James Collisher be appointed Overseer of the road in place of Isham Richardson & that the same hands work under the said Isham Richardson & all others within the bounds of sd. road who have not been heretofore ordered to work on any other road.

(p-123) This day was produced in Open Court, the last will & Testament of Harriet Blakeney decd. & the execution thereof duly proven by the Oath of Francis Baker, one of the subscribing witnesses thereto, who deposeth that he became a subscribing witness to the said will at the request of the said deceased.— whereupon Thomas Blakeney Senr., the executor named in said will, came into Open Court & entered into bond & security, satisfactory to the Court, & took the oath prescribed by law & it is ordered that letters testamentary be granted to said Thomas Blakeney on the estate of the said decd.

Robert G. Johnson & Abner V. Hampton administrators of Philip Johnson decd. returned into Open Court, the Inventory and account sales of the goods & chattles, rights & Credits of the said Philip Johnson decd. & qualified to the same agreeable to law & on motion ordered to be Recorded.

A Deed of Bargain & Sale between John Edmonson of the one part, and James Fowler of the other part for 100 Acres of land, was produced in Open Court & the execution thereof duly acknowledged by the said John Edmonson to be his act & deed for the purposes therein mentioned, & on motion ordered to be Certified for registration.

A Deed of Bargain & Sale between Hayden E. Wells of the one part and Josiah Morrison of the other part for 200 Acres of land, was produced in Open Court & the execution thereof duly acknowledged by the said Hayden E. Wells to be his act & Deed for the purposes therein contained, & on motion ordered to be ~~/////////~~ Certified for registration.

A Power of attorney from William Haynes to William E. Williams, was produced in Open Court & the execution thereof duly acknowledged by the said William Haynes to be his act and deed for the purposes therein contained & on motion ordered to be Certified.

William Newel, John H. Marable, Heydon E. Wells & Francis Carter, commissioners appointed to settle with Samuel Craft, & Henry D. Jamison administrators (p-124) of Nathan Peeples decd. make report of said settlement to this Court, & it appearing from ~~////~~ the report of the said commissioners, that the late firm of Craft & Peeples are indebted to the said Samuel Craft one of the administrators aforesaid & surviving partner of said Craft & Peeples (in the sum of thirteen hundred & sixty three dollars & sixty seven cents) & it further appearing to the Court, that the said estate of Nathan Peeples ought to be chargeble with onehalf of said sum & on motion therefore ordered, that said administrator be Credited with the sum of $681.63½ cents & that the Clerk of this Court enter on said report a credit of the said sum of $681.63½ Cents & on motion ordered that the same be Recorded.

This day came into Court John Alcock a mulatto man of about the age of eighteen years and it appearing satisfactorily to this Court that said John Alcock is free born and has been raised in this County, On motion ordered ~~////~~ that the same be certified by the Clerk of this Court under the seal of this Court & &.

Court adjourned untill ~~////////~~ Monday morning to meet at nine O'clock.

John McCauley
Samuel Smith
Jas. Barret

The Worshipful Court of Montgomery County have met according to adjournment Monday January 27th 1823——
    Present

John McCauley ⎫
Samuel Smith ⎬ Esquires
& James Barret ⎭ Justices

(p-125) On motion ordered by the Court, that Ambrose Maddison be permitted to give in his list of Taxable property for 1822 & that it be annexed to said years tax list.

On motion ordered by the Court, that Samuel White be permitted to give in his list of Taxable property for 1822 & that it be annexed to said years Tax list.

On motion ordered by the Court that William Corbin be appointed Guardian to Melbry Wilkins, Permelia, Telitha, & Charnall Corbin deced. whereupon the said William Corbin came into Open Court, & entered into bond & security satisfactory to the Court, & quallified agreeable to law.

WOOLFOLK & GOULD for the }
benefit of MATTHEW WATSON }
    VS   } Debt
WILLIE BLOUNT }

And now at this day came the defendant by attorney & prayed an appeal in the nature of a writ of Error, to the Circuit Court of Montgomery County, & having given bond & security agreeable to law the same is allowed.

Same }
vs } Debt
Same }

And now at this day came the defendant by attorney & prayed an appeal to the Circuit Court of Montgomery County, in the nature of a writ of Error & having given bond & security satisfactory to the Court the same is allowed.

STATE OF TENNESSEE }
    VS   } Indict.
HENRY W. MERRIWETHER }

This day came the Solicitor General in behalf of the State & the defendant Henry W. Merriwether in custody of the sheriff, & thereupon was arraigned & upon his arraignment pleads not Guilty to the Bill of Indictment & for his trial puts himself upon the Country as does the Solicitor General likewise, & thereupon came a jury of good & lawful men to wit, Edward S. Walton, Samuel Kerchival, Stephen Mallory, John P. Epps, Philmor Whitworth, Needham Whitfield, William Stewart Sr., Samuel White, Dray H. Whipple, James Price Sr., William Carter (p-126) & Matthew Ogburn, who being duly elected, tried & sworn the truth to speak upon the issue of Traverse upon their Oaths do say that the defendant Henry W. Merriwether is not Guilty, as is charged in the Bill of Indictment. It is therefore considered by the Court, that the defendant be hence discharged & it appearing to the Court that said prosecution is frivolous & without any just grounds. It is therefore ordered that Jeffry Sims, the prosecutor in this case be taxed with the costs & that the State of Tennessee recover of said Jeffry Sims the Costs of this prosecution.

STATE OF TENNESSEE }
    VS   } Presentment
WILLIAM BRANTLEY }

JOHN HAMPTON }
VS } Original
WILLIAM WHIPPLE } Attach't.

This day came the plaintiff by his attornies & thereupon came a
jury of good & lawful men, to wit, Henry Weeks, Jesse Oldham, Labon
Holt, Charles D. McLean, John Bell, Ambrose Madison, Balum Bull, Reuben
Hold Sr., Edward Trice, William L. Williams. (p-127) Vincent Cooper &
William Sulivant, who being duly elected tried & sworn, well & truly, to
assess the plaintiffs damages in this case upon their Oaths do say that
they assess the said plaintiffs damages to One hundred dollars besides
his Costs.
Therefore it is considered by the Court that the plaintiff John Hampton,
recover of the defendant William Whipple the aforesaid sum of One hundred
dollars, the damages so assessed, by the jury in form aforesaid, together
with his costs by him about his suit in this behalf Expended.

HUGH H. SPARKMAN assee }
VS }
CALEB WILLIAMS, } Debt
GEORGE WEST & }
JOHN HAYSE }

This day came the plaintiff by his attorney William A. Cook esquire,
& says he will no further prosecute his said suit against the defendants,
but dismisses the same. It is therefore considered by the Court, that
said defendants go hence without day, & recover of the plaintiff the
Costs in this behalf Expended.

THOMAS SHELBY }
VS }
W. C. JAMISON & } Case
ANTHONY B. SHELBY Admr. }

On motion of the plaintiff by atto. it is ordered that a Scieri
Facias issue against John Shelby Executor of William C. Jamison decd.
returnable & &.

Inserted page was omitted.

This day came the Solicitor General in behalf of the state, & the defendant William Brantly in Custody of the Sheriff & was thereupon arraigned & upon his arraignment pleads not guilty to the Bill of presentment, & for his trial puts himself upon his Country as does the Solicitor General likewise, & thereupon came a jury of good & lawful men, to wit, Edward S. Walton, Samuel Kerchival, Edward Trice, John P. Epps, Philmer Whitworth, Needham Whitfield, William Stewart Sr., Samuel White, Pray H. Whipple, James Trice Sr., William Porter & Matthew Ogburn, who being duly elected tried & sworn the truth to speak upon the issue of Traverse upon their Oaths do say that the defendant is not Guilty as is charged in the bill of Presentments— It is therefore considered by the Court that said defendant William Brantly be hence discharged, & that the County of Montgomery pay the costs of this prosecution.

SAMUEL C. HAWKINS)
    VS   ) Original
ISAAC SHELBY) Attach't.

This day came the plaintiff by his attornies & the defendant Isaac Shelby being solemnly called to come into Court & replevy his property ////// and plead to the plaintiffs action, failed so to do. It is Therefore considered by the Court, that said plaintiff Samuel C. Hawkins, recover of the said defendant Isaac Shelby, the sum of Two hundred dollars the debt in the declaration mentioned & also the sum of twelve dollars & seventy five cents, damages for the detention of said debt, together with his Costs by him about his suit in this behalf Expended, & that a Venditioni (p-128) Exponas issue directing the sale of the negroe levied on by virtue of the said attachment, to satisfy the said debt, damages & Costs.

On motion ordered by the Court, that John Edmonston be allowed the sum of Forty dollars, for keeping & maintaining William Walker a Pauper from April Term 1821 to April Term 1822 & that the County Trustee pay the same out of any monies not otherwise appropriated.

JOHN LOWE, DAVID LOWE
by their next friends PERKINS
ROBINSON & WIFE LAVINA
    VS
ELI LOCKERT & SARAH LOCKERT admrs.

This day came said plaintiffs by their attorney, William A. Cook esquire, & says he will no further prosecute their said suit against the sd. defendant but dismisses the same.
It is therefore considered by the Court, that the defendants recover of the sd. plaintiff, John Loove, Miles Loove & ////// Perkins Robinson, the Costs in this behalf Expended & &.

Court adjourned untill Tomorrow to meet at 9 O'clock.
                John McCauley
                Thos. Smith
                Samuel Smith

The Worshipful Court of Montgomery County have met according to adjournment Tuesday January 28th 1823.

Present John McCauley)
     Thomas Smith) Esquires
     Samuel Smith) Justices

On motion Ordered by the Court, that Daniel Moore be appointed Overseer of the road, from John F. Vaughan's Mill to Palmyra, & that the following hands work on said road, to wit, John F. Vaughan's hands, Gully (p-129) Moore's hands, Stephen Noblett & hands, & William Parker & hands.

On motion Ordered by the Court, that Alexander M. Rogers, be exonerated from the payment of any thing to the County Trustee, for two stray cattle viz, one small Bull & one small Steer, posted by said Rogers in December 1821, one of which strays was proven to be the property of Samuel Smith esquire, & the other having died within the year.

Alexander M. Rogers Guardian of the children of Epps Barns decd. returned into Court an Inventory of the property received from said children, & also an account of the hire of negroes for the present year & on motion Ordered to be Recorded.

Thomas Epps by his Guardian Wyatt Epps files in Court his petition against William Allen former Guardian & his given bond & security for the prosecution of the suit.

On motion ordered by the Court, that James Carr, Joseph Woolfolk & Matthew Ryburn esquires or any two of them, be appointed Commissioner to take the privy examination of Mrs. Mary Prince touching the execution of a deed of Conveyance, executed by Francis Prince & the said Mary Prince, to Joel Grizard, & certify the same to our next, agreeable to law.

The Court proceeded to appoint Justices to receive the lists of Taxable property for 1823, who are as follows, to wit, John Kerchival esqr. appointed to receive the list of Taxable property in Cap't John Moore's Company.

James Carr esqr. in Cap't. Worthington's Company.
Robert Vance esqr. appointed to receive the list of Taxable property in Cap't. Epps Company.

Alexander M. Rogers appointed to receive the list of Taxable property in Cap't. John Cook's Company.

Charles Bailey esqr. appointed to receive the list of Taxable property in Cap't. C. Crusman's Company.

(p-130) Francis Carter esqr. appointed to receive the list of Taxable property in People's Company.

John McCauley esqr. appointed to receive the list of Taxable property in Cap't. Simon Holme's Company.

Lewis C. Taylor esqr. appointed to receive the list of Taxable property in Cap't. Joseph Shenwell's Company.

Valentine Allen esqr. appointed to receive the list of Taxable property in Cap't. John M. Smith's Company.

Abner Harris esqr., of McAdo, appointed to receive the list of
Taxable property in Capt. Andrew Sims Company.

Matthew D. Ryburn esqr. appointed to receive the list of Taxable
property in Cap't. James William's Company.

Stephen Pettus esqr. appointed to receive the list of Taxable property
in Cap't. Philip William's Company.

STATE OF TENNESSEE
      VS   } Sci Fa
RICHARD T. MERRIWETHER

This day came the Soliciter General in behalf of the State, & the
defendant being solemnly called to come into Court & answer to the Scire
Facias against him failed so to do. It is therefore considered by the
Court, that the judgment nisi rendered at July Court 1822, for the sum
of Five dollars, be made final, & that said State of Tennessee recover
of the defendant, said sum of Five dollars & also the Costs on former
judgment as well as the Costs of sueing forth & prosecuting this Scieri
Facias & it is ordered that the above judgment be suspended untill the
next term of this Court.

STATE OF TENNESSEE }
      VS   } Sci Fa
RICHARD ANDERSON

This day came the Soliciter General in behalf of the State & the
defendant being Solemnly called to come into Court & plead to the Scieri
Facias against him, failed so to do.
It is therefore considered by the Court, that the judgment nisi rendered
rendered against said Richard Anderson at the last Term of this Court,
for the sum of Ten dollars, be made final, & that said State of Tennessee
recover of the defendant said sum of Ten dollars & also the Costs on
former judgment as well as the costs of sueing forth (p-131) & prosecuting this writ of Scieri Facias & it is ordered by the Court that $5—
of the above fine be remitted.

STATE OF TENNESSEE }
      VS   } Indict. for
DEMPSEY BULL   } a Riot

This day appeared in Open Court, Balum Bull & Laban Holt, and
acknowledged themselves indebted to the state of Tennessee, in the sum of
Two hundred & fifty dollars each, to be levied of their proper goods &
chattles, lands & Tenements to be void on condition that said Dempsey Bull,
doth make his personal appearance before the justices of the County Court
of pleas & quarter sessions for Montgomery County at the Courthouse in the
town of Clarksville on the first thursday after the third Monday in April
next, then & there to answer said State of Tennessee on a Bill of Indictment against him, for a Riot & for his not departing, without leave of
Court.

ISRAEL MCLAUGHLIN)
VS) Case
ISAAC W. VANLEER)

Whereas it being suggested to the Court, that no person has administered on the estate of the defendant Isaac W. Vanleer, it is therefore
ordered by the Court, that a Scieri Facias issue against the Heirs of the
said defendant to revive said suit.

LEMUEL PETERS)
VS) Case
CONSTANT H. P. MARR)

This day came the defendant by his attorney Cave Johnson esquire
& the plaintiff being solemnly called to come into Court & prosecute his
said suit, came not, nor does he prosecute the same.
It is therefore considered by the Court, that said suit stand dismissed,
& that the defendant go hence without day & recover of the plaintiff,
the costs in this behalf Expended.

EDMUND TAYLOR)
VS)
ANTHONY B. SHELBY,) Case
HENRY H. BRYAN)

This day came the plaintiff by his attorney, & the defendant, being
solemnly called to come into Court & answer the plaintiffs action failed
so to do but because the said Court do not know what damages the plaintiff
hath sustained.
(p-132) It is therefore considered by the Court that a Writ of Enquiry
be awarded returnable to next Court to enquire of the same.

JOSHUA PIKE)
VS) Certiorari
CHRISTOPHER BUTTS) Supersedias

This day came the parties by their attornies & thereupon came a
jury of good & lawful men, to wit, Edward S. Walton, Samuel Kerchival,
Philmer Whitworth, Henry Weeks, William Stewart Sr., Samuel White, Fray
H. Whipple, James Trice Sr., William Porter, Burrell Bayliss, Matthew
Ogburn & Edward Trice, who being duly elected, tried & sworn, the truth
to speak upon the matters of Controversoy between the parties, upon their
Oaths do say that they find for the plaintiff & do assess his damages to
Forty Two dollars & twenty cents besides his Costs.
It is therefore considered by the Court, that the plaintiff Joshua Pike
recover of the defendant Christopher Butts & on motion against Constant
H. P. Marr the security for the prosecution of said Writs of Certiorari &
Supersedias, the said sum of Forty two dollars and twenty cents, the
damages so assessed by the jury in form aforesaid together with his costs
by him about his suit in this behalf Expended, this judgment is for the
benefit of Joshua P. Vaughan.

WILLIAM PHILIPS)
VS) Debt
ROBERT SEARCY)

This day came the parties by their attornies & thereupon all and singular the matters of law arrising on the defendants demurrer to the plaintiffs declaration, being argued & by the Court fully understood. Because it seems to the Court that the matters of law arrising on the defendants demurrer are not sufficient.

It is therefore considered by the Court that said demurrer be overruled, & that the plaintiff recover of said defendant the sum of Two hundred dollars & seventy five cents, the debt in the declaration mentioned, & also the sum of six dollars and twenty two cents damages sustained by reason of the (p-133) detention of said debt as also the Costs in this behalf Expended, & the plaintiff agrees to stay the execution untill the first of April 1823.

JESSE SULIVANT Guardian of WILLIAM SULLIVANT SR., V S BALUM BULL, WILLIAM SULIVANT & WILSON SULIVANT	Case

This day came the parties by their attornies & thereupon came a jury of good and lawful men, to wit, Josiah G. Duke, William Brantly, John Williford, Elisha Willis, Joseph Heathmen, John B. Persise, Jesse Oldham, Washington Oldham, Joshua Pike, John Bell, John Dougherty, & Jourdan Lisles, who being duly elected, tried and sworn the truth to speak upon the issue joined between the plaintiff and one of the defendants Balum Bull, upon their Oaths do say that they find the issue between the plaintiff & said defendant Balum Bull in favour of the defendant. Therefore it is considered by the Court, that the sd. defendant Balum Bull go hence without day and recover of the plaintiff Jesse Sullivant Guardian as aforesaid, the costs in this behalf Expended.

Court adjourned untill tomorrow morning to meet at 9 O'clock.
John McCauley
Thos. Smith
James Dennison

The Worshipful Court of Montgomery County have met according to adjournment, Wednesday January 29th 1823---Present

John McCauley Thomas Smith & Isaac Dennison	Esquires Justices

The Grand jury appeared in Open Court, & returned a Bill of Presentment against James McGee an Overseer of a Road.

(p-134) On motion ordered by the Court that Philmor Whitworth, be permitted to give in his list of Taxable for the year 1822 & that the same be annexed to said years tax list.

Joshua F. Vaughn & Thomas Smith esqrs. Commissioners appointed to settle with Drewry Harrison administrator of Jane Alcock decd. make their report to this Court & on motion ordered to be Recorded.

CAVE JOHNSON VS ROBERT SEARCY	Debt

This day came the defendant Robert Searcy into Open Court and freely confesses that he is indebted to the plaintiff, the sum of One hundred and fifty one dollars and thirteen Cents.
It is therefore considered by the Court that the plaintiff Cave Johnson, recover of the defendant Robert Searcy, the aforesaid sum of One hundred & fifty one dollars and thirteen cents, confessed as aforesaid & also the Costs in this behalf Expended.

On motion ordered by the Court, that, Joshua P. Vaughan & Thomas Smith esqrs. be appointed commissioners to settle with Drewry Harrison admrs. of Jane Alsock decd. & make report to this Court.

```
RICHARD BROWN   )
      VS        ) Appeal
JOHN RINEHART   )
```

This day came the parties by their attornies & thereupon came a jury of good & lawful men, to wit, Edward S. Walton, Stephen Mallory, John P. Epps, Philmer Whitworth, Needham Whitfield, William Stewart Sr., Samuel White, Pray H. Whipple, James Trice Sr., William Porter, Burrell Bayliss, & Matthew Ogburn, who being duly elected tried & sworn & sworn the truth to speak upon the matters in controversey, between the parties, upon their Oaths do say, that they find for the defendant.
Therefore it is considered by the Court that the defendant John Rinehart go hence & recover of the plaintiff Richard Brown & on motion against Valentine Pryors the security the (p-135) Cost in this behalf Expended.

```
RICHARD BROWN )
      VS      ) Appeal
JOHN RINEHART )
```

This day came the parties by their attornies & thereupon came a jury of good & lawful men, to wit, Edward S. Walton, Stephen Mallory, John P. Epps, Philmer Whitworth, Needham Whitfield, William Stewart Sr., Samuel White, Pray H. Whipple, James Trice Sr., William Porter, Burrell Bayliss & Matthew Ogburn & Philmer Whitworth, who being duly elected, tried and sworn, the truth to speak upon the matters of controversey between the parties, upon their Oaths do say that they find for the defendant.
It is therefore considered by the Court, that the defendant John Rinehart, go hence & recover of the plaintiff Richard Brown & on motion against Valentine Powers, the security for said appeal, the costs in this behalf Expended.

On motion ordered by the Court that the witnesses summoned in the Case of Jesse Sulivant Guardian of William Sr., against William Porter & others be permitted to prove their attendance in each seperate case respectively.

```
(p-136)   WILLIAM PORTER        )
               VS               ) Motion
          JESSE SULIVANT Guardian)
```

This day came the plaintiff by his attorney Cave Johnson esquire &
says he will no further prosecute his said motion against the defendant
but dismisses the same.

Therefore it is considered by the Court, that the defendant Jesse Sulivant
Guardian as aforesaid ////// go hence and recover of the plaintiff William
Porter, the Costs in this behalf Expended.

> HAYDEN E. WELLS Guardian
> of HARRIET PEEPLES (now Harriet Harris)
> VS
> SAMUEL CRAFT & HENRY D. JAMISON Admrs.
> of NATHAN PEEPLES decd.
>   Case

This day came the parties by their attornies & thereupon came a jury
of good & lawful men, to wit, Edward S. Walton, Stephen Mallory, John P.
Epps, Philmer Whitworth, Needham Whitfield, William Stewart Sr., Samuel
White, Pray H. Whipple, James Trice Sr., William Porter, Burrell Bayliss
& Matthew Ogburn, who being duly elected, tried & sworn, the truth to
speak upon the issues joined upon their oaths do say they find the issues
in favour of the plaintiff & do assess his damages to Three hundred and
thirty seven dollars and seventy five cents & find that said defendants
have fully administered all & singular the goods & chattles, rights and
credits of Nathan Peeples decd. which have come to their hands to be
administered.

It is therefore considered by the Court, that the said plaintiff Hayden
E. Wells Guardian as aforesaid recover of the sd. defendants the said
sum of Three hundred and thirty seven dollars & seventy five cents, the
damages so assessed by the jury in form aforesaid, to be levied of the
goods and Chattles rights and credits of Nathan Peeples decd. that may
hereafter come to the hands of the said administrators to be administered,
& the Costs to be levied of the said defendants own proper goods and
chattles (p-137) lands & Tenements.

> JAMES ELDER
> VS
> WILLIAM L. WILLIAMS
> & JAMES BARRET
>   Covenant
> Broken

This day came the plaintiff by his attorney & the defendants William
L. Williams & James Barret in proper person & say they cannot gainsay the
plaintiffs action, but freely acknowledges that they are indebted to the
sd. plaintiff in the sum of Nine hundred and eighteen dollars and seventy
five cents, balance of debt, & also the sum of twenty dollars & sixty six
cents, the damages sustained by the detention of said debt, besides his
costs.

Therefore it is considered by the Court, that the plaintiff James Elder,
recover of the defendants William L. Williams & James Barret the sum of
Nine hundred and thirty nine dollars and forty one cents, the debt &
damages, as aforesaid confessed, together with his costs by him about his
suit in this behalf Expended & &.

> WOOLFOLK & GOULD
> VS
> AMBROSE MADISON
>   Case

This day came the parties by their attorneys & by consent, this cause is transferred to the Circuit Court of Montgomery County for trial to be had thereon.

BURRELL BAYLESS
VS.   } Sci Fa
JOSEPH & JOHN BOWERS

This day came the parties by their attornies & thereupon came a jury of good & lawful men, to wit, Edward S. Walters, Stephen Mallory, John P. Epps, Philmer Whitworth, Needham Whitfield, William Stewart Sr., Sam'l White, Iray H. Whipple, James Trice Senr., William Porter, Matthew Ogburn, & Edward Trice, who being duly elected, tried & sworn the truth to speak upon the issue joined upon their oaths do say that the said defendants have not paid the Debt in the Sci fa mentioned as they have alledged by their plea—& all & singular the matters & law arising on the plea nul tiel record being fully heard & understood by the Court here. (p-138) It is considered by the Court here that there is such a Record as mentioned & described the said Scire facias.
It is therefore further considered by the Court here that the said plaintiff recover of the said Defendant the sum of sixty eight dollars with interest from 20th July 1817 & also $40.35 costs on the former judgment in the Scire facias mentioned and the Costs in this behalf expended.

STATE OF TENNESSEE
VS
THOMAS ROBERTS,   } Bastardy
PETER P. ROBERTS &
HEYDON E. WELLS

This day came the //////// // ///// Solicitor General in behalf of the State and the said defendant being solemnly called to come into Court, and answer the state of Tennessee on a charge against said Thomas Roberts for the support of a Bastard Child, failed so to do—
It is therefore considered by the Court, that said State of Tennessee recover of the said defendants Thomas Roberts, Peter P. Roberts & Heydon E. Wells, the sum of Twenty dollars for the support of a Bastard child begotten on the body of Esther Cooper by the said Thomas Roberts for the last two years from the January Term 1821, to the present Term & also the Costs in this behalf Expended.

Court adjourned untill tomorrow morning to meet at 9 O'clock.
                              John McCauley
                              James Dennison
                              Jas. Barret

The Worshipful Court of Montgomery County have met according to adjournment Thursday January 30th 1823.
                    Present—   John McCauley)
                               Isaac Dennison) Esquires
                               & James Barret) Justices

WILLIAM H. MCLAUGHLIN Assee ⎫
⎬ Debt
VS ⎟
JAMES SMITH ⎭

This day came the said defendant James Smith into Open Court & says he cannot (p-139) gainsay the plaintiff's action, but freely acknowledges, that he is indebted to the said plaintiff in the sum of sixteen hundred & twleve dollars & fifty one cents including interest on said debt.
It is therefore considered by the Court, that the plaintiff William H. McLaughlin assee as aforesaid recover of the defendant James Smith said sum of sixteen hundred and twelve dollars and fifty one cents, the debt aforesaid confessed, together with his costs by him about his suit in this behalf Expended & the plaintiff agrees to stay Execution twelve months.

MATTHEW RYBURN Guardian ⎫
⎬ Petition
VS ⎟
JOSHUA P. VAUGHN Guardian ⎭

This day came the parties by their attornies & thereupon by consent, the order of reference made in this case is set aside, & the cause transfered to the Circuit Court of Montgomery County to stand for trial at the first Term thereof.

DAVID VAUGHAN ⎫
⎬ Sci Fa
VS ⎟
REBECCA SMITH ⎭

This day came the plaintiff by his attorney, & the defendant being solemnly called to come into Court & answer said Scieri Facias failed so to do.
It is therefore considered by the Court, that the judgment nisi rendered against the said Rebecca Smith at the July Term 1822 for one hundred and twenty five dollars, be made final, & that said plaintiff recover of the defendant Rebecca Smith, said sum of One hundred & twenty five dollars as mentioned in said Scieri Facias & also the Costs on former judgment as well as the costs of sueing forth & prosecuting this writ of Scieri Facias.

CONSTANT H. P. MARR ⎫
⎬ Appeal
VS ⎟
RICHARD K. TYLER ⎭

This day came the parties by their attornies & thereupon came a jury of good & lawful men, to wit, Edward S. Walton, Stephen Mallory, John P. Epps, Philmer Whitworth, Needham Whitfield, William Stewart Sr., Samuel White, Pray H. (p-140) Whipple, James Trice Sr., William Porter, Burrell Bayliss, & Matthew Ogburn, who being duly elected, tried & sworn the truth to speak upon the matters in Controversey between the parties upon their Oaths, do say that find for the plaintiff, and do assess his damages to Eighty three dollars & twenty five cents—besides his costs—Therefore it is considered by the Court that the plaintiff Constant H. P. Marr, recover of the defendant Richard K. Tyler, said sum of Eighty three dollars & twenty five cents, the damages so assessed by the jury in form aforesaid, together with his Costs by him about his suit in this behalf Expended.

From which said judgment, the defendant being dissatisfied hath prayed an appeal to the Circuit Court of Montgomery County & entered into bond & security satisfactory to the Court, & the same is allowed.

DREWRY BELL)
  VS) Debt
JAMES GORDON)

This day came the parties by their attornies & thereupon by consent, this cause is transferred to the Circuit Court for Montgomery County for trial to be had thereon.

JOHN BELL JR.)
  VS) Debt
JAMES GORDON)

This day came the parties by their attornies & thereupon by consent this cause is transferred to the Circuit Court for Montgomery County for trial to be had thereon.

PHILIP BARBOUR for the benefit)
of ELIAS DAVIS)
  VS) Debt
RICHARD COCKE)

This day came the parties by their attornies & thereupon ⫫ ⫫ by consent, this cause is transferred to the Circuit Court of Montgomery County, for trial to be had thereon.

SUSAN COCKE by her Guardian Jno. Cocke)
  VS) Petition
EDWARD HEBLETT)

This day came the parties by their attornies (p-141) & the plaintiff excepts to said defendants answer to said petition, and after the same being argued and by the Court here fully understood, it is considered by the Court, that said defendants answer & show more particularly what amount of money & he received from the said Susan Cocke & at what time, & file the same ready for trial at the next term of this Court.

MORGAN HOPSON Guardian)
of the heirs of Edward Boyd)
  VS) Covenant
DAVID TALLY) Broken

This day came the plaintiff by his attorney F. W. Huling esquire & says he will no further prosecute his said suit against the defendant, but dismisses the same.
It is therefore considered by the Court that the said suit stand dismissed, and that the defend't. David Tally, go hence & recover of the plaintiff Morgan Hopson Guardian as aforesaid, the Costs in this behalf Expended.

DAVID ANDERSON)
  VS) Appeal
BURRELL BAYLISS)

This day came the defendant by attorney, & the plaintiff being solemnly called to come into Court & prosecute his said suit, came not, nor does he prosecute the same.
It is therefore considered by the Court, that said suit stand dismissed & that the defendant go hence & recover of the plaintiff the costs in this behalf Expended.

On motion ordered by the Court, that James Barret & Isaac Dennison esquires, be appointed commissioners to settle with Edward Neblett his Guardianship of Elizabeth Cooke & make report to the next term of this Court.

On motion ordered by the Court that Stephen Cooke & Sterling Neblett Esquires be appointed Commissioners to settle with Alexander M. Rogers Guardian of Elizabeth Waller & make report to the next Term of this Court.

(p-142) On motion and for reasons appearing satisfactory to the Court, it is ordered that Richard Daly Esqr. be released from the payment of Five dollars, the state & County Tax, laid on a Gigg given for taxes by the said Richard Daly for the year 1822, & that the same be erased from the tax list.

On motion ordered by the Court, that Alexander M. Barker, be appointed Guardian to Joseph Fowlkes a minor of John A. Fowlkes decd. whereupon the said Alexander M. Barker came into Court & entered into bond & security, in the sum of Ten thousand dollars conditioned as the law directs, & quallified agreeable to law, all of which is satisfactory to the Court.

On motion ordered by the Court that William Allen be appointed Overseer of the road from Peter Holt's ferry to Peter P. Robert's & that the following hands work on said road, to wit, Thomas Orgain & hands, Samuel Creath & hands, the hands of said William Allen, William Good Jr., John Good & Peter P. Roberts & hands.

On motion ordered by the Court, that William L. Williams, be permitted to take out Tavern Licence for the next twelve months, whereupon the said William L. Williams came into Court & entered with bond & security satisfactory to the said Court, & took the oath prescribed by law.

On motion ordered by the Court, that Wm Reasons be permitted to give in his list of Taxable property for 1822 & that it be annexed to said years tax list.

A Transfer from Thomas Watson to John Steele Administrator of John Steele decd., for a judgment against Isaac & Anthony W. Vanleer, was produced in Open Court & the execution thereof duly proven by the Oaths of Naco F. Trice & James Barret, the subscribing witnesses thereto, & on motion ordered to be Recorded.

(p-143)   The commissioners appointed at the last Term of this Court, to make division of the real estate of John Shelby decd. between the heirs of the said John Shelby decd. make their report, together with John Caldwell surveyor, that they have made division of a lott of ground in the town of Clarksville & on motion the same is ordered to be Recorded.

On motion ordered by the Court, that the order made at the last Term of this Court, appointing commissioners to make division of the real estate of John Shelby decd. between the heirs be continued & that the same commissioners, or any five of them together with John Caldwell (the County surveyor) be appointed to make division of said estate agreeable to the former order, except one Lott in the town of Clarksville, the division of which has already been made, & it is ordered that said Commissioners make report of said division to the next term of this Court.

The Commissioners appointed at the last Term of this Court to make division of the lands and slaves of David Harrison decd. between Mary Harrison widdow of the said David decd. & the heirs of said decd. make their Report to this Court & on motion ordered to be Recorded.

The Court proceeded to appoint Jurors to the next April County Court, who are as follows (to wit) Dawson Bayliss, John Bayliss, John Barber, Matthew Rogers, William Wickham, James Fentress Jr., John Martin, William Daniel, David McManus, Henry Williams, Barnet Gaines, Wilson Gibson, John Hampton, Henry Northington, Starkey Norfleet, John King, Benjamin Mallory, Samuel Bagwell, George Kirk, Griffin Mills, William Thompson, William Corlew, Henry Noblett, Frederick Moody, Josiah Hoskins, & James Trice Sr.,
Samuel Creath & William E. Dancy are appointed constables to attend the next April Court.

(p-144)   EPHRAIM H. FOSTER assee }
                      VS   } Debt
    CHARLES BAILEY   }

And now at this day came the defendant & prayed an appeal to the Circuit Court of Montgomery County & having given bond & security satisfactory to the Court the same is allowed.
Court adjourned untill tomorrow morning to meet at 9 O'clock.

                                 Chas. Bailey
                                 James Dennison
                                 Jas. Barret

The Worshipful Court of Montgomery County have met according to adjournment Friday January the 31st 1823.

                        Present   Charles Bailey   }
                                        Isaac Dennison   } Esquires
                                        & James Barret   } Justices

⦻⦻⦻⦻⦻⦻⦻ 7. 7. ⫲⫲⫲⫲
    JOSHUA PIKE
            VS
    CHRISTOPHER BUTTS &} Certiorari &
    G. H. P. MARR   } Supersedias

And now at this day came the defendant by attorney, & prayed an appeal to the Circuit Court of Montgomery County, & having given bond & security satisfactory to the Court & the same is allowed.

    JESSE SULIVANT Guardian &&}
            VS   } Case
    BALUM BULL & others   }

This day came the plaintiff by attorney & being dissatisfied with the judgment in this case, hath prayed an appeal to the Circuit Court of Montgomery County & having given bond & Security satisfactory to the Court the same is allowed & it is ordered that the same be made as of Wednesday last.

JESSE SULIVANT Guardian & ⎫
     VS   ⎬   Case
SAMUEL SMITH & others ⎭

And now at this day came the defendant Samuel Smith & prayed an appeal to the Circuit Court of Montgomery County (p-145) & having given bond & security satisfactory to the Court the same is allowed, & it is ordered that the same be made as of Wednesday last.

This day was produced in Open Court, Thomas Crutcher's receipt, Treasurer of West Tennessee to Andrew Vance Clerk for the State Tax, by him collected, for the year 1822, which the said Andrew Vance is bound to account for agreeable to his return ending first Octo'r. 1822, which is satisfactory to the Court.

On motion ordered by the Court, that James York, be allowed the sum of Four dollars & twenty five cents,--for leg Irons, & for spikes to repair the Jail, as per a/c rendered to this Court & filed, & that the County Trustee pay the same out of any monies not otherwise appropriated.

STATE OF TENNESSEE ⎫
     VS   ⎬
ROBERT HOWLAND, ⎪
GUTHRIDGE LYONS ⎪
JOHN WYATT, ⎪
RICHARD TAYLOR & ⎪
WILLIAM BLAIR ⎭

It appearing to the Court that said defendants were duly summoned as jurors to this Term, ordered by the Court that each be fined the sum of five dollars unless they appear on or before the next Term of this Court & shew good Cause to the Court for their delinquency & in case they or either of them do not appear & shew cause as afores'd. that Sci Fa. Issue from the next Term as required by law.

JOHN WOOLFOLK ⎫
     VS   ⎬
JOSEPH WOOLFOLK ⎭

This day came the pl't'ff. by attorney & the defendant being called came not---
Therefore It is considered by the Court that the pl't'ff. recover against sd. Defendant his damages sustained by reason of the nonperformance of the assumtcous in the declaration mentioned (p-146) to be enquired of by a jury at next Court.

DAVID VAUGHN ⎫
     VS   ⎬   Sci Fa
JAMES BAKER ⎭

This day came said def't. by attorney and It appearing to the satisfaction of the Court from aff't. of said def't. ordered that said defendant be exonerated from the forfeiture in said writ of Sci Fa specified & that he be hence discharged on paying costs of said writ of Sci Fa.

JAMES H. BRYAN
VS   } Debt
WILLIAM M. BELL & CO.

This day came the plaintiff by his attorney, & on motion leave is granted to the said plaintiff to take the deposition of John Bell, upon giving Ten days notice to James Gordon, one of the defendants, & in Case of his absence out of the State, notice shall be given to his attorney Cave Johnson esquire.
Court adjourned untill Court in Course.

Chas. Bailey
James Dennison
Jas. Barret

(p-147)   The Worshipful County Court of Montgomery hav met according to adjournment Monday April 21st 1823

Present

Alexander M. Rogers)
John McCauley   } Esquires
& Abner Harris   ) Justices

On motion it is ordered by the Court Horrace Bailey Admr. of Nancy Ury dec'd. proceed to sell the Perishable property of said dec'd. on a credit of nine months after advertising the same agreeable to law.

On motion ordered by the Court that Lewis C. Taylor, Francis, Carter & Valentine Allen, be appointed to settle with Thomas White administrator of the estate of John White administrator of the estate of John White dec'd. & make report to next Court.

On motion ordered by the Court that Braxton Wall admr. of Johnson Wall dec'd. be permitted to sell two negroe women, named Sarah & Nancy for the purpose of settling up said estate.

On motion ordered by the Court that James Barret & Isaac Dennison & Joel C. Rice be appointed Commissioner to settle with Robert C. Johnson surviving admr. of Philip Johnson dec'd.

Ordered by the Court that Abner Harris esqr., James Carr esqr. & Zachariah Grant, be appointed commissioners to settle with James Hollis Guardian of Charles Parker*& make report to the next term of this Court.

On motion ordered by the Court that Philmer Whitworth be appointed Guardian of Charles Parker, Rebecca Parker and Sabra Parker, in place of James Hollis the former Guardian & the said Philmer Whitworth entered into bond & security satisfactory to the Court & quallified agreeable to law & it is ordered that the securities of the said James Hollis be released from any further responsibility in his said bond as Guardian aforesaid.

(p-148)   On motion ordered by the Court that, John Carter, Thomas Carraway & Neal Blue be appointed Commissioner to lay off and allot to Ellenor Adams, widow of John Adams dec'd. her dower of the personal estate of said Adams dec'd. & make report to next Court.

On application & it appearing to the satisfaction of the Court, that Morgan W. Brown has been a resident of Montgomery County for twelve months immediately proceeding this date, that he has a good moral Character & has attained the age of twenty one years, It is ordered that a Certificate issue accordingly.

On application & it appearing to the satisfaction of the Court, that Thornton H. Cook has been a resident of Montgomery County for twelve months immediately proceeding this date that he has a good moral character & has attained the age of twenty one years—it is ordered that a certificate issue accordingly.

On application and it appearing to the satisfaction of the Court, that Philander McBride Priestly has been a resident of Montgomery Counry for the twelve months immediately proceeding this date, that he has a good moral character & has attained the age of twenty one years, it is ordered that a certificate issue accordingly.

*Richard Parker & Sarah Parker

A Deed of Conveyance from John Steele admr. of John Steele dec'd. to John Kegee for 75 acres of land was produced in Open Court & the execution thereof duly acknowledged by the said John Steele to be his act & deed for the purposes therein contained & on motion ordered to be certified for registration.

A Deed of Conveyance from Grizzel Jordan to William L. Williams for 9½ Acres land, was (p-149) produced in Open Court & the execution thereof duly proven by the oath of Jordan Banks & William Jourdan, two of the subscribing witnesses thereto & on motion ordered to be Certified for registration.

A deed of conveyance from Ananias Boatwright to William Yarborough for 77 acres land was produced in Open Court & the execution thereof duly proven by the oaths of John Mathis & Josiah Baggett the subscribing witnesses thereto & on motion ordered to be certified for Registration.

A Bill Sale from John Bayliss to Burrell Bayliss, for a negroe girl named Dinah, was produced in Open Court & the execution thereof duly acknowledged by the said John Bayliss to be his act & deed for the purposes therein mentioned & on motion ordered to be Recorded.

A Deed of Conveyance from Stephen Pettus to Needham Whitfield for 200 acres land, was produced in Open Court & the execution thereof duly acknowledged by the said Stephen Pettus as his act & Deed for the purposes therein contained & on motion ordered to be certified for registration.

A Deed of Conveyance from John Trousdale to Thomas Magehee for 43 Acres land, was produced in Open Court & the execution thereof duly proven by the oaths of Joshua R. Smith & William Smith two of the subscribing witnesses thereto, & on motion ordered to be Certified for registration.

A Deed Conveyance from John McGuire to John Northington for 60 acres land was produced in Open Court & the execution thereof was duly proven (p-150) by the Oath of Samuel Northington & William S. Perry, two of the subscribing witnesses thereto & on motion ordered to be certified for registration.

A Deed Conveyance from Lewis Tyer to Bird Hardy for 30 acres land was produced in Open Court & the Execution thereof duly proven by the oaths of John Williams & Council Tyer two of the subscribing witnesses thereto & on motion ordered to be certified for registration.

A Deed Conveyance from William E. Williams to Hampton Powell for 210 Acres land, was produced in Open Court & the execution thereof, duly acknowledged in Open Court by the said William E. Williams as his Act and deed for the purposes therein contained & on motion ordered to be certified for registration.

A Deed Conveyance from John Cryer to Edmond Taylor for 30 Acres of land was produced in Open Court & the execution thereof duly proven by the oath of John Caldwell & J. J. Williams, two of the subscribing witnesses thereto, & on motion ordered to be Certified for registration.

A Deed Conveyance from Thomas Blakeney to David McManus for 180 acres land was produced in Open Court & the execution thereof duly proven by the Oath of Shaderick Trawel & Hugh Blakney two of the subscribing witnesses thereto & on motion ordered to be certified for registration.

A Bill Sale or Deed Gift from William Dicks Sr. to John Dicks for a negroe Boy named Dave, was produced in Open Court & the execution thereof duly proven by the Oath of Isaac Dennison & James Barret the subscribing witnesses thereto & on motion Ordered to be Recorded.

A Conveyance from David Outlaw to William Haynes for three negroes, was produced in Open Court & the execution thereof duly proven by the Oaths (p-151) of Absalom L. Dennis one of the subscribing witnesses thereto & on motion ordered to be Recorded.

A Deed Conveyance from Henry H. Bryan, Edward Neblett, John Neblett Jr. & Benjamin Neblett, to Eli Lockert for 2 Town Lotts, was produced in Open Court & the execution thereof duly proven by the Oath of Thomas Ogburn & William K. Turner as to the execution & delivery of said deed by Henry H. Bryan, the execution of said deed by the other parties has heretofore been duly proved in Open Court, & on motion the same is ordered to be Certified for registration.

A Deed Conveyance from Drewry Bagwell to his son Nicholas Bagwell for 370 acres land, was produced in Open Court & the execution thereof duly acknowledged by the said Drewry Bagwell to be his act and Deed for the purposes therein contained & on motion ordered to be Certified for registration.

A Deed Conveyance from James Martin to John French was produced in Open Court, & the execution thereof duly proven by the oath of John B. French & Lemuel B. Lizenby the subscribing witnesses thereto & on motion ordered to be Registered for 27 acres land.

A Deed of Bargain & Sale from Stephen Tyer to Michael Tyer for 71 acres of land was produced in Open Court & the execution thereof duly proven by the Oath of Bird Hardy & John Bayliss the subscribing witnesses thereto & on motion ordered to be Certified for registration.

An Indenture of Bargain & Sale from Peter Teasly to Lewis C. Taylor for 71 acres land was produced in Open Court & the execution thereof duly proven by the oath of J. J. Williams & Thomas Williams the subscribing witnesses thereto & on motion ordered to be Certified for registration.

A Deed of Bargain of Sail between John Wyatt & William Neblett of the one part & Drewry Matthis of the part for 332½ Acres land, was produced in (p-152) Open Court & the execution thereof duly proven by the Oaths of John S. Mosley, as to the execution of said deed by John Wyatt & acknowledged by William Neblett as his act & deed for the purposes therein mentioned & on Motion the same if ordered to be certified.

An Indenture of Bargain & Sale between Stephen Pettus of the one part & Needham Whitfield of the other part for 150 Acres of land, was produced in Open Court & the execution thereof duly Acknowledged by the said Stephen Pettus as his act & deed for the purposes therein contained & on motion ordered to be Certified for registration.

An Indenture of Bargain & Sale from Lewis B. Allen to David B. Allen, for 461 acres land, was produced in Open Court & the execution thereof duly acknowledged by the said Lewis B. Allen as his act & deed for the purposes therein contained & on motion ordered to be Certified for registration.

An Indenture of Bargain & Sale between John McGill of the one part & Willis Short of the other part, for 170 Acres land was produced in Open Court & the execution thereof duly proven by the Oaths of John Caldwell & Richard Nasworthy two of the subscribing witnesses thereto & on motion ordered to be Certified for registration.

An Indenture of Bargain & Sale between Francis Ford of the one part & Willie Parker of the other part for 23 acres of land, was produced in Open Court & the execution thereof duly proven by the oaths of Joel Grizard & Philip Ford subscribing witnesses thereto & on motion ordered to be Certified for registration.

A Deed of Bargain & Sale from Lewis C. Taylor to Edmond Taylor for 71 acres land was produced in Open Court & the execution thereof duly proven by the Oaths of James McClure & James Elder two of the subscribing witnesses thereto & on motion ordered to be Certified for registration.

(p-153)   This day was produced in Open Court a platt & certificate and the assignments thereon, and was duly acknowledged by Hugh Ducas as his act & Deed & the same was ordered to be Certified.

A Power of Attorney from Joel C. Rice to Thomas W. Nantz, was produced in Open Court & the execution duly acknowledged by the said Joel C. Rice as his act & deed for the purposes therein contained & on motion ordered to be Certified.

A Bill Sale from Burrell Bayliss to James H. Brigham was produced in Open Court & the execution thereof duly acknowledged by the said Burrell Bayliss as his act & Deed and the same was ordered to be Certified.

A Power of Attorney from George Pardue & Sally Pardue to Lewis Reeves was duly proven in open Court by the Oath of Matthew Rybourn & Thomas Adkins subscribing witnesses thereto & the same is ordered to be Certified.

A deed of conveyance from Hugh F. Bell to William B. Nelson for five hundred acres of land on waters of Red River was duly proven in Open Court by the Oath of Jno. Dicks & Cornelius Crisman subscribing witnesses thereto & the same is ordered to be certified.

A deed of conveyance from James Johnson to William E. Dancy for 200 acres of land on the waters of Red River was duly proven by the Oath of Alexander M. Barker a subscribing witnesses thereto & the same having been proven by the oath of John Neville at the January Term 1823 of this court the same is ordered to be certified to be registered.

A deed of Conveyance from Jehu Parker to John Taylor for 48 3/4 on Brush Creek was duly proven by the Oath of John H. Williams & John (p-154) Parker subscribing witnesses thereto & the same is ordered to be certified.

A Deed of conveyance from Michael Tyer To Bird Hardy for 53 acres of land on Blooming Grove was duly acknowledged in Open Court & the same is ordered to be certified.

Ordered by the Court that Alexander Barker, John Wilcox, William Morrison, James Morrison & Joseph Morrison work be added to the hands of Leroy Kezee to work on the road under his direction as overseer.

Ordered by the Court that Robert West be appointed guardian for Benett B. Corban & Olive Corban infants & heirs at law of Charnal Corban deceased, who entered into bond and security agreeable to law & was duly qualified.

On motion it is ordered by the Court that William Bonds be bound to Alexander M. Rogers until the age of twenty one, Whereupon the said A. M. Rogers entered into bond & security agreeable to law.

On motion it is ordered by the Court that John Hampton & Wilson Gibson be appointed Administrators of the estate of Abner C. Hampton deceased, And thereupon the said John Hampton & Wilson Gibson entered into bond and security satisfactory to the Court and were duly qualified and it is therefore ordered that letters of Administration issue to said John Hampton & Wilson Gibson accordingly.

On motion it is ordered by the Court that Elaner Adams be appointed guardian of Elijah Adams, Shelby Adams, Susannah Adams, John Adams, Emma Adams, Anderson Adams, Jackson Adams, Amanda Adams and Amelia Adams, whereupon (p-156) the said Elanor Adams entered into bond on security satisfactory to the Court and were duly qualified.

On motion it is ordered by the Court that Horace G. Barbee be appointed Administrator of the estate of Nancy Ury deceased and that letters of administration issue accordingly Whereupon the said Horace G. Barbee entered into bond & security and was duly qualified.

This day appeared in Open Court Prudence Outlaw & her securities as guardian, and on motion it is ordered by the Court that she renew her Bond & give other securities Whereupon the said Prudence Outlaw came into Court and entered into bond & security agreeable to law & was duly quallified & on motion it is ordered by the Court that her former securities be released from any further responsiblity on their bond aforesaid.

On motion it is ordered by the Court that Alexander M. Rogers be appointed Guardian to Thomas G. Hutcheson in the place of Samuel Vance deceased--Whereupon the said Alexander M. Rogers entered into bond & security approved of by the Court and was duly qualified.

On motion it is ordered by the Court that Robert Vance & Andrew Vance be appointed guardian to Joseph Brunson, Penelope Brunson and Ashbel Brunson in the place of Samuel Vance deceased and were duly qualified and entered into bond and security approved of by the Court.

This day comes into Court William L. Brown, Robert Vance & Elizabeth Vance and produced to the Court the last will and testament of Samuel Vance deceased which was duly proven by the oath (p-156) of John H. Marable a subscribing witnesses thereto & on motion the same is ordered to be recorded.

Whereupon the said William L. Brown, Robert Vance and Elizabeth Vance executor named in said will were duly qualified as executors of the said Samuel Vance deceased & it is ordered that letters Testamentary issue to said Executors on the estate of the said deceased.

There was present the following justices to wit, Matthew Ryburn, John McCauley, Stephen Cooke, A. M. Rogers, Robert Vance, Abner Harris, Francis Baker, Stephen Pettus, James Barret & Isaac Dennison. Whereas it appears to the Court, that part of the Register Books of the Court are much worn & torn to pieces & that part of the said Books should be transcribed in a well bound book or Books in a good & plain legible hand write--It is therefore ordered by the Court, that the said Books marked & known by letters A. B. C. D. E.F. be transcribed & that Edward H. Steele be allowed the sum of six hundred dollars, as full compensation for transcribing said books, the said Edward H. Steel to furnish the necessary Books of a good quality & that Cave Johnson, James Barret, Charles Bailey & William A. Cook or any two of them be appointed commissioners to examine said books when transcribed for and in behalf of the County & that the work to be done in the Course of fifteen months.

This day appeared in Open Court Edward A. Lucy & Francis Baker, and was thereupon appointed Administrators of Thomas Blakeney decd. & entered into bond & security approved of by the Court & qualified agreeable to law, It is therefore ordered by the Court that Letters of administration issue to said Admr. on the estate of said decd.

(p-157)   On motion it is ordered by the Court that letters of Administration be granted to Thomas W. Frazier & Joel C. Rice on the estate of Richard Cooke dec'd. Whereupon the said Thomas W. Frazier & Joel C. Rice, came into Open Court & entered into bond & security in the penal sum of Fifty thousand dollars which (was approved of by the Court) & the said admr. qualified agreeable to law.

George B. Hopson appeared in Open Court & with the assent of the Court renewed his bond as administrator of Valentine McCutcheon dec'd. & give a new bond & security in the penal sum of two thousand dollars & qualified agreeable to law, which was approved of by the Court, It is therefore considered by the Court that the security on the former bond be reseased from any further responsibility on their bond aforesaid.

On motion it is ordered by the Court, that Thomas W. Nantz be appointed Guardian to John W. Cooke son of Richard Cooke dec'd. whereupon the said Thomas W. Nantz came into Court & entered into bond & security in the penalty of twelve thousand dollars, which was approved of by the Court & qualified agreeable to law.

Court adjourned untill tomorrow morning to meet at nine O'clock.
Chas. Bailey
Jas. Barret
A. M. Rogers
Stephen Cooke

(p-158)   Tuesday morning April 22nd 1823 the Court met according to adjournment.

Present the Worshipful   Stephen Cooke
                            Alexander M. Rogers
                            Richard B. Blount

Esquires, justices for said County

```
WILLIAM M. BELL        )
       VS              )
GEORGE BELL,           )
BRITTAIN NICHOLSON,    )   Petition
JAMES H. BRYAN,        )
GEORGE READ,           )
LEWIS DICKINSON        )
```

This day came the parties by their attornies and therefore it appearing to the satisfaction of the Court, that the matters and things in the plaintiff's petition set forth are true and it further appearing to the Court that the said William M. Bell hath been confined in the prison rules of the County of Montgomery for the space of twenty days next before prefering the said petition on the several processes stated in said petition and that the said George Bell, James H. Bryan, Brittain Nicholson and Lewis Dickson has been notified of this motion agreeable to law more than ten days before this Court, and the said William M. Bell having in Open Court taken the oath prescribed by law & having delivered Action in Court a schedule of his property— It is therefore considered by the Court a schedule of his property—It is therefore considered by the Court and it is ordered and adjudged accordingly, that the said William M. Bell be discharged from the prison rules of said County and that a warrant issue to the sheriff and other officers having him in custody ///////// for his discharge and it is ordered that George Bell pay the costs in this behalf expended & that a Fi Fa issue for the same.

```
(p-159)    WILLIAMS & WALL        )
               VS                 )
           STEPHEN G. JONES &     )   Sci Fa
           ABRAHAM McCORKLE       )
```

This day came into Court Stephen G. Jones & surrendered the body of Charles Ferrell in discharge of himself as appearance bail and in behalf of Abraham McCorkle who was also appearance bail for the said Charles Ferrell & it is ordered that said Charles Ferrell be delivered into the Custody of the sheriff of this County, and it is further ordered by the Court that said Stephen G. Jones & Abraham McCorkle be taxed with the Costs of sueing forth & prosecuting said Scieri Facias & that a Fi Fa issue accordingly.

```
WILLIAM S. WHITE        )
       VS               )   Case
WILEE SEAGRAVES         )
```

This day came the parties by their attornies and thereupon the plaintiff saith, that he will no further prosecute his said suit against said Defendant and the Defendant in proper person comes into Court and assumes the one half of the cost of said suit. Therefore it is ordered by the Court that the Defendant depart without day and recover of the Plaintiff the one half of the Cost by him about his suit in this behalf expended and that the Execution issue against said plaintiff accordingly & that an Execution issue against said Defendant for the other half of said Cost.

THOMAS SHELBY)
VS)
WM. C. JAMISON &) Case
ANTHONY SHELBY) Admrs.

This day came the parties by their attornies, and thereupon the plaintiff saith that he will no further prosecute his said suit against said Defendant but freely dismisseth the same. Therefore it is ordered by the Court, that the Defendant go hence without day and recover of the plaintiff his Cost by him about his suit in this behalf expended.

(p-160)   SAM'L. YOUNG)
VS) Appeal
WILLIAM BROWN)

This day came the parties by their attornies and thereupon the plaintiff saith that he will no further prosecute his said suit, against said Defendant but freely dismissed the same.
Therefore it is ordered by the Court that the plaintiff go hence and recover of the Defendant his Cost about his suit in this behalf expended.

GEORGE F. NAPIER)
VS) Debt
WILLIAM L. WILLIAMS)

This day came the parties by their attornies and thereupon came a Jury of good & lawful men, to wit, William Daniel, Barnet Gains, James Trice Sr., George Kirk, Henry Williams, Douglass Meriwether, Archibald Walker, William Hunt, Mark Booth, Amos Hatcher, John Steele, & William Brantly, who being duly elected tried and sworn, the truth to speak upon the issues joined, upon their Oaths do say that they find the issue in favour of the plaintiff, that the Defendant hath not paid the Debt in the Declaration mentioned of Three hundred and thirty five Dollars, and do assess his damages to nine dollars and fifty cents, by reason of the detention of said debt besides his cost.
Therefore it is considered by the Court that the plaintiff George F. Napier recover of the defendant William L. Williams the Bal. of Debt of three hundred and forty four dollars & fifty cents, the Debt and damages so assessed by the jury in form aforesaid, together with his Costs about his suit in this behalf expended.

ELIAS W. NAPIER)
VS) Debt
WILLIAM L. WILLIAMS)

This day came the parties by their attornies and thereupon came a Jury of (p-161) good and lawful men, to wit, William Daniel, Barnet Gains, James Trice Sr., George Kirk, Henry Williams, Douglass Meriwether, Archibald Walker, William Hunt, Mark Booth, Amos Hatcher, John Steele, & William Brantly, who being duly elected tryed and sworn, the truth to speak

upon the issue joined, Upon their Oaths do say, that they find the issue
in favour of the plaintiff, that the Defendant hath not paid the Debt in
the declaration mentioned of seven hundred and Eighty Dollars and do
assess his damages to seventy seven Dollars seventy five cents, by reason
of the detention of said Debt besides his Cost.
Therefore it is considered by the Court that the plaintiff Elias F. Napier,
recover of the Defendant William L. Williams, the sum of seven hundred &
Eighty dollars the Debt and seventy seven Dollars seventy five cents the
damages so assessed by the Jury in form aforesaid together with his Costs
about his suit in this behalf expended.

John Mallory Admr. of Francis Mallory dec'd. returned into Court an
Inventory of the estate of said dec'd. agreeable to law & on motion
ordered to be Recorded.

John B. French & Thomas W. Atkinson commissioners appointed to
settle with Francis Baker Guardian of Mary Davis, make their report to
this Court & on motion ordered to be Recorded.

Isaac Dennison & James Barret, esquires commissioners appointed at
the last term of this Court, to settle with Edward Neblett Guardian of
Elizabeth J. Cooke make their report to this Court & on motion ordered
to be Recorded.

The Commissioners appointed to settle with James Adams Admr. of
Daniel Venable dec'd. make their report to this Court, & on motion ordered
to be Recorded.

William Trigg & Richard B. Blount esquires Commissioners appointed
at the last Term of this Court to settle with Richard Fortson admr. of
Mildred Fortson dec'd. make their report to this Court & on motion ordered
to be Recorded.

(p-162)   Francis Baker & Thomas W. Atkinson commissioner appointed to
settle with John B. French Guardian of the children of Aquilla Tubbs dec'd.
make their report to this Court & on motion ordered to be Recorded.

On motion it is ordered by the Court that Joseph Woolfolk & James
Carr esquires be appointed commissioners to settle with William McGowen
Executor of Samuel Wilcox dec'd. & make report to the next Court.

Ordered by the Court, that Samuel Smith and Robert Vance, be appointed
commissioners to let out the paupers immediately, and make report to the
present Term of this Court.

On motion ordered by the Court, that Abner Gupton, Matthew Ryburn
esqrs. & Howel V. Adkins, be appointed Commissioners to settle with James
Hollis Guardian for the minor heirs of Thomas Parker dec'd. & make report
to the next Term of this Court.

On motion ordered by the Court that the talesmen Jurors that served
at last Circuit Court be allowed pay agreeable to law for whatever they
did serve.

Horrace G. Barbee admr. of Nancy Ury dec'd. returned into Court an
Inventory of said estate & quallified to the same agreeable to law & on
motion ordered to be recorded.

Richard B. Blount & Joseph Woolfolk commissioners appointed at the last Term of this Court to settle with William Trigg admr. of Daniel Collier dec'd. make their report to this Court & on motion ordered to be Recorded.

Robert Wade admr. of William Faulkner dec'd. returned into Court an account of the hire of Negroes & & on motion the same is ordered to be Recorded.

(p-163)   From the affidavit of Starkey Norfleet it is ordered by the Court that he be exonerated from serving as a juror at this Court.

On motion ordered by the Court that Thomas Dodd, Joseph Martin, Aaron Smith, John French & P. H. Marr, be appointed a jury of View, or any three of them, to view the road leading from Clarksville to Robert Searcy's between John French's & the first fork of said road, this side of William Holloway's, and make report thereof to the next Term of this Court.

On motion ordered by the Court that Henry Weeks, Thomas Williford, John Stone, John Williford & Thomas McGehee be appointed a jury of View (or any three of them) for the purpose of straightening the road through Henry Week's land & make report to the next Term of this Court.

Ordered by the Court that Matthew Simmons & hands be annexed to the hands that works on the road from Peter Holts ferry, to where the same intersects the road from Vick's ferry.

On motion ordered by the Court that John Matlock be appointed overseer of the road leading from Peter Holts ferry to Peter P. Robert's is in place of William Allen who has resigned & that the same who were ordered to work under the said William Allen work under the said John Matlock.

On motion ordered by the Court that the following hands be added to the list of hands now working under Joel Grizard overseer of the road from Port Royal to Weekley's ferry, to wit, Thomas Carney, Daniel Holt, John Holt, Reuben Holt, Lewis Holt, Christopher Holt, William Coon, G. Pickering, Joseph Smith, David Cooper, L. Lemaster, Robert Davis, Asa Hooper, John T. Dabney's hands Alsy McGuire, & Samuel Parker.

(p-164)   On motion ordered by the Court, that William Hogan be appointed Overseer of the road, that leads from Jeremiah Browns to Well's ferry and that the following hands work under said Overseer on the road, to wit, Drewry Bagwell's hands, Nicholas Bagwell & hand, Samuel Bagwell, Pleasant Bagwell, James Morrow, the Rineharts, John Thompson, William Dunlop, Joseph Harrison, Philip Crotzer, Richard Anderson & John Delph & all other hands within the bounds of said road, who have not heretofore been ordered to work on any other road.

On motion ordered by the Court that Nicholas Bagwell, William Morrow, William Hogan, Philip Crotzer, John Thompson, Samuel Bagwell & James Morrow, or any five of them be appointed a jury of View to review that part of the road, that leads through Henry Funk's plantation, said road to be turned to the right of said Henry Funks field so as to intersect with Well's ferry road, on the ridge above James Donnelly's the nearest & best way & make report thereof to the next Term of this Court.

Ordered by the Court, that James Thomas be appointed Overseer of the road from the mouth of Yellow Creek to the Dickson County line, & that James Whitsell, Samuel Whitsell, Lewis Thomaswork on said road under the said Overseer & all other hands within the bounds of said road who have not heretofore been ordered to work on any other road.

On motion ordered by the Court, that John A. B. McBride be appointed overseer of the road in place of William Handlin removed & that the same hands which worked under the said William Handlin work under the said John A. B. McBride.

(p-165)   On motion ordered by the Court, that Daniel Morrison be appointed overseer of the road, leading from Levi Smith's old ferry to the forks of the road near widow Penrice's in place of James H. Roberts & that the same hands that worked under the said James H. Robert's work under the said Daniel Morrison overseer of the road leading from Vick's ferry to where it intersects the road leading from Well's ferry to Benjamin Whitehead's who are as follows, to wit, James H. Roberts & hands, Edward Neblett & hands, Whitmill Harper, Widow Cook's hands, Benjamin Orgain Sr., hands, William Haile, James Powel, John Haile, William Good Jr., James Good, John //////// Peter P. Roberts & hands, Josiah Morrison & Wallace Branch and all other hands within the bounds of said road who have not heretofore been ordered to work on any other road.

On motion ordered by the Court that the following hands work under Daniel Moore overseer of the road from John P. Vaughn's Mill to Palmyra, to wit, John P. Vaughan & hands, Cully Moore's hands, Stephen Neblett & hands, William Parker & hands, William Moore & hands & William Lyons & all the other hands who live within the bounds of said road who have not heretofore been ordered to work on any other road.

On motion ordered by the Court that Burrell Bayliss be appointed overseer of the road leading from the mouth of Blooming Grove Creek to the   (p-166) Hopkinsville road in place of James McGehee & that the same hands that worked under the said James McGehee work under the said Burrell Bayliss, & all other hands within the bounds of said road who have not heretofore been ordered to work on any other road.

On motion ordered by the Court that John Williford be appointed overseer of the road leading from Clarksville to the Stewart County line, near where Alexander Trousdale formerly lived, begining where the said road leaves the Palmyra road & to continue thereon four miles, (in place of Henry Weeks resigned) & that the same hands work under the said John Williford that worked under the said Henry Weeks, & all others within the bounds of said road who have not heretofore been ordered to work on any other road.

On motion ordered by the Court, that Elijah Raimey be appointed overseer of the road in place of Jesse Cooksey & that the same hands that worked under the said Elijah Raimey & all other hands within the bounds of said road who have not heretofore been ordered to work on any other road.

William Wickham a juror at this Time is exonerated from any further attendance during the Term & has filed his affidavit relative thereto.

Samuel Smith & Robert Vance Esqrs. who were appointed commissioners to lett out the paupers of this County, have returned the Bonds into Court & the same is ordered to be filed in the Clerk's office.

A Bill of Sale from James Smith to James H. Brigham for a negro Boy named Davy was duly acknowledged in Open Court by the said James Smith as his act and deed for the purposes therein contained, & on motion ordered to be Recorded.

(p-167)   A Bill Sale from Stephen Pettus to John H. Marable & Needham Whitfield for certain negroes therein named & discribed, was produced in Open Court & the execution thereof duly acknowledged by the said Stephen Pettus as his act & deed for the purposes therein contained & on motion ordered to be Recorded.

A Deed Conveyance from ~~///// //////~~ David Anderson, Joseph Bowers, Trustee to James Smith for 520 Acres land, one town Lott & Sundry other property was produced in Open Court & the execution thereof duly proven by the oaths of John Bowers & James N. Smith subscribing witnesses thereto, & on motion ordered to be certified for registration.

A Deed of Bargain & Sale from William H. Marshall to Henry Horn for one half of 640 acres of land, was produced in Open Court, & the execution thereof duly acknowledged by the said William H. Marshall as his act & Deed for the purposes therein contained, & on motion ordered to be certified for registration.

A Deed conveyance from Christopher C. Clements & John G. Collier Executors of William Clements dec'd. to Mary Jourdan for 320 Acres land, was produced in Open Court & the execution thereof duly proven in Open Court by the Oath of William Hankins a subscribing witnesses thereto it having also been proven by William Thomas the other subscribing witness at the October Term 1822, & on motion the same is ordered to be certified for registration.

The following persons were duly elected empaneled sworn & charged as a grand jury to enquire for the body of the Court, to wit.

BENJAMIN MALLORY Fourman

JOHN BAYLISS	WILSON GIBSON
JOHN MARTIN	MATTHEW ROGERS
SAMUEL BAGWELL	WILLIAM CORLEW
(p-168) JOHN BARBOUR	HENRY NORTHINGTON
JOHN KING	DAVID MANNUS
HENRY NEBLETT	JOHN HAMPTON having

received their charge retired to consider of their presentments.

Samuel Creath was sworn as a Constable to attend the Grand jury at this Term.

Court adjourned untill tomorrow morning to meet at nine O'clock.

Isaac Dennison
Stephen Cocke
James Carr

The Worshipful Court of Montgomery County have met according to adjournment Wednesday April 23rd 1823.

Present   Isaac Dennison)
Stephen Cocke) Esquires
James Carr) Justices

William McDaniel, Thomas Hunter & Joseph Wilson Commissioners appointed at the last Term of this Court to settle with Britain Nicholson & Dempsey Hunter Exrs. of Allen Hunter dec'd. & on motion ordered to be Recorded.

William McDaniel, Thomas Hunter & Joseph Wilson Commissioners appointed at the last Term of this Court to settle with Britain Nicholson & Dempsey Hunter Exrs. of Allen Hunter dec'd. & on motion ordered to be Recorded.

A Bill Sale from Joseph Corban to Thomas Batson for sundry property was produced in Open Court & the execution thereof duly proven in Open Court by the oath of Thomas H. Batson a subscribing witness thereto & on motion ordered to be recorded.

Joseph Hopson's probate respecting the freedom of James Liles, Daniel Liles, Betsy Liles, John Liles, Joshua Liles, & Mahalia Liles people of colour was produced in Court & on motion ordered to be Recorded.

John B. French & Thomas W. Atkinson commissioners appointed at the last Term of this Court to settle with Francis Baker Guardian of the heirs of Charles Wall dec'd. make their report, & on motion ordered to be recorded.

(p-169)   WILLIAM S. WHITE)
VS)
JAMES MALLORY former sheriff)
of Stuart County, HOSEA H. LEAGUE) Motion
& WILLIAM KING)
his securities in office.)

This day came the plaintiff by his attorney & moves the Court for a judgment against the said Mallory & his securities for office & thereupon it appearing to the Court that the said James Mallory as sheriff of Stuart County had recovered of an execution for the said William S. White the sum of one hundred and twenty dollars which the said Mallory had failed & refused to pay over when application was made to him for that purpose and it also appearing to our said Court that the said Mallory had more than Ten days notice of this motion and that Horace H. League & William King were his securities in office. It is thereupon considered by the Court that the said William S. White recover of the aforesaid Defendants the sum of one hundred and thirty three dollars the sum of money collected by him as aforesaid on the 9th of June 1821 and interest to this time and also the sum of Fifteen dollars & ninety six cents, the damages by law allowed for the failure of the said sheriff to pay the same and also the Costs in this behalf expended.

PETER N. MARR
    VS   Garnishment
SAM'L VANCE

Upon motion of pl't'ff. and it appearing to the Court that Sam'l Vance hath departed this life since the last term of this Court, it is ordered by the Court that the said //// ////// suit be be revived by Scieri Facias against the Executors of the said Sam'l. Vance.

(p-170)   ERWIN MCLAUGHLIN & CO
             VS
      JOSIAH C. SMITH

This day came the pl'ff. by Open Court & by consent permit that //// //// James Elder & Joel C. Rice the appearance bail be released from their obligation for his appearance and it is thereupon ordered that they be released & forever discharged from any further responsibility for the appearance of the said Josiah C. Smith.

On motion ordered by the Court, that James Carr, Maj'r. Sam'l. Northington & Cordall Norfleet be appointed Commissioners // ////// ////// to make division of the personal estate of Valentine McCutcheon dec'd. between the widow of said deceased & the heirs of said McCutcheon dec'd. and make report to the next Term of this Court shewing distinctly their respective portions of said estate agreeable to law.

A Power of attorney from Forest Hunter to Samuel Dabney, was produced in Open Court & the execution thereof duly proven by the oath of Douglass Merriwether a subscribing witness thereto & on motion ordered to be Recorded.

Alexander M. Barker Guardian for Joseph Foulks returned into Court an Inventory of the property rec'd. in his hands as Guardian of the said Joseph Foulks & on motion ordered to be Recorded.

Lewis Terrell, Richard B. Blount & Stephen W. Carney commissioners appointed at the last Term of this Court to divide the estate of William Fortson & Mildred Fortson that was left there by Elizabeth Johnson & after the death of Mildred to the heirs at law make their report to this Court & on motion Ordered to be Recorded.

On motion ordered by the Court, that Samuel Smith & Francis Carter Esquires, be appointed to Examine a poor person by the name of Mary Barlow not at the house of Parson Harris in this County (p-171) and make report to this Term whether she ought to be put on the list of paupers of this County.

Thomas Williams Admr. of William McCauley dec'd. returned into Court an a/o Sales of the balance of the property belonging to the estate of said dec'd. & on motion ordered to be recorded.

Braxton Wall admr. of Johnson Wall dec'd. returned into Court an account Sales of the property of sd. Johnson Wall dec'd. & on motion ordered to be recorded.

A.M. Rogers & Robert Vance commissioners appointed to settle with Prudence Outlaw Guardian of her son Wright Outlaw, make report to this Court & on motion ordered to be Recorded.

On motion ordered by the Court that A. M. Rogers & Robert Vance be appointed Commissioners to settle with Prudence Outlaw Guardian of Wright Outlaw & make report to this Court.

Joshua P. Vaughn, John McCauley & Stephen Cooke commissioners appointed at the last Term of this Court to settle with Jesse Sulivant Guardian of William Sulivant Sr., make their report to this Court & on motion ordered to be recorded.

On motion ordered by the Court that Charles A. Hutcheson be allowed to establish a ferry across Cumberland River, at or near the place where Isham Richardson obtained an order for keeping a ferry at the last Term of this Court, the said Isham Richardson appeared in Open Court & consented to the same, whereupon the said Isham ~~Richardson~~ Charles A. Hutcheson entered into bond & security agreeable to law.

On motion, ordered by the Court that Daniel Tolson, be allowed the sum of Twenty five dollars, for keeping & maintaining a boy by the name of Levi Carter for the year last past ending 15th of this month (April 1823) & that the (p-172) County Trustee pay the same, out of any monies in the Treasury not otherwise appropriated.

On motion ordered by the Court that Armstead Grant be allowed the sum of one hundred & seventy dollars for keeping Lydia Copeland, a pauper, for the last year ending 15th April 1823 & that the County Trustee pay the same out of any monies in the Treasury not otherwise appropriated. Present when the above appropriations were made.
Valentine Allen, Stephen Pettus, Robert Vance, Joshua P. Vaughn, Thomas Smith, Stephen Cooke, A. M. Rogers, John McCauley & James Barret Esqrs. Justices.

A Deed of Bargain & Sale from Obediah Woodson to Thomas S. Ferrell for 367 acres land was produced in Open Court, & the execution thereof duly acknowledged by the said Obediah Woodson, as his act & deed for the purposes therein contained & on motion ordered to be Certified for registration.

Matthew Ryburn & Abner Gupton Commissioners appointed at the last Term of this Court to settle with Thomas Williams admrs. of John Everit dec'd. make their report to this Court & on motion ordered to be Recorded.

On motion ordered by the Court, that Francis Baker & Edward A. Lucy admrs. of Thomas Blakeney decd. be permitted to sell the Perishable property of the said Thomas Blakney dec'd. on a credit of nine months, after advertising the same agreeable to law.

Ordered by the Court that Valentine Allen, John Kerchival & John Blair be appointed commissioners to settle with Thomas Smith Guardian of Plumer Smith & Tabitha Smith & make report to the next Term of this Court.

(p-173)

STATE
VS } Contempt
WILSON GIBSON

On motion it is ordered by the Court that Wilson Gibson be fined the sum of Five dollars for not attending as a juror agreeable to his summons, he being solemnly called, but failed to appear, & it is ordered that a Scieri Facies issue commanding him to appear at the next term of this Court & shew cause why the Judgment should not be made final.

THOMAS ORGAN
VS } Appeal
JAMES HUBBARD

This day came the plaintiff by his attorney and the said James Hubbard being solemnly called to come into Court and prosecute his said appeal failed so to do—It is therefore considered by the Court that the said Thomas Organ recover of the said James Hubbard the sum of Seventy dollars and also of James Mickle his securities in appeal the amount or the Judgment below and also the costs in this behalf expended.

JAMES HUBBARD
VS } Appeal
RICHARD DAILY

This day came the Def'd't. by his attorney and the said plaintiff being solemnly called to come into Court and prosecute his appeal failed so to do—It is therefore considered by the Court that the said Defendant go hence without day and recover of the plaintiff the costs in this behalf expended.

(p-174)

DAVID G. THOMPSON
VS
The Adm'rs. of PHILIP } sci fa
JOHNSON Dec'd.

This day came the parties by their attornies and it being suggested here that Abner Hampton one of the administrators hath departed this life since the last term of this Court, the said Robert G. Johnson the surviving administrator is permitted to defend the said suit alone— and thereupon came a jury of good and lawful men, to wit, Matthew Rogers, Benjamin Mallory, Samuel Bagwell, John Barbour, Henry Northington, John King, David McManus, Henry Noblett, William Daniel, Barret Gains, James Trice Sr., and George King who being duly elected tried and sworn the chattles, lands & tenements of the said Robert, said execution also to issue against Eli Lockert, the other Defendant in the said action of Debt on the judgment aforesaid.

(p-175) STEPHEN CANTRELL)
VS)
JOHN H. MARABLE &)
NEEDHAM WHITFIELD)

This day came John H. Marable and Needham Whitfield into Open Court and acknowledged themselves indebted to Stephen Cantrel in the sum of Eleven hundred and twenty dollars and forty one and one half cents——It is therefore considered by the Court that the said Stephen Cantrell recover of the said John H. Marable and Needham Whitfield the sum of eleven hundred and twenty dollars and forty one and one half cents and also the costs in this behalf expended.

CORNELIUS CRUSMAN)
VS)
JOHN H. MARABLE &)
NEEDHAM WHITFIELD)

This day came into Open Court John H. Marable and Needham Whitfield and acknowledged themselves indebted to Cornelius Crusman the sum of ninety six dollars & sixty seven & one half cents——It is therefore considered by the Court that Cornelius Crusman recover of the said John H. Marable & Needham Whitfield the said sum of ninety six dollars & sixty seven & one half cents as aforesaid confessed and also the costs in this behalf expended.

EDMOND TAYLOR)
VS) Case
HENRY H. BRYAN,) on
ANTHONY B. SHELBY) writ
& ALFRED M. SHELBY Exrs.) of
of JOHN SHELBY DEC'D.) Enquiry

This day came the pl'ff. ///// by his attorney, & thereupon came a jury of good & lawful men, to wit, William Nelson, John Matlock, Samuel Bristoe, Wells Fowler, Lewis Terrill, John B. Persise, George Humphreys, Stephen G. Jones, Hugh Bakeney, Thomas Cherry, David Anderson & William Corlew, who being duly elected (p-176) tried & sworn the truth to speak well & truly to assess the plaintiffs damages in this case, upon their Oaths do say that they find for the plaintiff & do assess his damages to sixty three dollars & forty six cents by reason of the several promises & undertaking in the declaration mentioned besides his Costs.
Therefore it is considered by the Court that Edmund Taylor recover of the said defendants the sum of sixty three dollars and forty six cents the damages so assessed by the jury in form aforesaid together with his Costs by him about his suit in this behalf Expended to be levied of the goods & chattles of the sd. John Shelby deceased which have come to their hands to be administered if so much they have if not then the costs to be levied of their own proper goods & chattles lands & tenements.

JOHN WOOLFOLK   }
    VS   }   Case
JOSEPH WOOLFOLK } on Writ of Enquiry

This day came the plaintiff by his attorney & thereupon came a jury of good & lawful men to wit—William Nelson, John Matlock, Samuel Bristoe, Wells Fowler, Lewis Terrell, John B. Persise, George Humphreys, Stephen G. Jones, Hugh Blakeney, Thomas Cherry, David Anderson, William Corley, who being duly elected tried & sworn the truth to speak & well & truly do assess the plaintiffs damages to one hundred & eighteen dollars by reason of the several promises & undertakings in the plaintiffs declaration mentioned besides his costs.
Therefore it is considered by the Court that the plaintiff John Woolfolk recover of the defendant Joseph Woolfolk the said sum of One hundred & eighteen dollars, the damages so assessed by the jury in form aforesaid, together with the Costs on this behalf Expended.

HOPSON & ALLEN for the benefit }
of ROBERT BAXTER   }
      VS   }
WILLIE BLOUNT   }

This day came the parties ///////// by their attornies & thereupon came a jury of good & lawful men, to wit, William Daniel, Barnett Gaines, James Trice Sr., George Kirk, Henry Williams, Douglas (p-177) Merriwether, Archibald, Walker, William Hunt, Mark Booth, Amos Hatcher, John Steele, & William Brantly, who being duly elected, tried & sworn the truth to speak upon the issues joined upon their oaths do say that they find the issues in favour of the plaintiff & that the defendant doth owe to the plaintiff the sum of one hundred & eighty two dollars & thirty three cents the debt in the declaration mentioned and do assess the plaintiffs damages to thirteen dollars & sixty cents by reason of the detention of said debt besides his Costs.
Therefore it is considered by the Court, that the plaintiff Hopson & Allen (for the benefit of Robert Baxter) recover of the defendant Willie Blount the sum of one hundred and ninety five dollars ninety three cents the debt & damages so assessed by the jury in form aforesaid together with the Costs in this behalf Expended.

BURNARD & ANTHONY W. VANLEER }
      VS   } Debt
WILLIAM WICKHAM & JOHN WICKHAM }

This day came the parties by their attornies & thereupon came a jury of good & lawful men, to wit, William Daniel, Barnett Gaines, James Trice Sr., George Kirk, Henry Williams, Douglass Merriwether, Archibald Walker, William Hunt, Mark Booth, Amos Hatcher, John Slate & William Brantly, who being duly elected, tried & sworn the truth to speak upon the issues joined upon their Oaths do say that they find the issues in favour of the plaintiffs & find that the defendent doth owe to the plaintiff the sum of Two hundred & twelve dollars seventy two & ½ cents, balance of Debt, & the further sum of thirty six dollars & eleven cents the damages sustained by reason of the detention of said debt besides his Costs.
Therefore it is considered by the Court that the plaintiffs Burnard & Anthony W. Vanleer recover of the defendants William Wickham & John Wickham

the sum of Two hundred & forty eight dollars (p-178) & eighty three cents, the debt & damages so assessed by the Jury in form aforesaid together with his costs by him about his suit in this behalf Expended.

AMOS HATCHER
VS
JOHN BELL &
HUGH F. BELL
} Debt

This day came the parties by their attornies & thereupon came a jury of good & lawful men, to wit, William Daniel, Barnett Gaines, James Tribe Sr.; George Kirk, Henry Williams, Douglass Merriwether, Archibald Walker, William Hunt, Mark Booth, Amos Hatcher, John Steele, & William Brantly, who being duly elected, tried & sworn the truth to speak upon the issue joined upon their Oaths do say that they find the issue in favour of the plaintiff & find that the defendants doth owe to the plaintiff the sum of one hundred & forty two dollars, balance of Debt, & do assess the plaintiffs damages to seven dollars & seventy five cents by reason of the detention of said debt besides his Costs. Therefore it is considered by the Court that the plaintiff recover of the sd. defendant John Bell & Hugh F. Bell, the sum of one hundred & forty nine dollars & seventy five cents, the debt & damages so assessed by the jury in form aforesaid together with his costs by him about his suit in this behalf Expended.

HOPSON & ALLEN for the benefit
of LEWIS B. ALLEN
VS
ELIZA SMITH
} Debt

This day came the parties by their attornies & thereupon came a jury of good & lawful men, to wit, William Nelson, John Medlock, Samuel Bristoe, Wells Fowler, Lewis Terrell, John B. Persise, George Humphreys, Stephen G. Jones, Hugh Blakeney, Thomas Cherry, David Anderson, & William Corlew who being duly elected tried & sworn the truth to speak upon their oaths do say that they find the issues in favour of the plaintiff & find that (p-179) the defendant doth owe to the plaintiffs the sum of one hundred & thirty two dollars & eighty cents balance of debt & do assess the plaintiffs damages to ten dollars & fifty cents by reason of the detention of said debt besides his Costs.— Therefore it is considered by the Court that the plaintiff's Hopson & Allen for the benefit of Lewis B. Allen, recover of the defendant Eliza Smith, the sum of one hundred & forty three dollars & thirty Cents, t he debt & damages so assessed by the Jury in form aforesaid, together with the Costs in this behalf Expended.

PETER N. MARR)

issue joined upon their oaths do say that they find the issue in favour of the plaintiff & find that the defendants doth owe to the plaintiff the sum of Two hundred dollars, the debt in the declaration mentioned & do assess the plaintiffs damages to nine dollars by reason of the detention of sd. debt besides his Costs.

Therefore it is considered by the court that the plaintiff Peter N. Marr recover of the defendants James Trice & Mordica Reed, the sum of Two hundred & nine dollars the debt & damages so assessed by the jury in form aforesaid together with his costs by him about his suit in this behalf Expended.

PETER N. MARR
VS } Debt
NATHAN VICK

This day came the parties by their attornies & thereupon came a jury of good & lawful men (p-180) to wit, William Nelson, John Mattock, Samuel Bristoe, Wells Fowler, Lewis Terrell, John B. Peraise, George Humphreys, Stephen G. Jones, Hugh Blakeney, Thomas Cherry, David Anderson & William Corlew, who being duly elected tried & sworn the truth to speak upon the issue joined upon their oaths do say that they find the issue in favour of the plaintiff & find that the defendant doth owe to the plaintiff the sum of Ninety five dollars, the debt in the declaration mentioned & do assess his damages to one dollar & ninety cents by reason of the detention of said debt besides his costs.

Therefore it is considered by the Court, that the plaintiff Peter N. Marr, recover of the defendant Nathan Vick the sum of ninety six dollars & ninety Cents, the debt & damages, so assessed by the jury in form aforesaid together with his costs by him about his suit in this behalf Expended.

STEPHEN CANTRELL, assee of
ALFRED DATCH
VS } Debt
WILLIAM L. WILLIAMS

This day came the parties by their attornies, & thereupon came a jury of good & lawful men, to wit, William Nelson, John Mattock, Samuel Bristoe, Wells Fowler, Lewis Terrell, John B. Peraise, George Humphreys, Stephen G. Jones, Hugh Blakeney, Thomas Cherry, David Anderson & William Corlew, who being duly elected tried & sworn the truth to speak upon the issue joined upon their Oaths do say that they find the issue in favour of the plaintiff & find that the defendant doth owe to the plaintiff, the sum of Five hundred & thirty three dollars & seven cents, Debt & do assess the plaintiffs damages to Fifty three dollars & eighteen cents by reason

JOSEPH & ROBERT WOODS assignee)
            vs   }   Debt
CONSTANT H. P. MARR & ROBERT SEARCY)

This day came parties by their attornies & thereupon came a jury of good & lawful men, to wit, William Nelson Sr., John Mattock, Samuel Bristoe, Wells Fowler, Lewis Terrell, John B. Persise, George Humphreys, Stephen G. Jones, Hugh Blakeney, Thomas Cherry, David Anderson & William Corlew, who being duly elected, tried & sworn the truth to speak upon the issue joined upon their oaths do say, that they find the issues in favour of the plaintiffs & that the defendants doth owe to the plaintiffs the sum of Two hundred and thirteen dollars & ninety four cents, the debt in the declaration mentioned & do assess the plaintiffs damages to six dollars forty three & three fourth cents, by reason of the detention of said debt besides their Costs.
Therefore it is considered by the Court, that the plaintiffs Joseph & Robert Woods assignee, as aforesaid recover of the defendants Constant H. P. Marr & Robert Searcy the sum of Two hundred & twenty dollars, thirty seven & three fourth cents, the debt & damages so assessed by the jury in form aforesaid together with their Costs by them about their suit in this behalf Expended.

(p-182)   LEWIS DICKENSON)
                VS   }   Debt
      WILLIAM M. BELL)

This day came the parties by their attornies & thereupon came a jury of good & lawful men, to wit, William Nelson Sr., John Mattock, Samuel Bristoe, Wells Fowler, Lewis Terrell, John B. Persise, George Humphreys, Stephen G. Jones, Hugh Blakeney, Thomas Cherry, David Anderson & William Corlew, who being duly elected tried & sworn the truth to speak upon the issues joined upon their Oaths do say they they find the issues in favour of the plaintiff & find that the defendant doth owe to the plaintiff the sum of One hundred & sixty dollars balance of debt & damages thereon by reason of the detention of said debt, besides his Costs.
Therefore it is considered by the Court, that the plaintiff Lewis Dickenson recover of the defendant William M. Bell, the said sum of One hundred & sixty dollars, the balance of debt & damages so assessed by the jury in form aforesaid together with his costs by him about his suit in this behalf Expended.

HAYDEN E. WELLS assee)
of RANDOLPH RAMEY   )
         vs   }   Debt
GEORGE HUMPHREYS   )

This day came the parties by their attornies & thereupon came a jury of good & lawful men, to wit, William Daniel, Barnett Gaines, James Trice Sr, George Kirk, Henry Williams, Douglass Merriwether, Archibald Walker, William Hunt, Mark Booth, Amos Hatcher, John Steele & William Brantly, who being duly elected tried & sworn the truth to speak upon the issues joined upon their oaths do say, that they find the issues in favour of the plaintiff / //// /// ///// // ////// // /// /////// & find that the said defendant doth owe to the plaintiff the sum of One thousand and fifty four dollars the debt in the declaration mentioned & do assess his damages to Eighty four dollars & fifty cents by reason of the detention of said debt besides his costs.

(p-183) Therefore it is considered by the Court, that the plaintiff Hayden E. Wells assignee as aforesaid recover of the defendant George Humphreys the sum of Eleven hundred & thirty eight dollars & fifty cents the debt & damages so assessed by the jury in form aforesaid together with his Costs by him about his suit in this behalf Expended. From which said Judgment the defendant George Humphreys hath prayed an appeal in the nature of a writ of Error to the Circuit Court of Montgomery & entered into bond & security satisfactory to the Court & the same is allowed.

ABNER GUPTON assee)
of SAMUEL LYNES   )
        VS   } Debt
PETER H. COLE   )

This day came the plaintiff by his attorney & the defendant in proper person, & thereupon came a jury of good & lawful men, to wit, William Daniel, Barnet Gaines, James Trice Sr., George Kirk, Henry Williams, Douglass Merriwether, Archibald Walker, William Hunt, Mark Booth, Amos Hatcher, John Steele & William Brantly, who being duly Elected, tried & sworn the truth to speak upon the issue joined upon their oaths do say, that they find the issue in favour of the plaintiff & find that the said defendant doth owe to the plaintiff the sum of one hundred dollars & sixty eight cents, balance of debt in the declaration mentioned & do assess his damages to three dollars & ninety one cents by reason of the detention of said debt, besides his Costs—Therefore it is considered by the Court that the plaintiff Abner Gupton assignee as aforesaid recover of the defendant Peter H. Cole the sum of One hundred & four dollars and fifty one cents, the debt & damages so assessed by the jury in Form aforesaid together with his Costs by him about his suit in this behalf Expended.

(p-184) Court adjourned untill tomorrow morning to meet at 9 O'clock.

Chas. Bailey
Isaac Dennison
Jas. Barret

The Worshipful Court of Montgomery County have met according to adjournment Thursday April 24th 1823.

                    Present   Charles Bailey)
                                   James Barret   } Esqrs.
                                   Isaac Dennison) Justices

ASHBEL BRUNSON)
      VS   } Motion
JAMES R. NAPIER)

This day came the plaintiff by his attorney and moved the Court for a judgment against the defendant—- And thereupon It appearing to the satisfaction of the Court here, that at the April Term of the Court of Pleas and quarter sessions for the County of Davidson at the January Term 1823 thereof, the Bank of the state of Tennessee recovered a judgment against George West the said Ashbell Brunson and the said James R. Napier for the sum of two hundred and sixty six dollars and ninety cents and the further sum of one dollar sixty five cents cost of suit—- And it also appearing to the satisfaction of the Court, that the said Ashbell Brunson

& James F. Napier were securities for the said West jointly & equally
liable as such, And it further appearing to the Court that an execution
(p-185)   issued to the sheriff of Montgomery County and made the said
execution and costs of the property of said Brunson together with the
said sheriff's fees amounts to the sum of two hundred and eighty two
dollars & seventy cents.
It is therefore considered by the Court that the plaintiff Ashbel Brunson
recover of the defendant James R. Napier the sum of one hundred and forty
one dollars and thirty five cents with costs of this motion and that
execution issue accordingly.

```
WILLIAM H. MARSHALL )
         VS          )
BURRELL BAYLISS      )   Debt
& JOHN H. MARABLE    )
```

This day came into Court the defendants Burrell Bayliss & John H.
Marable, and freely acknowledged themselves indebted to the said plaintiff
William H. Marshall, in the sum of Four hundred dollars —
It is therefore considered by the Court that the said William H. Marshall
recover of the said Burrell Bayliss & John H. Marable the said sum of
Four hundred dollars confessed as aforesaid & also the costs in this
behalf Expended.

```
GEORGE W. L. MARR )
      VS          )
SAMUEL LYNES      )
```

This day came Samuel Lynes into Open Court and freely acknowledges
himself indebted to the said George W. L. Marr in the sum of One hundred &
fifty four dollars & fourteen cents the principal & Interest due on a note
executed by Alexander Martin & the said Samuel Lynes to the said George
W. L. Marr—
It is therefore considered by the Court that the said George W. L. Marr
recover of the said Samuel Lynes the sum of One hundred & fifty four
dollars & fourteen cents the principal & Interest due on a note executed
by Alexander Martin & the said Samuel Lynes to the said George W. L. Marr—
It is therefore considered by the Court that the said George W. L. Marr
recover of the said Samuel Lynes the sum of One hundred & fifty four
dollars & fourteen cents so confessed as aforesaid & also the costs in
this behalf Expended & the plaintiff agrees to stay Execution——months.

```
(p-186)   ANTHONY W. VANLEER & CO )
             VS                   )   Appeal
          BURRELL M. WILLIAMSON   )
```

This day came the parties by their attornies & it is suggested
here to the Court, that Isaac W. Vanleer one of the firm of Anthony W.
Vanleer & Co. hath departed this life, which is not denied.

```
JOHN HAMILTON )
     VS       )   Appeal
JOHN EDMONSON )
```

This day came the parties by their attornies & the plaintiff here
in Open Court says he will no further prosecute his said suit against the
defendant, but dismisses the same & the defendant John Edmonson came into
Court & assumes the payment of his own Costs, & the said plaintiff agrees
to pay his part of the Costs on said suit.
It is therefore considered by the Court that the parties recover of each
other the Costs in this behalf Expended—agreeable to the above agreement,
& that a Fi Fa issue against each party for his respective part of the
Costs as aforesaid.

    JOHN T. DABNEY)
         VS   ) Debt
    JOHN J. BELL.   )

This day came the plaintiff John T. Dabney in proper person, & says
he will no further prosecute his said suit against the defendant, but
dismisses the same.
It is therefore considered by the Court that said suit stand dismissed,
& that the defendant go hence without day & recover of the plaintiff the
Costs in this behalf Expended.

    RICHARD GREGORY)
         VS   ) Case
    SAMUEL CREATH   )

This day came the parties by their attornies, & by consent all
matters in dispute relative to this (p-187) case is left to the arbitration of Frederick W. Huling Esquire, & his award to be made the final
Judgment of this Court, & to be returned to the July Term 1823 of said
Court.

    ELI LOCKERT   )
         VS   )
    ROBERT G. JOHNSON &) Debt
    ABNER V. HAMPTON admr's.)

This day came the parties by their attornies & it is suggested
here to the Court that Abner V. Hampton one of the defendants in this
case, has departed this life since the last term of this Court & the
same is not denied.

    STEPHEN CANTRELL Exr. of)
    GEORGE DEDRICK dec'd. assee)
         VS   ) Debt
    SAMUEL VANCE   )

Upon the motion of the plaintiff & it appearing to the Court, that
Samuel Vance hath departed this life, since the last Term of this Court.
It is therefore ordered by the Court that the said suit be revived by
Scieri Facias against the Executors of the said Samuel Vance dec'd.

    SAMUEL VANCE   )
         VS   )
    ROBERT G. JOHNSON, surviving admrs.) Debt
    of PHILIP JOHNSON dec'd.)

This day came the plaintiff by his attorney William A. Cook esquire & says he will no further prosecute his said suit against the defendants but dismisses the same and the said defendants by their attorney F. W. Huling appeared in Open Court & assumes the payment of all the Costs—
It is therefore considered by the Court that the plaintiff recover of the said defendant the costs in this behalf expended.

SAMUEL VANCE
    VS   } Debt
R. G. JOHN *surviving admr. }

This day came the plaintiff by his attorney William A. Cook esquire & says he will no further prosecute his said suit against the the defendant, but dismisses the same. (p-188) and the defendant Robert G. Johnson surviving admr. as aforesaid assume the payment of the Costs.
It is therefore considered by the Court that the plaintiff, recover of said defendant the costs in this behalf Expended.

SAMUEL VANCE
    VS   } Case
ROBERT G. JOHNSON surviving Admr. }

This day came the plaintiff by his attorney William A. Cook esquire & says he will no further prosecute his said suit against the defendant but dismisses the same and the said defendant assumes the payment of all the Costs.
It is therefore considered by the Court that the plaintiff recover of said defendant Robert G. Johnson surviving admr. as aforesaid the costs in this behalf Expended.

JOHN M. WILLIS }
    VS   } Appeal from a Justices Court
DAVID ANDERSON } on a writ of Enquiry.

This day came the parties by their attornies & thereupon came a jury of good & lawful men to wit, Matthew Rogers, Benjamin Mallory, Samuel Bagwell, John Barbour, Henry Northington, John King, David McManus, Henry Neblett, William Daniel, Barnett Gaines, James Trice Sr. & George Kirk, who being duly elected tried & sworn the truth to speak & well & truly to assess the damages in this case, upon their Oaths do say that they find for the Defendant.
Therefore it is considered by the Court that the defendant David Anderson go hence & recover of the plaintiff John M. Willis the costs in this behalf Expended.

(p-189) WILLIAM H. MARSHALL)
              VS   )
    SAMUEL CRAFT &   } Debt
    BURRELL BAYLISS   )

This day came the plaintiff by his attorney William B. Turley esquire & says he will no further prosecute his said suit against the defendants but dismisses the same & the said defendants by their attorney C. Johnson in proper person assumes the payment of all the Costs.
Therefore it is considered by the Court that the plaintiff William H. Marshall recover of the the said defendant Samuel Craft & Burrell Bayliss, the Costs in this behalf Expended.

*JOHNSON

JOHN METCALF)
    VS   ) Case
OLLIVER B. HAYS)

This day came the plaintiff by his attornies & say they will no further prosecute his said suit against the defendant, but dismisses the same & the said Olliver B. Hays by his attorney William A. Cook in proper person assumes the payment of all the costs.
Therefore it is considered by the Court that the plaintiff John Metcalf recover of the defendant Olliver B. Hays the costs in this behalf Expended.

NOBLE OSBURN)
& JOHN LONG)
    VS   ) Debt
HUGH CAMPBELL)

This day came the defendant in proper person & says he cannot gainsay the plaintiffs action but acknowledges that he is indebted to the plaintiff Noble Osburn & John Long assee in the sum of One hundred & ten dollars. Therefore it is considered by the Court that the plaintiffs Noble Osburn & John Long recover of the defendant the said sum of One hundred & ten dollars aforesaid confessed together with the Costs in this behalf Expended.

CHARLES BARKER assee)
    VS   )
JOHN CARTER &   ) Debt
THOMAS RAILSBACK   )

This day came the plaintiff Charles Barker in proper person, & says he will no further prosecute his said suit against the defendants but dismisses the same.
(p-190)   It is therefore considered by the Court, that the said suit stand dismissed, & that the defendants go hence without day & recover of the plaintiff the costs in this behalf Expended.

STATE   )
    VS   ) Riot
DEMPSEY BULL)

This day came the said Defendant Dempsey Bull & acknowledged himself bound & indebted to the state of Tennessee in the sum of Five hundred dollars to be levied of the proper goods & chattles, lands & tenements of the said Dempsey Bull, to be void on condition that he doth make his personal appearance at the Court house in the town of Clarksville on the first Thursday after the third Monday in July next, to answer the state of Tennessee on a Bill of Indictment for a Riot & for not departing without leave of Court.

STATE OF TENNESSEE)
    VS   ) Presentment for
JOHN DARE   ) Lewdness

This day came the Solicitor General in behalf of the State & says he will no further prosecute another said Bill of Indictment against the defendant but dismisses the same.

Therefore it is considered by the Court that said Bill of Indictment be dismissed & that the County of Montgomery pay the Costs of this prosecution.

```
        STATE OF TENNESSEE )
            VS             )  Presentment
        WILLIAM B. NELSON  )
```

This day came the Soliciter General in behalf of the State & says he will no further prosecute said Bill of presentment against the defendant & by permission of the Court enters a Nolle prosiqui—
It is therefore considered by the Court, that said suit stand dismissed & that the County of Montgomery pay the Costs of this prosecution.

```
(p-191)   STATE OF TENNESSEE )
              VS             )  Indict. for
          JOHN COOPER        )  an asst. & battery
```

This day came the Soliciter General in behalf of the State, and the soliciter General in behalf of the state, and the defendant John Cooper in proper person, & was thereupon arraigned and upon his arraignment pleads not Guilty to the Bill of Indictment, & for his trial puts himself upon his Country, as does the Soliciter General likewise & thereupon came a jury a jury of good & lawful men (to wit) James Trice Sr. David McManus, George Kirk, William Corlew, William Daniel, John Martin, John Bayliss, John Barbour, Matthew Rogers, Henry Northington, Benjamin Mallory & John King who being duly elected tried & sworn the truth to speak upon the issue of Traverse, upon their Oaths do say that the defendant John Cooper is guilty of an assault & Battery in manner & form as charged in the Bill of Indictment—
Therefore it is considered by the Court that the said defendant John Cooper be fined the sum of Five dollars & that he pay the costs of this prosecution.

```
        STATE OF TENNESSEE )
            VS             )  Indict. for an
        DANIEL COOPER      )  an asst. & Battery
```

This day came the Soliciter General in behalf of the State, and the defendant David Cooper in proper person & was thereupon arraigned & upon his arraignment pleads not guilty to the Bill of Indictment, & for his trial puts himself upon his country as does the Soliciter General likewise & thereupon came a jury of good & lawful men, to wit, James Trice Sr., David McManus, George Kirk, William Corlew, William Daniel, John Martin, John Bayliss, John Barbour, Matthew Rogers, Henry Northington, Benjamin Mallory & John King, who being duly elected tried & sworn the truth to speak upon the issue of Traverse (p-192) upon their oaths do say that they find the defendant guilty in manner & form as charged in the Bill of Indictment—
Therefore it is considered by the Court that the said defendant David Cooper be fined the sum of Five dollars & that he pay the Costs of this prosecution.

```
        STATE OF TENNESSEE  )
            VS              )  Indict. for an
        OBEDIAH BROOKFIELD  )  asst. & Battery
```

This day came the said defendant Obediah Broomfield & acknowledged himself bound & indebted to the state of Tennessee in the sum of Five hundred dollars & his security William B. Dancy in the sum of Two hundred & fifty dollars to be levied of their proper goods & chattles, lands & tenements to be void on condition that the said Obediah Broomfield doth make his personal appearance at the Court house in the town of Clarksville on the first Thursday after the third Monday in July next, then & there to answer the state of Tennessee on a Bill of Indictment against him for an assault & Battery & not depart without leave of Court.

```
STATE OF TENNESSEE )
         VS        )   Indict for an
JOSEPH WOOLFOLK    )   ass't. & Battery
```

This day came the Solicitor General in behalf of the state & the defendant Joseph Woolfolk in proper person & was thereupon arraigned & upon his arraignment pleads not Guilty to the Bill of Indictment & for his trial puts himself upon his Country as does the Solicitor General likewise & thereupon came a jury of good & lawful men, to wit, James Trice, Sr., David McManus, George Kirk, William Corlew, William Daniel, John Martin, John Bayliss, John Barbour, Matthew Rogers, Henry Northington, Benjamin Mallory & John King, who being duly elected tried & sworn the truth to speak upon the issue of Traverse (p-193) upon their Oaths do say that the defendant Joseph Woolfolk, is not Guilty of an assault & battery as charged in the Bill of Indictment.

It is therefore considered by the Court that the defendant be hence discharged, & it appearing to the Court that said prosecution is frivolous and without any just grounds, It is therefore ordered & adjudged by the Court that Jesse Smith the prosecutor in this case be taxed with the costs of this prosecution & that a Fi Fa issue for the same.

```
WILLIAM L. WILLIAMS )
        VS          )
SAM'L ELAM          )   Motion
```

This day came William L. Williams by his attorney & moves the Court for a judgment against Sam'l Elam & produces to the Court here a Bill single signed by the said Elam & said Williams for one hundred & sixty Three dollars payable twelve months after date to Benjamin Williams & dated the 23rd of August 1821 upon which said Bill, the judgment was rendered at the January term of the County Court 1823 against William L. Williams and the said Williams now moves the Court here for a judgment against sd. Elam as his security in the aforesaid bill single and because the Court do not know whether the said Williams was the security or not of said Elam in the said Bill single therefore there came a jury of good and lawful men of our County, to wit, James True Sr. David McManus, George Kirk, Wm Corbin, William Daniel, John Martin, John Bayless, John Barbour, Matthew Rogers, Henry Northington, Benjamin Mallory, & John King, who being duly elected tried & sworn the truth to speak whether or not the said Williams was security in the said Bill single for the said Elam or not upon their oaths do say that the said Williams was only the security for the said Elam in the aforesaid Bill single and it further appearing to our said Court that judgment to as rendered against Williams at the Jan'y . Term 1823 for $177.76 besides the Costs.

It is therefore considered by the Court that the said Williams recover of the said Elam the said sum of of one hundred & seventy seven dollars & seventy six cents & the further sum of Two dollars & sixty six cents interest thereon to this time (p-194) and also the costs expended in the defence of the said suit of Benjamin Williams against William L. Williams and also the Costs of this motion.

```
WILLIAM L. WILLIAMS )
         VS          } Motion
SAM'L. ELAM          )
```

This day came the said Williams and moves the Court for a judgment against said Elam, the said Williams alledging that he was only security in a Bill single which is here produced to the Court signed by Samuel Elam & William L. Williams payable to Alfred Balch or order for five hundred and Thirty Three dollars and seven cents with interest from the date one year after date & dated the 23rd day of August 1821 and because the said Court do not know whether the said Williams is the security in the said ///// note, therefore there came a jury of good and lawful men, to wit, James Trice Jr., David McManus, George Kirk, William Corlew, William Daniel, John Martin, John Bayless, John Barbour, Mathew Rogers, Henry Northington, Benjamin Mallory & John King who being duly elected; tried & sworn the truth to speak upon the issue afpresaid, upon their oaths do say that the said William L. Williams is only security in the said Bill single & it appearing to the Court here that a judgment had been rendered on the said note in behalf of Stephen Cantrell at the April Term 1823 of the County of Montgomery against said Williams for the sum of five hundred and eighty six dollars & twenty five cents & the costs of suit.
It is therefore considered by the Court here that the said Williams recover of the said Elam the aforesaid sum of five hundred and eighty six dollars and twenty five cents & the costs of the former suit and also the costs in this behalf expended.

```
(p-195)    STATE OF TENNESSEE )
                VS            } Indict. for
           HENRY HOLLIS       } a Riot
```

This day came the Solicitor General in behalf of the state & the defendant Henry Hollis in proper person & was thereupon arraigned & upon his arraignment pleads Guilty to the Bill of Indictment & submits to the Court whereupon the evidence being heard—— It is considered by the Court that the defendant Henry Hollis be fined the sum of Five dollars & that he pay the costs of this prosecution.

```
STATE OF TENNESSEE )
        VS         }
WILSON GIBSON      )
```

On motion it is ordered by the Court that the judgment nisi
           rendered against said Wilson Gibson for not attending as a
Cost paid   juror // ////////// be set aside upon the payment of the
           costs.   It is therefore considered by the Court that the
State of Tennessee recover of said defendant the costs in this behalf
Expended.

PETER H. BARR
VS
JAMES TRICE JR. &} Debt
MORDICA REDD

And now at this day came the said defendants & prayed an appeal to the Circuit Court of Montgomery County & having given bond & security satisfactory to the Court the same is allowed.

STEPHEN CANTRELL
VS
THE HEIRS OF } Debt Sci Fa
B. SEARCY DEC'D.

This day came the plaintiff by an attorney and the said Charles D. McLean Guardian of Maria D. & Marcia S. McLean heirs at law of Bennett Searcy Dec'd. being solemnly called to come into Court & shew Cause if any they had why execution should not issue on the judgment in the said Scire facias mentioned to be levied of the real estate of Bennett Searcy Dec'd. that have descended to them as his heirs at law—and the said C. D. McLean Guardian as aforesaid failing to come in & to answer or shew any cause—— It is therefore considered by the Court here that an execution issue on the judgment (p-196) aforesaid to be levied of the real estate of the said Bennett Searcy Dec'd. that descended to the said Maria D. & Marcia S. McLean for the judgment aforesaid and the costs of said judgment and also the Costs in this behalf Expended.

JOHN ALLENSWORTH
& JAMES MILLER
VS } Debt
ROBERT G. JOHNSON Admr.
of P. Johnson Dec'd.

This day came the plaintiffs by atto. & suggest to the Court here that Abner V. Hampton one of the administrators hath departed this life since last Court & the said Robert is permitted to defend alone & thereupon pleads the plea of fully administered upon which there is issue joined & thereupon came a jury of good & lawful men, James Trice Senr. David McManus, George Kirk, Wm. Corlew, William Daniel, John Martin, John Bayless, John Barbour, Mathew Rogers, Henry Northington, Benjamin Mallory and John King who being duly elected tried & sworn the truth to speak upon the issue joined upon their oaths do say, that the said Defendant Robert G. Johnson hath fully administered all and singular the goods & chattles rights & credits of Philip Johnson Dec'd. that have come to his hands to be administered—— ~~It is therefore considered by the Court~~ & they also find for the said plaintiffs his Debt in the Declaration mentioned amounting to $163.50 & also the sum of three dollars & twenty seven cents damages for the detention of the same. It is therefore considered by the Court that the said plaintiffs recover of the Defendant the sum of one hundred and sixty six dollars & seventy six cents to be levied of the goods & chattles rights & credits of Philip Johnson Dec'd. that may hereafter come to the hands of the said Robert to be administered & the Costs to be levied of the proper goods & chattles, lands & tenements of said Robert.

(p-197)   ELI LOCKERT
            VS
    ROBERT G. JOHNSON admrs. of) Debt
    P. JOHNSON dec'd.

        This day came the parties by their attorney and the said pl'ff.
suggesting to the Court here that Abner V. Hampton has departed this life
since last Court & the said Robert is permitted to defend alone & pleads
the plea of fully administered upon which issue is taken by the said
plaintiff & thereupon there came a jury of good & lawful men, to wit,
James Trice Sr., David McManus, George Kirk, William Corlew, William
Daniel, John Martin, John Bayless, John Barbour, Mathew Rogers, Henry
Northington, Benjamin Mallory & John King who being duly elected tried &
sworn the truth to speak upon the issue joined upon their oaths do say
that they find that the said Robert G. Johnson both fully administered all
& singular the goods & chattles, Rights & credits of Philip Johnson Dec'd.
that has come to his hands to be administered & they also find that there
is a balance of debt due the plaintiff amounting to the sum of one hundred
and eighteen dollars & sixteen cents—
It is therefore considered by the Court here that the said plaintiff
recover of the Defendant the said sum of one hundred & eighteen dollars
& sixteen cents to be levied of the goods & chattles, rights & credits of
Philip Johnson Dec'd. that may hereafter come to the hands of the said
Robert G. Johnson to be administered and the costs to be levied of the
goods & chattles lands & tenements of the said Robert G. Johnson.

(p-198)   JAMES H. BRYAN)
            VS
    WILLIAM M. BELL) Debt
    & JAMES GORDON)

        This day came the plaintiff by attorney and the defendant
William M. Bell being solemnly called came not but made default.
It is therefore considered by the Court that the plaintiff recover of the
said William M. Bell the sum of three hundred and eighty five dollars &
twenty cents the debt in the declaration mentioned and also the further
sum of fifty one dollar thirty cents his damages by the Court here awarded
for the detention of said suit together with his costs by him about his
suit in this behalf expended.

    JAMES H. BRYAN)
            VS
    WILLIAM M. BELL) Debt
    & JAMES GORDON)

        This day came the parties by their attornies and thereupon all and
singular the matters and things in the defendant James Gordon's one of
said defendants demurrer to the plaintiff's declaration being heard and
fully understood.
It is considered by the Court that said demurrer be sustained and that
the defendant James Gordon go hence without day and recover of the plaintiff his costs about his defence in this behalf expended.

JAMES H. BRYAN)
VS)
WILLIAM M. BELL,) Debt
& JAMES GORDON)

This day came the plaintiff in open Court and prayed an appeal in
this case to the Circuit Court (p-199) and having entered into bond
and security agreeable to law the same is allowed.

BRITTAIN NICHOLSON
VS
WILLIAM M. BELL
& JAMES GORDON

This day came the plaintiff by attorney & thereupon the defendant
William M. Bell being solemnly called came not but made default.
It is therefore considered by the Court, that the plaintiff recover of
the defendant William M. Bell the sum of three hundred and sixty nine
dollars twenty five cts. the debt in the declaration mentioned and also
the sum of thirty two dollars sixty two cents for the detention of said
debt besides his costs by him about his suit in this behalf expended.

BRITTAIN NICHOLSON
VS
WILLIAM M. BELL
& JAMES GORDON

This day came the parties by their attornies and thereupon all and
singular the matters and things contained in the defendant James Gordons
demurrer to the plaintiffs declaration being heard & fully understood
it is considered by the Court that said demurrer be sustained & that the
defendant James Gordon go hence without day and recover of the plaintiff
his costs by him about his suit in this behalf expended.

BRITTAIN NICHOLSON)
VS)
WILLIAM M. BELL,) Debt
& JAMES GORDON)

This day came with Court the plaintiff by attorney and prayed an
appeal in this suit to the Circuit Court and (p-200) having entered
into bond & security the same is allowed.

Court adjourned untill tomorrow morning to meet at 9 O'clock.
Chas. Bailey
Stephen Cooke
Isaac Dennison
Francis Baker

Friday morning 25th April 1823 Court met according to adjournment
Present the Worshipful---
Isaac Dennison
Stephen Cooke
Charles Bailey
Francis Baker

SAMUEL C. HAWKINS)
   VS   ) Motion
HARVEY SHELBY)

This day came said plaintiff by his attorney and It appearing to
the satisfaction of this Court that heretofore two alias executions were
Issued from the Docket of Stephen Thomas formerly a justice of the Peace
for this County now resigned by the Clerk of this Court on the 11th April
1823 one for the sum of ~~$$$ $$$ $$$ $$$ $$~~ $2.70 and $1.12½ cents costs
and the other for $64.00 & 1.00 costs on Judg'ts. rendered before said
Stephen Thomas the 9th February 1821 which said executors came to the
hands of Cornelius Crusman sheriff on said 11th April 1823, who has returned thereon that he can find no personal property of said Shelby the
defendant, to make said money & costs & in default thereof has levied the
said executions on all the right & title ~~$$$$~~ that said defendant has in
& to a tract of land whereon said Defendants' mother now lives which
discended to said defendant as one of the heirs (p-201) of his father
Isaac Shelby Deceased.
On motion therefore it is considered by the Court and ordered that a
Venditioni exponas Issue directing the Sheriff to expose said land so
levied to date to satisfy said sums of money called for in said Executions
as also the costs of this motion.

THOMAS SMITH)
   VS   ) Case
JOSEPH TOCKINGTON)

This day came into Open Court Matthew Dougherty and filed his
answer as garnishee in this case which is received by the Court.

THOMAS SMITH)
   VS   ) Case
JOSEPH TOCKINGTON)

This day came the plaintiff by attorney and thereupon the said
Joseph Tockington being solemnly called came not but made default be
rendered against the said Joseph Tockington, but because the Court are
not advised what damages the plaintiff hath sustained, let a writ of
enquiry issue returnable to the next term of this Court to ascertain &
assess the same.

JAMES W. BLAKES assee)
   VS   ) Debt
MOSES COLLIER)

Upon motion of the defendant by his attorney it is ordered by the
Court, that said defendant have liberty to take the depositions of David
G. Williams & Freeman Williams residents of the State of Virginia upon
giving the adverse party thirty days notice of time & place, to be read
as evidence in the suit aforesaid.

(p-202) JOEL BAYLISS)
     VS   ) Case
   WILLIAM WHITEHEAD)

This day came the plaintiff by his attorney C. Johnson Esquire & says he will no further prosecute his said suit against the defendant, but dismisses the same---Therefore it is considered by the Court that said suit stand dismissed, & that the def't. William Whitehead go hence without day & recover of the plaintiff Joel Bayless the costs in this behalf Expended.

```
DAVID ANDERSON for the benefit )
of JAMES SMITH                 )
        VS                     )   Case
CONSTANT H. P. MARR            )
```

Upon motion of defendant by his attorney it is ordered by the Court that said defendant have permission to take the deposition of Henry Jackson resident of the City of New Orleans State of Louisiana to be read as evidence in the suit aforesaid, upon giving the adverse party thirty days notice of time & place.

```
MARTIN THOMAS                      )
        VS                         )
ROBERT G. JOHNSON Admr. of         )   Debt
PHILIP JOHNSON dec'd.              )
```

This day came the parties by their attornies, & the said plaintiff suggesting to the Court here, that Abner V. Hampton one of the admrs. of said Philip Johnson dec'd. hath departed this life since the last Term of this Court & the said Robert G. Johnson is permitted to defend alone & thereupon pleads the plea of fully administered upon which there is issue joined & thereupon came a jury of good & lawful men (to wit), James Trice Sr., David McMannus, George Kirk, William Corlew, William Daniel, John Martin, John Bayliss, John Barbour, Matthew Rogers, Henry Northington, Benjamin Mallory & John King, who being duly elected tried & sworn the truth to (p-203) to speak upon the issue joined, upon their oaths do say, that the said Robert G. Johnson hath fully administered all and singular the goods & chattles, rights & credits of the said Philip Johnson dec'd. that have come to his hands to be administered, & they also find that there is a balance of debt due the plaintiff amounting to the sum of One hundred & twenty dollars the debt, & the further sum of three dollars & sixty cents the damages thereon by reason of the detention of said debt. It is therefore considered by the Court here that the said plaintiff recover of the defendant, the sum of One hundred & twenty three dollars & sixty cents, the debt & damages so assessed by the jury in form aforesaid, to be levied of the goods and chattles, rights & credits of Philip Johnson dec'd. & it being suggested to the Court here that lands have descended to the heirs of said Philip Johnson ordered that Fieri Facias issue against them & & and the costs to be levied of the proper goods & chattles, lands & tenements of the said Robert G. Johnson admrs.

```
GEORGE F. NAPIER      )
        VS            )   Debt
WILLIAM L. WILLIAMS   )
```

And now at this day came the defendant & prayed an appeal in the nature of a writ of Error, to the Circuit Court of Montgomery County & given bond & security satisfactory to the court the same is allowed.

> ELIAS W. NAPIER
> VS   } Debt
> WILLIAM L. WILLIAMS }

And now at this day came the defendant & prayed an appeal in the nature of a writ of Error, to the Circuit Court of Montgomery County & having given bond & security satisfactory to the Court the same is allowed.

> JOSEPH & ROBERT WOODS assee }
> VS   }
> CONSTANT H. P. MARR   } Debt
> & ROBERT SEARCY   }

And now at this day came the defendants & prayed an appeal to the Circuit Court of Montgomery County & having given bond & security satisfactory to the Court the same is allowed.

> (p-204)   HOPSON & ALLEN for the benefit }
>   of LEWIS B. ALLEN   }
>   VS   } Debt
>   ELIZA SMITH   }

And now at this day came the defendant by her attorney William A. Cook esquire & prayed an appeal to the Circuit Court of Montgomery County & having given bond & security satisfactory to the Court the same is allowed.

On motion it is ordered by the Court that Francis Baker be appointed Administrator (with the will annexed) of Harriet Blakeney dec'd. & the said Francis Baker came into Court & entered bond & security satisfactory to the Court & the same is allowed, & it is therefore ordered by the Court that letters Testamentary issue to the said Francis Baker on the estate of the said dec'd.

Francis Baker adm'r. of Harriet Blakeney dec'd. & on motion ordered to be Recorded.

Alexander M. Rogers, William E. Williams & Thomas Wyatt commissioners appointed at the last Term of this Court to settle with John & Elijah Martin Executors of Jesse Martin dec'd. make report to this Court & on motion ordered to be recorded.

James Barret & Manoah Bostick commissioners appointed at the last Term of this Court, to settle with James Trice Jr., & John Long Admrs. of this Court, to settle with James Trice Jr., & John Long Admrs. of Dolphy Mitchel dec'd. make their report to this Court & on motion ordered to be Recorded.

James Fentress, Francis Carter & Robert Vance commissioners appointed at the last Term of this Court to ~~//////~~ ~~////~~ lay off a years provision for Elizabeth Corbin, widow of Charnell Corbin dec'd. make their report to this Court & on motion ordered to be Recorded.

(p-205)   A Deed of Bargain & Sale from Britain Bayless to John Williams for 171 Acres of land, was produced in Open Court & the execution thereof duly proven by the Oaths of Bird Hardy & Michael Tyer, the subscribing witnesses thereto & on motion ordered to be Certified for registration.

A Deed of Bargain & Sale from Philip Delph to George Kirk for 62 acres of land, was produced in Open Court & the execution thereof duly acknowledged by the said Philip Delph to be his act and deed for the purposes therein contained & on motion ordered to be certified for registration.

A Deed of Bargain & Sale from Jacob Rudolph to Philip Delph for 62 Acres of land was produced in Open Court & the execution thereof duly proven by the Oaths of George Kirk & Richard Brown, two of the subscribing witnesses thereto, & on motion ordered to be certified for registration.

A Deed of Bargain & Sale from Cave Johnson to William J. Lynes, for one town Lott in Clarksville, was produced in Open Court & the execution thereof duly acknowledged by the said Cave Johnson as his act & deed for the purposes therein contained & on motion ordered to be certified for registration.

A Deed of conveyance from David Outlaw to his son, William Outlaw for 520 Acres of land & other personal property, was produced in Open Court, & the execution thereof duly acknowledged by the said David Outlaw as his act & deed for the purposes therein mentioned & on motion ordered to be certified for registration.

The Grand jury appeared in Open Court & returned a Bill of Indictment the State of Tennessee against John Davie for an assault & Battery a True Bill & it is ordered that the same be made as of yesterday.

(p-206)   Stephen Pettus esquire returns into Court the list of Taxable property taken in Cap't. Philip William's Company for 1823.

James Carr Esqr. returns into Court, the list of Taxable property taken in Cap't. James Hamlett's Company for 1823.

Abner Harris esquire returns into Court, the list of Taxable property taken in Cap't. Andrew Simm's Company for 1823.
Charles Barley esqr. returns into Open Court, the list of Taxable property taken in Cap't. Bridges after Company for the year aforesaid.

Francis Carter esquire returns into Court, the list of Taxable property taken in Cap't. Samuel T. Allen's Company for the year aforesaid.

William Trigg esquire returns into Court the list of Taxable property taken in Cap't. John Moore's Company for the year aforesaid.

John McCauley Esquire returns into Court the list of Taxable property taken in Cap't. Simon Holmes Company for the year aforesaid.

Francis Baker esquire, returns into Court the list of Taxable property taken in Cap't. Shamvell's Company for the year aforesaid.

Matthew Ryburn esquire returned into Court the list of Taxable property taken in Cap't. James Williams Company for the year aforesaid.

On motion ordered by the Court that the order appointing Commissioners to settle with William O. Robbins & Nancy Henelson admr. of Burgess Henelson admr. of Burgess Henelson dec'd. at the last Term of this Court, be continued & that the same commissioners be appointed & make report to the next Term of this Court.

(p-207)   SUSAN COCKE by her Guardian)
             vs   ) Petition
    EDWARD NEBLETT   )

This day came the parties by their attornies & thereupon all & singular the matters & things arising on said petition and answer & Replication being fully heard & understood, it is ordered adjudged & decreed by the Court here that the said petitioner recover of the said Edward Neblett the sum of fourteen dollars & sixty one cents & the Costs in this behalf expended.

    CULLEN BAYLESS   )
    & JAMES ELDER   )
          VS   ) Motion
    JOHN BOWERS Constable)

This day came the plaintiff by his attorney & moves the Court for a judgment against John Bowers a constable of said County & thereupon it appearing to the Court here, that John Bowers had collected the sum of Thirty nine dollars & sixty one cents as a constable of said County and that he had more than Ten days notice of this motion and that the said Cullen Bayless & James Elder were entitled to the said money and that application had been made for said money of said John Bowers.
It is therefore considered by the Court that the said Cullen Bayless & James Elder recover of the said John Bowers the sum of thirty nine dollars so collected by him as aforesaid and also the sum of Four dollars & seventy five cents damages at the rate of $12\frac{1}{2}$ pr. centum and also the costs of this motion.

    Court adjourned untill tomorrow morning to meet at 9 O'clock.
                         Isaac Dennison
                         Chas. Bailey
                         Jas. Barret

(p-208)   Saturday morning 26th April 1823
Court met according to adjournment.
Present the Worshipful

                         Charles Baily)
                         James Barret) Justices
                         Isaac Dennison)

    ABRAHAM BRANTLEY Guardian for   )
    ELISHA BENNETT & GEORGE BENNET   )
    of LIDIA BENNET of MOSES OLDHAM   ) Justices
    JOHN R. DOUGHERTY & NANCY DOUGHERTY)

This day came said petitioners by Guardian & Counsel and it appearing
to the Court & by consent of his Counsel that one of said petitioners
Polly Daugherty is not a distributer of said intestate.
Therefore ordered that as to said Polly said petition be dismissed—
And it appearing to the Court as to the other petitioners, that the subpoena & copy of petition in this case was duly served on said Defendant
more than ten days before the last Term of this Court that the said defendant
has failed to appear & plead answer or demurrer to said petition that the
same is hereby taken for confessed, & now has upon the hearing of said
Petition it appearing as charged in said petition that on the —day of—
1818 by the sale of the personal & perishable property of said Moses
Deceased there came to the hands of said defendant as admr. the sum of
$216.21½. That afterwards on the —day of —1819 there was made by the sale
of negroes & other property the sum of $316.00 all of which were due &
owing on the 21st February 1820, making together the sum of $3552.21½ and
it further appearing by the settlement made with the commissioners by the
consent of said petitioners (p-209) That said Oldham has disbursed in
expenses & in payment of Debts about said Estate the sum of $470.21½ which
ought to be deducted from said sum of $3552.21½ and leaves a ballance
of Principal of $3082.00 in the hands of said Def't. as administrator for
distribution, that on said sum there is Interest due from said 20th
February 1820 to this time being three years & two months being the sum
of $581.78 making together the sum of $3643.78 subject to distribution—
and it further appearing to Court that by the deed of Gift ////s///
/////// of said Moses in his life time duly proven & &. That said
petitioner is intitled to distribution in the following proposition, To wit,
Elisha Bennet, George Bennet and Lydia Bennet one sixth as the sum of
$607.29 Moses Oldham to one sixth being the sum of $607.29 John R. Daugherty
& Nancy L. Daugherty to one sixth of the sum of $607.29. Whereupon the
premises considered this Court do think fit to order, adjudge & decree, and
do hereby order adjudge & decree that Def't. Elisha R. Oldham admr.
aforesaid do pay to said petitioners George & Elisha by their Guardian
A. Brantly & to Lydia Bennet said sum of $607.29 to wit, two thirds to
said Guardian & one third to said Lydia—That he pay to said Moses Oldham
the sum of $607.29 being his proportion or one sixth—
That he pay to said John R. Daugherty in his own Right and as guardian for
Nancy L. Daugherty the sum of $607.29 and also that said defendant pay
the Costs of this suit.
That said Petitioner's have execution for their respective parts as at
common law.

(p-210)   SOLOMON HUNT)
                VS   )
           JOHN ROOK &   )   Debt
           SAMUEL CREATH   )

        This day came the plaintiff by his attorney & the defendants
being solemnly called, to come into Court & plead to the plaintiffs declaration failed so to do.
It is therefore considered by the Court that the said plaintiff Solomon
Hunt recover of the defendants John Rook & Samuel Creath the sum of One
hundred & fifty dollars, the debt in the declaration mentioned & the
further sum of Three dollars the damages sustained by the detention of
said debt & also the Costs in this behalf Expended.

AMBROSE MADDISON)
      VS   )
JONATHAN JOHNSON)   This day came the Defdt. in open court and
                          acknowledges himself indebted as the security
of Philip Johnson Decd on a note of hand executed by the said Philip &
himself to Ambrose Maddison in the sum of two hundred and forty five
dollars & fourteen & three fourth cents-
It is therefore considered by the court here, that the said Ambrose
Maddison recover of the said Johnathan Johnson the aforesaid sum of Two
hundred and forty five dollars and fourteen & three fourth cents and the
costs in this behalf expended

Execution stayed by consent until October Term 1823-

    HOPSON & ALLEN)
        VS   )   came the defendant
    WILLIE BLOUNT) This day again/by his attorney and prays an appeal
                      in the nature of a writ of Error to the Circuit
Court & having entered into Bond & security according to law the same is
allowed him

(p-211) JONATHAN JOHNSON)
        VS   )   Motion
    ROBERT G JOHNSON ADMR OF) This day came the said plaintiff by his
    PHILIP JOHNSON DECD   ) attorney and moves the court for a
                      judgment against the said Robert as
admr. of Philip Johnson Decd as security on a Bill single executed by the
said*Philip payable to Ambrose Maddison upon which there is a balance
due at this time of Two hundred & forty five dollars & 14 3/4 and the
said administrator being present court admits the said Johnathan Johnson
was the security of the said Philip in the execution of the aforesaid
bill single and the said Robert also here shews to the Court that he has
fully administered all & singular the goods & chattles which were of the
estate of Philip Johnson Decd and the same is admitted by the said Jonathan
Johnson & it further appearing on the motion aforesaid that a judgment
had been rendered on the aforesaid Bill single against the said Jonathan
Johnson for the sum of Two hundred & forty five dollars & fourteen &
three fourth cents at the April Term 1823 of the County Court of Montgomery
& for the Costs- It is therefore considered by the court here that the said
Jonathan Johnson recover of the said Robert G. Johnson the aforesaid sum
of Two hundred and forty five dollars & 14 3/4 cents and also the costs
of the judgment of Madison against Jonathan Johnson to be levied of the
goods & chattles of the said Philip Johnson Decd.- and because it is here
suggested to our said court that real estate hath descended to the heirs
of the said Philip Johnson, It is thereupon further ordered by the court
that a Sciere facias issue against said heirs of said Philip Johnson
* Jonathan Johnson & the said

(p-212) JOHN ROOK)
       VS   )   Sci fa
THE HEIRS OF N.PEEPLES DECD) This day came the said plaintiff by his attorney
                      and the said Polly Peeples Guardian of David
Peeples, William Peeples, Agatha Peeples,   Burrell Peeples, Patsy Peeples,

& Nathan Peeples -- the heirs at law of Nathan Peeples Decd being
solemnly called to come into Court & show cause upon the said Scire
Facias failed so to do - It is thereforeconsidered by the court here
that ~~the~~ an execution issue on the judgment mentioned in the said Scire
Facias to be levied of the ~~lands~~ real estate of Nathan Peeples Decd
that descended to his aforesaid heirs as his heirs at law to satisfy
the said debt due to the said John Rook

ALLY DILLARD GUARDIAN OF THE)
HEIRS OF LUKE DILLARD DECD)
      VS)   Debt
HUGH F. BELL & WILLIAM E. DANCY) This day came the defendant by their
                      attorney & thereupon the plaintiff
being solemnly called to come into court & prosecute her said suit, failed so to do.
It is therefore considered by the court that said suit be dismissed &
that the defendants go hence & recover of the plaintiff the costs in this
behalf Expended

On motion it is ordered by the court that the order appointing Stephen
Cocke & A.M. Rogers Esqr. commissioners to settle with Isham Trotter
Guradian of Abraham & Polly Cocke at the last term of this court, be
continued & that they make report to next Court-

A deed of Conveyance from Willie Segraves & his wife Elizabeth Segraves
to Samuel Lynes for their Interest in the estate of John Sims decd was
produced in open court & the execution thereof was proven by Stramler &
Cole the subscribing witnesses thereto to have been executed and delivered by Willie Seagraves & it is ordered by the court that P-213
Matthew Ryburn & Thomas Smith Justices of the peace for said County
examined privately Elizabeth Segraves relative to the execution of the
same and certify such examination to this court
In pursuance of the above order of court we have caused Elizabeth Segraves
to come before us & upon her examination seperate & appart from her husband she acknowledges she executed the above deed of conveyance freely
voluntarily & of her own accord & for the purposes therein mentioned &
without compulsion of constraint from her husband - In testimony where
of we have hereto set our hands & seals this 21st of April 1823-
                       Signes Matthew Ryburn J.P.
                       Samuel Smith   J.P.
& it is ordered by the court, that the same be certified for registration

HAYDON E. WELLS GUARDIAN)
      VS)   Sci Fa
THE HEIRS OF NATHAN PEEPLES) This day came the plaintiff and the
                      defendants being called came not but
made default on motion Therefore considered by the court that said plaintiff recover against said defendants the sum of three hundred and thirty
seven dollars & 75 cents the debt in said writ of Sci Fa specified with
interest thereon from 25th Jany 1823 untill paid as also the sum of
$9.46½ costs in said writ specified and his costs about his suit in this
behalf expended to be levied of the lands & tenements which were of said
Nathan Peeples at his death & which have descended to his heirs the said
defendants

JOHN COCKE GUARDIAN	)	
VS	)	This day came the petitioner and prays an
EDWARD NEBLETT	)	appeal to the Circuit Court & enters into
		Bond & security & the same is allowed him-

(p-214) Ordered that John Edmonson be permitted to give in his list of Taxable property for the year 1823 &that it be annexed to the present years tax list-

A Bill Sale from Stephen Pettus to Stephen P. Cook for four negros was produced in Open Court & the execution thereofwas duly acknowledged by the said Stephen Pettus as his act & deed for the purposes therein contained & on motion ordered to be recc/rded-

A Deed of settlement between Joseph Ligon & Nathaniel D. Terry was produced in open court & the execution thereof was duly proven by the oaths of Frederick W. Huling & James Barret subscribing witnesses thereto & on motion ordered to be recorded-

A Deed of relinquishment from Nathan D. Terry to Joseph Ligon for a negro girl named Peggy was duly proven in open court by the oaths of Frederick W. Huling & James Barret subscribing witnesses thereto & on motion ordered to be recorded

A Deed Gift from Joseph Ligon to Elizabeth W. Terry for a negro girl named Peggy was produced in open court & the execution thereof duly proven by the oaths of Frederick W. Huling & James Barrett subscribing witnesses thereto & on motion ordered to be recorded

William Trigg, William R. Gibson & Richard B. Blount commissioners appointed at the last term of this court to make division of the property left to Francis Isbel & Patsey Isbel make their report to this court & on motion ordered to be recorded

On motion ordered by the court that the order appointing Francis Baker Nathan Hester & Samuel Haggard commissioners to settle with Robert Wade admr of William Faulkner decd be continued & that the same commissioners make report to next court-

(p-215) On motion ordered by the court that Robert T. Williams be allowed the sum of Three dollars & fifty cents it being for an error in gividing in his tax list for the year 1821 as appears from the affidavit of the said Robert T. Williams filed here in court, that he has paid the sheriff said sum ofThree dollars & fifty cents more than he was bound to pay. It is therefore ordered by the court that the said Robert T. Williams be allowed said sum of three dollars & fifty cents & that the county Trusteepay the same out of any monies in the Treasury not otherwise appropriated-

From the report of Samuel Smith & Francis Carter commissioners appointed to examin into the situation of Mary Barlow now at the house of Parson Haynes in this County - It is considered by the court that the said Mary Barlow be placed on the paupers list of this county for her support-

Richard Overton Edward A. Lucy Samuel Haggard Joseph Shanwell Lewis Bush commissioners appointed to settle with William Cooper admr of Charles Wall decd make their report to this court & on motion ordered to be recorded-

Edmund Taylor John Brodie Lewis C. Taylor & James Bowers commissioners appointed to settle with William Cooper admr of Charles Wall decd make their report to this court & on motion ordered to be recorded

On motion it is ordered by the court that Louisa Taylor a minor be bound to Robert McClure untill she shall attain to the age of Eighteen years & thereupon the said Robert McClure came into court entered into bond agreeable to law-

Ordered by the court that David R. Slatter be permitted to give in his list of Taxable property for the year 1823 & that it be annexed to the present years tax list-

(p-216) Ordered by the court that Solomon Hunt be permitted to give in his list of Taxable property for 1823 & that it be annexed to said years tax list-

On motion ordered by the court that Monoah Taylor be appointed overseer of the road from the mouth of the West fork to Thomas Watsons on the West fork & that the following hands work on said road underthe all said overseer (to wit) Mr. Hinsly & hands Obediah Broomfields hands Stephen Pettus hands Spirus Herring & hands John Herrington Nathaniel Herrington & the hands of Reuben Pollard & all other hands within the bounds of said road, who have not heretofore been ordered to work on any other road-

On motion ordered by the court that John Clark a witness in the Circuit Court in the case of the State of Tennessee against Stephen D.B.Stuart be allowed the sum of Four dollars & seventy eight cents agreeable to his certificate from the clerk of the Circuit Court filed in this Court & that the County Trustee pay the same outof any monies in the treasury not otherwise appropriated-

On motion ordered by the court that Harbert Walker be allowed the sum of Ten dollars a yearfor the support of a pauper Boy named William Bond now bound to the said Harbert Walker-

On motion it is ordered by the court that Letters of administration be granted to Rebecca Council on the estate of David Council decd. whereupon the said Rebecca Council came into open court & entered into bond & security satisfactory to the court & qualified agreeably to law-

Alexander M. Rogers Edward Neblett & Benjamin Orgain commissioners appointed at the last Term of this court to settle with Elias F. Foppe-

(p-217) Guardian of Drew Smith make their report to this court & on motion ordered to be Recorded-

On motion ordered by the court that Sterling Neblett A.M.Rogers & Capt John Taggart be appointed commissioners to settle with Abner Harris Guardian of John Fritchard (Idiot) & make report to the next Term of this court

On motion ordered by the court that Francis Baker Admr, of Harriet Blakeney decd by be permitted to sell the perishable property of said estate upon a credit ofninemonthss after advertising the same agreeable to law-

On motion ordered by the court that Jacob Rudolph be allowed a credit for the tax on 500 acres of land it being that much charged him too much by mistake in giving in his list of Taxable property for the year 1822 & that the sheriff be allowed the sum of One dollar eighty seven & ½ cents in his settlement with the County Trustee in paying the County Tax

A Bill Sale from John King to Madison King for a negroe Boy names Henry was Produced in Open Court & the execution thereof duly proven by the oaths of B. King & John King Jr. subscribing witnesses thereto & on motion ordered to be Recorded-

A Bill Sale from John King to Kincheon Washington King was produced in open Court & the execution thereof duly proven in Open Court & by the Oaths of Benjamin King & John King Jr. subscribing witnesses thereto & on motion ordered to be Recorded-

A power of Attorney from John W. Barker Mary W. Barker his wife Richard T. Merriwether & Thomas L. Merriwether to Peter N. Merriwether was produced in open Court & the execution thereof duly proven by the (p-218) Oath of William Chiles a subscribing witness thereto, & the execution of the same was also acknowledged in open court by John W. Baker & Richard T. Merriwether two of the parties thereto to be their act & deed for the purposes therein contained & on motion the same is ordered to be certified-

The Court proceeded to appoint Jurors to the July Term 1823 as follow (to wit) Thomas H . Oneal Peter Oneal Jacob Corban John Linch Gibson Mills Aquilla Johnson Meridith Williams Hervey McFall Jr. Robert Nowland Thomas Railsback Lewis Trice James Hamplett James Thackston Thomas Moon John Darnal John Williams Samuel Jordan William Clifton Darvin E.Barton John Rudolph Jr. (McAdoe) Jacob Foust John Cooke Jr. Benjamin E. Orgain Joseph Bowers James Bayliss & Christopher N. Carney-

Zachariah Grant & John Moore are appointed constables to the next July Term 1823-

The court proceeded to appoint jurors to the next August Circuit Court to wit John McCauley George J.McCauley Thomas Adams David B. Allen James Fentress Sr. John Russel William B. Nelson John Henderson William S. White Rowland Peterson Reuben Pollard John Nevill David Ellipott James Smith N.York Joseph Ogburn Richard Taylor Robert Searcy James Wilson Kencheon W. King Robert McMordie Solomon Hunt Hayden E Wells Samuel Bumpass Sr. Jacob Bailey & Thomas Batson & James Bowers

Samuel Creath & Howel U. Atkins are appointed constables to the next Augst. Circuit Court

(p-219) ANTHONY B. SHELBY)
VS) Sci Fa
BENJAMIN NEBLETT &) This day came the parties by their attornies &
SAMUEL MCFALL) thereupon by consent of parties this cause is
transfered to the Circuit Court for trial to be
had thereon-

Court adjourned untill Monday morning to meet at 9 O'clock-

Chas Bailey
Isaac Dennison
Jas Barret

The Worshipful court of Montgomery County have met according to adjournment Monday April 28th 1823

Present Charles Bailey) Esquires
James Barret   ) Justices
Issac Dennison

Thomas Epps his Guardian
     WYATT EPPS)
         VS   ) Petition
     WILLIAM ALLEN)   This day came the parties by their counsel and there
                     upon argument being had on the petitioners Demurer
to Defendants Plea ~~being printed/argued~~ & by the court here fully understood It is ordered by the court that said Demurrer be sustained and it
is further ordered that said deft ~~is further ordered that said deft~~
answer immediately to said petition-

This cause is by consent of Parties transferred to the Circuit Court of
Montgomery County for trial & C

     STATE OF TENNESSEE)
         VS   )   It appearing to the court that said defendant
     DAWSON BAYLISS   )   was duly summoned as a juror to this term
                           ordered by the court that he be fined the sum
of Five dollars unless he appearson or before the next Term of this court &
shews good cause to the court to the contrary & in case he does not appear
and shew (p-220) sufficient cause as aforesaid that scieri Facias issue
from the next Term of this court as required by law-

Court adjourned untill court in course

Chas Bailey
Isaac Dennison
Jas Barret

The Worshipful court of Montgomery County have met according to adjournment Monday July 21st 1823-
Present Valentine Allen Lewis C. Taylor & James Carr Esqurs Justices

Ordered by the court that James Barret & Charles Bailey Esq's be appointed
commissioners to settle with William Jordan admr. of William Elliott decd
& make report to this court

On motion ordered by the court that Gideon Pace Hardy Pace Kamp Holt
Charles Parker & Shaderick Lee's hands work on the road under James Hollis
overseer of that part of the road leading from Nashville to Clarksville
it being the part of the road he has worked on heretofore in addition to
the ~~said~~ hands already ordered to work on said road & that said hands
be excused from working under John Major as heretofore ordered-

On motion ordered by the court that John Carter Neal Blue & Thomas Carraway be appointed commissioners to lay off and allot to Ellinor Adams her dower of the personal estate of said Adams decd & make report to next court-

Ordered by the court that John Edmondson be allowed the sum of Ten Dollars for keeping William Walker a pauper for twelve months ending April Term 1823 & that the County Trustee pay the same out of any monies not otherwise appropriated-

(p-221) On motion ofdered by the court that Reuben N. Bullard be allowed the sum of Twenty Dollars for keeping Patsey Brannon from the 8th untill the 16th May a poor helpless woman who came to his house sick and died and for furnishing // coffin &c & that the County Trustee pay the same out of any monies not otherwise appropriated-

Present Lewis C. Taylor Abner Gupton Thomas W. Atkinson Samuel Smith Valentine Allen Francis Cartee Robert Vance Alexander M. Rogers & James Carr Esquiers justices

On motion ordered by the court that Cornelius Crusman Sheriff of Montgomery County be allowed the sum of fifty Dollars for his Exofficio services from July Term 1822 to this date & that the County Trustee pay the same out of any monies in the treasury not otherwise appropriated-

On motion ordered by the court that John H Marable be appointed Guardian to Plumer & Tabitha Smith in the place of Thomas M. Smith their former guardian whereupon the said John H Marable came into court & entered into Bond & security satisfactory to the court & quallified agreeable to law & it is ordered by the court that said Thomas M. Smith's securities be exonerated from any further responsibility as securities for the said Thomas Smith as guardian aforesaid-
Present- Lewis C Taylor Abner Gupton Thomas W Atkinson Samuel Smith Valentine Allen Francis Carter Robert Vance Alexander M Rogers & James Carr Esqrs Justices-

On motion ordered by the court that James Haynes be allowed the sum of thirty Dollars for keeping Polly Barlow three months & for Burying expenses & that the County Trustee pay the same out of any monies not otherwise appropriated-

(p-222) On motion ordered by the court that Alsey Jones & hands James Jones Julias Johnson Edwin Clifton William Plasters & David Jones be annexed to the list of hands heretofore ordered to work on the road leading from Weakleys to the Robertson County line under William Stewart overseer of said road

On motion ordered by the court thatthe following hands work under Joel Grizard overseer of the road from Port Royal to Thomas W. Carney's (to wit) Thomas Carney & hands John T Dabney & hands Alsy McGuire Samuel Parker Reuben Holt Joab C Acre & the hands of Joel Grizard

On motion ordered by the court that Asa W Hooper be appointed overseer on that part of of that part of the road leading from Thomas Carney's to the cross roads above Thomas Weaklys & that the following hands work on said road under him (to wit) Robert Davis Lemuel Lemaster Joseph Smith William Coon Canals T Pickering Daniel Holt John Holt Lewis Holt Christopher Holt John Holt Sr. & David Cooper

On motion by the court that Wyatt Epps be appointed overseer of the road leading from Well's ferry to Benjamin Whiteheads in place of Daniel Rook resigned & that the following hands work on said road in addition to the hands heretofore ordered to work on said road to wit James Allen & hands & John Cocke & hands and all others who live within the bounds of said road who have not heretofore been ordered to work on any other road-

On motion ordered by the court that Israel Robinson be appointed overseer of the road from Clarksville to said Robinson's ferry (to wit) J.P.Vaughn's hands M.D.Summons & hands Uriah Humphreys & hands John Kay Mrs Duff's hands & the hands of Mark Boothe-

(p-223) On motion ordered by the court that Peter Oneal be appointed over seer of the road from Clarksville to Wine Millers old place in place of Norfleet Smith resigned & that all the hands that were ordered to work under the said Smith work under Peter Oneal & all others within the bounds of said road-

On motion ordered by the court that Robert Baker be appointed overseer of the road from Palmyra by//XXXXXX widow Potters to the Dickson County line in place of Joseph Haynes resigned & that the following hands work on said road XX XXX Abraham Baggot & hands John Yarborough & William his father Robert Baker & son William Rye Thomas & Abealom Rye Francis & Barney Powers

John Allen Joseph Baggot Enuch Edwards William & Moses Bone James Hayns & hands John Matthis Allen Baggot Micajah Baggot & John Baggot-

On motion ordered by the court that William S. White be appointed overseer of the road from Thomas Cherrys to the six mile tree on the Russellville road & that the following hands work on said road to wit the hands of William S. White Benjamin Herring Mrs. Rosa Cherry's hands William Dikis Eli Dikis Henry Johnson Mr. -- Reed John Johnson's hands James Riggs William Watwood Enoch Carver John Edwards John Hamilton Solomon Grace & Mr.   Brantly Nicholas Bagwell John Thompson William Morrow William Hogan Samuel Bagwell & Philip Crotzer Jury of view who were appointed at the last term of this court to view that that part of the road that leads through Henry Funks plantation so as to intersect with Well's ferry road make report we the undersigned according to appointment & do say the road shall run down (p-224) the creek round William Hogan's fence by Crotzer's mill leaving the widow Staly's plantation to the right Thence on to the Road leading to Well's ferry acting agreeable to order-

The jury of View who were appointed at the last term of this court to view a road make the following report (to wit) This is to certify that we the undersigners have and have viewed the way for the road toview and think it the nearest rout and as good a way as the other given under our hands this day & date above writen said road to run to the right of the Pond thence straight to weeks lane-

On motion ordered by the court that Capt Thomas Rivers Henry W & Valentine Merriwether John Carter & Thomas Walker be permitted to give in their lists of taxable property for the year 1823 & that the same be annexed to the Present years list

On motion ordered by the court that Anthony B Foster The Hrs. James Gray & George S. Gray be permitted to give in their lists of Taxable property for the year 1823 & that it be annexed to the present years list-

Ordered by the court that Francis Carter John Kerchival & Henry McFall Jr. be appointed inspector of the election for the August election John Kezee Thomas W. Atkinson & William J. Lyons are appointed inspectors of the next August election at Clarksville-

Ordered that James Matthew Liggon & James W. Carney are appointed inspector of the next August Election at Port Royal

Matthew Ryburn & Abner Gupton commissioners appointed at the last Term of this court to settle with James Hollis guardian for the Hrs. of Thomas Parker decd make their report & on motion ordered to be Recorded

(p-225) Francis Baker & Edward A Lucy admrs of Thomas Blakeney decd returned into court an inventory and account sales of the goods chattles rights & credits of Thomas Blakeney decd quallified agreeable & on motion the same is ordered to be Recorded-

On motion ordered by the court that John F. Epps & hands & John Neblett Jr & hands be added to the list of hands who work under Arthur Harris overseer of the road leading by A. M. Rogers & Abner Harris' into the Dickson road in place of Benjamin Whiteheads hands taken off-

The commissioners appointed at the last Term of this court to settle with Abner Harris Guardian of John Pritchet (Idiot) make report to this Term & on motion ordered to be Recorded-

Present Samuel Smith Val Allen Francis Baker Stephen Cocke James Carr Robert Vance Lewis C Taylor Joshua P Vaughn Abner Gupton & Francis Carter Esqrs Justices- The court proceeded proceeded to the appointment of constable and after the votes being counted out there appeared a majority of votes for Joseph John Harris who was duly appointed constable whereupon the said Joseph J Harris came into court and entered bond & security satisfactory to the court & quallified agreeable to law-

Sterling Neblett admr of Charnal Corbin decd returns into court an Inventory and acct sales Of the goods & chattles rights & credits of Charnall Corbin decd & quallified agreeable to law & on motion ordered to be recorded

(p-226) Horace Barbee admr of Nancy Ury returns into court an Inventory or acct sales of the property of said decd was quallified agreeable to law & on motion ordered to be Recorded

On motion ordered by the court tha. Ambrose Martin be appointed Guardian to Jesse Martin whereupon the said Ambrose Martin entered into Bond with Daniel Rook John Wyatt & William Hale his securities in the penal $\not s \not u \not m$ one thousand Dollars conditioned as the law directs & quallified agreeable to law-

Joseph Woolfolk & James Carr commissioners appointed at the last Term of this court to settle with William M. Gowan Exer of Saml. Wilcox decd. make their report & on motion ordered to be recorded-

Ellinor Wray Guardian of her son Joseph Wray returns into court her a/c as Guardian against said Joseph Wray & on motion ordered to be Recorded

John Hampton & Wilson Gibson admrs of Abner V. Hampton decd returned into court an Inventory (and acct sales of the perishable property of said decd & on motion ordered to be Recorded

On motion ordered by the court that Thomas Cherry be appointed constable in place of Elisha R. Oldham whereupon the said Thomas Cherry come into court and entered into Bond & security satisfactory to the court & was duly quallified agreeable to law-

Joel Grizard admr of Samuel Hawkins decd returns into court an a/c sales of the property of Samuel Hawkins decd & on motion ordered to be Recorded

(p-227) On motion ordered by the court that Vallentine Allen Esqr Francis Baker Esqr & Isaac Dennison Esq & James Barret esquire or any three of them be appointed commissioners to settle with the admrs of John Adams decd and make report to next court-

This day come into court Solomon Hunt one of the Executors of Mesuier Mitchell decd and produced to the court the last will and Testament of the said Mesuier Mitchell decd which was duly proven proven by the oaths // of Lewis C Taylor and Philip Crotzer subscribing witnesses thereto & on motion ordered to be Recorded whereupon the said Solomon Hunt executor named in said will entered into bond & security satisfactory to the court & quallified agreeable to law & it is ordered that letters Testamentary issue to said Solomon Hunt on the estate of said decd.

On motion ordered by the court that Samuel Mann an orphan of Robert Mann decd be bound to John Roach & the said John Roach entered into a covenant with the court agreeable to law-

On motion ordered by the court that letters of administration be granted to Elizabeth Ingram on the estate of Sterling Ingram decd whereupon the said Elizabeth Ingram entered into Bond and security satisfactory to the court & was duly quallififed agreeable to Law-

On motion ordered by the court that Henry Small Hiram Bobo Isaac Weakly Thomas Hunter and John Caldwell surveyor be appointed to divide and lay off a tract of land agreeable to the petition of Wilson Sanderlin and William Barton and make report to the next term of this court with a destinct plat of the same-

(p-228) A.M. Rogers returns into court a list of Taxable property in Capt. John Cocks' Company for the year 1823-

John Kerchival esquire returns into court a list of Taxable property in Capt Josiah Ogburn's Company for the year 1823-

On motion ordered by the court that John Smith be appointed overseer of the road in place of Jacob Welker resigner- & that the same hands work under the said John Smith that were ordered to work under the said Jacob Welker

On motion ordered by the court that James Carr be appointed overseer of the road leading from Farson's Creek by way of Fort Royal to the Robertson County line - and that the hands of John Edmondston David Northington & hands Samuel Northington Sr. hands Henry Northington & hands John Northington & hands Fendall J. Sebree & hands Starkey Norfleet & hands Jonathan L. McFaddin Jesse Oldham & hands James Ford & S. Ford and other hands within the bounds of said road who have not heretofore been ordered to work on any other road-

On motion ordered by the court that Aron Smith be appointed overseer of the road in place of Andres Donnolson resigned & that the same hands work under the sd Aaron Smith who were heretofore ordered to work under the former overseer-

On motion ordered by the court thatValentine Merriwether Jacob Cordin William Guy Thomas Joiner William James be appointed to Patrole from Merriwethers ferry to William S. White's & throughout the neighbourhood & that Robert Nelson be appointed Capt. of said Patrolers-

(p-229) On motion ordered by the court that Francis Baker Samuel Jordan & Zebedee Dennis be appointed commissioners to lay off the protion of the estate of Robert Davie in the hands of his guardian in pursuance of the will of Ashburn Davie & make report to the next term of this court-

A Deed of Conveyance from William Stewart to Dudley Council for thirty six and one fourth acres of land was produced in open court and the execution thereof duly acknowledged by the said William Stewart to be his act and deed for the purposes therein contained and on motion ordered to be certified for Registration-

A Deed of Conveyance from Robert Weakly to William Stewart Sr. was produced in open court and the execution thereof duly proven by the oaths of Gideon Pace & John Pace the subscribing witnesses thereto and on motion ordered to be certified for Registration for One hundred acres of land-

A Deed of Conveyance from Andrew Stewart to William Stewart Senr. for four acres & one hundred and Twenty eight Poles was produced in open court and the execution thereofduly proven by the oaths of Dudley Council & James Barton two of the subscribing witnesses thereto and onmotion ordered to be certified for Registration-

A Deed of Conveyance from James Grant to Zachariah Grant for One hundred acres of land wasproduced in open court and the execution thereof duly proven by the oaths of A. W. Hooper & James Carr the subscribing witnesses thereto and on motion ordered to be certified for Registration-

A Deed of conveyance from Joseph Woolfolk to Zachariah Grant for three tracts of land containing one hundred and eighty seven acres was produced in open court and the execution thereof duly (p-230) duly proven by the oaths of James Carr & Maurice Morris the subscribing witnesses thereto and on motion ordered to be certified for Registration-

A Deed of conveyance or Deed of Gift from Sarah Lockert to Eli Lockert was produced in opencourt and the execution thereof duly proven by the oaths of Josiah Hoskins & Neander Hoskins the subscribing witnesses there to to be her act and Deed for the purposes therein contained and on motion ordered to be certified for Registration for two tracts of land containing one hundred and fifty five acres and sundry other personal property

A Deed Conveyance from Joseph Woolfolk to Andrew Peterson for fifty acres land was produced in open court and the execution thereof duly proven by the oath of Benjamin King a subscribing witness thereto as to the execution of said deed by said Joseph Woolfolk and the handwriting of Daniel Gould who is also a subscribing witness thereto was duly proven in open court by the oath of Zachariah Grant & on motion the same is ordered to be certified for registration-

A Bond for the conveyance of a land warrant for Fifty acres from John Rook & Daniel Rook Exrs of Rowland Vick decd to John Caldwell was duly acknowledged in Open Court by the said John Rook & Daniel Rook to be their act and deed for the purposes therein mentioned & on motion ordered to be certified for registration-

A Deed conveyance from John Wyatt & William Neblett to Drewry Mathis for three hundred thirty two & a half acres land was duly proven in open court by the oath of Benjamin Neblett a subscribing witness thereto- and the same being proven at the April Term 1823 by John S Mosley (p-231) a subscribing witness thereto as to the execution of said deed by John Wyatt and duly acknowledged at said April Term 1823 by William Neblett & on motion ordered to be certified for registration-

A Deed conveyance from William & Benjamin Whitehead Jr. to John Neblett Jr was duly proven in open court by the oath of Absolom Williams a subscribing witness thereto & the same being duly proven by the oath of John Caldwell a subscribing witness thereto at the January Term 1823 of said Court on motion the same is ordered by the court to be certified for registration-

Isham Trotter returns into court the commissioners report of settlement with him as Guardian of Polly Cocke & Abraham Cocke & on motion ordered to be Recorded-

Thomas W. Frazier & Joel C. Rice Admrs. of Richard Cocke decd returned into court an Inventory and a/c sales of the property of said decd & on motion ordered to be Recorded-

A Deed of Conveyance from John H Hyde Polly S. Hyde Sally F. Gray Anthony F. Gray Margaret Gray Elizabeth Gray French Gray William W Gray Martha Gray & George S. Gray to James McClure was produced in open court and the execution thereof duly proven by the oaths of Thomas Dunbar and Isaac Peterson Two of the subscribing Witnesses thereto and on motion ordered to be certified for / Registration for one hundred acres of land-

A Deed of conveyance from Robert Davis to Andrew Smith for one hundred and one and one third acres of land was produced in open court and the execution thereof duly acknowledged by the said Robert Davis to be his act and Deed for the purposes therein contained and on motion ordered to be (p-232) certified for Registration

A Deed of Conveyance from Richard Boyd to Robert Davis for one hundred and one and one third third acres was produced in open court & the execution thereof duly proven by the oaths of A.W. Hooper & Churchell Hooper the subscribing witnesses thereto and on motion ordered to be certified for Registration-

A Deed of conveyance from Elijah Hancock to Robert Sawyers was produced in open court and the execution there of duly proven by the oaths of Joseph Martin & Isaac Shelby Two of the subscribing witnesses thereto and on motion ordered to be certified for Registration for one hundred and Twenty two and a half acres of land-

A Deed of Conveyance from Wallis Branch to Edwd. Neblett for thirty one acres of land was produced in open court and the execution thereof duly proven by the oath of Thomas Orgain one of the subscribing witnesses thereto and on motion ordered to be certified-

A Deed of conveyance from Patrick H. Darby to James Trice Junr. for thirty three acres of land was produced in open court and the execution thereof duly proven by the oath of Joshua Pike one of the subscribing witnesses thereto and on motion ordered to be certified-

A Deed of Gift from Ransom N. Sexton to Thomas Evins was produced in open court and the execution thereof duly acknowledged by the said Ransom N. Sexton to be his act and deed for the purposes therein contained and on motion ordered ordered to be Recorded-

A Deed of conveyance from William Pogan to Henry Williams was produced in open court and the execution there of duly proven by the oaths (p-233) of Samuel Bagwell & Alexander Hogan the subscribing witnesses thereto and on motion ordered to be certified for Registration for / Twenty one and a half acres of land-

A Deed of conveyance from Samuel Edmonston to William Neblett for ninety six acres ten and one quarter poles of land was produced in open court and the execution thereof duly proven by the oaths of Benjamin Neblett & Benjamin Orgain two of the subscribing witnesses thereto and on motion ordered to be certified for Registration

A Deed of conveyance from Wilson Sanderlin to Frederick Davis for the undivided fifth part of six hundred and forty acres of land was produced in open court and the execution thereof duly acknowledged by the said Wilson Sanderlin to be his act and Deed for the purposes therein contained & on motion ordered to be certified for Registration-

Court adjourned untill tomorrow to meet at 9 O'clock-

> Jas. Barret
> Lewis C. Taylor
> Valentine Allen

The Worshipful court of Montgomery (p-234) The Court met according to adjournment present the Worshipful Vallentine Allen William Trigg & Lewis C. Taylor Esquires Justices

JOHN BELL)
VS) Trespass
CORNELISU CRUSMAN) This day came into court the parties by their
attornies & thereupon this cause is transfered by
consent to the circuit court for trial to be had thereon at the first term-

JOSIAH W. FORT)
VS) Case
CHARLES BAILY) This day came into open court the Plaintiff by his
attorney Cave Johnson Esquire and says he will
no further prosecute his said suit but dismisses the same-
Therefore it is considered by the court that the Defendant go hence without day & recover of the Plaintiff the costs about his suit in this behalf expended-

JACOB H. FORT)
VS) Case
HARVEY SHELBY) This day came into open court the Plaintiff by his
attorney Cave Johnson and says he will no further
prosecute his said suit but dismisses the same-
Therefore it is considered by the court that the Defendant go hence with out day and recover of the Plaintiff his costs about his suit in this be- half expended to be levied of the goods & chattles rights & credits of James Fort decd if so much he has if not to be levied of the goods & chattles of said Fort-

JESSE SULLIVANT GUARDIAN)
VS) Case
WILLIAM PORTER) This day came the parties by their attor-
nies and thereupon came a Jury (p-235)
of good andlawful men to wit Thomas Moore
Thomas Railsback Lewis Trice John H Williams John Cocke Mathew Daugherty William Brantly Abraham Brantly Bright Herring William Hunt Samuel Jordon & Joseph Bowers who being duly elected tried and sworn the truth to speak upon the issue joined upon their oaths do say that they find for the Plaintiff and do assess his damages to Twenty five cents-
Therefore it is considered by the court that the Plaintiff Jesse Sullivant Guardian as aforesaid recover of the Defendant William Porter the sum of Twenty five cents damages as assessed by the Jury in form afore- said assessed besides his costs about his suit in this behalf expended-

POLLY B. HATCHER FOR THE BENEFIT OF)
WILLIAM BRANTLY)
VS) Debt
WILLIAM & JOHN HUST) This day came into open court the
Defendants William Hust & John
Hust and freely acknowledged

themselves indebted (p-236)

JAMES HUTCHISON)
   VS) Debt
JOSIAH G. DUKE JEREMIAH) This day came into open court the Defend-
BROWN JACOB FOUST) ant Josiah G. Duke Jeremiah Brown Jacob
       Foust and freely acknowledged themselves
indebted to the Plaintiff James Hutchison the sum of two hundred Dollars
Debt and the further sum of Nineteen Dollars damages thereon sustained
by the detention of said Debt–

  Therefore it is considered by the court that the Plaintiff James
Hutchison recover of the Defendants Josiah G. Duke Jeremiah Brown &
Jacob Foust the sum of Two hundred and nineteen Dollars the Debt and
damages so confessed in form aforesaid together with his costs about his
suit in this behalf expended–

to the Plaintiff Polly B Hatcher for the benefit of William Brantly the sum
of One hundred and Twenty Dollars damages sustained b y reason of the detention of said Debt-

Therefore it is considered by the court that the Plaintiff Polly B
Hatcher recover of the Defendants William & John Hust the sum of One hundred
and Twenty six dollars the debt and damages so confessed in form aforesaid
together with his costs about his suit in this behalf expended ~~and that the~~
Plaintiff agrees to stay Execution three months-

     GEORGE ANDERSON FOR THE USE)
     OF JAMES GIVEN   )
          VS   ) Debt
     THOMAS MOORE   ) This day came into open court the Plaintiff
                        by his attorney and says he will no
                        further prosecute his said suit against
the Defendant but dismisses the same and the said Defendant T homas Moore
assumes the Payment of all Costs-

Therefore it is considered by the court that the Plaintiff George
Anderson recover of the Defendant Thomas Moore his costs about his suit
in this behalf expended-

     HINCHY HILL, GILFORD HILL, JOHN HILL,)
     JOHN WALKER & WIFE MELINDA WALKER   )
             VS   ) Case
     ABNER GUPTON   ) This day came into open court
                        ~~the~~ the Plaintiffs by their
attorney Cave Johnson Esquire and says he will no further prosecute his said
suit but dismisses the same-

Therefore it is considered by the court that the Defendant Abner
Gupton (p-237) go hence without day and recover of the Defendants the
costs about this suit in this behalf expended-

The Grand Jury appeared in open court & returned a Bill of Indictment the
state against Eliza Smith for an assault & Battery a True Bill also returned
a Bill of Indictment against Needham B Farrier & others for a Riot a
True Bill-

A Deed of conveyance from Samuel Craft to James Cummings & Benjamin Cummings
for three hundred and twenty acres of land was produced in open court and
the execution thereof duly proven by the oath of John H Marable a subscribing witness and on motion ordered to be certified-

A Deed of conveyance from Betsy A. West Executrix of Claibourn West Deed
to Ambrose Davis for three hundred and thirty one acres of land was produced
in open court and the execution thereof duly proven by the oath of J.B.
Flemming one of the subscribing witnesses thereto and on motion ordered to
be certified-

A Deed of conveyance from John Gately & wife to John Watt for thirteen acres
& fifty four poles poles was produced in open court and t he execution
thereof duly proven by the oaths of Randolph Ramey & Alexander Hogan
the subscribing witnesses thereto and on motion ordered to be certified for
Registration-

An obligation from Jonathan Wall to Nathan Hester for title to Ten acres of land was produced in open court and the execution thereof duly proven by the oath of Richard Jones a subscribing witness thereto and on motion ordered to be certified-

(p-238) A Deed of Gift from Elias F. Pope to Harris Pope was produced in open court and the execution thereof duly acknowledged by the said Elias F. Pope to be his act and Deed for the purposes therein contained and on motion ordered to be Recorded-

A Deed of Gift from Elisha Willis to John M. Creswell was produced in open court & the execution thereof duly acknowledged by the said Elisha Willis for the purposes therein contained and on motion ordered to be Recorded-

On motion ordered by the court that Elias McFall oversee the road from Palmyra to the forks of the Road leading from Yellow Creek to New York and that one half of the hands that live most convenient thereto which worked under Archibald Jackson work thereon-

On motion ordered by the court that one half of the hands which formerly worked under Archibald Jackson work on the road leading from the mouth of Yellow Creek to the Dickson County line and that James Thomas the overseer notify them thereof-

On motion ordered by the court that the Road leading up the East fork of Yellow Creek by Stepehen Handlin's be taken on the old West by the Widow Potters-

On motion it is ordered by the court that Capt John Taggart John Steele & Israel Robertson lay off the years provision of Mrs. Elizabeth Ingram out of the Estate of Sterling Ingram Decd and report to the next Term of this court-

On motion ordered by the court that Joseph Liggin be permitted to give in his list of (p-239) Taxable property for 1823 and that it be added to the Tax list for the present year-

Valentine Allen returns into court a list of the Taxable property taken in Capt. John M. Smith's Company for the year 1823

This day was produced in open court the last will and Testament of Dowell Young decd and the execution thereof duly proven by the oaths of John Jamison & Henry McFall Jr. Subscribing witnesses thereto & on motion ordered to be Recorded

On motion and for reasons appearing satisfactory to the court it is ordered that John Cocke be exonerated from serving as a juror at this Term-

On motion and for reasons appearing satisfactory to the court it is ordered that Jacob Foust and Thomas Denton be Exonerated from serving as jurors at this Term-

On motion ordered by the court that the order made at the last Term of
this court appointing commissioners to make division of the real estate of
John Shelby decd. between Jesse A. Brunson and Levisa his wife Clark Molton
Shelby & Alfred M. Shelby heirs of said John Shelby decd. be continued and
that the same commissioners who were appointed at the October Term 1822
or any five of them together with John Caldwell the County surveyor make
division of said estate agreeable to the former order except one Lott in
the Town of Clarksville the division of which has already been made & it
is ordered that said commissioners make report of said division to the
next Term of this Court with a distinct plat of the same-

(p-240) WILLIAM DEAN   )
              VS   ) Case
           RANSOM SEXTON   ) This day came the defendant by his attorney
                             Richard Daly Esqr and enters a motion to dismiss
said suit-

     JACOB H. FORT FOR WISTER PRICE & WISTER)
              VS   )
     PETER N. MARR & C.H.P. MARR   )   This day came the plaintiff
                                                  by attorney & the Defendants
                                                  being solemnly called to come
into court & bring with them the body of George Crutcher and answer the
aforesaid Scire facias failed so to do - It is therefore considered by the
court here that the said Plaintiff recover of the said Peter N. Marr & C.
H. P. Marr the sum of Fifty dollars - being the balance of the money yet
due the plaintiff on the said Scire facias principle & interest up to this
time & also the costs in the bahalf expended-

     CLAIBORNE WEST   )
          VS   ) It having been suggested to the court here that the
     ROBERT HESTER   ) said Claiborne West had departed this life more
                        then two terms ago & the same not being revived nor
any person appearing as his Representative to prosecute said suit-
It is therefore considered that the said suit abate-

     JAMES CUMMINS   )
          VS   ) This day came the plaintiff by his attorney and the
     ROGER SHACKLEFORD &   ) Defendants Roger Shackleford & George West being
     GEORGE WEST   ) solemnly called to come into court & defend said
                             suit failed so to do - It is therefore considered
                             by the court that the said James Cummins recover
of the said George West & Roger Shackleford the sum of Three hundred &
forty Three dollars Eighty three ½ cents the Debt in the declaration mentioned and also the sum of Thirty four dollars 38½ cents damages for the
detention of said debt and also the costs in this behalf expended-

(p-241) DAVID ANDERSON FOR THE USE OF JAS. SMITH)
              VS   ) Case
           C. H. P. MARR   )   Upon affidavit of
                                                   the defendant & by per-
mission of the court this cause is continued untill the next term of this
court upon the payment of the costs accrued at this Term-
     Therefore it is considered by the court that the plaintiff recover
of the defendant the costs as aforesaid & that a Fi Fa issue for the same-

CHARLES BOGARD & JOSEPH BOGARD)
    VS   )
WILLIAM COOPER & BRAXTON WALL ADMRS) This day came the plaintiff by
                their attorney C. Johnson esquire
& say they will no further prosecute their said suit against the defendants
but dismisses the same and Lewis Whitfield assumes the payment of all the
costs-

  Therefore it is considered by the court that the plaintiffs recover
of Lewis Whitfield the costs in this behalf Expended & c C. Johnson the
plaintiffs attorney//////////// //// releases his tax fee-

ALLY DILLARD GUARDIAN)
    VS   ) Debt
HUGH F. BELL, WILLIAM)
S. WHITE, & JOHN NEVELLE) This day came the plaintiff by his attorney F.
            W. Huling Esqr. and says he will no further
prosecute her said //// suit against the defendants and Hugh F. Bell are of
said defendants assumes the payment of Five dollars of the costs of said suit
& the plaintiff agrees to pay the balance of the costs on said suit-

  Therefore it is considered by the court that the plaintiff recover of
said Hugh F. Bell said sum of Five dollars in part of said costs & that
said defendants recover of the plaintiff the balance of the costs in this
behalf Expended-

(p-242) The following persons were duly elected empaneled /sworn and charge
ed as a Grand Jury to enquire for the body of the County to wit-
Henry McFall Foreman, James Thackston - John Lynch - James Hamlet - Henry
McFall Jr. - Gibson Mills - William Clifton - John Darnall - Thomas H.
ONeal - Benjamin E. Orgain - John Rudolph Jr. - Darvin D. Barton - Meridith
Williams - John Williams - having received their charge retired to consider
of their presentments-

Court adjourned until tomorrow 9 O'clock-
            Valentine Allen
            Jas Barret
            Lewis C. Taylor

Court met according to adjournment Wednesday July 23rd 1823-
Present   Valentine Allen)
          James Barret &) Esquire
          Lewis C. Taylor) Justices

JESSE SULLIVANT GUARDIAN)
    VS   ) Appeal
WILLIAM PORTER   ) This day came the Defendant by his attorney
           and prays an appeal to the circuit Court for
Montgomery County and having entered into Bond satisfactory to the Court the
same is allowed-

JESSE SULLIVANT)
    VS   ) Appeal
WILLIAM PORTER) This day came into open court the Plaintiff by his
         Attorney and being (p-243) dissatisfied with
the verdict of this case prays an appeal to the Circuit Court, and having
entered into Bond and security agreeable to law, and satisfactory to the
court the same is allowed him-

JESSE SULLIVANT)
     VS   ) Case
William PORTER) This day came the Parties by their attornies and
                  there upon came a Jury of good and lawful mento
wit Thomas Railsback Lewis Trice Thomas Moore Samuel Jordan John Cocke
Joseph Bowers John H Williams James Broom Abraham Brantly William Hunt
Mathew Dougherty & William Brantly who being duly elected tried and sworn
the truth to speak upon the issue joined upon their oaths do say that they
find for the Defendant

    Therefore it is considered by the court that the Defendant William
Porter recover of the Plaintiff Jesse Sullivant the costs in this behalf
expended

JAMES MCCAULY)
     VS   ) Case
DEMPSY BULL &) This day came the Plaintiff by his attorney into
PETER P. ROBERTS) open court and says he will no further prosecute
                  his suit but dismisses the same and thereupon the
Defendant assumes the costs-

    Therefore it is considered by the court that the Plaintiff recover
of the Defendants the costs in this behalf expended and that the said
suit stand dismissed-

JAMES CROCKET)
     VS   ) Case
JESSE SULLIVANT) This day came into open court the Parties by their
                  attornies and thereupon came a Jury of good and
lawful men to wit James Trice ser. (p-244) William Allen John Cocke
Samuel Bagwell Jesse Baily Edward S. Walton Wells Fowler Thomas Moore
Lewis Trice John H. Williams Thomas Railsback & Saml. Jordan/XXX/ who
being duly elected tried and sworn the truth to speak upon the issue
joined upon their oaths do say that they find for the Plaintiff and do
assess his damages to seventy six dollars & Eight and three fourth cents
by reason of the several non performances and undertakings mentioned in
the Plaintiffs declaration

    Therefore it is considered by the court that the Plaintiff recover
of the Defendants the said sum of seventy six dollars & eight and three
fourth cents the damages so assessed by the Jury in form aforesaid together
with his costs about his suit in this behalf expended-

JOHN OGBURN)
     VS   ) Debt
STEPHEN HARRIS &) This day came the Parties by their attornies and
DORRELL Y. HARRIS) thereupon came a Jury of good and lawful men to
                  wit Thomas Railsback Lewis Trice Thomas Moore
Samuel Jordan John Cocke Joseph Bowers John H. Williams James Brown Abraham
Brantly William Hunt Mathew Daugherty & William Brantly who being duly
elected tried & sworn the truth to speak upon the issue joined upon their
oaths do say that the Defendant doth owe to the Plaintiff the sum of one
hundred and Twenty six Dollars & eighty two cents the Debt in the Declaration mentioned as also the sum of nine Dollars damages sustained by reason
of the detention of said Debt besides his costs- Therefore it is (p-245)
considered by the court that the Plaintiff John Ogburn recover of the
Defendants Stephen Harris & Dorrell Y. Harris the sum of One hundred and
thirty five dollars and eighty two cents the Debt and damages so assessed

NO PAGE 149

by the Jury in form aforesaid together with his costs about his suit in this behalf expended

JOHN BELL)
VS) Certiorari & Superceedeas
ELIJAH HUGHES) This day came into open court the Plaintiff by his attorney Cave Johnson and says he will no further prosecute his said suit but dismisses the same and the Defendant assumes the costs-

Therefore it is considered by the court that the Plaintiff recover of the Defendant the costs in this behalf expended and that the same stand dismissed-

FRANCIS MCMORDIE)
VS) Debt
CHARLES BAILEY) This day came into open court the Plaintiff by his attorney Fred W. Huling Esquires and says he will no further prosecute his said suit but dismisses the same and the Defendant and the Defendant assumes the costs of said suit-

Therefore it is considered by the court that the Plaintiff Frances McMordie recover of the Defendant Charles Baily the costs as aforesaid and the same stand dismissed-

ROBERT WADE)
VS) Debt
ROBERT SEARCY &) This day came into opencourt the Plaintiff by his
FRANCES BAKER) attorney (p-246) Frederick W. Huling and says he will no further prosecute his said suit but dismissed the same and the Plaintiff assumes the cost of suit-

Therefore it is considered by the court that the Defendant go hence without day and recover of the Plaintiff the costs in this behalf expended

JESSE WATKINS)
VS) Original attchs.
PRECILLA JEFFREYS) This day came the Defendants by their attorney
& BAYLISS E. PRINCE) Cave Johnson and enters a motion to dismiss said suit

CULIEN BAYLISS & CO)
VS) Debt
JESSE CRAFT) This day came into open court the parties by their attornies and thereupon came a Jury of good and lawful men to wit Thomas Railsback Lewis Trice Thos Moore Samuel Jordon John Cocke Joseph Bowers John H. Williams James Brown Abraham Brantly William Hunt Mathew Dorherty & William Brantly who being duly elected tried and sworn the truth to speak upon the issue joined upon their oaths do say that they find the issue in favor of the Plaintiff that the Defendant doth owe to the Plaintiff the sum of Tow hundred & Six Dollars & Twentynone cents the Debt in the Declaration mentioned and also the sum of six dollars and eighteen cents the damages by reason of the detention of sd Debt-

Therefore it is considered by the court that the Plaintiff (p-247) recover of the Defendant the sum of Two hundred and Twelve dollars & forty seven cents the Debt and damages so assessed by the Jury in form aforesaid together with his costs by him about his suit in this behalf expended-

FRANCIS MCMURDY)
      VS)   Debt
JOHN BELL)   This day came into court the Parties by their
& HUGH F. BELL)   attorney and thereupon came a jury of good and
                  lawful men to wit Thomas Railsback Lewis Trice
Thomas Moore Samuel Jordon John Cooke Joseph Bowers John H. Williams James
Brown Abraham Brantly William Hunt Mathew Dougherty & William Brantly who
being duly elected tried & sworn the truth to speak upon the issue joined
upon their oaths do say that they find the issue in favor of the Plaintiff
& find that the Defendants doth owe to the Plaintiff the sum of One Hundred
& ninety seven Dollars the Debt in the Declaration mentioned and also the
sum of thirteen Dollars and seventy cents the damages sustained by reason
of the detention of said Debt besides his costs-

    Therefore it is ordered by the court that the Plaintiff recover of
the Defendant the sum of Two hundred and ten Dollars & seventy cents the
Debt and damages so assessed by the Jury in form aforesaid together with
his costs by him about his suit in this behalf expended-

JAMES SNEED)
     VS)   Debt
JAMES HULING)   This day came the parties by their attornies and
               thereupon came a Jury (p-248) of good and lawful
men to wit Thomas Railsback Lewis Trice Thomas Moore Saml Jordan John Cooke
Joseph Bowers John H. Williams James Brown Abraham Brantly William Hunt
Matthew Dorherty & William Brantly who being duly elected tried and sworn
the truth to speak upon the issue joined upon their oaths do say that they
find the issue in favor of the Plaintiff and find that said Defendant doth
owe to the plaintiff the sum of Five hundred and Twenty five Dollars and
seventy cents the debt in the declaration mentioned and do assess his damag
ges to forty four dollats and sixty nine cents by reason of the detention
of said debt besides his costs costs-

    Therefore it is considered by the court that the Plaintiff recover of
the Defendant the sum of Five hundred and seventy Dollars and thirty nine
cents the debt and damages so assessed by the Jury in form aforesaid together with his costs by him about his suit in this behalf expended-

RICHARD C. GREGORY)
      VS)   Debt
SAMUEL CREATH)   This day came the parties by their attornies
               & it is suggested here to the court that the
the defendant Samuel Creath hath departed this life and the same is not
denied-

GILFORD MILLS)
     VS)   Debt
ASHBELL BRUNSON)   This day came the Parties by their attornies and
              thereupon came a Jury of good and lawful men to wit
Thomas Railsback Lewis Trice Thomas Moore Samuel Jordon John Cooke Joseph
Bowers John H. Williams James Brown Abraham Brantly William Hunt Mathew
Dorherty & William Brantly who being duly elected tried and sworn the truth
to speak upon the issues joned upon their oaths do say that they find
the issues in favor of the Plaintiff and that the said Defendant doth owe
to the Plaintiff and that the said Defendant doth owe to the Plaintiff the

sum of Two hundred and seventeen Dollars sixty two and a half cents the debt in the declaration mentioned and do assess his damages to/////// Eight Dollars seventy and a half cents by reason of the detention of said Debt besides his costs-

Therefore it is considered by the court that the Plaintiff Gilford Mills recover of the Defendant Ashbell Brunson the sum of Two hundred and and Twenty six Dollars & thirty three cents the Debt and damages so assessed by the Jury in form aforesaid - together with his costs by him about his suit in this behalf expended-

GILFORD MILLS)
     VS)   Debt
ASHBEL BRUNSON) This day came the Parties by their attornies and //// thereupon came a Jury of good & lawful men to wit Thimas Railsback Lewis Trice Thomas Moore Samuel Jordan John Cocke Joseph Bowers John H. Williams James Brown (p-249) Abraham Brantly William Hunt Mathew Dotherty & William Brantly who being duly elected tried and sworn the truth to speak upon the issue joined upon their oaths do say that they find the issues in favor of the Plaintiff and that the Defendant doth owe to the Plaintiff the sum of two hundred and Twenty six dollars the debt in the declaration mentioned and do assess his damages to six dollars and seventy eight cents by reason of the detention of said debt besides his costs-

Therefore it is considered (p-250) by the court court that the Plaintiff recover of the Defendant the sum of Two hundred and thirty two Dollars & seventy eight cents the debt and damages so assessed by the Jury in form aforesaid together with his costs by him about his suit in this behalf expended-

FREDERICK W. HULING)
     VS)   Original attachment
GUSTAVUS E. EDWARDS) This day came into open court the Plaintiff
 & GEORGE BROWN) Fredrick W. Huling by his attorney Cave
                  Johnson Esquire and the Defendants Gustavus
E. Edwards & George Brosn being solemnly called to come into court and repl/ evy their property & plead to the Pltff's action came not but made default

Therefore it is considered by the court that the Plaintiff Frederick W Huling recover of the Defendants Gustavus E. Edwards & George Brown the sum of Three hundred and Twenty six Dollars sixty six and one third cents the debt in the declaration mentioned and also the sum of Fifty eight dollars & seventyseven cents the damages sustained by reason of the detention of said Debt together with his costs by him about his suit // in this behalf expended and that a Venditioni Exponas issue directing the sale of the lands and Lotts levied on by virtue of the Said attachment / to satisfy the said debt damages and costs

HUGH & JAMS MCCLURE)
     VS)   Debt
PETER P. ROBERTS &)   /
EDWARD NEBLETT)

Court adjourneed until tomorrow 9 O'clock

Jas. Barret
Isaac Dennison
Stephen Cocke

(p- 251) The Worshipful Court of Montgomery County have met according to adjournment Thursday July 24th 1823-

Present James Barret)
Isaac Dennison) Esquires
Stephen Cocke) Justices

JESSE SULLIVANT)
VS) Forfeiture
STEPHEN ELEAZER) This day came the Plaintiff by his attorney Richard Daly Esquire & Stephen Eleazer a witness in said cause for the said Jesse Sullivant being solemnly called to come into court and to give testimony in behalf of the said Jesse Sullivant on the said cause between the said Jesse Sullivant and William Porter failed so to do-

It is therefore considered by the court that the said Jesse Sullivant recover of the said Stephen Eleazer the sum of One hundred & Twenty five Dollars for not appearing and giving evidence in pursuance of the summons unless the said Stephen Eleazer appear here at the next Court and shew cause if any he can why the said forfeiture should be set aside and that a sciere facias issue & c-

STATE OF TENNESSEE)
VS) Riot
NEEDHAM B FARRIER) This day came the said Defendant Needham B Farrier and acknowledges himself bound and indebted to the state of Tennessee in the sum of Five hundred Dollars and his securities Thomas Cherry and David Bunting to the sum of Two hundred and fifty Dollars each to be levied of their proper goods & chattles lands and tenements to be void on condition that the said Needham B. Farrier doth make (p-252) his personal appearance at the Court house in the Town of Clarksville on the first Thursday after the third monday in October next then and there to answer the state of Tennessee on a Bill of Indictment for a Riot against him and not to depart without leave of court-

STATE OF TENNESSEE)
VS) Riot
WILLIAM DICAS) This day came the said Defendant William Dicas and acknowledged himself bound and indebted to the state of Tennessee in the sum of Five hundred Dollars and his securities Needham B. Farrier & Edward Dicas in the sum of Two hundred and fifty Dollars each to be levied of their proper goods and chattles lands & tenements to be void on condition that the said William Dicas doth make his personal appearance at the court house in the Town of Clarksville on the first Thursday after the third monday in October next then and there to answer the state of Tennessee in a Bill of Indictment for a Riot against him and not to depart without leave of court-

STATE OF TENNESSEE)
VS) Riot
JAMES W. CARVER) This day came the said James W. Carver and acknowledges himself bound and indebted

to the State of Tennessee in the sum of Five hundred Dollars and his securit
ies Needham B. Farrier in the sum of Two hundred and fifty Dollars each to
be leviedof their proper goods and chattles lands and tenements to be void
on condition that the said James W. Carver doth make his personal appearance
at the Court house (p-253) in the Town of Clarksville on the first Thurs-
dayafter the Third monday in October next then and there to answer the State
of Tennessee on a Bill / of Indictment for a Riot against him and not to
depart without leave of court-

<pre>
STATE OF TENNESSEE   )
        VS   )   Riot
JOHN EDWARDS   )   This day came the said John Edwards and acknow-
                           ledges himself bound & indebted to the State
</pre>
of Tennessee in the sum of Five hundred Dollars and his securities Needham
B. Farrier and David Dunting in the sum of Two hundred and Fifty Dollars
each to be levied of their proper goods & chattles lands and Tenements to
be void on condition that the said John Edwards doth make his personal
appearance at the court house in the Town of Clarksville on the first
Thursday after the Third monday in October next then and there to answer
the State of Tennessee in a Bill of Indictment for a Riot against him
and not to depart without leave of court-

<pre>
STATE OF TENNESSEE   )
        VS   )   Indict. for a Riot
DEMPSEY BULL   )   This day came the soliciter General in behalf
                           of the state and the defendant Dempsey Bull
</pre>
in proper person & was thereupon arraigned & upon his ar aignment pleads not
guilty to the Bill of Indictment & for his trial puts himself upon his
county as does the soliciter General likewise & thereupon came a jury of
good and lawful me; (to wit) James Thackston John Lynch James Hamlet
Henry McFall Gibson Mills William Clifton John Darnall John Williams
Benjamin E. Orgain John Rudolph Darvin E. Barton & Merrideth Williams who
(p-254) being duly elected tried & sworn the teuth to to speak upon the
issue of Traverse upon their their oaths do say that the defendant
Dempsey Bull is guilty of a riot in manner and form as charged in the Bill
of Indictment and that he be fined the sum of Twenty Dollars besides the
costs of this prosecution-

Therefore it is considered b, the court that the State of Tennessee
recover of the defendant Dempsey Bull the sum of Twenty dollars the fine
assessed by the jury in form aforesaid & that he pay the costs of this
prosecution & it is ordered by the court that he be ordered in // to the
custody of the sheriff untill said fine & costs are paid and the said defend
ant being dissatisfied with the judgment of the court prays an appeal to
the Circuit Court of Montgoery County and came into open court and acknowledged himself indebted to the State of Tennessee in the sum of Two hundred
& fifty dollars & his securities William Peay & Balum Bull appeared in open
court and acknowledged themselves indebted to the State of Tennessee in the
sum of one hundred & twenty five dollars to be levied of their propper goods
and chattles lands and Tenements to be void on condition that said defend-
and Dempsey Bull doth make his personal appearance before the judge of the
Circuit Court on the third monday in August next and on the states day of
said Tenn. then and there to answer to answer the State of Tennessee on a
Bill of Indictment against him for a Riot & not depart without leave of
Court-

STATE OF TENNESSEE)
VS) Assault & Battery
OBEDIAH BROOMFIELD) This day came the solicitor General on behalf
of the state and the Defendant Obediah
Broomfield in proper (p-255) person and was thereupon arraigned and upon
his arraignment pleads not guilty to the Bill of Indictment and for his
trial puts himself upon his country as does the solicitor General likewise
and thereupon came a Jury of good and lawful men to wit Thomas Railsback
Lewis Trice Thomas Moore Samuel Jorden John Cocke Joseph Bowers John H.
Williams John Shelby Robert McMurdy Benjamin Herring William Brantly &
Abraham Brantly who being duly elected tried and sworn the truth to speak
upon the issue ot Traverse upon their oaths do say that the Defendant Obediah
Broomfield is guilty of assault & Battery in manner and form as charged in
the Bill of Indictment and that he be fined the sum of twenty Dollars besides
the costs of this prosecution-

Therefore it is considered by the court that the State of Tennessee
recover of the Defendant Obediah Broomfield the sum of Twenty Dollars the
fine assessed by the Jury in form aforesaid and that he pay the costs of
this prosecution - and the said Defendant being dissatisfied with the
Judgment of the court prays an appeal to the Circuit court of Montgomery
County and came into open court and acknowledged himself bound and indebted to the State of Tennessee in the sum of Two hundred and fifty dollars
and his security Henry Williams appeared in open court and acknowledged him
self bound and indebted to the State of Tennessee in the sum of one hundred
and Twenty five Dollars to be levied of their proppergoods and chattles
land and thenements to be void on condition that said Defendant Obediah
Broomfield doth make his personal appearance before the Judge of the Circuit court on the third monday in August next- and (p-256) on the states
day of said Term then and there to answer the State of Tennessee on a Bill
of Indictment against him for an assault and battery and not depart without
leave of court-

STATE OF TENNESSEE)
VS) Riot
JOHN M. HOLLIS) This day came the solicitor General on the part
of the state and the Defendant John M. Hollis
in propper person and was thereupon araigned and upon his arraignment
pleads guilty to the Bill of Indictment and submits this case to the court
and after the evidence being heard it is consideredby the court that the
Defendant John M. Hollis be fined the sum of Five dollars It is therefore
considered by the court that the State of Tennessee recover of said Defendant James Hollis said sum of money the fine so assessed as aforesaid & togeth
er with the costs of this prosecution-
(This Judgt. is entered in another - see this day Error)

STATE OF TENNESSEE)
VS) Riot
WILLIAM CHANCE) This day came the solicitor General on behalf
of the state and the Defendant William Chance
in propper person and thereupon was arraigned and upon his arraignment
Plead not guilty to the Bill of Indictment and for his trial puts himself
upon his Country as does the solicitor General likewise and thereupon came
a Jury of good and lawful men to wit Thomas Railsback Lewis Trice Thomas Moore
Samuel Jordon John Cocke Joseph Bowers John H Williams John Shelby Robert
McMurdy Benjamin Herring William Brantly Abraham Brantly who being duly
elected tried and sworn the (p-257) truth to speak upon their oaths do say

that the Defendant William Chance is not guilty of a Riot in manner & form
as charged in the bill of Indictment-

Therefore it is considered by the court that the Defendant William Chance
be dismissed and that the County of Montgomery pay the costs of this prosecution

On motion ofdered by the court that Anthony B. Shelby & John Shelby be appo
ointed Guardians to Jenkins W. Shelby Laetetia Shelby Tennessee Shelby and
Alfred Shelby minor heirs of Isaac Shelby Decd whereupon the said Anthony
B. Shelby & John Shelby came into court and entered into Bond and security
satisfactory to the court the same is allowed -

On motion ordered by the court that letters o administration be granted to
Mary Creath on the Estate of Samuel Creath Decd. Whereupon the said Mary
Creath entered into Bond & security satisfaction to the court and was duly
quailified agreeable to law-

A Bill Sale from Stephen Cocke to Sam'l Vance for two negros Peter & Rachel
was duly proven in open court by the oaths of Edward H. Steele & Josiah G.
Duke the subscribing witnesses thereto & on motion ordered to be Recorded

William Allen a constable appeared in open court and renewed his bond
as constable for the next two years & the said William Allen came into court
and entered into bond & security satisfactory to the court & quallified a
agreeable to law-

On motion ordered by the court that John Rice Capr. William Allen Elisha
Clark be appointed commissioners to lay off one years provision to Nancy
Creath the late widdow of Sam'l Creath decd & make report to next Court-

(p-258)   STATE OF TENNESSEE)
              VS   ) Peace Warrant
           JOHN DAVIE   ) This day came the said John Davie and acknow-
                                ledges himself bound and indebted to the State
of Tennessee in the sum of Two hundred & Fifty dollars and his security
Stephen G. Jones in the sum of One hundred and Twenty five Dollars to be levi
ied of their propper goods and chattles lands & Tenements to be void on
condition that the said John Davie doth make his personal appearance at the
court house in the Twon of Clarksville on the first Thursday after the third
Monday in October next then and there to answer the State of Tennessee on a
Bill ofIndictment for a Riot against him and not depart without leave of
court-

           JAMES MCCLURE)
              VS   )   Motion
           JAMES BOWERS   )   This day came the Plaintiff by his attorney Nathaniel
                               H. Allen Esquire and thereupon it appearing to the
Court that Valentine Allen Esquire had issued an Execution in behalf James
McClure against James Bowers directed to any lawful officer in said county
directing that of the goods and chattles lands & Tenements of the said James
Bowers to make the sum of six dollars and fifty cents to satisfy a Judgment
pf said James McClure rendered 2nd day of July 1823 placed in the hands of
William H. Allen a constable for said County for collection upon which the
said William H. Allen levied on Eighty four acres of land near New York on
the north side of Cumberland River the Tract whereon the said James Bowers
now lives for the want of personal property-

Upon motion of said Plaintiff by attorney it is ordered by the court that a Venditioni Exponas issued to the sheriffof Montgomery County commanding him to expose to sale (p-259) said tract of land to satisfy said Judgment and costs and also the cost of this motion-

DENNIS DORHERTY)
VS) Motion
JAMES BOWERS) This day came the Plaintiff by his attorney Nathan
H. Allen Esquire and thereupon it appearing to the court that Valentine Allen Esquire had issued and Execution in behalf of Mathew Dorherty against James Bowers directed to any lawful officer in said county directing that of the goods and chattleslands and Tenements of said James Bowers to make the sum of Five Dollars to satisfy a Judgment of said Mathew Dorherty rendered 2nd day of July 1823 placed in the hands of William H. Allen a constable of said County for collection upon which the said William H Allen levied on Eighty four acres of land near New York River the tract whereon the said James Bowers now lives for the want of personal property - Upon motion of said Plaintiff by attorney it is ordered by the court that a Venditioni Exponas was issued to the sheriff of montgomery County commanding him to expose to sale said Tract of land to satisfy said Judgment and costs and also the cost 1f this motion-

HUGH & JAMES MCCLURE)
VS) Motion
JAMES BOWERS) This day came the Plaintiff by his attorney
Nathaniel H. Allen Esquire and thereupon it appearing to the court that Valentine Allen Esquire had issued an Execution in behalf of Hugh & James McClure against James Bowers directed to any lawful office in said County directing that of the goods and chattles lands and Tenements of said James Bowers to make the sum of fifteen Dollars and forty one cents to satisfy a Judgment of (p-260) Hugh & James McClure rendered 2nd July 1823 placed in the hands of William H. Allen a constable in said County for collection upon which the said William H. Allen levied on Eighty four acres of land near New York on the north side of Cumberland River the tract whereon the said Bowers now lives for the want of personal property - Upon motion of said Plaintiffs by attorney it is ordered by the court that a Venditioni Exponas issue to the sheriff of Montgomery County Commanding him to expose to sale said Tract of land to satisfy said Judgment and costs and also the cost of this motion-

CULLEN BAYLISS & CO)
VS) Motion
JAMES BOWERS) This day came the Plaintiff by his Attorney
Nathaniel H. Allen Esquire therupon it appearing to the court that Valentine Allen Esquire had issued an Execution in behalf of Cullen Bauliss & Co. against James Bowers directed to any lawful officer in said County Directing that of the goods and chattles lands and Tenements of Said James Bowers to make the sum of Eighteen dollars and fifty cents to satisfy a Judgment of Cullen Bauliss & Co. rendered qnd day of July 1823 placed in the hands of William H. Allen a constable in said county for collection upon which the said William H. Allen levied on Eighty four acres of land near New Your on the North side of Cumberland River the tract whereon the said Bowers now lives for the want of personal property - Upon motion of said Plaintiff by attorney it is ordered by the court that a Venditioni Exponas issue to the sheriff of Montgomery County commanding him to expose to sale said Tract of land to satisfy said Judgment and costs and also the cost of this motion-

(p-261) STATE   )
                VS   )   Indict-
         GEORGE CHANCE)   This day came as will the solicitor General by said
                           defendant & the solicitor General here in court
says he intends no farther to prosecute this Indictment. It is therefore
considered by the court that said defendant be hence discharged & that the
County pay the pay the costs-

         STATE OF TENNESSEE)
                VS   )   Indict.
         ROBERT CHANCE   )   This day came the solicitor General as well as
                                 said defendant & the solicitor says he intends
no further to prosecute his said said Indictment against the defendant
         It is therefore considered by the court that said defendant be hence
discharged & that the county of Montgomery pay the costs of this prosecution

Court adjourned until tomorrow 9 O'clock

                                        Isaac Dennison
                                        Jas. Barret
                                        Thos W. Atkinson

         The Worshipful Court of Montgomery County have met according to adjourn-
ment Friday July 25th 1823-

                          Present Isaac Dennison) Esquires
                                   James Barret   ) Justices
                                   Thomas W. Atkinson)

         STATE OF TENNESSEE)
                VS   )Indt for a Riot
         JOHN M. HOLLIS   ) This day came the solicitor General in behalf
                               of of the state & the defendant in proper person
& was thereupon arraigned & upon his arraignment pleads guilty to the Bill
of Indictment & submits to the court & after the (p-262) evidence being
heard it is considered by the Court that the defendant be fined the sum of
Five Dollars & that he pay the costs of this prosecution and James Hollis
appeared in open court and assumed the payment of said fine & costs -
         Therefore it is considered b y the court that the state of Tennessee
recover of the defendant and the said James Hollis the fine and costs
aforesaid & that a Fi Fa issue for the same-

         ABRAHAM BRANTLY)
                VS   )
         DANIEL KYLE   )   Appeal
                             This day came the parties by their attornies and
thereupon came a Jury of good and lawful men to wit. James Thackston John
Lynch James Hamlet Henry McFall Jr. Gibson Mills William Clifton John Darnall
Thomas H. Oneal Benjamin E. Orgain John Rudolph Jr. Darwin E. Barton & Mered-
ith Williams who being duly elected tried & sworn the truth to speak upon the
matters of controversy between the Parties upon their oaths do say that they
find for the Plaintiff and do assess his damages to Fifteen Dollars & seven
ty five cents-
         Therefore it is considered by the court that the Plaintiff Abraham
Brantly recover of the Defendant Daniel Kyle & on motion against C.H.F.
Marr security for appeal the aforesaid sum of fifteen Dollars and seventy

five cents so assessed by the Jury in form aforesaid together with his costs by him about his suit in this behalf expended-

CHARLES COOKE ASSEE) Debt
VS)
WILLIAM BARTON) This day came the parties by their attornies and ther upon came a Jury of good and lawful men to wit Thomas Railsback Thomas Moore John H. Williams John Cocke Luther Laird Lewis Trice Samuel Jordan (p-263) Joseph Bowers Haydon E. Wells John Williams Wills Fowler & Daniel Kyle who being duly elected tried and sworn the truth to speak upon the issue joined upon their oaths do say that they find the issues in favor of the Plaintiff and that the Defendant doth owe to the Plaintiff the sum of One hundred Dollars the Debt in the declaration mentioned and do assess the Plaintiffs damages to twenty Two dollars by reason of the detention of said Debt besides his costs- Therefore it is considered by the court that the Plaintiff recover of the Defendant the sum of One hundred and Twenty Two dollars the debt and damages so assessed by the Jury in form aforesaid together with his costs in this behalf expended-

STERLING NEBLETT ADMR.) Debt
VS)
JOHN WATSON & STEPHEN) This day came the Parties by their attornies
NEBLETT) andthereupon came a Jury of good and lawful men to wit Thomas Railsback thomas Moore John H. Williams John Cocke Luther Laird Lewis Trice Samuel Jordon Joseph Bowers Haydon E. Wells John Williams Wells Fowler & Daniel Kyle who being duly elected tried and sworn the truth to speak upon the issue joined upon their oaths do say that they find the issue in favour of the Plaintiff that the Defendant doth owe to the Plaintiff the sum of One hundred and Thirty Dollars the Debt in the declaration mentioned and do assess the Plaintiffs damages to Four Dollars & fifty five cents by reason of the defention of said debt besides his costs-

Therefore it is considered by the court that the Plaintiff recover of the Defendant the sum of One hundred and thirty four // dollars (p-264) and fifty five cents the debt and damages so assessed by the Jury in form aforesaid together with his costs by him about his suit in this behalf expended-

NATHAN YARBOROUGH) Case
VS)
DAVID BRODIE) This day came the Parties by their attornies and therupon came a Jury of good and lawful men to wit Thomas Railsback Thomas Moore John H Williams John Cocke Luther Laird Lewis Tirce Samuel Jordon Joseph Bowers Haydon E. Wells John Williams Wells Fowler & Daniel Kyle who being duly elected tried and sworn the truth to speak upon the issue joined upon their oaths do say that that find for the Plaintiff and do assess his damages to one hundred and Twenty Two dollars & sixty four cents by reason of the several non performances and undertakings in the Plaintiffs declaration mentioned-

Therefore it is considered by the court that the Plaintiff Nathan Yarborough recover of the Defendant David Brodie the said sum of One hundred & Twenty two dollars and sixty four cents so assessed by the Jury in form aforesaid and the costs in this behalf expended - From which said Judgment the Defendant being dissatisfied prays an appeal to the Circuit Court of Montgomery County and having entered into Bond & security satisfactory to the court that same is allowed-

JOSEPH OGBURN)
  VS   ) Debt
JAMES SMITH) This day came the Plaintiff by his attorney Mortimer
        A Martin and the Defendant James Smith being solemnly
called (p-265) came not but made default-

Therefore it is considered by the court that the Plaintiff Joseph/Ogburn
Ogburn recover of the Defendant James Smith the sum of Four hundred & twelve
dollars twenty nine & cents Debt and the further sum of thirty nine dollars
forty six & & cents the damages sustained by the detention of said debt &
also the costs in this behalf expended-

STERLING NEBLETT GUARDIAN OF SALLY COCKE)
      VS   ) Debt
Henry Odonley & John Rook   ) This day the defendants Henry
                 Odonley & John Rook and freely
acknowledged themselves indebted to the plaintiffs Sterling Neblett Guardian
as aforesaid in the sum of Eighty three dollars & fifty cents ballance of
debt and the further sum of None dollars and seventy six cents the damages
thereon sustained by the detention of said debt besides his costs-

Therefore it is considered by the court that the plaintiff recover of
said defendants the sum of ninety Dollars & twenty six cents the debt and
damages so assessed as aforesaid & also the costs in this behalf Expended
& the plaintiff agrees to stay execution six months-

HUGH & JAMES MCCLURE)
   VS   ) Debt
PETER P. ROBERTS &)
EDWARD NEBLETT   ) This day came one of the defendants Peter P.
            Roberts the sum of one hundred & ninety nine
dollars & nine cents the debt and damages so confessed as aforesaid & also
the costs of this suit- Execution stayed untill next October Court-

(p-266) RICHARD C. GREGORY)
      VS   ) Debt
SAMUEL CREATH   ) This day came the plaintiff by his attorney
           Richard Daly Esqr. & upon motion it is order-
ed by the court that said suit be revived by Scieri Facias against the administratrix of Samuel Creath decd (the plff. Creath having been suggested here
tofore)

EPHRIAM H FOSTER ASSEE)
    VS   ) Debt & Sci Fa
JOHN ROOK & DANIEL ROOK EXRS) This day came the parties by their attor-
             nies & thereupon came a Jury of good &
lawful men (to wit) Thomas Railsback Thomas Moore John H Williams John Cocke
Jr., Luther Laird Lewis Trice E. Wells Samuel Jordon Joseph Bowers Hayden
E. Wells John Williams Wells & Daniel Kyle who being duly elected tried &
sworn the truth to speak upon the issues joined upon their oaths do say they
find the issues in favor of the plaintiff & find that the defendants doth owe
to the plaintiff the sum of Two hundred & thirty dollars the debt in the
declaration mentioned & do assess his damages to Twenty one Dollars & seventy
cents sustained by reason of the detention of debt besides costs-

Therefore it is considered that the plaintiff recover of the defendants
John Rook & Daniel Rook Executors as aforesaid the sum of Two hundred & fifty
one dollars & seventy one cents the debt and damages so assessed by the jury

in form aforesaid together with his costs by him about his suit in this behalf expended to be levied ½ of the goods and chattles & Rights and credits which were of Rowland Vick at the time of his death and which have come to the hands of his Executors to be administered if so much he has if so much he has not then the costs to be levied of the proper goods & chattles lands and tenements of said Executors

(p-267) JOHN BRODIE   )
              VS   ) Motion
         PATRICK H DARBY)
         & WILLOUGHBY WILLIAMS) This day came the Plaintiff by attorney and says he
                                 will no further prosecute his said suit but dismisses
the same—
     Therefore it is considered by the court that the Defendant go hence without day and recover of the Plaintiff the costs in this behalf expended—

         GIVEN MCALISTER & GIVEN)
                  VS   ) Debt
         William Whitehead   ) This day came the plaintiffs by their attorney and
         JOHN T. WHITEHEAD   ) thereupon came a jury of good and lawful men to wit
                                   Thomas Railsback Thomas Moore John H Williams John
Cocke Luther Laird Lewis Trice Samuel Jordon Joseph Bowers Haydon E. Wells John Williams Wells Fowler & Daniel Kyle who being duly elected tried and sworn the truth to speak upon the issues joined upon their oathsdo say that they find the issues infavour of the Plaintiffs that the Defendants doth owe to the Plaintiffs the sum of Two hundred and sixty Dollars Balance of Debt in the Declaration mentioned and do assess his damages to seventeen dollars & fifty five cents by reason of the detention of said Debt besides their costs—
     Therefore it is considered by the court that the plaintiff recover of the Defendants the sum of Two hundred and seventy seven dollars and fifty five cents the Balance of Debt and damages so assessed by the Jury in form aforesaid together with their costs by them about their suit in this behalf expended—

(p-268) ARCHIBALD D. MURPHY FOR THE)
         BENEFIT OF HERNDON HARALSON)
                  VS   ) Debt
         JOHN S. MOSELY ADMR.   ) This day came into open court the Parties by
                                        their attornies and thereupon this cause is
Transferred by consent to the Circuit Court for trial to be had thereon—

         STEPHEN CANTRELL EXR OF)
         GEORGE N. DEDRICK ASSEE)
                  VS   ) Debt
         WILLIAM L. BROWN, ROBERT) This day came the parties by their attornies &
         VANCE & ELIZABETH VANCE EXRS) thereupon came a jury of good and lawful men to
                                        wit Thomas Railsback Thomas Moore John H. Williams
John Cooke Luther Laird Lewis Trice Samuel Jordon Joseph Bowers Hayden E. Wells John Williams Wells Fowler & Daniel Kyle who being duly elected tried and sworn the truth to speak upon the issues joined upon their oaths do say that they find the issues infavor of the plaintiff and find that the defendants doth owe to the plaintiff the sum of sixteen hundred & sixty six Dollars Sixty Six and two third cents the debt in the declaration mentioned & do assess his damages to sixty dollars by reason of the detention of said debt besides costs—

Therefore it is considered by the court that the plaintiff Stephen Cantrell Executor as aforesaid recover of the defendants William L. Brown Robert Vance & Elizabeth Vance Executors of Samuel Vance Dec'd the sum of seventeen hundred and twenty six dollars sixty six & two third cents the debt and damages so assessed by the Jury in form aforesaid together with his costs by him about his suit in this behalf Expended- to be levied of the goods and chattles rights and credits which were of Samuel Vance decd at the time of his death (p-269) and which have come to the hands of his Executors to be administered if so much he has if not then the costs to be levied of the proper goods and chattles lands and tenements of the said Executors-

ROBERT WEAKLY	)	
VS	)	Original Attachment
REUBEN OGLESBY	)	The Plaintiffs in this case failing to appear and prosecuting his suit-

Therefore it is ordered by the court that said suit be dismissed and that the Defendant Reuben Oglesby go hence without day and recover of the Plaintiff Robert Weakly the costs in this behalf Expended

OREN D. BATTLE BENEFIT OF	)	
JOSIAH W. FORT	)	
VS	)	Covenant Broken
JOHN PATTON	)	This day came the parties by their attornies & thereuponall and singular the matters and things

arrising in law upon the defendants Demurrer &c the plaintiffs declaration being heard and by the court here fully understood it appearing to the court that the matters arrising in law upon said demurrerare not sufficient to bar the plaintiff from having and maintaining his action - It if therefore considered by the court that said demurrer be overruled & that the plaintiff recover against said defendant his damages sustained by reason of the nonperformances of the covenants in the declaration mentioned but because the amt. of damages are unknown to the court let a jury come here at next court and assess the same-

(p-270) STATE OF TENNESSEE	)	
VS	)	Bastardy
MAJOR BARBEE GEORGE	)	Upon motion it appearing to the court that Major
BARBEE & ELISHA	)	Barbee had been charged as the father of a Bastard
WILLIS	)	child begotten upon the body of Polly Chumney and had been ordered at the April Term 1820 of the

County Court of Montgomery to pay annually for the maintainance of the same the sum of Twelve dollars and it further appearing that the said child was yet living & that the said Major Barbee had neglected to comply with the order of said court relative thereto It is thereupon ordered by the court that the said Major Barbee pay the sum of Thirty six dollars in pursuance of the order of the court as heretofore made and that a Fieri Facias issue therefor against the said Major Barbee & also against Joseph Barbee & Elisha Willis who are his securities of Record for the performance of the said order & that he pay the costs in this behalf expended-

JACOB H. FORT ADMR	)
VS	)
PETER H. COLE &	)
WILLIAM J. LYNES	)

De bt.

This day came the parties by their attornies and thereupon came a Jury of good and lawful men to wit, Thomas Railsback Thomas Moore John H. Williams John Cocke Luther Laird Lewis Trice Samuel Jordon Joseph Bowers Heydon E. Wells John Williams Wells Fowler & Danile Kyle who being duly elected tried and sworn the truth to speak upon the issue joined upon their oaths do say that they find the issue in favor infavour of the Plaintiff that the Defendants doth owe the Plaintiff the sum of Two hundred dollars the Debt in the Decl. mentioned & they do assess his damages to seven dollars for the detention of the sum - It is thereupon considered by the court that the said Plaintiff Jacob H. Fort recover of the said Defendants P ter H. Cole and William J. Lynes the said sum (p-271) of Two hundred & seven dollars the debt & damages so as found by the Jury aforesaid and also the costs in this behalf expended-

```
STATE          )
   VS          )    Bastardy
VINSON ENNIS)
& JOHN EDMONDSON)
& JOHN WEAKLY HIS SECURITIES)
```
Upon motion it appearing to the court that Vinson Ennis had been charged as the father of a Bastard child begotten on the body of Kesiah Mathews and that he had been charged with the maintainance of the same at the April County Court 1819 & that he had entered into Bond with Dr. Edmondson and Wealky his securities for paying annually Twelve dollars for that purpose and that the child was yet living & that the last two years remain due & unpaid - It is thereupon ordered by the court that a Fiere Facias issue against the said Vinson Ennis & John Edmonson & John Weakly his securities for Twnety four dollars and also for the costs of this motion -

```
STATE               )
   VS               )    Riot
NEEDHAM FARRIER & OTHERS)
```
Lewis C. Hurt Edmund Winston & Wm. Griffith witnesses in behalf of the state personally appeared in open court & acknowledged themselves severally indebted to the state of Tennesseein the sum of one hundred & twenty five dollars each to be levied respectively of their goods & chattles lands & tenements &c to be void on condition that they make their personal appearance before the County Court of Montgomery at the ourt House in Clarksville on the Thursday after the third monday in October next then & there to give testimony in behalf of the state of Tennessee against the said Needham Farrier and others & not depart without leave of the court first had & obtained &c -

```
(p-272)  ISRAEL MCLAUGHLIN   )
              VS            )
         ISAAC W. VANLEER   )
```
Upon motion of the plaintiff and it appear ing to the court that Israel Vanleer had departed this life & that no person had administered on his estate & that James C. Napier & wife are the heirs at law of the said Isaac W. Vanleer, It is the eupon ordered by the court that a Soire issue &c to revgive the same against the heirs-

Ordered by the court that Letters of administration issue to Henry Mc
Fall Junr. on the Estate of Dorrell Young Decd. whereupon the said Henry
McFall came into open court and entered into Bond & security satisfactory
to the court and was qualified agreeable to law-

Samuel Smith Esquires administrator returns into court an Inventory of
the estate of David Council Decd. and on motion ordered to be Recorded
and that the property contained in said Inventory be sold upon said
Samuel Smith Administrator as aforesaid advertising the same agreeable to
law-

On motion ordered by the court that Abner Harris be permitted to give
in his list of Taxable property for the year 1823 and that it be annexed
to the present years list-

On motion ordered by the court that Arthur Harris be permitted to give
in his list of Taxable property for the year 1823 and that it be annexed
to the present years Tax list

On motion ordered by the court that Joseph J Harris be permitted to give
in his list of Taxable property for the year 1823 and that it be annexed
to the present years Tax list-

DORRELL Y. HARRIS & WIFE)
    VS   ) Petition
HAYDON E WELLS GUARDIAN) For reasons appearing to the court upon
                     the affidavit of the defendant this cause
is continued & the said defendant is permitted (p-273) to amend his
answer upon paying the costs accrued at this Term & it is ordered that
said amended answer be filed on or before the 15th Sept. next & that a
Fi Fa issue for said Costs-

JAMES BLANKS ASSEE)
    VS   ) Debt
MOSES COLLIER) Upon motion of the plaintiff by his attorney
             leave is granted him to take the deposition
of in the State of Virginia County upon giving the adverse
party thirty days notice of time & place-

Rebecca Council admrs. of David Council decd. returns into court an
Inventory of said estate & on motion ordered to be Recorded-

On motion ordered by the court that Rebecca Council admr. of David
Council decd. be permitted to sell the personal property of said decd.
after advertising the same agreeable to law-

STATE OF TENNESSEE)
    VS   ) Sci Fa
WILLIE SEGRAVES) This day came the Solicitor General in be-
            half of the state & the defendant being
solemnly called to come into court & plead to the Scieri Facias against
him failes so to do-
It is therefore considered by the court that the Judgt. nisi rendered
against said Willie Segraves at the January Term last for Two Dollars

& fifty cents be made final—

It is therefore considered by the court that the state of Tennessee recover of said defendant Willie Segraves said sum of Two dollars & fifty cents & the costs in this behalf Expended as well as the costs of the former Judgt.

Court adjourned untill tomorrow morning to meet at 9 O'clock.

Isaac Dennison
Stephen Cocke
Thos. Smith

(p-274) The Worshipful Court of Montgomery County have met according to adjournment —

Saturday July 26th 1823
Present Isaac Dennison)
Stephen Cocke) Esquires
Thomas Smith) Justices

EDWARD H STEELE & THOMAS BARNET)
VS) Debt
WILLIAM MCCULLOCK) This day came into court thereupon the defendant being solemnly called came not but made default it is therefore considered by the court that the plaintiffs Edward H. Steele & Thomas Barnet recover of the defendant the sum of eighty eight dollars & fifteen cents the debt in the declaration mentioned & the further sum of twenty five dollars seventy two cents & damages for the detention of Sd. debt besides his costs about his suit in this behalf expended—

HUGH & JAMES MCCLURE)
VS) Debt
PETER P. ROBERTS &) This day came the Plaintiff by his attorney
EDWARD NEBLETT) Willie B. Johnson esquires and Edward Neblett one of the Defendants being solemnly called to come into court and answer to the Plaintiffs declaration failed so to do, but made default—

Therefore it is considered by the court that the Plaintiff recover of the defendant Edward Neblett together with Peter P. Roberts the other Defendants in this suit the sum of one hundred & (p-275) ninety five dollars the debt in the declatation mentioned and the further sum of four dollars & nine cents the damage sustained by reason of the detention of said debt besides this costs in this behalf expended— the plaintiff agrees to stay Execution untill next October Court—

WILLIAM E WILLIAMS))
VS) Admr.) Motion
CHARLES D MCLEAN)) This day came the Plaintiff and thereupon it appearing to the court that Andrew Vance clerk of the county court of pleas and quarter sessions had issued an Execution from the docket of Stephen Thomas Esqr. in behalf of William E. Williams against Charles D. McLean administrator directed to any lawful officer in said county directing that of the goods and chattles lands and Tenements of said Charles D. McLean administrator to

makenthe sum of Forty five Dollars & twenty five cents including costs to satisfy a Judgment of William E. Williams rendered 17th October 1820 placed in the hands of Samuel M. Stramler a constable in said County for collection upon which the said Samuel M. Stramler levied on Lotts No. 39&40 being near the River in the Old Town of Clarksville for the want of personal property- Upon motion of said Plaintiff it is ordered by the court that a Venditioni Exponas issue to the sheriff of Montgomery County commanding him to expose to sale said Twon Lotts No. 39 & 40 to satisfy said Judgment and costs and also the cost of this motion-

On motion it is ordered by the court that Thomas Dunbar be permitted to give in his list of Taxable property and that it be annexed to the present years list-

On motion ordered by the court that Samuel Gordon be permitted to give in his list of Taxable property for 1823 and that it be annexed to the present years Tax list-

(p-276) On motion ordered by the court that Abraham Brantly be permitted to give in his list of Taxable property for the year 1823 and that it be annexed to the present years Tax list-

On motion ordered by the court that James Reeves be permited to give in his list of Taxable property for the year 1823 and that it be annexed to the present years Tax list-

On motion ordered by the court that John John Hinton Exr be permitted to give in the list of Taxable property of the Estate of Kimbrough Hinton for the years 1822 & 1823 & that it be annexed to the present years Tax list

On motion ordered by the court that Peter Oneal be appointed Overseer of the Road leading from Clarksvilleto Wine Miller's old place in the place of Mathew Dorherty and that the same hands work under him that worked under him that worked under the said Mathew Dorherty-

On motion ordered by the court that William J. Lynes account as Jailor of Montgomery County amounting to sixty six Dollars thirty seven and a half cents be allowed & that the county Trustee pay the same out of any monies in his hand not otherwise appropriated-

Ordered by the court that Cypress Hensley be appointed overseer of the road from the mouth of the West fork towards Pettis's mill to the Ford of Spring Creek and that the following hands work under him, to wit John Herndon Nathaniel Herndon Alexander Sims Burnett Sims, Willie Segraves Reuben Pollard & hand James Pollard Hewel Pollard & William Spead-

(p-277) On motion ordered by the court that Pettus cook be appointed overseer of the road from the ford of Spring Creek at Obediah Bromfields to Thomas Watson's mill & that said Obediah Bromfield's hands Stephen Pettus & hands & all other hands about said Pettus's mill work on said road-

The jury of view appointed at the last Term of this court to view the road leading from Clarksville to Robert Searcy's between John Frenchs

and the first fork of said road this side of William Holloways make the
following the following report we Thomas Dodd Joseph Martin John French
Jr., & Peter N. Marr jurors of view to view the within described road
being duly sworn & strictly examined the said road report & say as follows
(to wit) that we think (the John French road) aforesaid would be much
better to leave the present road about three fourths of a mile beyond
William Holloway's running as marked by us leaving said Holloway's to the
north about three hundred yards & intersecting the old road about half a
mile on this side of said Holloway's—

On motion ordered by the court that Andrew Donnolson overseer of the road
from Clarksville to Robert Searchs out out the road as viewed & marked
by the jury appointed at last court to leave the present road about three
fourths of a mile beyond William Holloway's runing as marked leaving said
Holloway's to the north about three hundred yards and to intersect the old
road about half a mile this side of said Holloway—

On motion ordered by the court that Edwin H. Adams be appointed overseer
of the road leading from Clarksville to half pone from Jeremiah Bowers to
Brush Creek in place of John Barton former overseer & that the following
hands work on said road (to wit) George Humphreys & hands Yancy Kelley
Joseph Kelley Joel Mann the hands of Sanford Wilson James Roach Charles
Roach William Raimey Andrew Linn Jarrat Perdue David Cavnes & all other
hands within the bounds of said road who have not heretofore been ordered
to work on any other road—

(p-278) Deed of conveyance from John H. Poston & wife Nancy George B.
Nelson & Robert Nelson to Cullen Bayliss for a tract of land around
Dover and also for their interest in the town of Dover was produced in
open court and the same was duly acknowledged by John H. Poston & George
B. Nelson and It was ordered by the court that Isaac Dennison & James
Barrett Esquires Justices of this court take the privy examination of
Nancy L. Poston relative to theexecution of said Deed and she having
been duly examined by the said Dennison & Barrett menbers of this court
seperate & apart from her husband & upon such privy examination she
having acknowledged that she executed the same freely & voluntarily &
without the constraint & Compulsion of her husband—
    It is thereupon ordered by the court that the said Deed be certified
for Registration as to the said John & Nancy & George Nelson—

```
PETER N MARR      )
        VS        )   Garnishment
BROWN & VANCE&)
WM. VANCE EXECUTORS)   This day came the parties by their attornies
OF SAML.VANCE DECD )   & thereupon all & singular & matters of things
                       arrising on said motion being fully heard &
understood—
```
    It is considered by the court that the said plaintiff recover of the
said Wm. L. Brown Elizabeth Vance & Robert Vance Executors as aforesaid
the sum of Eighteen dollars & seventy five cents & costs of this suit to
be levied of the goods & chattles rights & credits of Sam'l Vance Decd
in the hands of his Executors if so much there be, if not then the costs
to be levied of the goods & chattles of the said Executors—

The Heirs of John Minor is permitted to give in their list Taxable property for 1822 & 1823 & that it be annexed to the present years tax list & that they be exonerated from the double tax for the year 1822-

(p-279)   STATE   )
              VS   )   Forfeiture
         JAMES KING) This day came the solicitor Genl. in behalf of the
                              state & the Defendant being solemnly called to come
into court & answer the charge against him failed so to do. It is therefore considered by the court that the state of Tennessee recover of the said James King the sum of Five hundred dollars unless he make his appearance before our County Court at the next term thereof and shew cause &c and that a Scire Facias issue-

         STATE   )
              VS   )   Forfeiture
         JESSE BOOKSEY) This day came the Solicitor General in behalf of the
                              State and Jesse Cooksey being solemnly called to come
into court & bring with him the body of James King agreeably to his recognisance failed so to do. It is therefore considered by the court that the state recover of the said Jesse Cooksey the sum of one hundred dollars unless he makes his personal appearance at next Court & shew cause &c and that a Sci fa issue &c-

         STATE   )
              VS   )   Forfeiture
         JOSHUA HUTCHISON) This day came the Solicitor General in behalf of
                              the State & the Defd. sd. Joshua Hutchinson being
Solemnly called to come into court & produce the body of James King agreeably to the recognisance failed so to do. It is therefore considered by the court that the state of Tennessee recover of the said Joshua Hutchison the sum of one hundred dollars unless he makes his personal appearance at the next term of our said court and shews cause &c and that a Scire facias issue &c-

(p-280)   JACOB H FORT ADMR.)
                     VS   ) Debt
PETER H. COLE & WILLIAM J LYNES) This day came the Defendant by their att-
                              ornies and prays an appeal to the Circuit
Court of Montgomery Counry in the nature of a writ of Error whereupon the said Defendants entered into Bone & security satisfactory to the court and the same is allowed-

This day was presented to the court Lucy Blackburn for the purpose of being placed on the list of Paupers of this county and thereupon it was ordered by the court that James Barret and Abner Gupton Esquires examine the said Lucy Blackburn and report to the next Term of this Court-

A Deed of conveyance from Cornelius Gusman sheriff of Montgomery County to William B. Nicholson for three Tracts of Land containing 914 acres was produced in open court and the execution thereof was duly acknowledged in open court by the said Cornelius Crusman to be his act and deed for the purposes therein contained and on motion ordered to be certified for Registration-

A deed of conveyance from James Trice to Dennis Dorherty for fifty and one half acres of land was produced in open court and the execution thereof was duly proven by the oaths of Lee Trice and Quintus C. Atkinson the subscribing witnesses and on motion ordered to be certified for Registration

Francis Baker Nathan Hester & Samuel Haggard Commissioners appointed at the last Term of this court to settle with Robert Wade administrator of William Faulkner Decd make their report to this Term and on motion ordered to be recorded-

(p-281) John H. Poston & Isaac Dennison commissioners appointed at the last Term of this court to settle with William O. Robbins administrator of Burges Hardson Decd. make their return to this Term and on motion ordered to be recorded-

On motion ordered by the court that a License issue to Samuel Lynes to keep an ordinary in the Twon of Clarksville whereupon the said Samuel Lynes entered into Bond and security agreeable to law and took the oath prescribed by law-

Francis Baker administrator of the Estate of Harriet Blackney Decd. returned into court an Inventory of said decd. and on motion ordered to be Recorded-

James Barret & Charles Baily commissioners appointed at the last Term of this court to such with the Administrator of William Elliott deceased make their report to this Term and on motion ordered to be Recorded-

Francis Baker Administrator of Harriet Blackney Decd returns into court an account of sales of the property of said deceased and on motion ordered to be Recorded

John W. Barker Stephen Pettus & Ellinor Adams admr. of John Adams decd. returns into court the a/c sales of the property of said decd. sold at two different times & on motion ordered to be Recorded-

On motion ordered by the court that Isaac W. Jones an orphan of Isaac Jones decd. be bound to Daniel Ogalsby whereupon the said Daniel Ogalsby came into and entered into bond with the court agreeable to law-

Robert Vance returns into open court a list of Taxable property in Capt. James Mannell's company for the year 1823-

(p-282) A Deed of conveyance from Zebedee Dennis to Robert Sawyer for 92¾ acres of land was produced in open court and the execution thereof duly acknowledged by the said Zebedee Dennis to be his act and and deed for the purposes therein contained and on motion ordered to be certified for Registration-

The court proceeded to appointed Jurors at the next October Court to wit, Thomas Collier John Williams James Wilson Levi P. Allen Jefferson Weakley Mathew Ogburn Mathew Rogers James Trice Washington Lee Jesse

Baily & Uriah Humphreys Alexander Hamilton John Barton Nicholas Bagwell
George Blanks Henry Taylor James Allen Robert Bumpass Thomas Carraway
Stephen Mallory Ambrose Martin James Trotter Fred rick Rudolph Nathaniel
Thaxton William McClure & James Hubbard.

Samuel M. Stramller & Nace F. Trice are appointed comstables to the next
October County Court.

On motion ordered by the court that the order appointing commissioners at
the last Term of this court to settle with Robert G. Johnson surviving
admr of PhilipJohnson decd be continued & that the same commissioners
report to next court.

```
ELI LOCKERT        )
        VS         )              Debt entered as of Tuesday
PHILIP JOHNSON'S ADMRS)  This day came said parties by their attornies
                           & thereupon came a jury of good & lawful
```
men to wit Thomas Railsback Thomas Moore John H. Williams John Cooke
Luther Laird Lewis Trice Samuel Jordan Joseph Bowers Haydon E. Wells
John Williams Wells Fowler Daniel Kyle who being duly elected tried &
sworn the truth to speak on the Issue Joined upon their oath do say as to
first Issue that the defendant has fully administered all and singular
the goods & chattles rights & credits which were of the said Phillip
Johnson at the time of his death, & which have come to the (p-283)
hands of said administrators to be administered except the sum of five
hundred dollars which remains in their hands yet unadministered and the
jurors aforesaid on their oaths aforesaid do further sau as to the second
issue that said defendants have not paid the debt in the declaration
mentioned but that there is owing to the plaintiff the sum of fifteen
hundred thirty three dollars & thirty three cents Bal. of Debt & the
further sum of sixty dollars damages sustained by the detention of said
debt.
     Therefore it is considered bythe court that the plaintiff recover
against the defendants said sum of $1533.33 balance of Debt aforesaid
& said sum of $60.00 damages aforesaid in form aforesaid assessed & his
costs by him about his suit in this behalf expended- five hundred dollars
of said debt to be levied of the goods & chattles rights & credits which
were of said Phillip Johnson to the hands of said admr. to be administered
as to the Ballance of said debt to be levied of the estate of Phillip
Johnson where assets may be found &c & that he have Sci Fa against the
heirs of Intestate for ballance of said Debt & Damages &c-

```
HENRY WILLIAMS     )
        VS         )  Debt
ROBERT SEARCY      )  This day came the Plaintiff by his attorney Cave
                        Johnson Esquire and the Defendant Robert Searcy
```
being solemnly c lled came not but made default-
     Therefore it is considered by the court that the Plaintiff Henry Wil-
liams recover of the defendant Robert Searcy the sum of Two Hundred and
Twenty dollars the debt in the declaration mentioned and the further sum
of Two Dollars and Twenty cents the damages sustained by reason of the
detention of said debt besides his costs in this behalf expended-

(p-284)

JONATHAN JOHNSON)
   VS) Sci Fa
THE HEIRS OF PHILIP) The Scire Facias inthis case have been returned
JOHNSON DECD) & specifying & shewing that many of the heirs
           of Philip Johnson Decd. are not in habitants
of this state and also specifying that Roobert G. Johnson John Johnson
Whitfield Killebrew & wife f Fanny & George W. Killebrew are also heirs
at law of the said Philip - It is thereupon ordered by the court that an
alias Scire facias issue &c-

Court adjourned until Monday Morning to meet at 9 O&clock
            Isaac Dennison
            Chas, Bailey
            Jas. Barret

Court met according to adjournment Monday 28th July 1823
       Present   Isaac Dennison)
           Charles Bailey) Esqrs. Justices
           James Barret)

Elizabeth Vance, Robert Vance & William L. Brown executors of the estate
of
  SAMUEL VANCE DECD)
     VS   ) This day came into court the parties by their
  CHARLES BAILEY) attornies & thereupon by consent of parties
          It is ordered and adjurdged by the court
here that a judg ment heretofore rendered in favour of Samuel Vance in
his lifetime against D. Bailey on the 22nd day of January 1823 for the sum
of one hundred and sixty five dollars sixty two and a half cents be revived in the name of the sd. executors & that execution issue accordingly &
the plaintiffs agree to & stay execution two months & within fifteen days
before the next term of this court-

(p-285) It is ordered by the court that William Killebrew be appointed
Guardian for George W. Killebrew for the purpose of defending the suits of
Jonathan Johnson against the heirs of Philip Johnson Decd. Eli Lockert
against the heirs of Philip Johnson Decd.
John Allensworth & James Miller against the heirs of Philip Johnson Decd.
and Martin Thomas against the heirs of Philip Johnson Decd.

  ELI LOCKERT)
    VS   ) Upon application of the plaintiff it is
  THE HEIRS OF) ordered by the court that an alias Scire
  OHILIP JOHNSON DECD) facias issue against the heirs of Philip
Johnson Decd.

  MARTIN THOMAS   )
    VS   ) It is ordered by the court that an alias
  THE HEIRS OF PHILIP) scire facias issue against the Heirs of
  JOHNSON DECD   ) Philip Johnson Decd.

  ALLENSWORTH MILLER)
    VS   )
  THE HEIRS OF PHILIP)
  JOHNSON DECD   )

It appearing to the court from the return of the sheriff that William Nelson & wife Mary Bernard Reynolds & wife Suey Mille Stephens James Shackleford & wife Sally Henry Hodges & wife Nancy Robert Goodloe & Wife Agnes part of the Heirs of Phillip Johnson Decd. are now residents- It is therefore ordered that an alias Scire facias issue-

H & J. MCCLURE
VS
C. D. MCLEAN

It is ordered by the court that the pltff have leave to amend his declaration upon payment of the costs of the amendment- and that the same stand for trial at next court

(p-286) DAVID ANDERSON
VS
CLARK CABLE

Case
It appearing to the court that no step has been taken to prosecute this case for more than two Terms- It is therefore ordered by the court that said suit be dismissed & that defendant Clark Cable go hence without day and recover of theplaintiff David Anderson the costs in this behalf Expended-

ANDREW MCFADDIN & DAVID COFIELD   VS
JOHN JARRAT ADMR

Case
This day came the plaintiffs by their attorney C. Johnson Esquire and say they intend no further to prosecute their said suit against the defendant but dismisses the same - It is therefore considered by the court that said suit be dismissed & that the defendant recover of the Plaintiff the costs in this behalf Expended-

Upon the petition of Cave Johnson it is ordered by the court that Lewis Trice Dennis Doherty Nace F. Trice Samuel McNichols May Trice ~~Samuel~~ ~~McNichols~~ Wm. Chism William Lee Washington Lee or any five of them be appointed commissioners to view & mark out a road from the mouth of Red River to cross the West fork at Reuben Pollards and make return thereof to next Court-

It is ordered by the court that William S. White David Fields Reuben Pollard John Pollard John Johnson and William Reasons or any five of them be appointed commissioners to lay off & mark a road from Reuben Pollards to intersect the Russelbille road near William S. White & ~~make~~ make return thereof to the next term of this court-

(p-287) Court adjourned until court in course-

Isaac Dennison
Thos. W. Atkinson
Jas. Barret

The Worshipful court of Montgomery County have met according to
adjournment Monday October 21st 1823-
Present

Alexander M. Rogers)
Abner Harris)Esquires
Valentine Allen) Justices
Thos. W. Atkinson)

On motion ordered by the court that Stephen Cooke Valentine Allen
Esquires be appointed to settle with Samuel Smith Guardian for the heirs
of Elizabeth Harvey Deceased and make report to the next term of this
court-

A Bill of Sale from John Neblett Junior to Alexander M. Rogers was produced
in open court and the execution thereof duly acknowledged by the said
John Neblett Junr. to be his act and deed for the purposes therein
named and on motion ordered to be recorded-

A Bill of Sale from John Neblett Junr. and Alexander M. Rogers to John
Wyatts for negro slave Watt was produced in open court and the Execution
thereof duly acknowledged by the said John Neblett and Alexander M. Rogers
to be their act and deed for the purposes therein mentioned and on motion
ordered to be recorded-

On motion ordered by the court that Andrew W. Hail be appointed Guardian
for his Children Sally Hale Elizabeth Hail G.D. Hale James J. Hale Alexander B. Hale Matilda Hale & Andrew Hale whereupon the said Andrew W.
Hale entered entered into Bond and security satisfactory to the court and
the same is allowed-

On motion ordered by the court that Lewis Whitfield be appointed Guardian
to Joseph Sally Needham Robert Lewis George & Elizabeth Whitfield minor
heirs of the said Lewis Whitfield whereupon the said Lewis Whitfield entered into Bond & security satisfactory to the court and the same is allowed

On motion ordered by the court that Joseph Caldwell be appointed Guardian
to William Rogers & Louisa Rogers minor heirs of Isaac Rogers deceased
Whereupon the said Joseph Caldwell entered into Bond & security satisfactory to the court and the same is allowed-

On motion ordered by the court that Mary Duff be appointed Guardian to
Frances Duke in the place of Joseph C. Patterson former Guardian who has
been removed by the court as Guardian aforesaid-
Whereupon the said Mary Duff came into court and entered into Bond
and security the same is allowed-

On motion ordered by the court that Letters of Administration issue to Joel
Bayless on the Estate of John Ridsdale Deceased0 (p-289) Whereupon the
said Joel Bayliss came into court and entered into Bond and security
satisfactory to the court and qualified agreeable to law- from which proceeding Thomas Ridsdale one of the heirs of said Deceased preyed an
appeal to the circuit Court of Montgomery County at the next February Term
whereupon the said Thomas Ridsdale came into court and entered into Bond
and security satisfactory to the court and the same is allowed-

On motion ordered by the court that letters of administration issue to Archibald Y. Donnalson and Adaline Mallory on the estate of George Mallory Deceased whereupon the said Archibald Y. Donnalson and Adaline Mallory came into court and entered into Bond & security satisfactory to the court and qualified agreeable to law-

On motion ordered by the court that Ross Jones be furnished with letters of administration on the Estate of Joseph Gee Decd. whereupon the said Ross Jones came into court and entered into Bond and security satisfactory to the court & qualified agreeable to law-

On motion ordered by the court that Lewis Whitfield be furnished with Letters of administration on the Estate of Johnson Wall Deceased in the place of Braxton Wall the former administrator on said Estate and that said Braxton Wall be released from any further responsibility as administrator aforesaid whereupon the said Lewis Whitfield entered into Bond & security satisfactory to the court and qualified agreeable to law-

This day came into open Court Samuel Caldwell one of the Executors of John Caldwell Deceased (p-290) and produced to the court the last will and Testament of the said John Caldwell deceased which was duly proven by the oath of Sterling Neblett one of the subscribing witnesses thereto and the name of John Steele Decd. One of the witnesses to said will was proven by the oath of John Steele Junr. to be the hand write of the said John Steele Decd. in his life time & on motion ordered to be recorded-Whereupon the Samuel Caldwell one of the Executors in said entered into Bond & security satisfactory to the court and was qualified agreeable to law, and it is ordered that letters Testamentary issue to sd. Samuel Caldwell on the Estate of the said Deceased-

This day came into open court Thomas Brodie the Executor of John Watkins Deceased and produced to the court the last will & Testament of the said John Watkins Deceased which was duly proven by the oaths of Samuel B. White and Thomas B. White two of the subscribing witnesses thereto and on motion ordered by the court to be Recorded-
Whereupon the said Thomas Brodie the Executor aforesaid entered into Bond & security satisfactory to the court and was qualified agreeable to law and it is ordered that letters Testamentary issue to the said Thomas Brodie on the estate of the said Deceased-

This day came into open court John H. Hinton and Peter N. Marr the Executors of Peter H. Cole Decd. and produced to the court the last will and Testament of the said Peter H. Cole Deceased which was duly proven by the oaths of Mary H. Minor (p-291) and Ann G. Marr the subscribing witnesses thereto and on motion ordered to be recorded- Whereupon the said John H. Hinton & Peter N. Marr Executors aforesaid entered into Bond and security satisfactory to the court and qualified agreeable to law-

On motion ordered by the court that James Hamilton a Juror in the case of the State of Tennessee against Stephen B. Stewart be allowed for three days attendance as a Talesman Juror in said case and that the county Trustee pay the same out of any monies in his hand not otherwise appropriated-

On motion ordered by the court that Thomas Frazer David Bunting William
Trigg Esquire John Hampton Richard Meriwether John Carter Bright Herring
Reuben Pollard & John Johnson or any seven of them be appointed a comm-
ittie to view and report to the next Term of this court whether the old
road from the state line near Rice Colemans where the Dover Road intersects
the same to Watson's mill ought to be Established as a public road-

On motion ordered by the court that the following hands work on the Road
from New York to the second fork To wit the hands in New York and that
Thomas Siles be appointed overseer of said Road-

On motion ordered by the court that Burrell Bayliss be appointed overseer
of the Road from the second fork by sd. Burrell Bayless to Mr. Perry's on
Stewart line and that the following hands work under him To wit Mr. ɸɸȻȻ
Collier's hands Mr. McGee Mrs. Hitchers Mrs. Tire Mr. Bowers H. Horn Mr.
Hathcock Mr. Johnson (p-292) V. Cooper Mr. Kercheval James Nelson Mr.
Morrow & Mr. Cates-

On motion ordered by the court that the following hands work under Thomas
Carraway overseer of the Road from the forks of the Road in the hollow
at John Trice's farm to River's mill to wit said Carraway & hands Noble
Osburn and hands Hugh McClure's hands Ross Jones Sheppard Trice's hands
& Hugh Campbell's hands-

On motion ordered by the court that John P. Epps be appointed overseer of
the Road leading by A.M.Rogers & Abner Harris's into the Dickson Road in
the place of Arthur Harris removed and that the same hands work under the
said John P. Epps that worked under the said Arthur Harris-

On motion ordered by the court that Thomas Joiner be appointed overseer
of the road from the mouth of the West fork to Thomas Cherry's in the
place of Jeffrey Sims former overseer & that the same hands work under
the said John P. Epps that worked under the said Arthur Harris-

On motion ordered by the court that Thomas Joiner be appointed overseer
of the road from the mouth of the West fork to Thomas Cherry's in the place
of Jeffrey Sims former overseer & that the same hands work under him
that worked under said sims and that William Speed Jeffrey Sims James Sims
& Thomas Cherry be added to the former list of hands on said Road-

On motion ordered by the court that Richard P. King be appointed overseer of the Road from Mossley's ferry to Springfield in the place of
Rich'd T. Ryburn resigned and that the same hands work under him that
worked under the said Ryburn-

On motion of ordered by the court that Mary Harrison John Steele David
Wood Frances McMurdy Robert McMurdy Richard H. Adams and Samuel Edmonston
be permitted to give in their list of Taxable property for the present
year-

(p-293) On motion ordered by the court that Urey a negro woman belonging
to Mary B. Cocke deceased ward of Sterling Neblett be sold by said

Sterling Neblett Guardian of said ward and others her Brothers and sisters upon a credit of Twelve months with a view of making a division between the surviving wards-

By the consent and upon the petition of the heirs & distributers of Abner V. Hampton Decd. Ordered by the court that they have leave and are hereby authorised to sell for the purpose of a division the following slaves To wit James Abram David Venira & her two children also a tract of land of Two hundred acres deeded by Larkin Rogers to Mary N. Hampton and by her to Abner V. Hampton fifty acres deeded by Joseph Woolfolk to Abner V. Hampton also the rent corn on said land and that Richd B. Blount & William S. White be appointed commissioners to make said sale-

On motion ordered by the court that Joseph Woolfolk William Trigg & Rich'd B. Blount be appointed commissioners to settle with George W. Nevill as Executor of George Nevill Decd. and make return to the next Term of this court-

The commissioners at the last Term of this court to lay off one years provision for Elizabeth Ingram out of the Estate of Sterling Ingram Decd make their report to this Term and on motion ordered to be Recorded-

John Rook & Daniel Rook returns into court as Executors of Rowland Vick and Inventory of the Estate of said deceased and on motion ordered to be recorded-

(p-294) On motion order d by the court that John Kezee be entitled to the sum of five dollars for attending at the August Circuit Court five days as a Talisman Juror agreeable to the certificate of P.N.Marr clerk of said Circuit Court and that the County Trustee pay the same out of any monies in his hands not otherwise appropriated-

The commissioners appointed at the last Term of this court to lay of the protion of the Estate of Robert Davie in the hands of his Guardian make their report to this Term and on motion ordered to be recorded-

On motion ordered by the court that the Executors of Issac Rogers have leave to make sale for the purpose of a division on a credit of Twelve months the following negroes and other property to wit, Davy Waltham Manoa Reuben and all the perishable property belonging to the legatees of said Isaac Rogers-

On motion ordered by the court that Willi am McDaniel & Lemuel H. Clifton be appointed commissioners to settle with Thomas Williams administrator of the Estate of William McCauly Deceased and make report to the next Term of this Court-

Francis Baker and Edward A. Lucy administrators of the Estate of Thomas Blakeney Decd. returns into court an additional Inventory of the estate of said Decd. and on motion ordered to be Recorded-

Joel Bayliss Administrator of the Estate of John Ridsdale Decd. returns into court an Inventory of said Decd. and on motion ordered to be Recorded (p-295) John Steele administrator of the Estate of John Steele Decd. returns into court an Inventory of the notes and accounts of said

John Steele Decd. and on motion ordered to be Recorded-

Archibald Donalson and Adaline Mallory administrators of the Estate of George Mallory Decd returns into court and Inventory of the Estate of said Decd. and on motion ordered to be Recorded-

Elizabeth Ingram administratrix of the Estate of Sterling Ingram Decd. returns into court an Inventory of said Estate and on motion ordered to be Recorded-

Braxton Wall administrator of the Estate of Johnson Wall Decd Returns into court the account of sales of the property of said Decd and on motion ordered to be Recorded-

John Steele Administrator of the Estate of John Steele Decd returns into court the account of sales of the Estate of said Deceased and on motion ordered to be Recorded-

Present Alexander M. Rogers Abner Harris Stephen Cooke Thomas W. Atkinson Joshua P. Vaughn Valentine Allen Frances Baker James Barret Isaac Dennison & Sterling Neblett The court proceeded to the appointment of a constable in the place of John Moore Resigned and after the votes were counted out there appeared to be a majority in favour of Merideth Williams who was duly and constitutionally elected - Whereupon the said Merideth Williams entered into Bond and security satisfactory to the court and qualified agreeable to law-

On motion ordered by the court that Alexander M. Rogers Joshua P. Vaughn & Thomas Smith (p-296) be appointed commissioners toto settle with Stephen Cooke & Mary Duff, administrators of the Estate of Barney Duff Deceased and make Report to the next Term of this court-

On motion ordered by the court that Isaac Darnall be allowed as a pauper & parishioner by the county at the same rate at which he was formally allowed by this court from the time his former allowance ceased - & it is ordered that he be allowed the sum of Twenty dollars-

James Smith Senr. & James Smith Junr. & others of near New York and Felix Allen are permitted to give in their list of Taxable property for the present year - and that the same be annexed to the present years Tax list

Guthridge Lyons came into court and makes oath that he is charged with a Town Lott in his Tax list that the same is unjust that he has none said charge being made by mistake and for such reasons the court exonerates the said Lyons from the payment of said Tax-

On motion ordered by the court that Council Tyer be appointed overseer of the Road from Blooming Grove Creek to where the Dover road crosses the same and that the following hands work under him to wit, Thpmas McGehee and Vincent Cooper's Boys, Timothy Harris Henry Boyd James McGehee

Michael Tyer Mitchel Ther Thomas Tyer and all the hands within said bounds-

On motion ordered by the court that Sanford Wilson be permitted to renew his Tavern License to keep a house of entertainment at his dwelling house in this county and the said Sandford Wilson entered into Bond and security satisfactory to the court and the same is allowed-

(p-297) A Deed of Gift from Solomon Hunt to Absolom D. Sneed was this day produced in open court and the execution thereof duly acknowledged by the said Solomon Hunt to be his act and deed for the purposes therein mentioned and on motion ordered to be Recorded-

A Deed of Conveyance from John Reed to John D. Hargrove for one hundred and sixty and a half acres of land was produced in open court and the Execution thereof duly proven by the oaths of Benjamin W. Trotter & Ambrose Martin the subscribing witnesses thereto and on motion ordered to be certified for Registration-

A Deed of Conveyance from David W. Williamson to Samuel Grant for one hundred and thirty five acres of land was produced in open court and the execution thereof duly proven by the oath of Stephen W. Carney & Charles Grant subscribing witnesses thereto and on motion ordered to be certified for Registration-

A Deed of conveyance from Braxton Wall for one hundred and thirty three acres of land to Moses Oldham was produced in open court & the execution thereof duly acknowledged by the said Braxton Wall to be his act and deed for the purposes therein mentioned and on motion ordered to be certified for Registration-

A Deed of Conveyance from Felix Allen to James Grant for two hundred and Twenty and a quarter acres of land was produced in open court and the execution thereof duly proven by the oaths of David B. Allen Rich'd B. Blount & William E. Dney the subscribing witnesses thereto and on motion ordered to be certified for Registration-

A Deed of conveyance from Betsey A. West to Ambrose Davie for three hundred and thirty three acres of land was produced in open court and (p-298) the execution thereof duly proven by the oaths of J.B.Fleming at April Term 1823 and by the oath of Jones Davie at this Term two of the subscribing witnesses thereto and on motion ordered to be certified for Registration

A Deed of conveyance from William Jordon to Samuel Wilson for three acres of land was produced in open court and the Execution thereof duly acknowledged by the said William Jordon to be his act and deed for the purposes therein mentioned and on motion ordered to be certified for Registration -

A Deed of conveyance from John Faulkner to Ambrose Davie for one hundred & sixty three acres of land was produced in open court and the execution thereof duly proven by the oaths of Gabriel Davie & John Davie the subscribing witnesses thereto and on motion ordered by the court to be Certified for Registration-

A Deed of conveyance from Vincent Ennis to James Wilson for thirty five acres of land was produced in open court and the Execution thereof duly acknowledged by the said Vincent Ennis to be his act and Deed for the purposes therein mentioned and on motion ordered to be certified for Registration—

A Deed of ~~Deed~~ Mortgage from William L. Williams to Fielding S. Williams of Lynchburgh Virginia for certain lands mentioned therein was produced in open court and the execution thereof duly proven by the oaths of William B. Turly & Frederick W. Huling the subscribing witnesses thereto and on motion ordered to be certified for Registration—

A Deed of conveyance from William L. Williams to Alley Dillard for two tracts of land containing (p-299) two hundred acres was produced in open court and the Execution thereof duly acknowledged by by the said William L. Williams to be his act and deed for the purposes therein mentioned and on motion ordered to be certified for Registration —

A Deed of Gift from Ambrose Davie to John Davie & Elizabeth Davie was produced in open court and the Execution thereof duly acknowledged by the said Ambrose Davie to be his act and Deed for the purposes therein mentioned and on motion ordered to be Recorded—

A Deed of conveyance from William L. Williams to James Barret & ~~James~~ Samuel Dabney for Twon Lotts in the Tewn of Clarksville known by numbers fifty eight and fifty where the Tavern house and stables now stand now occupied by Williams & Barret was produced in open court and the execution thereof duly proven by the oaths if Isaac Dennison & William Turly the subscribing witnesses thereto and on motion ordered to be certified for Registration —

A Power of Attorney from Alexander Steele of the County of Campbell and state of Virginia to Philip Chapman and Moses Steele of the County of Williamson & State of Tennessee was produced in open court and it appearing to the court that said Power of attorney came duly certified with the seal annexed of the said County of Campbell it is ordered to be recorded—

A Deed of Conveyance from William McDaniel to Samuel K. Clifton for seventy six acres of land was produced in open court and the execution thereof duly proven by the oath of Thomas Williams & Thomas Hunter the (p-300) the subscribing witnesses thereto and on motion ordered to be certified for Registration —

The commissioners appointed at the last Term of this court to settle with Robert O. Johnson Decd. make their report to this court and on motion ordered to be Recorded—

On motion ordered by the court that David Hubbard be appointed Guardian to Henry Harris & Malvina Harris the minor heirs of Nancy Ury Decd. whereupon the said David Hubbard entered into Bond and security satisfactory and the dame is allowed—

The commissioners appointed at the last Term of this court to make division of the Real Estate of John Shelby Decd, between Jesse A. Brunson & Levisa his wife Clark Motton Shelby and Alfred M. Shelby make their Report to this Term with a destinct platt of the same and on motion ordered to be recorded

Court adjourned tomorrow untill 9 O'clock

Robert Vance
William Trigg
J.P.Vaughn

The Worshipful court of Montgomery County have met according to adjournment October 21st 1821-

Present A.M.Rogers Abner Harris & Joshua P. Vaughn

This day appeared in open court Joseph Woodson & Sally his wife by atto. and it appearing to this court from the petition of said Woodson & wife that they said Sally Woodson is entitled to dower in the lands in said petition specified that notice was duly given as required by law- It is therefore ordered by the court that a writ Issue &c Directed &c & that (p-301) the sheriff have dower assigned as required by law in the lands specified on said petition & make return to next Court-

Bytheconsent of the mother of William Neblett formerly Nancy Vaughn and Richard H. Adams to whom said William Neblett was bound at the January Term 1822 of this court - It is now ordered by the court that said William neblett may now leave said Adams and that said Adams be released from all further responsibilityin consequence of his Bond now filed in this office and that said Bond be considered from this date null & void to all intents and purposes-

On motion ordered by the court that Francis Baker Elijah Hancock Stephen G. Jones and John French Junr. be appointed to settle with Braxton Wall administrator of Johnson Wall decd. and make report to the next Term of this Court-

On motion ordered by the court that letters of administration issue to Nancy Young on the Estate of Dorrell Young Decd. Whereupon the said Nancy Yound entered into Bond & security satisfactory to the court and qualified agreeable to court-

On motion ordered by the court that Benjamin Rye have letters of administration on the Estate of Absalom Rye decd, Whereupon the said Benjamin Rye came into court and entered into Bond and security satisfactory to the Court, and qualified agreeable to law-

Stephen Mallory makes oath and for reasons appearing satisfactory to the court the said Stephen Mallory is exonerated from attending as a Juror at this Term-

(p-302) On motion ordered by the court that John H. Marable be appointed overseer of the Road from the Stewart County Line to the Widow Armfields in place of Henry D. Thornton and that the same hands work under him that worked under the said Thornton-

On motion ordered by the court that Bernard Powers be appointed overseer
of the Road from Yellow Creek Iron Works to the Ridge between the East
fork of Yellow Creek & the East fork of Yellow Creek & the Barron fork of
Bartons Creek and that the same hands work under him that worked under
John A.B.McBride on said Road-

On motion ordered by the court that Peter Oneal & William Killebrew be
permitted to give in their list of Taxable property for the present year
and that the same be added to the present years Tax list-

Robert Vance returns into court his resignation as a Justice of the peace
for Montgomery County-

On motion ordered by the court that James Elder John H. Poston & Joel C.
Rice be appointed commissioners to settle with Henry Small as late Treasurer of Montgomery County and make report to the next Term of this Court

On motion ordered by the court that Henry Taylor be appointed overseer
of the Road from Brushy fork to the state line and that the following
hands work under him To wit Robert Searoyes hands Edmund Taylors hands
Edwd. A. Lucyes hands Thomas Hester Lewis C. Taylor's hands Philip Dukes
hands Sam'l Davis Widow Radford's hands Zonas Bush & James Goyne-

(p-303) A Deed of Mortgage from Joseph Woolfolk to Cave Johnson for
certain property described therein was produced in open court and the
execution thereof duly acknowledged by the said Joseph Woolfolk to be his
act and deed for the purposes therein mentioned and on motion ordered to
be certified for Registration-

Ordered by the court that Mathew Ogburn be exonerated from attending as a
Jurror at this Term

On motion ordered by the court that Samuel White James N. Smith & Thomas
Brodie be appointed to mard and lay off the Road leading from the forks of
the Road two and a half miles from Moores mill and leading to intersect
the Saline old Road leading to the green Tree Grove that papers by John
Perry's to intersect said Road at or near the big meadow and that James N
Smith be appointed overseer of said Road-

This day was produced in open court the nuncupative will of Carter Marshall
decd. and was proven by the oaths of Josiah W. Fort and Richard Fortson who
prove that said will was written within three days after the death of
said Decd. and that the question was asked by said Josiah Fort and by him
reduced to writing at this dwelling house and that the said will is the
last will of the said Carter Marshall and on motion ordered to be Recorded

On motion ordered by the court that John H. Marable be exonerated from
the payment of Taxes on five four wheel carriages as is charged against
him on on the Tax list, the said charge should be for five Town lotts
and that he pay for five Town lotts instead of five four wheel carriages

(p-304)   GEORGE GRACE   )
                 VS   )   Case
           WILLIAM KILLEBREW)   This day came into court the parties 𝗑#/
                                 in this case and whereupon the same is
left to the arbitration of Hugh F. Bell Bright Herring Henry Small Charles
Bailey Stephen Pettis or a majority of them and their award to be the
Judgment of this court-

           JOSEPH FALKINGTON)
                 VS   )   Debt
           MATHEW DAUGHERTY)   This day came into court the Plaintiff by his
                                  attorney Frederick W. Huling and says he will
no further prosecute his suit but dismisses the same- Therefore it is
ordered by the court that the Defendant Mathew Dougherty go hence without day and recover of the Plaintiff Joseph Talkington the cost in this
behalf expended and that said suit stand dismissed-

           THOS. ALLISON   )
                 VS   )   Appeal
           SAMUEL C HAWKINS)   This day came into court Thomas Allison the Plaintiff
                                 in this and says he will no further prosecute his
𝗑𝗑𝗑𝗑 said suit but dismisses the same-
     Therefore it is ordered by the court that said suit stand dismissed
and that the Defendant Sam'l C Hawkins go hence without day and recover of
the Plaintiff the cost in this behalf expended-

           SAM'L M PUCKET & W M. P. PUCKET)
                 VS   )   Debt
           PETER P. PUCKET   )   This day came into court the Defend-
                                               ant Peter P Pucket & acknowledges
himself indebted to the Plaintiffs in the sum of one hundred and Thirty
one dollars thirty five cents Debt and the further sum of none dollars
and nineteen cents damages (p-305) sustained by reason of the detention
of said debt-
     Therefore it is considered by the court that the Plaintiffs Sam'l M
Pucket & William P Pucket recover of the Defendant Peter P Pucket the
sum of one hundred and forty dollars & fifty four cents the debt and
damages so confessed and the cost in this behalf expended-
Present - Joseph Woolfolk A.M. Rogers James Carr Charles Bailey W.R.
Gibeon Vale Allen Rich'd B. Blount Sterling Neblett William Trigg James
Barret Mathee Ryburn Thomas Smith Sam'l Smith Stephen Cooke Joshua P.
Vaughn Francis Carter Robert Vance Stephen Pettis & Francis Baker Esquires
Justices and after solemn proclamation the court proceeded to the Election
of County Register to fill the vacancy occasioned by the death of Peter
H. Cole and after balloting for the same and the votes being counted out
it appeared to the court that John Dicks had the number of Eighteen votes
more than a majority of all the Justices present-
     Therefore it is considered by the court that John Dicks is duly
elected as Register of Montgomery County and is ordered that he said
Dicks be appointed as such upon his giving Bond and security agreeable
to law-

Justices present as above and after solemn proclamation the court proceeded to the Election of County Trustee in the place of Henry Small resigned, and after balloting for the same and the votes being counted out there appeared a majority in favour of Edw'd H. Steele

Therefore it is considered by the court that Edwd H. Steele be appointed Trustee of Montgomery County upon his giving Bond and security agreeable to law-

(p-306)   MARTIN THOMAS   )
          VS   )   Debt
    SAM'L SMITH   )   This day came into court the Plaintiff by his
                            attorney and says he will no further prosecute
his suit but dismisses the same and the Defendant assumes the cost of suit-

Therefore it is considered by the court that said suit stand dismissed and that the Plaintiff recover of the Defendant the costs in this behalf expended-

Court adjourned untill Tomorrow 9 O'clock-

                        Wm. Trigg
                        Abner Harris
                        J.P.Vaughn

The worshipful court of Montgomery County have met according to adjournment October 22nd 1823

          Present Wm. Trigg   )
               Joshua P. Vaughn) E squires
               Abner Harris   ) Justices

ROBERT G. JOHNSON   )
       VS   )   Debt
  JESSE CRAFT &   )   This day came said plaintiff by his attorney
JOHN H. MARRABLE   )   & thereupon John H. Marrable asse of said
                        defendants being solemnly called to plead &
defend this suit came not and thereupon came a jury of good and lawful men to wit Henry C Taylor Thomas Carraway Frederick Rudolph William Peay Charles P. Robertson Jeffry Sims Valentine Powers Thomas Merriwether William Brantly Elijah Lewis Mark Booth John W. Usery who being duly elected tried & sworn to well & truly the Issues Joined between the said plaintiff and one of said defendants Jesse Craft on their oath do say they find the Issue in favor of the Pltff. that said defendant doth not owe said plaintiff the sum of one hundred & eighty six dollars & they asses the plaintiffs damage by reason of the detention of said debt to Eight dollars & twenty five cents- (p-307) It is therefore considered by the court that said plaintiff recover of said defendants Jesse Craft & John H. Marrable said sum of one hundred & Eighty six dollars the debt aforesaid as also the further sum of Eight dollars & twenty five cents the damages aforesaid in form aforesaid assessed & his costs by him about his suit in this behalf expended &c-

A Deed of conveyance from Andrew Walker to Henry Minor for twenty five acres of Land was produced in open court and the execution thereof was acknowledged by the said Andrew Walker to be his act and Deed for the purpose therein named and on motion ordered to be certified for Registration-

The commissioners appointed at the last term of this court to settle with John W. Barker administrator of John Adams Decd. make their report to this court and on motion ordered to be Recorded-

A Deed of conveyance from Francis McMurdy to Amos Hatcher for one hundred acres of land was produced in open court and the Execution thereof duly proven by the oaths of John Dicks and John Caldwell the subscribing witnesses thereto and on motion ordered to be certified for Registration-

This day came into court John Dicks and entered into Bond and security satisfactory to the court as Register of Montgomery County and it is ordered by the court that the same be Recorded and the said Dicks was qualified agreeable to law-

This day was produced in open court the last will and Testament of Sam'l Creath Decd. and there being no witnesses subscribed (p-308) thereto ordered by the court that John B. Rice and Elisha Clark be permitted to qualify as to the hand writing of the said Sam'l Creath and the said John B. Rice and Elisha Clark came into court and swore that the name subscribed to the said will was the hand writing of the said Samuel Creath and on motion ordered to be Recorded-

JOHN P IRWIN & CO)
VS) Case
WOOLFOLK & GOULD) This day came into court the Plaintiffs by their
attorney Cave Johnson Esquire and says he will
no further prosecute their said suit but dismisses the same-

Therefore it is considered by the court that the Defendants Woolfolk & Gould go hence without day and recover of thePlaintiffs the costs in this behalf expended-

FRANCIS CONNER)
VS) Debt
STEPHEN PETTIS &) This day came into court the parties by their
JNO. H. MARABLE) attornies and thereupon came a Jury of good
and lawful men to wit Henry Taylor Thomas
Carraway Frederick Rudolph William Peay Charles P. Robertson Jeffrey Sims Valentine Powers Thomas Merriwether William Brantly Elijah Lewis Mark Booth & John W. Ussery who being duly elected tried & sworn the truth to speak upon the issue Joined upon their oaths do say that the Defendants doth owe to the Plaintiff the sum of one hundred and three dollars the Debt in the declaration mentioned and the further sum of three three dollars (p-309) and fifty cents damates sustained by reason of the detention of of said debt-

Therefore it is considered by the court that the Plaintiff Francis Conner recover of the Defendants Stephen Pettis and John H Marable the sum of one hundred & six dollars and fifty cents the Debt and damages so assessed by the Jury in form aforesaid together with the cost in this behalf expended-

FRANCIS MCMURDY)
VS) Debt
CHARLES BAILEY) This day came into court the Parties by their
attornies and thereupon came a Jury of good

of good and lawful men to wit Henry Ta lor Thomas Carraway Frederick
Rudolph William Peay Charles P. Robertson Jeffrey Sims Valenting Powers
Thomas Merriwether William Brantly Elijah Lewis Mark Booth & John W
Ussery who boing duly elected tried and sworn the truth to speak upon
the issues joined upon their oath do say that they find the issues in
favour of the Plaintiff that the Defendant doth owe to the Plaintiff the
sum of six hundred and forty one dollars and sixty three cents the Debt
in the Declaration mentioned and the further sum of fifty five dollars
& fifty cents damages sustained by reason of the detention of said debt-

Therefore it is considered by the court that the Plaintiff Francis
McMurdy recover of the Defendant Charles Bailey the sum of six six hundred
and ninety seven dollars and thirteen cents the Debt and damages so assessed by the Jury in form aforesaid together with his costs by him
about his suit in this behalf expended-

(p-3p0) The commissioners appointed at the last Term of this court to
divide and lay off the lands of William Barton and Wilson Senderline
agreeable to the petition of the said parties make their report to this
court and on motion ordered to be Recorded-

A Bill of sale from Sam'l Smith to Polly B. Hatcher for negro Boy John
was prosuced in open court and the execution thereof duly acknowledged
by the said Sam'l Smith to be his act and Deed for the purposes therein
mentioned and on motion ordered to be Recorded-

Andrew Walker returns into court his Tax list for the present year and
on motion ordered that the same be allowed-

On motion ordered by the court that William Peay be exonerated from the
payment of a Tax on three four wheel carriages as is charged against him
on the present years tax list and that he pay for three Black poles
instead of three four wheel carriages-

KERCHEVALL & BAYLISS)
   VS   ) Debt
ASHBELL BRUNSON   ) This day came into court the parties by
          their attornies and thereupon came a Jury
of good and lawful men to wit Henry C Taylor Thomas Carraway Frederick
Rudolph William Peay Charles P. Robertson Jeffrey Sims Valentine Bowers
Thomas Merriwether William Brantly Elijah Lewis Mark Booth & John W. Ussery
who being duly elected tried and sworn the truth to speak upon the issue
joined upon their oaths do say that they find the issue in favour of the
Plaintiffs that the Defendant (p-311) doth owe to the Plaintiffs the
sum of One hundred and Eleven Dollars and fifry cents the debt in the
declaration mentioned and the further sum of Five dollars thirty seven
& one half cents damages sustained by reason of the detention of said
Debt - Therefore it is considered by the court that the Plaintiffs
recover of the Defendant the sum of One hundred and sixteen dollars
Eighty seven and One half cents the Debt and damages so assessed by the
Jury in form aforesaid together with his cost by him about his suit in
this behalf espended-

NO PAGE 186

SAM'L & JOHN KERCHEVAL)
    VS   ) Debt
ASHBELL BRUNSON   ) This day came the parties by their attor-
            nies and thereupon came a Jury of good
and lawful men to wit Henry C Taylor Thomas Carraway Frederick Rudolph
William Peay Charles P. Robertson Jeffrey Sims Valentine Powers Thomas
Merriwether William Brently Elijah Lewis Mark Booth & John W. Ussery who
being duly elected tried and sworn the truth to speak upon the issue
joined upon their oaths do say that they find the issue in favour of
the Plaintiffs that the Defendant doth owe to the Plaintiffs the sum of
Forty Eight Dollars & Twenty five cents damages sustained by reason of
the detention of said Debt—
  Therefore it is considered by the court that the Plaintiff recover
of the Defendant the sum of five hundred and Eighteen dollars (p-312)
and Twenty five cents the debt & damages so assessed by the Jury in form
aforesaid together with their costs by them about their suit in this
behalf expended—

THOMAS W ATKINSON)
   VS   ) Debt
ELLINOR SHELBY   ) This day came into court the parties by their
           attorneyies and thereupon came a Jury of
good and lawful men to wit Henry C Taylor Thomas Carraway Thomas Carraway
Frederick Rudolph William Peay Charles P. Robertson Jeffrey Sims Valentine
Powers Thomas Merriwether William Brantly Elijah Lewis Mark Booth &
John W. Ussery who being duly elected tried & sworn the truth to speak
upon the issue joined upon their oaths do say that they find the issue
in favour of the Plaintiff that the Defendant Ellenor Shelby doth owe to
the Plaintiff Thos. W. Atkinson the sum of one hundred and sixty six
dollars eleven and one half cents the Debt in the declaration mentioned
and the further sum of five dollars & seventy five cents damages sustained
by reason of the detention of said Debt—
  Therefore it is considered by the court that the Plaintiff Thomas
W. Atkinson recover of the Defendant Ellinor Shelby the sum of one
hundred and seventy one dollars and Eighty six and a half cents the debt
and damages so assessed by the Jury in form aforesaid together with his
cost by him about his suit in this behalf expended—

DAVID NORTHINGTON ASSEE*)
    VS   ) Debt
ANDREW PETERSON   ) This day came the Parties by their attor-
          nies and (p-313) thereupon came a Jury
of good and lawful men to wit Henry C Taylor Thomas Carraway Frederick
Rudolph William Peay Charles P. Robertson Jeffrey Sims Valentine Powers
Thomas Merriwether William Brantley Elijah Lewis Mark Booth & John W.
Ussery who being duly elected tried and sworn the truth to speak upon the
issue joined upon their oaths do say that they find the issue infavour
of the Plaintiff that the Defendant doth owe to the Plaintiff the sum of
Two hundred and fifty dollars the debt mentioned in the declaration and
the further sum of five dollars damages sustained by reason of the detention
of said debt—
  Therefore it is considered by the court that the Plaintiff David Northington assee as aforesaid recover of the Defendant Andrew Peterson the

sum of Two hundred and fifty five dollars the Debt and damages so assessed by the Jury in form aforesaid together with his cost by him about his suit in this behalf expended-

R.G. JOHNSON & A.V. HAMPTON)
VS) Appeal
AMBROSE MADISON) This day came the Parties by their attornies and thereupon came a Jury of good and lawful men to wit Henry C Taylor Thomas Carraway & Frederick Rudolph William Peay Charles P Robertson Jefferson Sims Valentine Powers Thomas Merriwether William Brantley Elijah Lewis Mark Booth & John W. Ussery who being duly elected tried and sworn the truth to speak upon the matter of controversey between the parties upon their oaths do say that they (p-314) find for the Defendant-

Therefore it is considered by the court that the Defendant Ambrose Madison be hence discharged and recover of the Robt. G. Johnson surviving administrator for the cost in this behalf expended -

JESSE SULLIVANT GUARDIAN)
VS) Case
WILLIAM SULLIVANT &) This day came the parties by their
WILSON SULLIVANT) attornies and thereupon came a Jury of good and lawful men to wit Henry C Taylor Thomas Carraway Frederick Rudolph William Peay Charles P. Robertson Jeffrey Sims Valentine Powers Thomas Merriwether William Brantly Elijah Lewis Mark Booth & John W Ussery who being duly elected tried & sworn the truth to speak upon the issue joined upon their oaths do say that they find for the Plaintiff and do assess his damages to forty five Dollars for the several non performances & undertakings in the Plaintiffs declaration mentioned-

Therefore it is considered by the court that the Plaintiff Jesse Sullivant Guardian as aforesaid recover of the Defendants William Sullivant & Wilson Sullivant the said sum of forty five dollars the damages so assessed by the Jury in form aforesaid and the cost in this behalf expended-

State of TENNESSEE)
VS) Sci Fa
ROBERT NOWLAND & OTHERS) This day came into court Robert Nowland and renders his excuse on oath for non attendance as a Juror at the January Term 1823 and for reasons satisfactory to the (p-315) court it is ordered that the fine assessed against him for non attendance as aforesaid be set aside and that said Nowland pay the cost that has accrued in this behalf expended and that a fieri facias issue accordingly-

STATE)
VS) Sci fa
JOHN WYATTE) This day came into court John Wyatte and on oath renders his excuse for non attendance as a Juror at the January Term 1823 and for reasons satisfactory to the court it is ordered that the fine assessed against him for non attendance as aforesaid be set aside and that said Wyatt pay the cost that has accrued in this behalf expended-

ANTHONY W VANLIER & CO)
VS) Appeal
B/URRELL M WILLIAMSON) This day came into Court Stephen Eleazer
and renders an excuse for non attendance
as a witness at the July Term 1823 of this court in the case of Jesse Sullivant against William Porter on the part of said Sullivant and for reasons
appearing satisfactory to the court it is ordered that the fine assessed
against him at said July Term 1823 be set aside and that Jesse Sullivant
pay the cost in this behalf expended-

STERLING NEBLETT)
VS) Debt
JOHN J BELL) This day came into court the parties by their
attornies and thereupon all and (p-316) singular
the matters and things arising in law upon the defendants demurrer to the
plaintiffs declaration being heard and by the court here fully understood
and it appearing to the court that the matters arising in law upon said
demurrer are not sufficient to bar the plaintiff from having and maintaining his action-

Therefore it is considered by the court that the Plaintiff Sterling
Neblett recover of the Defendant John J Bell the sum of six hundred and
forty three dollars the Debt in the declaration mentioned and the further
sum of thirty two dollars and fifteen cents damages sustained by reason
of the detention of said debt and the cost in this behalf expended-

Court adjourned untill Tomorrow morning 9 O'clock

Wm. Trigg
J.P. Vaughn
Abner Harris

The Worshipful Court of Montgomery County have met according to adjournment October 24th 1823-

Present Wm. Trigg
Joshua P. Vaughn
Abner Harris

MARY WAGERS)
VS) Debt
ANDREW LYNN &) This day came the parties by their attornies and
SIMON HEFLIN) thereupon came (p-317) a Jury of good and law-
ful men to wit Henry C. Taylor Thomas Carraway
Frederick Rudolph William Peay Charles B. Robertson Jeffrey Sims Valentine
Powers Thomas Merriwether William Brantley Elijah Lewis & Mark Booth who
being duly elected tried and sworn the truth to speak upon the issue joined
upon their oaths do say that they find the issue infavour of the Plaintiff
that the Defendants doth owe to the plaintiff the sum of one hundred and
Twenty five dollars the debt in the declaration mentioned and the further
sum of seventeen dollars and fifty cents damages sustained by reason of
thedetention of said debt-

Therefore it is considered by the court that the Plaintiff recover
of the Defendant the sum of one hundred and forty two dollars and fifty
cents the debt and damages so assessed by the Jury in form aforesaid together with the cost in this behalf expended-

HUGH & JAMES MCCLURE)
VS) Debt
CHARLES D MCLEAN) This day came the parties by their attornies

and thereupon came a Jury of good and lawful men to wit George W. Blanks
James Trotter Jefferson Weakley Washington Lee Nathaniel Thaxton Levi
P. Allen Jesse Bailey Ambrose Martin Robert Bumpass Uriah Humphreys James
Bumpass Uriah Humphreys James Hubbard & James Trice who being duly
elected tried andsworn the truth to speak upon the issue joined upon
their oaths do say that they find the issue in favour of the Plaintiffs
that the Defendant doth owe to the Plaintiffs the sum of Two hundred and
thirteen Dollars and thirty six cents the debt in the (p-318) declaration
mentioned and the further sum of Ten dollars and sixty six cents damages
sustained by reason of the detention of said debt-

  Therefore it is considered by the court that the Plaintiffs recover
of the Defendants the sum of Two hundred and Twenty four dollars and two
cents the Debt and damages so assessed by the Jury in form aforesaid together
with their cost by them about their suit in this behalf expended-

  HENRY GARDNER)
    VS   ) Appeal
  JOHN BELL) This day came into court the Plaintiff by his
         attorney James B Reynolds Esquire and says he
will no further prosecute his said suit but dismisses the same-

  Therefore it is considered by the court that the Defendant John Bell
go hence without day and recover of the Plaintiff the cost in this behalf expended-

  WILLIAM FITZGERALD)
  & WIFE ELIZABETH FITZGERALD) Case
) This day came into court the Parties by
         their attornies & thereupon this cause
is transferred by consent of the Circuit Court for trial to be had thereon

  OREN D BATTLE FOR THE USE OF J.W. FORT)
     VS   ) Covenant Broken
  JOHN PATTON   ) This day came the parties by
           their attornies and thereupon
came a Jury of good and lawful men to wit James Trotter Jefferson Weakley
Washington Lee Nathl. Thaxton Levi P. Allen Jesse Bailey Ambrose Martin
Robert Bumpass Uriah Humphreys (p-319) George W Blanks James Hubbard &
James Trice who being duly elected tried and sworn the truth to speak upon the matter of controversy between the parties upon their oaths do say
that they find for the plaintiffs and do assess his damages to two hundred and seventy six dollars for the several sd. non performances &
undertakings in the Plaintiffs declaration mentioned-

  Therefore it is considered by the court that the Plaintiff recover
of the Defendant the said sum of Two hundred and seventy six dollars so
assessed by the Jury in form aforesaid together with his cost by him
about his suit in this behalf expended-

  DAVID ANDERSON BENEFIT)
  OF JAMES SMITH   )
     VS   ) Case
  JOHN BRODIE   ) This day came into court the parties by
         their attornies and thereupon this cause
is continued on affidavit of Defendant upon due payment of the cost of
this Form-

STATE OF TENNESSEE)
    VS)   Riot
JOHN EDWARDS)   This day came the soliciter General in behalf
    of the state and the Defendnnt in proper
person and was thereupon arraigned and upon his arraignment plead guilty
to the Bill of Indictment and submits to the court and after the evidence
being heard it is considered by the court that the Defendant be fined the
sum of one cent/ and that he pay the cost of this prosecution - Therefore
it is considered by the court that the state of Tennessee recover of the
Defendant the fine and cost as aforesaid & that a fiere facias issue
accordingly -

(p-320)   STATE OF TENNESSEE)
    VS)   Riot
    NEEDHAM B FARRIER)   This day came the soliciter General in
    behalf of the state and the Defendant in
proper person & was thereupon arraigned and upon his arraignment pleads
guilty to the Bill of Indictment and submits to the court and after the
Evidence being heard it is consid red by the court that the Defendant
be fined the sum of Five dollars and that he pay the cost of this prosecution
Therefore it is considered by the court that the State of Tennessee recover
of the Defendant the fine and costs as aforesaid and that a fiere facias
issue accordingly-

STATE OF TENNESSEE)
    VS)   Debt
WILLIAM DIKAS)
    This day came the Soliciter General in behalf
    of the state and the Defendant in proper per-
son and was thereupon arraigned and upon his arraignment plead guilty to
the Bill of Indictment and submits to the court and after the evidence
being heard it is considered by the court that the Defendant be fined the
sum of five dollars and that he pay the cost of this prosecution-
    Therefore it is considered by the court that the State of Tennessee
recover of the Defendant the fine and cost as aforesaid and that a fiere
facias issue accordingly-

STATE OF TENNESSEE)
    VS)   Riot
WILLIAM GENTRY)   This day came the soliciter General on behalf
    of the state and the (p-321) Defendant in
proper person and was thereupon arraigned and upon his arraignment pleads
guilty to the Bill of Indictment and submits to the court and after the
evidence being heard it is considered by the court that the Defendant be
fined the sum of one cent/ and that he pay the cost of this prosecution
Therefore it is considered by the court that the state Of Tennessee
recover of the Defendant the fine and cost as aforesaid and that a fiere
facias issue accordingly -

STATE OF TENNESSEE)
    VS)   Riot
JAMES W. CARVER)

This day came the Solicitor General in behalf of the state and the Defendant in proper person and was thereupon arraigned and upon his arraignment plead guilty to the Bill of Indictment and submits to the court and after the evidence being heard ## it is considered by the court that the Defendant be fined the sum of one cent and the cost of this prosecution -

Therefore it is considered by the court that the State of Tennessee recover of the Defendant the fine and costs as aforesaid and that a fiere fafcias issue accordingly-

STATE OF TENNESSEE)
VS) Riot
ELI DIKAS)

This day came the Solicitor General in behalf of the State and the Defendant in proper person and was thereupon arraigned and upon his arraignment plead guilty to the Bill of Indictment and submits to the court and after the evidence being heard it is considered by the court that the Defendant be fined the (p-322) sum of one cent and that he pay the cost of this prosecution-

Therefore it is considered by the court that State of Tennessee recover of the Defendant the fine and costs as aforesaid and that a fiere facias issue accordingly-

This day was produced in open court a Bill of sale from Benjamin King to be his act and deed for the purposes therein mentioned and on motion ordered to be Recorded-

This day Edward H. Steele entered into Bond & security as County Treasurer and thereupon it is considered by the court that the security is sufficient and that the same be allowed and the said Edward H Steele took the oath prescribed by law-

STATE OF TENNESSEE)
VS)
JOHN DAVIE) Peace Warrant

This day came the Solicitor General in behalf of the state and the Defendant in proper person and was thereupon arraigned and upon his arraignment plead not guilty to the Bill of Indictment and for his trial puts himself upon his country as does the solicitor General likewise and thereupon came a Jury of good and lawful men to wit David Anderson Thomas Carraway Samuel Haggard William Trammell Richard Jones Henry C Taylor Solomon Grasse Rice Coleman Frederick Rudolph Jesse Bailey Charles P Robertson & Sam'l Smith who being duly elected the Trugh to Speak upon the issue of Traverse upon their oaths do say that the Defendant (p-323) ## ## John Davie is not guilty in manner & form as is charged in the Bill of Indictment-

Therefore it is considered by the court that the Defendant John Davie go hence & be discharged and that William Cooper the prosecutor be taxed with the prosecution of this cause - & that a fiere facias issue for the same-

STATE)
  VS) Sci fa
MOSES OLDHAM) This day came the solicitor General in behalf of the
      state and it appearing satisfactorily to the court here
that the said Moses Oldham was not a citizen of the County at the time of
his appointment as Juror to this court - It is therefore considered by the
the court that the forfeiture and fine aforesaid be set aside and that
the county pay the costs in this behalf expended-

STATE)
  VS) Sci fa
MOSES OLDHAM) This day came the solicitor General in behalf of the
     state and it appearing satisfactorily to the court
here that the said Moses Oldham was not a citizen of the County at the
time of his appointment as Juror to this court - It is therefore considered
by the court that the forfeiture and fine aforesaid be set aside and that
the county pay the costs in this behalf expended-

STATE)
  VS) Sci fa
WILLIAM BLAIR) upon motion of the Defendant it appearing to the court
     that William Blair was the overseer of one of the
public roads in the county at the time of his appointment as a Juror-
It is thereupon ordered by the court that the fine heretofore entered
against said Blair as a delinquent juror be set aside & that the county
pay the costs in this behalf expended-

STATE)
  VS) Upon motion of the Solicitor Gen'l & by the permission
JAMES KING) of the court a nolle prosique is permitted to be entered
     in this case & thereupon the Defd't assumes all costs
It is therefore considered by the court that the state recover of the De-
fendant the costs in this behalf expended-

JOSEPH BARBEE)
  VS) This day came the Defendant by his atto. and the
GEORGE W.L.MAIR) plaintiff Joseph Barbee being solemnly called to
     come into court & prosecute his said suit failed
so to do - It is therefore considered by the court that the Defendant go
hence without day and recover of the plaintiff the costs in this behalf
expended-

(p-324) CHARLES P ROBERTSON)
    VS) By the consent of the parties it is ordered
   RALPH CUSHMAN) by the court that the said parties have
      leave to take Depositions out of the State
by giving Twenty days notice & in the state by giving Ten days notice-

ELIZABETH VANCE)
   VS   )
MARGARET L VANCE)
MORGAN B VANCE)
WILLIAM L B VANCE)
ELIZABETH VANCE)

v & Samuel Vance heirs at law of) Petition for Dower
Samuel Vance Deceased   )   This day came into court the petitioner
                        by her attorney & filed her petition
for Dower whereupon it being suggested to the court that the defendants
are all infants under the age of Twenty one years & that the petitioner
is their regular guardian it is ordered that Jo/el C. Rice be & he is
hereby appointed guardian for said defendants to appear & defend this
suit for them & on their behalf-

Court adjourned untill tomorrow 9' O'clock-
                            Wm. Trigg
                            J.P. Vaughn
                            Abner Harris

The Worshipful court of Montgomery County have met according to adjournment October 25th 1824- Present-

       WILLIAM & ALEXR. MCCLURE)
              VS   ) motion
       ABRAHAM MCCORKLE   ) This day came the Plaintiffs by their
                        Attorney and says he will no further
prosecute his said suit but dismisses the same -
Therefore it is considered by the court that the Defendant Abraham
McCorkle (p-325) go hence without day and recover of the Plaintiffs
in this behalf expended-

       ALEXANDER MCCORKLE)
             VS   ) Motion
       ABRAHAM MCCORKLE   ) This day the Plaintiff by his attorney
                        Alexander McClure and says he will no fur-
ther prosecute his said suit but dismisses the same -
Therefore it is considered by the court that the Defendant go hence
without day and recover of the Plaintiff the cost in this behalf expended

       DAVID ANDERSON   )
             VS   ) Case
       JESSE COBB   ) This day the parties by their attornies and
                        thereupon came a Jury of good and lawful men
to wit Haydon E. Wells Thos. Carraway Henry C. Taylor Frederick Rudolph
Dorrell Y. Harris James Hambleton James Hutcheson Charles P Robertson
Eli Lockert William Hust John Hampton & Robert Nelson who being duly
elected tried and sworn the truth to speak upon the matters of controversy
between the parties upon their oaths do say that they find for the
Plaintiff and do assess his damages to one hundred and forty four dollars
and ninety cents for the several non performances and undertakings in
the Plaintiffs declaration mentioned-
    Therefore it is considered by the court that the Plaintiff recover
of the Defendant the said sum of One hundred and forty four dollars and
ninety cents the damages so assessed by the Jury in form aforesaid and
the cost in this behalf expended-

(p-326)   JOSEPH COOK   )
               VS   ) Covenant Broken
        FRANKLIN SAUNDERS)

This day the parties by their attornies and thereupon came a Jury of good and lawful men to wit James Trotter John Barton Jefferson Weakley Washington Lee Nathaniel Thaxton Levi P Allen Jesse Bailey Ambrose Martin Robert Bumpass Uriah Humphreys George W. Blands James Hubbard who being duly elected tried and sworn the truth to speak upon the issue joined upon their oaths do say that they do find the issues in favour of the Plaintiff and do assess his damages to six hundred and fifty eight dollars and thirty nine cents by reason of the non performance of the covenant in the plaintiffs declaration mentioned-

~~Therefore it is considered by the court that the Plaintiff Joseph Cook recover of the Defendant Franklin Saunders the said sum of Six Hundred and fifty eight dollars and thirty nine cents and the costs in this behalf expended~~

GEORGE B HOBSON)
    VS   ) Case
SEPTEMUS WILLIAMS) This day came the parties by their attornies and thereupon by consent of parties this cause is transfered to the Circuit Court for trial to be had thereon-

On motion order ordered by the court that David Anderson a Juror in the case of the State of Tennessee against Stephen G. Stewart be allowed for three days attendance and that the County Trustee pay the same out of any monies in his hand not otherwise appropriated-

(p-327) JOHN EDMONSTON)
            VS   ) Trespass
      MARK THOMASON) This day came into court the Plaintiff by his attorney and says he will no further prosecute his said suit but dismisses the same - Therefore it is considered by the court that the Defendant go hence without day and recover of the Plaintiff the costs in this behalf expended-

SAME)
 VS   ) Case
SAME) This day came the plaintiff by his attorney and says he will no further prosecute his said suit but dismisses the same-
Therefore it is considered by the court that the Defendant go hence without day and recover of the Plaintiff the cost in this behalf expended

GEORGE W BLANKS)
    VS   ) Covenant Broken
ALFRED M. SHELBY) This day came the Plaintiff by his attorney and sayd he will not further prosecute his said suit but dismisses the same- Therefore it is considered by the court that the Defendant go hence without day and recover of the Plaintiff the cost in this behalf expended-

The Grand Jury appeared in open court & returned a Bill of Presentment the State of Tennessee against John Barker as overseer of a Road a true Bill - Also appeared in open court and returned a Bill of presentment the State of Tennessee against James Hollis as an overseer of a Road - A True Bill -

(p-328) WILSON GIBSON &   )
         JOHN HAMPTON ADMR)
              VS   )
         RICE COLEMAN   ) Certiorari & Superceedeas
) This day came the parties by their attornies
                                and thereupon all & singular the matters &
things arising on the plaintiffs motion to dismiss being fully heard and
understood - It is considered by the court that the said certiorari be
dismissed it is also further considered by the court that the said
Certiorari be dismissed and it is also further considered by the court
that the said plaintiffs recover of the said Rice Coleman & on motion
also of Charles Bailey his securities for the said certiorari the sum
of Twenty seven dollars & Eighty three cts. the amount of the judgment
below and interest thereon from the 20th day of Augt. 1823 the date of
the judgment below and also the costs in this behalf expended-

         JOSEPH WOOLFOLK   )
              VS   ) This day came the parties by their attornies &
         JESSE OLDHAM   ) thereupon came a jury of good & lawful men to
                                wit James Trotter Jno. Barton Jefferson Weakley
Washington Lee Nathl. Thaxton Levi P Allen Jesse Bailey Ambrose Martin
Robt Bumpass Uriah Humphries Geo. W. Blands & James Hubbard who being
duly elected tried & sworn the truth to speak upon the issue joined upon
their oaths do say that they find the issue in behalf of the plaintiff
and they find for the pltff, his debt in the Decl. mentioned the sum
of Four hundred & twenty dollars and also the sum of Twenty one dollars
for the detention of said Debt - It is therefore considered by the court
that the said plaintiff recover of the Defendant the aforesaid sum of
Four hundred & forty one dollars the debt & damages as aforesaid and also
the costs in this behalf expended-

(p-329) JONATHAN JOHNSON   )
              VS   ) Sci fa
         THE HEIRS OF PHILIP) This day came the plaintiff by his attorney
         JOHNSON DECD   ) & it appearing to the court that a Scire
                                Facias had heretofore issued against the
heirs of Philip Johnson Decd. & that the same had been returned that
William Nelson & Wife Mary Bernard Reynolds & Wife Lucy Mille Stephens
James Shackleford & wife Sally Henry Hodges & wife Sally Henry Hodges
& wife Nancy Robert Goodloe & wife Agnes were not found in his county
and are not inhabitants of the state of Tennessee and an alias having
issued and the same returned being made thereon by the sheriff of
Montgomery County and the said Scire facias having been executed on
Robert G. Johnson John Johnson Whitfield Killebrew & wife Fanny and on
William Killebrew the guardian of George W. Killebrew & on Robert G.
Johnson Guardian of John Johnson and they having failed to answer or
plead to the said scire facias - It is therefore considered by the
court that the said Jonathan Johnson recover of the aforesaid Defendants
the sum of Two hundred & forty five dollars & fourteen three fourth cents
the amount of the aforesaid judgment and also the sum of seven dollars
& Thirty five cents interest since the rendition of the aforesaid
judgments & also the costs aforesaid & the costs in this behalf expended
to be levied of the real estate of Philip Johnson Decd. that has descended
to the aforesaid Defendant as his heirs at law so that the judgment against
the admr as aforesaid of Philip Johnson Decd. may be satisfied out of the

real estate of the said Philip Johnson that has descended to his ~~heirs~~ heirs as aforesaid-

THE EXECUTORS OF SAM'L VANCE)
    VS   ) Sci fa
ISAAC H LANIER ADMR   ) This day came the parties by attornies
             & thereupon came a jury of good &
lawful men to wit George W Blanks James Trotter John Barton Jefferson
Weakley Washington Lee Nathaniel Thaxton Lewis P Allen (p-330) Jesse
Baily Ambrose Martin Robert Bumpass Uriah Humphreys James Hubbart who
being duly elected tried & sworn the truth to speak on the issue joined
on their oath do say that they find the issues in favor of the plaintiffs
& say that there remains in his hands unadministered one hundred &
forty two dollars & two cents being the amt. of the judgt. & interest-
Therefore it is considered by the court that the plaintiff recover against
the defendant the sum of one hundred & two dollars & fifty cents the
debt in said Sciere Facias Specified with interest thereon from the
day of April 1820 untill paid as also the sum of $ costs of former
suit as also as well his costs expended in suing forth & prosecuting
this writ of Sci Fa to be levied of the goods & chattles rights &
credits which were of said Burwell C Lanier at his death & which have
come to the hands of sued deft. as his admr. to be administered
If so much there is If nor then the costs of this writ to be levied of
his proper goods & chattles &c-

WILSON GIBSON & JOHN HAMPTON ADMR)
     VS   ) Certiorari & Superceedeas
RICE COLEMAN   ) This day came the parties by
             their attornies & thereupon all
and singular the matters and things arising on the plaintiffs motion to
dismiss being fully heard and fully understood, it is considered by the
court that the said Certiorari be set aside and it is also further considered by the court that the said Plaintiffs recover of the Defendant
Rice Coleman and on motion also against Charles ~~Bailey his~~ security
for the said Certrorari the sum of forty two dollars or thereabouts the
amount of the Judgment and Interest thereon from 20th day of Augt 1823
the date of the Judgment aforesaid and also the cost in this behalf
expended-

(p-331) WILSON GIBSON & JOHN HAMPTON ADMRS)
      VS   ) Certeorari
RICE COLEMAN   ) This day came their Parties
             & thereupon all and singular
the matters & things arising on the Plaintiffs motion to dismiss being
fully heard and understood - it is considered by the court that the
said Certiorari be set aside and it is also further considered by the
court that the said plaintiffs recover of the Defendant Rice Coleman and
on motion also against Charles Bailey his security for said Certiorari
the sum of Two dollars and Twenty five cents of thereabouts the amt.of
the Judgment and Interest thereon from 20th day of Augt, 1823 the date
of the Judgment aforesaid and also the cost in this behalf expended-

STERLING NEBLETT ADMR)
      VS   )   To the judgment of the court given on the
JOHN J BELL   )   hearing of this cause the Deft. being dis-
                    satisfied prays an appeal in nature of writ

of error & having given bond the same is allowed

Court adjourned till tomorrow nine OBclock

                        Isaac /Dennison
                        P.B.Blount
                        A.M.Rogers

JOSEPH COOK)
    VS   )
FRANKLIN SAUNDERS)

The Worshipful court of Montgomery County have met according to adjournment October 26th 1823-
               Present-

(p-332) JOSEPH COOK   )
          VS   ) Covenant
        FRANKLIN SAUNDERS) This day came the parties by their attornies
                      whereupon all and singular the matters &
things in the plaintiffs demurrer to the defendants second fourth fifth
& sixth pleas being heard & fully understood it is considered by the court
here that the demurrer to sd. pleas be sustained-

    It is therefore considered by the court that the Plaintiff recover
of the defendant the sum of six hundred & fifty eight dollars & thirty
nine cents the damages by the jury assessed as also his costs about his
suit in this behalf expended-

    ELIZABETH VANCE   )
         VS   ) Petition for dower
    THE HEIRS AT LAW   ) On motion it is ordered by the court that the
    OF SAM'L VANCE DECD) sheriff summon a jury of twelve men to lay off
                      the dower of Elizabeth Vance to the following
tracts of land to wit - One Tract of land containing 214 acres lying on
McAdo Creek deeded by Benjamin King Sheriff to Samuel Vance on the 21st
day of April 1821 also one other tract containing 640 acres lying on the
aforesaid McAdo Creek Deeded by John Neblett sheriff to said Sam'l
Vance on the 23rd day of October 1819 also one othertract of land containing 100 acres and lying on Yellow Creek deeded by the aforesaid John
Neblett sheriff to the said Samuel Vance on the 23rd day of October 1819
also one other tract containing 40 acres of land lying on the north
side of Cumberland River and on the south side of Red River deeded to
the said Sam'l Vance by John Neblett Jury (p-333) Edward Neblett Benjamin Neblett & Henry H Bryan on the 1st day of November 1821 also a
part of one lott in the Twon of Charlkville known and distinguished in
the plan of said Twon No. 66 Deeded by Henry H. Bryan and Ashbell
Brunson to said Samuel Vance on the 1st day of November 1821 and also
three others in the addition of said Twon known and distinguished in the
plan thereof by Nos. 54 & 53 & 52 One half of lott No. 74 - and make
report to the next Term of this court-

A Deed of conveyance from David Smith to C.H.P. Marr for one hundred
and sixty acres of land in the Illinoise was produced in open court and

and the execution thereof duly proven / by the oaths of Chs D. McLean & Isaac Dennison subscribing witnesses thereto and on motion ordered to be certified-

A Deed of conveyance from Sam'l Lynes to Joel C. Rice for part of Town Lotts in the Town of Clarksville Nos. 13 & 14 was produced in open court and the execution thereof duly acknowledged by the said Sam'l Lynes to be $ his act and deed for the purposes therin mentioned and on motion ordered to be certified for Registration -

A Deed of conveyance from Joseph White Margaret Bailey Mary Bailey Sarah Elliott & ony Bailey of the county of Perquimans & State of North Carolina to Wilson Sanderline for certain Tracts of land therein specified was prod/uced in open court by the said Wilson Saunderline and it appearing to the court that said Deed of Conveyance was acknowledged by Joseph White & Ony Bailey two of the Grantors therein mentioned in the Court of pleas and quarter sessions for Perquimans County & State (p-334) of North Carolina and that Joseph Jones and Benjamin Winslow the subscribing witnesses thereto proved the execution of said Deed of conveyance as to Margaret Bailey & Sarah Elliott all of which being regularly certified by John Wood clerk of the Court of Pleas and quarter sessions for said County of Perquimans & State of North Carolina it is ordered by the court that the same be certified for Registration-

A Deed of Conveyance from James Bowers Senr. & James Bowers Junr. for Eighty three acres of land was produced in open court and the execution thereof duly proven by the oaths of John Bowers & Joseph Bowers the subscribing witnesses thereto & on motion ordered to be certified for Registration -

On motion ordered by the court that letters of administration issue to John W. Prouty on the Estate of John Boutell Decd. Whereupon the said John W. Prouty entered into Bond & security satisfactory to the to the court and qualified agreeable to law-

On motion ordered by the court that Francis Baker & Joseph Herel be furnished with letters of adinistration on the Estate of Stephen G. Jones whereupon the said Francis Baker and Joseph Hewel entered into Bond & security satisfactory to the court and qualified agreeable to law-

```
DAVID ANDERSON    )
       VS         )   Case
JESSE COBB        )   This day came the Defendant by his attorney and
                      prays an appeal to the Circuit Court of Montgomery
```
County from the Judgment of this cause and having given Bond and security satisfactory to the court the same is allowed-

(p-335) This day came into court Josiah G. Duke and renewed his Bond as Inspector for the next Year and having entered into Bond and security satisfactory to the court the same is allowed-

This day came into court Thomas Smith and renewed his Bond as Inspector for the next year and having entered into Bond and security the same is allowed-

On motion ordered by the court that the administrators of Stephen G.
Jones be permitted to sell the perishable property of said Decd. by
giving notice thereof agreeable to law-

DORRELL Y HARRIS & WIFE)
VS   ) Petition
HAYDON E WELLS GUARDIAN   ) This day came the parties by their attornies
                             and on motion th/is cause if continued
on affidavit of Defendant on the payment of the cost of this Term-

NEEDHAM B FARRIER)
VS   ) Case
RICE COLEMAN   ) This day came the parties by their attornies
                     and ther upon this cause is continued on
affidavit of Defendant and on motion it is ordered by the court that
each party have leave to take depositions by giving then days notice in
the state and Twenty if taken out of the State-

(p-336) Present Joshua P Vaughn A.M.Rogers & S.Cocke Esqrs. Justices-

On motion ordered by the court that Andrew Vance clerk of Montgomery
County Court be allowed the sum of Forty Dollars for his Exofficio
services for the year 1823 ending 1st October in said year & that the
same be paid by the county Trustee out of any monies not otherwise
appropriated-

Same Justices Present -

On motion ordered by the court that Andrew /Vance ordered by the court
that Andrew Vance clerk of Montgomery County Court be allowed the sum
of Twenty five dollars for drawing & recording the tax list for the
present year & that the county Trustee pay the same out of any monies
in the Treasury not otherwise appropriated-

Same Justices Present -

On motion ordered by the court that Andrew Vance clerk of Montgomery
County court be allowed the sum of six dollars & ninety one cents for
sundry fees allowed him by law- and for issueing sixty four Jurors
Certificates for a/c rendered & filed - & that the same b/e paid out
of any monies in the Treasury not otherwise appropriated (&that the
county Trustee pay the same -

The Jury of view appointed at the last term of this court to lay off
and mark a road from Reuben Pollards to intersect the Russellville
road near William S. Whites make report as follows - We have reviewed
the road & agreed that the said road run from Pollards to David Field's
so as to intersect the Clarksville road to the South east corner of White
field - William S. White John E. Pollard David Field & John Johnson

(p-337) On motion ordered by the court that Benjamin Herring be appointed
overseer of the road as lately viewd & marked out from R. Pollard's to
intersect the Russelville road near Wm. S. Whites & to cut out said road
as marked out & that the following hands work under him on said road untill

said road is cut out to wit R. Pollards hands Cyprus Hensly & hands
John Henderson & hands Manoah Taylor & Hands Bright Herring Sr. &
hands John Johnson & hands & the hands of Wm. S. White -

Court adjourned to meet Monday morning at 9 O'clock-
        Chas. Bailey
        J.P. Vaughn
        Jas. Barret

Met according to adjournment Monday morning Oct. 28th 1823-
      Joshua P. Vaughn)
      Chas. Bailey   ) Esquires
      James Barret   ) Justices

On motion ordered by the court that Isaac Weakly Thos. Hunter Hyram Bobo
Jno. Major Henry Small John Williams William Neblett Abner Gupton & John
Caldwell surveyor be appointed commissioners to lay off and divide
certain land agreeable to the petition of Wilson Saunderlin and make
report to the next Term of this court -

Mrs. Mary Creath returns into Court and Inventory of the Estate of Sam'l
Creath Decd. and on motion ordered to be recorded-

JOHN STEELE ADMINISTRATOR OF THE ESTATE OF JOHN STEEL DECD)
       VS   ) Motion
   THOMAS ~~WATT~~ WATSON   ) This day
                  came into
court the plaintiff by William A Cook his attorney & thereupon it appearing to the ~~satisfa~~ satisfaction of the court here by inspection of the
records of this court that at July term 1822 thereof one Charles Barker
recovered of Thomas Watson & the plaintiff as administrator as aforesaid the sum (p-338) the sum of seven hundred & seventy eight dollars
& four cents on the 18th of July of sd. year 1822 besides the further
sum of   dollars cost of suit and it further appearing to
the satisfaction of the court that sd Judgment was founded on a bill
single executed by sd. intestate in his lifetime as security for sd.
Watson It is therefore considered by the court here that the plaintiff
recover of sd. Thomas Watson the said sum of seven hundred & seventy
eight dollars and four cents together with fifty nine dollars interest
on the same upto this time as also sd. costs in sd. suit as also the
costs of this motion -

  JOHN STEELE ADMINISTRATOR)
  OF JOHN STEELE DECD   )
       VS   )
  THOMAS WATSON   ) Motion
              This day came into court the Plaintiff
             by his attorney William A. Cook and
thereupon it appearing to the satisfaction of the court here by inspection
of the Records of this court that at July Term 1822 thereof on Charles
Barker recovered of Thomas Watson and the Plaintiff as administrator
as aforesaid the sum of Twenty two hundred and forty two Dollars 66 1/3
cents on the 18th July of said term 1822 besides the further sum of
dollars cost of suit and it further appearing to the satisfaction of
the court that said Judgment was founded on a bill single executed by
said intestate in his lifetime as security for said Watson -

It is therefore considered by the court that the Plaintiff recover here
of said Thomas Watson the said sum of Two thousand two h ndred and forty
two Dollars and sixty six and two thirds cents together with one hundred and seventy five Dollars and sixty four cents interest on the same
up to this time (p-339) as also said costs in said suit as also the
cost of this motion -

     JOHN STEELE ADMR OF)
           X/X
JOHN STEELE DECD VS   ) Motion
    THOMAS WATSON   ) This day came into court the Plaintiff
                 by his attorney William A. Cook and it
appearing to the satisfaction here by Inspection of the Records of this
court that at January Term 1823 on William Killebrew assee of Charles Barker
recovered of Thomas Watson and the Plaintiff as administrator the sum of
five hundred and forty two dollars & thirty two cents from which
judgment an appeal was taken to the Circuit court and Judgt. Rendered
thereon at their August Term 1823 for five hundred and Eighty three dollars
& forty two cents besides the costs of the court and it also appearing
to the satisfaction of the court that the said John Steele Decd. was
only security for the said Thomas Watson and that John Steele Jr. was
 the administrator on the estate of the said John Steele Decd. It is
considered by the court he e th t John Steele admr. as aforesaid recover
ofThomas Watson and the Plaintiff as administrator as aforesaid the sum
of Twenty two hundred and forty two dollars 66 1/3 cents on the 18th day
of July of said term 1822 besides the further sum of
dollars cost of suit and it further appearing to the satisfaction of
the court that said Judgment was founded on a bill single executed by
said intestate in his lifetime as security for said Watson -
It is therefore considered by the court that the Plaintiff recover here
 of said Thomas Watson the said sum of Two thousand two hundred and
forty two Dollars and sixty six and two thirds cents together with one
hundred and seventy five Dollars and sixty four cents interest on the
same up to this time (p-339) as also said costs in said suit as also
the cost of this motion -

     JOHN STEELE ADMR OF)
     JOHN STEELE DECD'   )
        VS   ) Motion
    THOMAS WATSON   ) This day came into court the Plaintiff by his
                 attorney William A Cook and it appearing to
the satisfaction here by Inspection of the Records of this court that
at January Term 1823 on William Killebrew assee of Charles Barker recovered
of Thomas Watson and the Plaintiff as administrator the sum of five hundred and forty two dollars & thirty two cents from which Judgment an appeal
was taken to the Circuit Court and Judgt. Rendered thereon at their
August Term 1823 for five hundred and Eighty three dollars & forty two
cents besides the costs of the court and it also appearing to the
satisfaction of the court that the said John Steele Decd. was only security for the said Thomas Watson and that John Steele Junior
was the administrator on the estate of the said John Steele Decd.-
It is thereupon considered by the court here that John Steele admr. as
aforesaid recover of the said Thomas Watson the sum of Five hundred
and eighty three dollars & forty two cents and also the sum of Twenty

dollars the costs in this behalf expended &c.

FRANCIS MCMURDY)
VS) Debt
CHARLES ~~XXXXX~~ BAILEY) This day came the Defendat by his attorney ~~XX~~
and prays an appeal to the Circuit Court of
Montgomery County from the Judgment of this cause and having entered
into Bond and security satisfactory to the court and the same is
allowed-

(p-340) JOSEPH COOK)
VS)
FRANKLIN SAUNDERS) This day came the Defendant by his attorney
and prays an appeal in the nature of a
writ of Error to the Circuit Court from the Judgment of this cause and
having entered into Bond and security satisfactory to the court the
same is allowed-

On motion ordered by the court that Mary Creath be furnished with letters
of administration with the will annexed on the Estate of Sam'l Creath
Decd. and having entered into Bond and security satisfactory to the
court the same is allowed -

On motion ordered by the court that Mary Creath administratrix of Sam'l
Creath decd. have leave to sell the perishable property of said Decd.

Upon the petition of James Barrett for the emancipation of a negro man
names Sampson belonging to him for meritorious and faithful services and
it appearing to our said court that the emancipation of the said Sampson
will not be contrary to the interest or policy of the state and the said
Bond & security agreeably to law. It is thereupon ordered by the said
court that the said Sampson be emancipated & freed and that he be en-
tit/led to all the privileges & rights of other free persons os color in
the state of Tennessee and that the same be certified ~~XXXX~~ accordingly

This day Martin Thomas appeared in Court and renewed his Bond for
retailing spirits and having given Bond and security satisfactory to the
court the same is allowed-
(
(p-341) On motion ordered by the court that John W. Prouty admr. of
John Boutell Decd. be permitted to sell the perishable property of said
Decd.

On motion ordered by the court that Benjamin Orgain Sr. and James Allen
be appointed Inspectors of Tobacco at Andrew Vance's warehouse in the
Town of Clarksville and Benjamin Orgain one of said Inspectors came into
court and entered into Bond and security and took the oath prescribed
by law-

The court proceeded to the appointment of Jurrors to the next County
Court in Jany. next to wit-
John D. Hargrove Drewry Mathews Alexander Hamilton Benjamin O'Donally
Samuel Grant James W. Carney William Newel Joshua Weakley William
Jackson Hiram Lankford Glidwell Killebrew Jacob Garret Willie Parker

Jesse CookseyThos. Wyatte John //////// Rook James Miller Warren Sikes
Thos. L. Merriwether John Pollard James B. Bayless & Joel Bayless and
Jurrors to the 2nd Cir/cuit Court To Wit. Mathew D. Simmons & Stephen
Cooke Samuel Smith William Porter Abner Harris Nicholas Bagwell Richard
Fortson Lewis Terrell Thos Batson Francis Carter Thos. Williams Francis
Williams Philip Duke John Davis James Hutchison Edward S. Walton Isham
Trotter John Neblett John Steele Francis Penrice Bryant Whitefield James
Pollard & William S. White Thimas Moore James Smith & Amos Hatcher Thomas
Cherry and Merideth Williams are // appointed as constables to the Jan-
uary County Court 1824-

Barlett Sullivant & William E. Dancy are appointed constables to the next
February Circuit Court-

(p-342) JOHN ALLINGSWORTH &   )
         JAMES MILLER   )
              VS   ) Sci fa
         THE HEIRS AT LAW OF   ) // On motion ordered by the court that an
         PHILIP JOHNSON DECD   ) alias Scieri facias issue against the
                                   said Heirs and made returnable to the

next Term of this court-

         MARTIN THOMAS   )
              VS   ) On motion ordered by the court that an
         THE HEIRS AT LAW OF   ) alias Scieri facias issue against the
         PHILIP JOHNSON DECD   ) heirs at law of said Decd. made returnable
                                   to the next Term of this court-

         ELI LOCKERT   )
              VS   ) On motion ordered by the court that an
         THE HEIRS AT LAW OF   ) alias Scieri facias issue against the
         PHILIP JOHNSON DECD   ) heirs at law of said Decd. and made
                                   returnable to the next Term of this Court

         PARKER'S HEIRS BY THEIR GUARDIAN)
                      VS   ) Petition
         JAMES HOLLIS   ) This day came the parties by
                                              their attornies and thereupon
it appearing to the court that the said James Hollis has recd Eighteen
dollars & Eighteen cents that he had not accounted for & refused to pay
over to their Guardian Philmer Whitworth-
It is thereupon ordered adjudged and decreed by the court that the said
petitioners recover of the Defdt. the aforesaid sum of money & also the
costs in this behalf expended-

(p-343) Court adjourned untill Court in course
                              Chas. Beiley
                              Isaac Dennison
                              J.P. Vaughn

The Worshipful court of Montgomery County have met according to adjournment Monday Jany, 19th 1824-

                              Present   A.M.Rogers
                                         Abner Harris
                                         Mathew Ryburn

On motion ordered by the court that Joel Bayliss be furnished with Letters of administration on the estate of John Ridsdale Deceased whereupon the said Joel B Bayliss came into court and entered into Bond and security agreeable to law and qualified accordingly-

On motion ordered by the court that letters of administration issue to Francies Johnson on the Estate of James Johnson Decd. Whereupon the said Francis Johnson came into court and entered into Bond & security satisfacroty to the court and qualified agreeable to law-

On motion ordered by the court that letters of administration issue to Jane Harris on the Estate of Samuel Harris Decd. Whereupon the said Jane Harris came into (p-344) Court and entered into Bond and security satisfactory to the court and qualified agreeable to law-

On motion ordered by the court that Letters of administration issue to Nancy Marshall on the Estate of Carter Marshall Decd. with the will annexed whereupon the said said Nancy Marshall came into court and entered into Bond and security agreeable to law and qualified accordingly-

On motion ordered by the court that John B French be furnished with Letters of administration on the Estate of Joseph B Flemming Decd. Whereupon the said John B French came into court and entered into Bond and security satisfactory to the court and qualified accordingly -

On motion ordered by the court that John H Poston & Isa ac Dennison be appointed commissioners to settle with Charles Lockert and David Bird Executors of Isaac Rogers Decd. and make report to the next Term of this court-

This day came into court Joseph Caldwell and surrenders his Guardianship to William and Louisa Rogers Infant heirs of Isaac Rogers Decd and on motion ordered by the court that Charles Lockert be appointed Guardian of said heirs and that said Joseph Caldwell Co. and he is hereby exonerated from any further responsibility as Guardian aforesaid-Whereupon the sd. Charles Lockert came into court and entered into Bond and security satisfactory to the court and qualified agreeable to law-

(p-345) On motion ordered by the court that Henry Small be permitted to keep a house of entertainment at his dwelling house- Whereupon the said Henry Small came into court and entered into Bond and security satisfactory to the court and qualified agreeable to law-

On motion ordered by the court that Burrel Corbin be appointed Guardian to Malberry Wilkins Permela Saletha and Charanel Corbin Infant heirs of Charnal Corbin Decd. Whereupon the said Burrel Corbin came into court and entered into Bond and security satisfactory to the court and qualified agreeable to law-

On motion ordered by the court that Benjamin King be appointed Guardian to Elizabeth S. Jenkins and John J. Jenkins Infant Heirs of John Jenkins decd. in the place of Joshua P. Vaughn former Guardian and that the said Joshua P. Vaughn be and he is hereby exonerated from any further responsibility as Guardian as aforesaid Whereupon the said Benjamin King came into court and entered into Bond and security satisfactory to the court and qualified agreeable to law-

This day came into court Lewis C. Taylor and surrenders his Guardianship as Guardian to Martha and Mary Kittrel Infant Heirs of Solomon A. Kittrell Decd. and on motion ordered by the court that Benjamin S. Harrison be appointed Guardian to said Heirs and that said Heirs and that said Lewis C. Taylor be and he is hereby exonerated from any further responsibility (p-346) as Guardian aforesaid Whereupon the said Benjamin S. Harrison came into court and entered into Bond and security satisfactory to the court and qualified agreeable to law-

This day came into court Alexander M. Barker and surrenders his Guardianship as Guardian to Joseph Faulks Infant heir of   Faulks Decd. and on motion ordered by the court that Henry W. Merriwether be appointed Guardian to said Joseph Faulk and that said Alexander M. Barker be exonerated from any further responsibility as Guardian aforesaid Whereupon the said Henry W. Merriwether came into court and entered into Bond & security satisfactory to the court and qualified agreeable to law-

This day came into court Richard Taylor and surrenders hos Guardianship as Guardian to Mildred N. & Sally W. Paine Infant heirs of Pain Decd. and on motion ordered by the court that Gerard Vanburin be appointed Guardian to the said Heirs and that the said Richard Taylor and his securities be and they are hereby exonerated from any further responsibility as Guardian aforesaid Whereupon the said Gerard Vanburin came into court and entered into Bond and Security satisfactory to the court and qualified agreeable to law-

On motion ordered by the court that C.D.McLean be allowed five dollars and seventy five cents for expenses and trouble as a Guard to Henry Johnson (p-347) to Charlott and that the County Trustee pay the same out of any monies in his hand not otherwise appropriated in his hands

On motion ordered by the court that Lewis T. Poindexter be allowed the sum of five dollars and seventy five cents for Expenses and troubles as one of the Guard to Henry Johnson a Criminal to Charlott and that the County Trustee pay the same out of any monies in his hands not otherwise appropriated-

On motion ordered by the court that Mr. Marshall be allowed the sum of five dollars and seventy five cents for Expenses and trouble as one of the Guard to Henry Johnson a Criminal to Charlott and that the County Trustee pay the same out of any monies in his hands not otherwise appropriated-

On motion ordered by the court that William J. Lynes be allowed the sum of five dollars and seventy five cents as one of the Guard to Henry Johnson a criminal to Charlott and that the Coutny Trustee pay the same out of any monies in his hands not otherwise appropriated-

On motion ordered by the court that letters of administration issue to James Dunbar and William Dunbar on the Estate of Ann Dunbar Decd. Of ~~the~~ Whereupon the said James and William came into court and entered into Bond and security satisfactory to the court qualified agreeable to law-

(p-348) Benjamin Rye administrator of the Estate of Absalom Rye Decd. returns into court the account of sales of said Decd. and on motion ordered to be recorded-

Mary Creath returns into court the acct of sales of the estate of Sam'l Creath Decd. and on motion ordered to be recorded-

This day came into Court Benjamin S. Harrison and presented the last Will and Testament of Sarah Ogburn Decd. which was proven by the oaths of Harbert Walker and Tabitha Walker Two of the subscribing witnesses thereto and on motion ordered to be recorded - Whereupon Benjamin S. Harrison the Executor named in said will came into court and entered into Bond and security satisfactory to the court and qualified agreeable to law and it is ordered that Letters Testamentary issue to the said Benjamin Harrison on the Estate of the said Estate-

This day came into court Samuel Grant and Charles Grant and presented the last will and Testament of Charles Grant Decd. which was proven by the oath of William Nelson one of the subscribing witnesses thereto and on motion ordered to be Recorded whereupon the said Samuel & Charles Grant Executors named in the said will came into court and Entered into Bond and security satisfactory to the court and qualified agreeable to law and it is ordered that letters Testamentary issue to the said Samuel and Charles Grant on the Estate of the said decd/

(p-349) This day came into court Joseph Caldwell and surrenders his Guardianship as Guardian to the Infant Heirs of Issac Rogers to wit of Louisa Rogers and William Rogers and on motion ordered by the court that Charles Lockert be appointed Guardian to said Heirs and that the said Joseph be exonerated from any further responsibility as Guardian aforesaid together with his securities whereupon the said Charles Lockert came into court and entered into Bond & security satisfactory to the court and qualified agreeable to law-

On motion ordered by the court that Christopher C. Clements be appointed Guardian to Catharine and Robert Clements infant Heirs of William Clements Decd. Whereupon the said Christopher C. Clements came into Court and entered into Bond and security satisfactory to the court and qualified agreeable to law-

John W. Prouty administrator of the Estate of John Boutell Decd. returns into court and Inventory of the Estate of said Decd & on motion ordered to be Recorded-

The commissioners appointed at the last Term of this court to settle with Thomas Williams admr. of William McCauly Decd. ~~admr~~ made their Report to this Term and on motion ordered to be Recorded-

On motion ordered by the court that William Sowry an illegitimate son of James Trousdale aged fourteen years be bound to Horace Barbee untill he attains to the age of Twenty one years Whereupon the said Horace Barbee came into court and (p-350) entered into Bond and security satisfactory to the court and qualified agreeable to law-

A Bill of sale from John Neblett to Peter Laird for negro Boy George was produced in open court and the Execution thereof duly acknowledged by the said John Neblett to be his act and Deed for the purposes therein mentioned and on motion ordered to be Recorded-

Cordall Norfleet Guardian to Philip Ford returns into Court and account against said Philip and on motion ordered to be Recorded-

A Deed of Gift from James Trice to Elizabeth Trice for negro Girl Milly was this day produced in open court & the Execution thereof duly acknowledged by the said James Trice to be his act and deed for the purposes therein mentioned and on motion ordered to be Recorded-

A Bill of sale from Richard Brown to Christopher N Carney for negro Boy Peter was produced in open court and the Execution thereof duly acknowledged by the said Richard Brown to be his act and deed for the purposes therein mentioned and on motion ordered to be Recorded-

On motion ordered by the court that Thomas Sills be permitted to keep a house of Entertainment at his dwelling house in New York whereupon the said Thomas Sills came into court and entered into Bond and security satisfactory to the (p-351) court and qualified agreeable to law-

On motion ordered by the court that Edward Trice be appointed first Inspector of Tobacco at the warehouse of Cave Johnson at the mouth of Red River whereupon the said Edward Trice came into court and entered into Bond & security satisfactory to the court and qualified agreeable to law-

On motion ordered by the court that James Trice be appointed second Inspector of Tobacco at the warehouse of Cave Johnson at the mouth of Red River Whereupon the said James Tricecame into court and entered into Bond and security satisfactory to the court and qualified agreeable to law-

This day came into court Zachariah Grant and renewed his Bond as Constable whereupon the said Zachariah Grant entered into Bond and security agreeable to law and qualified accordingly-

On motion ordered by the court that the Executor of Solomon A. Kittrell be permitted to sell the perishable property of said deceased on a credit of nine months by giving place and time and that Robert Hester Sam'l White and Andrew Walker be appointed commissioners to divide the Estate of the said deceased between Ann T. Harrison late Ann T. Kittrell and Mary Kittrell and Martha Kittrell Infant heirs of said Solomon A. Kittrell Decd. in conformity to the provisions of the will of the said Decd. and make report to the next Term of this court-

(p-352) A Bill of sale from Harden Crouch to James Dunbar for negro
Girl Suckey was produced in open court and the execution thereof duly
acknowledged by the said Harden Crouch to be his act and Deed for the
purposes therein mentioned and on motion ordered to be Recorded-

John W. Prouty administrator of John Boutell Decd returns into court the
account of sales of the said Decd. and on motion ordered to be Recorded

On motion ordered by the court that William Trigg John Hampton & Gilles
Johnson be appointed commissioners to settle with Alexander M. Barker
as Guardianof Joseph Faulks Decd. and make report to the next Term of
this court-

On motion ord ered by the court that Samuel Edmonston be appointed over-
seer of the Road from Israel Robertsons to John P. Vaughn's in the place
of Peter Given and that the following hands work under him to wit -
Ambrose Martin & hands John Neblett Junr. and hands Francis Neblett
Peter Given and hands Samuel Edmonston and hands Richard Daly and hands
Jordon Lyles Mickleberry Lyles George Yarborough James Channel and hands

The commissioners appointed at the last Term of this court to settle
with George W. Neville Executor of George Neville Decd. make their report
to this Term on motion ordered to be Recorded-

(p-353) This day came into court William E. Dancy and renewed his Bond
as constable and the said William E. Dancy entered into Bond and security
agreeable to law and qualified accordingly-

This day came into court Thomas Orgain and renewed his Bond as constable
and the said Thomas Orgain entered into Bond and security satisfactory
to the court and qualified agreeable to law-

This day came into court John W. Jones and renewed his Bond as constable
and the said John W Jones entered into Bond and security satisfactory
to the court and qualified agreeable to law-

On motion ordered by the court thatEdmund M. Simpson be permitted to
keep a house of Entertainment at his dwelling house in the town of
Cumberland Whereupon the said Edmund M. Simpson entered into Bond and
security agreeable to law and qualified accordingly-

On motion ordered by the court that Abner Gupton Benjamin King John King
Junr. Benjamin Mallory & Hyram Bobo or a majority of them be appointed
commissioners to divide the real Estate of Benjamin Willson Decd. and
make report to the next Term of this court-

On motion ordered by the court that James N. Smith be appointed overseer
of the Road from Charles A Hutcheson's ferry on Cumberland River to the
Dover Road & that Elisha Willis's hands John Smith's hands Valentine
Allen's hands Archibald McCorkle's hands William Wiggins & hands and
(p-354) James N. Smith and hands mark & cut out said Road-

On motion ordered by the court that that Charles A Hutcheson be appointed
overseer ~~of the Road~~ to cut out a Road from his ferry on Cumberland River
to the Clarksville Road and that William E. Williams hands Henry Smith
and hands John Marshall's hands David Hutcheson and hands Widow Hutcheson's
hands and John Steele and hands work under him—

On motion ordered by the court that James Carr and Richard B. Blount be
appointed commissioners to settle with Cordall Norfleet Guardian of
Philip Ford and make report to the next Term of this court—

On motion ordered by the court that Malachi Ford be allowed the sum of
nineteen dollars and seventy five cents for keeping a Pauper by the name
of Henry Soree from April 1821 untill April 1822 also that said Malachi
Soree be allowed the sum of Twenty four dollars and fifty cents for
keeping said Henry Soree from April 1822 untill April 1823 & that the
County Trustee pay the same out of any monies in his hands not otherwise
appropriated—
(This order was given to H.G. Barber to whom an order was given by said
Sory)

Nancy Marshall administratrix of Carter Marshall Decd returns into court
an Inventory of said Decd and on motion ordered to be Recorded—

On motion ordered by the court that Sterling Neblett and Valentine Allen
be appointed commissioners to settle with Mathew Ryburn (p-355) Guardian of Hyrem Jenkins and make report to the next Term of this court—

Thomas Williams administrator of John Everet Decd. produced in Court a Receipt
from the Legatees of said John Everet Decd. To wit Memory Tyner Peter
Teasel Aquilla Everet Mary Everet Precilla Everet Nancy Everet Delila
Everet Polly Everet and Rebecca Everet which was proven by the oaths of
Willis Harris and Thomas Bell the subscribing Witnesses thereto and on
motion ordered to ~~the~~ be Recorded—

This day came into court Nace F. Trice and renewed his Bond as constable
and the said Nace F. Trice entered into Bond and security satisfactory
to the court and qualified accordingly—

On motion ordered by the court that Elijah Martin be appointed overseer
of the Road leading by A.M.Rogers and Abner Harris's into the Dickson
road inthe place of John P. Epps and that the said Hands work under that
worked under the said Epps—

On motion ordered by the court that John Book be appointed overseer of
the Road from Nick's ferry to Peter Holt's Road on the Clarksville road
in the place of Wilson Vick and that the same hands work under him that
worked under the said Vick—

The commissioners appointed at the Term of this court to settle with
Richard Taylor Guardian of the Heirs of James Pain Decd. make their
report to this Term and on on motion ordered to be Recorded—

Mathew Ryburn Guardian for Harmon Jenkins returns into court an acount
against his (p-356) said ward and on motion ordered to be recorded—
) (Void)

The commissioners appointed at this Term to settle with Mathew Ryburn Guardian to Harmon Jenkins make their report and on motion ordered to be Recorded–

On motion ordered by the court that Thomas Batson & Frances Carter be appointed commissioners to sell all the negros belonging to the Estate of Charnal Corban Decd //// for the purpose of a division upon a credit of Twelve months by giving notice agreeable to law–

William Handlin administrator of John Handlin Decd returns into court an additional Inventory of said Decd and on motion ordered to be Recorded–

On motion ordered by the court that John Russell and Francis Carter be appointed commissioners to settle with William Handlin administrator of John Handlin Decd and make report to the next Term of this Court–

On motion ordered by the court that the following hands be added to the list of hands that work under Thomas Sills overseer of the New York Road – To wit James Bowers Jr. James McGhee Horace Barbee & Thomas Collier

On motion ordered by the court that Morgan Hopson Thomas Hester William Allen Perry W. Humphreys William E. Williams Thomas Bell & John Williams be permitted to give in their list of Taxable property for the year 1823 and that the same be added to last years Tax list–

(p-357) A Deed of Transfer from Even W. Shelby to John H. Marble for all the right title & Interest that he the said Evan has in the Estate of his father Isaac Shelby Decd. both real and personal was produced in open court and the execution thereof duly proven by the oaths of Willie B. Johnson and Nathaniel H. Allen the subscribing witnesses thereto and on motion ordered to be Recorded–

A Bill of sale from John H. Marable to William McClure for negro woman Sally and her two children was produced in open court and the execution thereof duly acknowledged by the said John H. Marable to be his act and deed for the purposes therein mentioned and on motion ordered to be Recorded–

A Bill of sale from John H. Marable to William McClure for negro Girl Lizy was produced in open court and the Execution thereof duly acknowledged by the said John H. Marable to be his act and Deed for the purposes therein mentioned and on motion ordered to be Recorded–

A Bill of sale from John Roach and Elizabeth his wife to Thomas Hunter for negro woman Mary and her child Arreno was produced in open court and the Execution thereof duly acknowledged by the said John Roach to be his act and deed for the purposes therein mentioned and on motion ordered to be Recorded–

Present Lewis C. Taylor Sterling Neblett Charles Bailey James McCauly Abner Harris T.W. Atkinson Isaac Dennison Stephen Cooke Mathew Ryburn James Carr Valentine Allen Abner Gupton A.M. Rogers J. Barret Thos. Smith R.B. Blount & J.P. Vaughn (p-358) The court proceeded to the appointment of a court of quorum for the present year and upon the votes being counted out there sumed a Majority in favour of A.M.Rogers Sterling Neblett and Thos.W. Atkinson and it is therefore ordered by the court that the aforesaid Rogers Neblett and Atkinson constitute a court of quorum for the present year as aforesaid-

TheExecutors of Isaac Rogers Decd returns into court the account of sales of said Decd. & on motion ordered to be Recorded-

A Deed of Gift from Burrell J. Fort to William Elias Fort and Eliza Ann Fort for certain negroes therein mentioned was produced in open court and theExecution thereof duly proven by the oaths of Christopher N. Carner and Felix Northington the subscribing witnesses thereto and on motion order d to be Recorded-

On motion ordered by the court that Joel Bayliss who was summoned as a Juror at this Term be exonerated from attending as such he being an overseer of a Road-

On motion ordered by the court that Gideon Pace be appointed overseer of the Road in place of James Hollis and that the same hands work under him that worked under the said Hollis-

On motion ordered by the court that Josel Bayliss admr. of the Estate of John Ridsdale Decd. be permitted to sell the perishiable property of said decd on a credit of nine months by giving notice thereof according to law-

Court adjourned untill Tomorrow morning 9 O'clock

(p-359) On motion it is ordered by the court that Jacob H. Fort administrator of the estate of James Fort deceased sell the following negroes of said estate for cash in hand to wit negro man Billy negro man Timothy negro man Abram negro woman Levy and her four children Cely Rachel Washington & Maddison also negro girl Mary & Negro girl Sarah Jane and that a certificate issue accordingly-

On motion ordered by the court that a precinct Election be established at the house of Sandford Wilson for the purpose of electing members of congress the Governor of the state and members of the State Legislature-

On motion ordered by the court that the County Tax be the same ratio & at the same rate at which it was assessed Last year-

Ordered b the court that James Barret be appointed to take the Tax list in Capt. Williams old company for the year 1824-

Ordered by the court that Lewis C. Taylor be appointed to take the Tax list in Capt. Shamwell's ompany for the year 1824-

Ordered by the court that Isaac Dennison be appointed to take the Tax list in the Town Company for the year 1824-

Ordered by the court that Martha Ryburn be appointed to take the Tax list for Capt. James Williams Company for the year 1824-

Ordered by the court that Abner Harris be appointed to Take the Tax list for ///// Capt. Bagwell's Company for the year 1824-

Ordered by the court that ///// Valentine Allen be appointed to take the Tax list for Capt. Smith's company forthe year 1824-

(p-360) Ordered by the court that A.M.Rogers be appointed to take the Tax list for Capt. Cook's company for the year 1824-

Ordered by the court that Francis Carter be appointed to take the list in Capt. Allen's old company for the year 1824-

Ordered by the court that James Carr be appointed to take the Tax list in Capt. Hamblett's Company for the year 1824-

Ordered by the court that John Kercheval be appointed to take the Tax list in Capt. Bowne's company for the year 1824-

Court adjourned untill Tomorrow 9 O'clock-

                              A.M.Rogers
                              Sterling Neblett
                              Thos. W. Atkinson

Worshipful county court met according to adjournment present-
                              Thomas W. Atkinson)
                              Sterling Neblett   ) Esquires
                              Alexander Rogers   )

        ELI LOCKERT   )
             VS   )
        THE HEIRS AT LAW   )
        OF P.JOHNSON DECD   )

On motion it is ordered by the court that William Killebrew be appointed guardian ad litem to defend the interest of George W. Killebrew in this suit-

On motion ordered by the court that Samuel M. Stramler be allowed the sum of five dollars and seventy five cents for costs and trouble going to Charlott as one of the Guard to Henry Johnson a criminal to Charlott and that the County Trustee pay the (p-361) same out of any monies in his hands not otherwise appropriated-

The Jury of view appointed at the last Term of this court to view the old Road from the State line near Rice Coleman's where the Dover Road Intersects the same to Watson's mill make their report to this Term and says that that the Road ought to be established as a public Road-

        JOHN GRUBBS ASSEE   )
             VS   ) Debt
        RICHARD T MERIWETHER   )

This day came into court the Plaintiff and says he will no further prosecute his said suit but dismisses the same—

Therefore it is considered by the court that the Defendant Richard T. Merriwether go hence without day and recover of the Plaintiff the costs in this behalf expended—

CHARLES PETERS)
VS) Debt
BEVERLY STUBBLEFIELD) This day came into court Charles Peters by attorney and says he will no further prosecute his said suit but dismisses the same and thereupon the Defendant assumes the costs in this case—

Therefore it is considered by the court that said suit stand dismissed and that the Plaintiff recover of the Defendant the costs in this behalf expended— '

ARTHUR M BOWEN)
VS) Debt
WILLIAM BISHOP) This day came into court the Plaintiff by his attorney William B. Turly and says he will no further prosecute (p-362) his said suit but dismisses the same—

Therefore it is considered by the court that the Defendant William Bishop go hence and recover of the Plaintiff the costs in this behalf expended—

Thomas Williams administrator of the Estate of Benjamin Willson Decd. returns into court the hire of the negroes of said Decd— for the year 1823 and on motion ordered to be Recorded—

On motion ordered by the court that Robert G. Johnson and John Johnson be permitted to give in their list of Taxable property for the year 1823 and that the same be added to the last years Tax list—

WILLIAM HUNT)
VS)
SOLOMON HUNT) Case This day came into court the Plaintiff by his attorney and says he will no further prosecute his said suit but dismisses the same—

Therefore it is considered by the court that the Defendant go hence without day and Recover of the Plaintiff the costs in this behalf expended—

On motion ordered that John S Williamson be permitted to keep a house of entertainment at his dwelling house in Port Royal whereupon the said John S. Williamson entered into Bond and security satisfactory to the court and qualified agreeable to law—

On motion ordered by the court that Jno. Perry be permitted to give in his list of Taxable property for the year 1822 and that he shall not be subject to a double tax and that the said list be annexed to the last year's Tax list (p-363) A Deed of Mortgage from William L. Williams to Willie B. Johnson for two negroes Dick and Jerry was produced in open court and the execution thereof duly acknowledged by the said William L. Williams to be his act and Deed for the purposes therein mentioned and on motion ordered to be Recorded—

A Deed of Mortgage from William L. Williams to James Barret for two negroes James and Mariah was produced in open court and the Execution thereof duly acknowledged by the said William L. Williams to be his act and deed for the purposes therein mentioned and on motion ordered to be Recorded—

A Bill of sale from John H Marable & Needham Whitfield to Nathaniel A. McNairy for two negro slaves Nathan & Sandy was produced in open court & the Execution thereof duly acknowledged by Marable and Whitfield to be their proper act and Deed for the purposes therein mentioned and on motion ordered to be Recorded—

A Bill of sale from Stephen W. Carney to Elizabeth Norfleet Carney for negro Woman Rhoda was produced in open court and the Execution thereof duly acknowledged by the said Stephen W. Carney to be his act and deed for the purposes therein mentioned and on motion ordered to be Recorded

A Bill of sale from John H. Marable & Needham Whitfield to John Sanderson for two negroes to wit Rosetta & her child was produced in open court and the (p-364) execution thereof duly was duly proven acknowledged by the said John H Marable and Needham Whitfield to be their act and deed for the purposes therein mentioned and on motion to be Recorded—

GEORGE SHALL ASSIGNEE)
       VS   ) Debt
WILLIE BLOUNT   )
                          This day came the parties by their attorneys
                          and thereupon came a jury of good
and lawful men to wit George W Blanks James Trotter Jefferson Weakley Washington Lee Nathaniel Thaxton Levi P Allen Jessee Baily Ambrose Martin Robert Bumpass Urish Humphreys James Hubbard & James Trice who being elected tried and sworn the truth to speak upon the issue joined between the parties aforesaid upon their oaths do say that the issue in favour of the plaintiff that the defendant doth owe the plaintiff the sum of two hundred and ninety eight dollars sixty five cents the debt in pltffs declaration mentioned together with the further sum of fourteen dollars damates sustained by reason of the detention of said debt wherefore it is considered by the court that the plff George Shall recover of the defendant Willie Blount the sum of three hundred and twelve dollars & sixty five cents the debt (p-365) and damages so assessed by the Jury inform aforesaid together with his costs by him about his suit in this behalf expended—

NOBLE OSBURN   )
       VS   ) Debt
MATHEW D SIMMONS   )
                          This day came the parties by their attornies
                          and thereupon came a jury of good and lawful men
to wit George Blanks James Trotter Jefferson Weakley Washington Lee

Nathaniel Thaxton Levi P. Allen Jessee Baily Ambrose Martin Robert
Bumpass Uriah Humphreys James Hubbard and James Trice who being duly
elected tried and sworn the truth to speak upon the issue found between
the parties aforesaid upon their oaths do say they find the issue in
favour of the plff that the defendant doth owe the the pleff. the sum
of one hundred and twenty dollars seventy three cents the debt in plff.
declaration mentioned together with the further sum of five dollars and
four cents damages accruing by reason of the detention of said debt-
Wherefore it is considered by the court that the plaintiff Noble Osburn
recover of the defendant Mathew D. Simmons the sum of one hundred and
twenty five dollars and seventy seven cents the debt and damages by the
Jury aforesaid assessed together with his costs by him about his suit in
this behalf expended-
(Entered in another place)

    ALFRED BATCH PLFF)
          VS   )   Debt
    WILLIAM L. WILLIAMS DEFT)   This day came the parties by their attornies
                         and thereupon came a jury of good and
lawful men to wit George Blanks James Trotter Jefferson Weakley Washington
Lee Nathaniel Thaxton Levi P. Allen Jessee Baily Ambrose Martin Robert
Bumpass Uriah Humphreys James Hubbard and James Trice who being duly
elected tried (p-366) & sworn the truth to speak upon the issues joined
between the parties aforesaid upon their oaths do say they find the
issues in favour of the plff and that the defendant doth owe the plff the
sum of five hundred and thirty three dollars and seven cents the debt
in plffs declaration mentioned together with the further sum of of
twelve dollars and eighty nine cents damages accrueing by reason of the
detention of sd. debt wherefore it is considered by the court that the plff.
Alfred Batch recover of the defendant William L. Williams the sum of five
hundred and forty five dollars ninety six cents the debt and damages by
the Jury aforesaid in form aforesaid assessed together with his costs by
him about his suit in this behalf expended-
(Entered in another place)

    WILLIAM HUNT   )
        VS   )   Case
    SOLOMON HUNT   )   This day came the plff. by his attorney and
                         says that he means no further to prosecuted
his suit against the d fendant whereupon it is considered by the court
that said suit with all the proceedings thereon be disrupted that the
defendant go hence without day and recover of the plff. his costs by
him about his defence in this behalf expended
(Entered in another place)

    PEYTON BUCKLEY   )
        VS   ) Petition
    FRANCES MALLORY &) This day came the petitioner by his attorney
    CHILDREN   ) into court and says he will no further prosecute
                        his petition against the defts. wherefore it
is considered by the court that said petition together with all the
proceedings thereon be dismissed and thereupon came the defendants in
open court and assumes upon themselves the payment of the costs of this
suit which is allowed

(p-367) PEYTON BUCKLEY)
                VS   )   Petition
FRANCIS MALLORY & CHILDREN) This day came the plff. by his attorney and
                             all the matters and things arising on the face
of said petition being fully heard &c understood by the court it is
considered by the court that said petition be dismissed and for reasons
appearing to the court it is further considered that the plff. recover
of the defendants his costs by him about his suit in this behalf expended

A Bill of sale from Stephen Pettis to John H. Marable for negro man slave
Daniel was produced in open court and the execution thereof duly acknowledged
by the said Stephen Pettis to be his act and deed for the purposes
thereinmentioned and on motion ordered to be Recorded-

A Deed of conveyance from John Berry & wife to Daniel Isbell for Eighty
five acres of land was produced in open court and the execution therof
duly proven by the oaths of David Bunting & Aquilla Johnson the subscribing
witnesses thereto and on motion ordered to be certified-

A Deed of conveyance from Tyomas Williams to Joseph Stroud for fifty acres
of land was produced in open court and the execution thereof duly acknowledged by the said Thomas Williams to be his act and deed for the purposes
therein mentioned and on motion ordered to be certified for Registration

A Deed of Conveyance from William Peay to Benjamin Orgain for seventy four
acres of land was produced in open court and the execution thereof duly
proven by the oaths of John Caldwell and Thomas Orgain two of the Subscribing witnesses (p-368) thereto and on motion ordered to be
certified for Registration

A Deed of Conveyance from Williams Peay to Thomas Orgain for two hundred
and Twenty six acres of land was this day produced in open court & the
execution thereof was duly proven by the oath of John Calwell & Benjamin
E Orgain subscribing Witnesses thereto & on motion it is ordered to be
Certified for registration-

        DORREL Y. HARRIS & WIFE   )
                VS   )
        HAYDON E. WELLS   )   Petition
                                      This day came the parties by their attorn-
                                   nies and thereupon all and singular
the matters of law arising upon the Plaintiffs petition being argued heard
& by the court here fully understood. It is considered by the court that
the said petition be dismissed and that the Defendant go hence without day
and recover of the said Plaintiffs his costs by him about his defence in
this behalf expended

        RICHARD C GREGORY   )
                VS   )
        MARY CREATH ADMRX   )   Debt
                                      This day came the parties by their attorneys
                                   and thereupon on motion this cause is refered
(by consent of the parties foressid) to the award of Frederick W. /

Huling Esquire to be returned to the present Term of this court upon award shall be the Judgment of /// this court-

(p-369) A Deed of conveyance from William Sheppard Egbert Sheppard and Jesse Blackfan for one hundred and thirteen acres of land by their attorney infact Frederick W. Huling to David Willeford was produced in open court and the Execution thereof duly acknowledged by the said Frederick W. Huling as attorney in fact as aforesaid to be his act and Deed for the purposes therein mentioned and on motion and on motion ordered to be certified for Registration -

A Deed of conveyance from A.M.Shelby by his attorney in fact Cave Johnson to William Daniel for ninety one and a half acres of land was produced in open court and the Execution thereof duly acknowledged by the said Cave Johnson as attorney aforesaid to be his act and Deed for the purposes thereinmentioned and on motion ordered to be certified for Ietistration-

A Deed of //////// conveyance from William Coly to James O'Donally for fifty one acres of land was produced in open court & the Execution thereof duly proven by the oaths of Solomon Hunt and Josiah Johnson the subscribing witnesses thereto and on motion ordered to be certified for Registration-

A Deed of conveyance from Richard Brown to Looky Brown for one hundred acres of land was produced in open court and the Execution thereof duly acknowledged by the said Richard Brown to be his act and Deed for the purposes therein mentioned andon motion ordered to be certified for Registration-

(p-370) A Deed of conveyance from Edmund Taylor to Marvel Lowe for six hundred and fifty one acres of land was produced in open court and the Execution thereof duly proven by the oaths of Washington Lowe and Thomas Williams two of the subscribing witnesses thereto and on motion ordered to be certified for Registration-

A Deed of conveyance from Richard Brown to William Morrow for ninety one acres of land was produced in open court and the Execution thereof duly acknowledged by the said Richard Brown to be his act and Deed for the purposes therein mentioned and on motion ordered to be certified for Registration-

On motion ordered by the court that Herbert Walker be allowed the sum of Ten dollars for keeping a Boy pauper and that the county Trustee pay the same out of any monies in his hands not otherwise appropriated-

A Deed of conveyance from John Watt Daniel Bevel Samuel Watt & Thomas T. Watt to John Parker for sixty six and two thirds acres was produced in open court and the Execution thereof duly proven by the oath of W.H.Williams at October Term 1823 and by the oath of John H. Williams at this Term two of the subscribing witnesses thereto and on motion ordered to be certified for Registration-

A Deed of conveyance from Francis Baker to Nathan Hester one of the Trustees of the Baptist church of Little River for one acre (p-371) of land was produced in open court and execution thereof duly acknowledged by the said Francis Baker to be his act & Deed for the purposes therein mentioned and on motion ordered to be certified for Registration

A Deed of conveyance from Benjamin O'Donally to Josiah Johnson for One hundred acres of land was produced in open court and the execution thereof duly acknowledged by the said Benjamin O'Donally to be his act and Deed for the purposes ther in mentioned and on motion ordered to be Certified for Retistration-

A Bill of sale from Samuel Craft to John H. Marable for negro Girl Caswell was produced in open court and the Execution thereof duly proven by the oaths of Jesse Craft and Thomas Bayliss the subscribing witnesses thereto and on motion ordered to be Recorded-

On motion ordered by the court that the order made at the July Term of this Court appointing commissioners to make division of the real Estate of John Shelby Decd between Jesse A. Brunson and his wife Louisa A.M. Shelby and Clark M. Shelby heirs of said John Shelby Decd. be continued and that the same commissioners who were appointed at the October Term 1822 or any five of them together with John Caldwell the county surveyor and it is further ordered that said commissioners make said division and make report to the next Term of this court with a distinct platt of the same-

A petition that was presented to this court for the purpose of changing the road from (p-372) Port Royal to Moseley's ferry ordered by the court that unless some person make himself a party to said petition on or before saturday next that said petition stand dismissed as an act of today-

ROBERT G JOHNSON ASSEE)
VS) Debt
PARRY W HUMPHREYS) This day came into court the parties by
their attornies and thereupon came a Jury
of Good and lawful men To wit Sam'l Grant William Jackson James W. Carney Hyram Lankford Thomas Wyatt Willie Parker John Pollard Dennis Daugherty Benjamin Trice John Edwards Nathan Vick William Killebrew & James Hambleton who being duly elected tried and sworn the truth to speak upon the issue joined upon their oaths do say that the Defendant doth owe to the Plaintiff the sum of Three hundred and fifty nine dollars and fifty cents the debt in the declaration mentioned and the further sum of Twenty three dollars and Thirty six cents the damages sustained by reason of the detention of said Debt-

Therefore it is considered by the court that the Plaintiff recover of the Defendant the sum of three hundred and seventy nine dollars and Eighty six cents the debt and damages so assessed by the Jury in form aforesaid together with his cost by him about his suit in this behalf expended-

GEORGE SHALL ASSEE)
VS) Debt
WILLIE BLOUNT)

This day came the parties by their attornies and thereupon came a Jury of good and lawful men to wit- (p-373) Sam'l Grant William Jackson James W. Carney Hyram Lankfort Thomas Wyatte Willie Parker John Pollard Dennis Daugherty Brigham Trice John Edwards Nathan Vick William Killebrew & James Hambleton who being duly elected tried and sworn the truth to speak upon the issue joined upon their oaths do say that they find the issue in favour of the Plaintiff that the Defendant doth owe to the Plaintiff the sum of two hundred and ninety eight dollars & sixty five cents the Debt in the declaration mentioned and the further sum of fourteen dollars damages sustained by reason of the detention of said Debt-

Therefore it is considered by the court that the Plaintiff recover of the Defendant the sum of Three hundred and Twelve dollars and sixty five cents the debt and damages so assessed by the Jury in form aforesaid together with his costs by him about his suit in this behalf expended-

```
ALFRED BALCH        )
    VS              )   Debt
WILLIAM L WILLIAMS)     This day came the parties by their by their
```
attornies and thereupon came a Jury of good and lawful men To wit Sam'l Grant William Jackson James W. Carney Hyram Lankfort Thomas Wyatte Willie Parker John ✗ Pollard Dennis Daugherty Brigham Trice John Edwards Nathan Vick William Killebrew & James Hambleton who being duly elected tried and sworn the truth to speak upon upon the issue joined upon their oaths do say that they find the issue in favour of the Plaintiff that the Defendant doth owe to the Plaintiff the the sum of five hundred and ninety seven (p-374) dollars and seven cents the debt mentioned in the declaration and the further sum of Twelve dollars and Eighty nine cents the damages sustained by reason of the detention of said debt-

Therefore it is considered by the court that the Plaintiff recover of the Defendant the sum of six hundred and nine dollars and ninety six cents the debt and damages so assessed by the Jury inform aforesaid together with his costs by him about his suit in this behalf-

```
NOBLE OSBURN        )
    VS              )   Debt
MATHEW D SIMMONS )      This day came the Parties by their attornies and
```
thereupon came a Jury of good and lawful men To wit Sam'l Grant William Jackson James W Carney Hyram Lankfort Thomas Wyatte Willie Parker John Pollard Dennis Daugherty Bingham Trice John Edwards Nathan Vick William Killebrew & James Hambleton who being duly elected tried and sworn the Truth to speak upon the issue joined upon their oaths do say that the Defendant doth owe to the plaintiff the sum of one hundred and Twenty dollars and seventy three cents the debt in the declaration mentioned and the further sum of five dollars and four cents damages sustained by reason of the detention of said Debt-

Therefore it is considered by the court that the Plaintiff recover of the Defendant the sum of one hundred and Twenty five dollars and seventy seven cents the debt and damages so assessed by the Jury in form aforesaid besides his costs by him about his suit in this behalf expended

(p-375) JAMES ELDER)
     VS) Debt
AQUILLA JOHNSON &) This day came into court the Parties by
WM. TRIGG) their attornies and thereupon came a **Jury**
                    of good and lawful men to wit Samuel

Grant William Jackson James W Carney Hyram Lankfort Thomas Wyatte **Willie**
Parker John Pollard Dennis Daugherty ⱡⱡ Bingham Trice John Edwards
Nathn Vick William Killebrew & James Hambleton who being duly elected
tried and sworn the truth to speak upon the issue joined upon their **oaths**
do say that they do find the issues in favour of the Plaintiff and **do say**
that the Defendant doth owe to the Plaintiff the the sum of Three **hund**
red dollars the Debt in the declaration mentioned and the further **sum of/ⱡ**
nineteen dollars and thirty seven and one half cents damages sustained
by reason of the detention of said debt-

Therefore it is considered by the court that the Plaintiff recover of
the Defendant the sum of Three hundred and nineteen dollars and thirty
seven and a half cents the Debt and damages so assessed by the Jury **in**
form aforesaid together with the his costs by him about his suit **in**
this behalf expended-

Court adjourned untill Tomorrow 9 O'clock-
                          Thos. W. Atkinson
                          Sterling Neblett
                          Isaac Dennison

(p-376) The Worshipful court of montgomery county have met agreeable
to adjournment
                      Present

                            A.M.Rogers   )
                            Sterling Neblett) Esquires
                            T.W.Atkinson) Justices

ELIZABETH ROBBINS)
     VS)
STEPHEN PETTIS) This day came into court the Parties by **their**
THOMAS WATSON &) attornies and thereupon came a Jury of good and
WM. PEAY) lawful men to wit Samuel Grant William Jackson
                  James W Carney Hyram Lankfort Thomas W Carney
                  Thomas Wyatte Willie Parker John ⱡⱡ Pollard
Dennis Daugherty Bingham Trice John Edwards Nathan Vick & Joshua Weekley
who being duly elected tried and sworn the truth to speak upon the **issue**
joined upon their oath do say that the Defendants doth owe to the **plaintiff**
the sum of Two hundred dollars the debt in the declaration mentioned and
the further sum of Thirteen dollars damages sustained by reason of the
detention of said Debt-
    Therefore it is considered by the court that the Plaintiff **recover**
of the Defendant the sum of Two hundred and thirteen dollars the Debt
and damages so assessed by the Jury in form aforesaid together with her
costs by him about her suit in this behalf expended-

WILLIAM THOMAS)
  VS   ) Covenant Broken
MAURICE MORRIS ADMR) This day came into court the Parties by their
            attornies and thereupon came a Jury of good
and lawful men to witSam'l Grant William Jackson James W. Carney (p-377)
Hyram Lankfort Thomas Wyatte Willie Parker John Pollard Dennis Dorherty
Bingham Trice John Edwards Nathan Vick & Joshua Weakly who being duly
elected tried and sworn the truth to speak upon the issue joined upon
their oaths do say that they find the issue in favour of the Plaintiff
and do assess his damage to four hundred and sixteen dollars and sixty
six cents by reason of the several non performances and undertakings in
the Plaintiffs declaration mentioned—

   Therefore it is considered by the court that the Plaintiff William
Thomas recover of Maurice Maurice Guardian the sum of four hundred and
sixteen dollars and si xty six cents the damages so assessed by the Jury
in form aforesaid together with his costs by him about his suit in this
behalf expended—

    STALEY STAILEY)
      VS   )
    ANDREW SMITH) Case
           This day came into court the parties by their
           attornies and thereupon came a Jury of good and
lawful men to wit David Davis C.D.McLean Needham B Farrier Payton Cock
John Hampton Jesse L. Smith Jeffrey Sims Moble Osburn Edward S. Walton
Dawson Bayliss Lorenzo Gibson & George S. McCauly who being duly elected
tried and sworn the truth to speak upon the issue joined upon their oath
do say that they find the issue in favour of the Plaintiff and do assess
her damage to one cent—

   Therefore it is considered by the court that the Plaintiff recover
of the Defendant the sum of one cent the damages (p-378) so assessed
by the Jury in form aforesaid together with her costs by her about
her costs in this behalf expended—

    ROBERT G JOHNSON ADMR)
        VS   ) Debt
    THOMAS JOLLY & WM. PEAY) This day came into court the Parties by
              their attornies & thereupon came a Jury of
good and lawful men to wit Sam'l Grant William Jackson James W. Carney
Hyram Lankford Thomas Wyatte Willie Parker John Pollard Dennis Dorherty
Bingham Trice John Edwards Nathan Vick & Joshua Weakley who being duly
elected tried and sworn the truth to speak upon the issues joined upon
their oaths do say that they find the issues infavour of the Plaintiff and
do say that the Defendant doth owe to the Plaintiff the sum of one hundred and two dollars and Twenty nine cents the Debt in the plaintiffs
declaration mentioned and the further sum of seven dollars and Twenty
five cents damages sustained by reason of the detention of said Debt—

   Therefore it is considered by the court that the Plaintiff recover
of the Defendant the sum of one hundred and Twenty nine dollars and
fifty four cents the debt and damages so assessed by the Jury in form
aforesaid together with his costs by him about his suit in this behalf
expended—

ROBERT G JOHNSON ADMR)
     VS)
WILLIAM PEAY & CHARLES BAILEY)   Debt

This day came into court the parties by their attornies by their attornies and thereupon came a Jury of good (p-379) and lawful men to wit Samuel Grant William Jackson James W Carney Hyram Lankford Thos. Wyatte Willie Parker John Pollard Dennis Daugherty Benjamin Trice John Edwards Nathan Vick & Joshua Weakley who being duly elected tried and sworn the truth to speak upon the issue joined upon their oaths do say that they find the issue in favour of the Plaintiff and do say that the Defendants doth owe to the Plaintiff the sum of Two hundred and Twelve dollars and forty one cents the Debt in the declaration mentioned and the further sum of fourteen dollars and ninety nine cents damages sustained by reason of the detention of said Debt—

Therefore it is considered by the court that the Plaintiff recover of the Defendant the sum of Two hundred and Twenty seven dollars & forty cents the debt and damages so assessed by the Jury in form aforesaid together with his costs about his suit in this behalf Expended—

NEEDHAM B FARRIER)
     VS)
RICE COLEMAN)   Case

This day came into court the Parties by their attornies and thereupon came a Jury of good and lawful men to wit Sam'l Grant William Jackson James W. Carney Hyram Lankfort Thomas Wyatte Willie Parker John Pollard Dennis Daugherty Bingham Trice John Edwards Nathan Vick & Joshua Weakley who being duly elected tried and sworn the truth to speak upon the issue joined upon their oaths do say that they find the issue in favour of the Plaintiff and do assess his damage to ninety nine (Original note— This Judgt entered on the other side)

(p-380)   THE PRESIDENT DIRECTORS & CO OF)
THE BANK OF KENTUCKY)
     VS)
JOHN STEEL ADMINISTRATOR OF THE)   Debt
ESTATE OF JOHN STEEL DECD)

This day came John Steel into open court and acknowledged that the said John Steel Decd in his life time was indebted to the President Directors & Co of The Bank of Kentucky in the sum of Two thousand Twenty five hundred and Thirty seven dollars & fifty cents being the balance of the money due the said Bank at this time on a note given by the said John in his life time to the said Bank – It is therefore considered by the court that the said plaintiffs recover of the said John Steel admr. as aforesaid the aforesaid sum of Twenty five hundred & Thirty seven dollars & fifty cents so as aforesaid acknowledged to be due to be levied of the goods & chattles of John Steel Decd in the hands of his administrator John Steel to be administered if so much therebe if not then the costs to be levied of the proper goods & chattles lands & tenements of the said John Steel &c

NEEDHAM B FARRIER)
     VS)   Case
RICE COLEMAN)

This day came the parties by their attorneys and thereupon came a Jury
of good and lawful men To wit Sam'l Grant William Jackson James W. Carney
Hyram Lankfort Thomas Wyatte Willie Parker John Pollard Dennis Daugherty
(p-381) Bingham Trice John Edwards Nathan Vick & Joshua Weakley who being
duly elected tried and sworn the truth to speak upon the issue joined upon
their oaths do say that they find the issue in favour of the Plaintiff
and do assess his damages to ninety nine dollars and fifty seven cents by
reason of the several non performances and undertakings in the plaintiffs
declaration mentioned—

Therefore it is considered by the court that the Plaintiff recover f
of the Defendant the sum of ninety nine dollars and fifty seven cents the
damages so assessed by the Jury in form aforesaid together with his costs
by him about his costs in this behalf expended— from which Judgment the
said Rice Coleman Defendant as aforesaid p rays an appeal to the Circuit
Court of Montgomery County and having entered into Bond and security
satisfactory to the court and the same is allowed—

JOHN L WYNN)
VS) Debt
RICE COLEMAN)
This day came the Parties by their attornies
and thereupon came a Jury of good and lawful
men Sam'l Grant William Jackson James t. Carney Hyram Lankfort Thomas
Wyatte Willie Parker John Pollard Dennis Saugherty Bingham Trice John
Edwards Nathan Vick & Joshua Weakley who being duly elected tried
and sworn the truth to speak upon the issue joined upon their oaths do
say that they do (p-382) find the issue in favour of the Plaintiff
the sum of one hundred and Eighteen dollars and Eighty cents the debt
in the declaration mentioned and the further sum of three dollars and
fifty six cents damages sustained by reason of the detention of said
debt—

Therefore it is considered by the court that the Plaintiff recover
of the Defendant the sum of one hundred and Twenty two dollars and
thirty six cents the debt and damages so assessed by the Jury in form
aforesaid together with his costs by him about his suit in this behalf
expended—

DAVID ANDERSON USE OF J. B. SMITH)
VS) Case
C. H. P. MARR)
This day came the parties by
their attornies and thereupon
this cause by consent of Parties is continued and leave given to take
depositions by giving the adverse party Twenty days notice thereof—

WILLIAM DEAN)
VS) Case
RANSOM SEXTON)
This day came the parties by their attornies and
thereupon this cause is continued on affidavit
of Defendant and leave given him to take the depositions of Davis Ferguson William Luke and John Hust in the state of Virginia by giving the
adverse party thirty days notice of time and place thereof—

LODERVICK BRODIE)
       VS   )   Debt
ROBERT SEARCY)   This day came the (p-383) Plaintiff by his
                            attorney and says he will no further prosecute
his said suit but dismisses the same and thereupon the Defendant by attorney assumes the payment of the costs that have accrued in this action –

    Therefore it is considered by the court that said suit be dismissedand that the Plaintiff recover of the Defendant the costs in this behalf expended–

JOHN MCCULLOCK)
       VS   )   Case
DAVID LOVE)   This day came into court Frederick W. Huling the
                            security for the prosecution of this case and
makes a motion to have said suit dismissed and it appearing to the court that said Plaintiff has removed out of the state and that no council is employed to prosecute said suit– Therefore it is consid'd by the court that said suit be dismissed and that the Defendant be hence discharged and recover of the Plaintiff and his ~~shall~~ security for the prosecution of said suit the costs in this behalf expended–

THOMAS STONE)
       VS   )   Case
SAMUEL JONES)   This day the Plaintiff by his attorney and says
                            he will no further prosecute his said suit but
dismisses the same – Therefore it is considered by the court that the Defendant go hence without day recover of the Plaintiff the costs in this behalf expended–

THOMAS W FRAZER)
       VS   )   Debt
ROBERT SEARCY)   This day came the Plaintiff by his attorney and
                            says he will (p-384) no further prosecute his
said suit but dismisses the same Whereupon the Defendant by attorney assumes the costs that have accrued in this case–

    Therefore it is considered by the court that ~~that~~ said suit stand dismissed and that the Plaintiff recover of the Defendant the costs in this behalf expended–

WILLIAM L WILLIAMS)
       VS   )   Debt
WILLIAM S WHITE & JOHN NEVILL)   This day came the parties by their
                            attornies and thereupon came a Jury
of good and lawful men to wit Samuel Grant William Jackson James W Carney Hyram Lankfort Thomas Wyatte & William Parker John Pollard Dennis Dorherty Bingham Trice John Edwards Nathan Vick & Joshua Weakley who being duly elected tried and sworn the truth to speak upon the issue joined upon their oaths do say that they fine the issue in favour of the Plaintiff that the Defendants doth owe ti the Plaintiff the sum of Three hundred and Twelve dollars the Debt in the declaration mentioned and the furtyer sum of fourteen dollars and four cents damages sustained by reason of the detention of said Debt–

Therefore it is considered by the court that thePlaintiff Recover of the Defendants the sum of Three hundred and Twenty six dollars and four cents the Debt and damages so assessed by the Jury in form aforesaid to - gether with his costs by him about his suit in this behalf expended-

(p-385) GEORGE GRACE)
VS) Case
WILLIAM KILLEBREW) This day came the Parties by their attornies & the arbitrators to whom this cause was submitted returned their award & thereupon said defendant enters his motion to shew cause why said award should be set aside and thereupon this cause is transfered to the Circuit Court of Montgomery County for trial to be had thereon and it is further agreed by said parties that this cause stand for trial on the Saturday of the fist week of said Circuit Court-

A Bill of Sale from Cornelicu Crusman sheriff of Montgomery County to Parry W Humphreys for certain negroes therein mentioned and on motion ordered to be Recorded- and the said Crusman acknowledges in open court the execution of the said Bill of sale to be his act and deed for the purposes therein mentioned-

Ordered by the court that Philip Duke Barney Duff's heirs and Bright Herring be permitted to give in their list of Taxable property for the year 1823 and that the same be annexed to thelast years Tax list-

Ordered by the court that Sam'l Kynes be fined Two dollars and fifty cents for refusing to serve as a Juror and for rendering no excuse why he did not serve as aforesaid-

On motion ordered by the court that Sterling Neblett and Alexander M. Rogers be appointed commissioners to settle with Abner Harris Guardian of John Pritchard (Idiot) and make report to the next Term of this Court

A certificate of land warrant No. 11058 for Twenty three and a half acres ofland from Willson Sanderlin to Reuben Ross was produced in open court and the Execution thereof duly acknowledged by the said Wilson Saunderline to be his act and deed for the (p-386) purposes therein mentioned and on motion ordered to be certified for Registration

JOHN BRODIE)
VS) Motion on Prison bond
PATRICK H DARBY &) This day came said parties by their attornies
WILLOBY WILLIAMS) and thereupon It appearing to this court here that heretofore to wit from the January Term 1823 of Montgomery County Court a Capias satisfacendum Issued to the sheriff of Davidson County at the suit of said Plaintiff against said defendant Patrick H. Darby on a judgment of said county court of Montgomery in favor of said plaintiff for the sum of three hundred and fifty two debt & Eight dollars nine cents cos a which said Capias ad satisfacundum came to the hand of said sheriff of Davidson by virtue of which the said sheriff arrested said defendant Patrick Patrick H Darby who thereupon to wit on the 20th day of March 1823 entered into bond to said sheriff of Davidson with said other Defendant Willoby Williams his security in the pebal sum of seven hundred and twenty dollars & Eighteen cents conditioned to well & truly keep & confine himself within the prison bounds

of ~~plaintiff will and other defendant~~ by the Justices of the County Court
of said County and should in no wise depart ~~thereupon~~ therefrom untill
he should have satisfied said sum of $352.00 and costs or be discharged
by the plaintiff or by due course of law which bond was duly assigned
by said sheriff to said plaintiff as required by law and it further appearing to this court that Defendant Darby in violation of his said bond did
bredk said bond without having paie said Debt & cost or being ~~discharged~~
discharged by due course of law of by said plaintiff and it further
appearing to this court that due notice as required by law of this motion
was given said defendents-

It is therefore considered by this court that said plaintiff recover
against said defendant the said sum of $352.00 Debt aforesaid with interest
thereon from the 22nd day of Jany. 1823 untill paid as also Eight dollars
& nine cents former costs as also his costs of this motion &c

Court adjourned untill Tomorrow 9 O'clock- (p-387)

Thos. W. Atkinson
Sterling Neblett
Chas. Bailey

The Worshipful court of Montgomery County have met according to adjourn-
ment-

Present
A.M. Rogers   )
S. Neblett   } Justices
T.W. Atkinson)

ELI LOCKERT   )
VS   ) Sci Fa
THE HEIRS AT*   ) This day came into court the plaintiff by his attorney
LAW OF PHILIP   ) and thereupon the defendants being solemnly called
JOHNSON DECD   ) ~~to~~ came not but made default-

It is therefore considered by the court here that the plaintiff recover of
the defendants Bernard Reynolds & Lucy his wife Milly Stephens Jonathan
Johnson William Nelson & Mary his wife James Shackleford & Sally his
wife Henry Hodges & his wife Nancy Robert Goodloe and his wife Agnes
Robert G. Johnson John Johnson Whitfield Killebrew & his Fanny & George
Killebrew who defends by his guardian William Killebrew the sum of one
thousand & ninety three dollars & thirty three cents debt and also the
sum of thirty two dollars and seventy nine and three fourth cents damages
for the detention of the same to be levied of the lands & tenements which
were of the said Philip Johnson deceased at the time of his death & which
have come to them of descent from D. Philip Johnson as his heirs at law
if so much there (p-388) can be found if not then the cases to be levied
of their own proper goods and chattles-

A Power of attorney from Frederick W. Huling to Daniel Johnson was produced
in open court and the Execution thereof duly acknowledged by the said
Frederick W. Huling to be his act and Deed for the purposes therein
mentioned and on motion ordered to be certified-

The commissioners appointed to lay off the dower of Mrs. Elizabeth Vance agree-
ableto the oetition of said Elizabeth Vance makd their Report to this
this Term and on motion ordered to be Certified for Registration-

The commissioners that were summoned to lay off the dower ofJoseph
Woodson & wife Sally agreeable to the petition of said Joseph & wife
make their Report to this Term & on motion ordered to be certified for
Registration -

A Bill of sake frôm Sam'l Craft to John H. Marable for Three negroes to
wit Celia a yellow woman Stephen & Silas was produced in open court and
the Execution thereof duly proven by the oaths of Russel B. Craft and
William Johnson two of the subscribing witnesses thereto and on motion
ordered to be Recorded-

A Deed of conveyance from Wyatte Epps to John B. Rice for one hundred and
Twenty one acres of land was produced in open court & the Execution
thereof duly proven by the oaths of William Corlew James Allen & Upton
Orgain the subscribing witnesses thereto and on motion ordered to be
certified for Registration -

(p-389) A Deed of conveyance from William A. Cook to Lewis W. Cook for
the one half of Lott No. 38 was produced in open court and the Execution
thereof suly proven by the oaths of William B. Turly and Frederick W.
Huling the subscribing witnesses thereto and on motion ordered to be certified for Registration-

A Bill of sale from Gabriel Loving and Sally Loving to John Roach for
negro woman Mary was produced in open court and the Execution thereof
duly proven by the oath of Abner Gupton one of the subscribing witnesses
thereto and on motion ordered to be Certified-

William S. White and Richard B. Blount commissioners appointed at the
last Term of this court to sell for the purpose of a division the Estate
of Abner V. Hampton decd. make their report to this Term and on motion
ordered to be Recorded-

A Deed of conveyance from Cornelisu Crusman Sheriff of Montgomery
County to Margaret Vance Morgan B. Vance William Vance & Elizabeth Vance
heirs at law of Sam'l V nce Decd. was produced in open court and the
execution thereof duly acknowledged by the said Cornelius Crusman to be
his act and Deed for the purposes therein mentioned and on motion ordered
to be certified for Registration for Town Lotts in the new addition to
the Town of Clarksville Nos. 52-53-&54-

On motion ordered by the court that Joel Grizzard Administrator of Sam'l
Hawkins Decd. be permitted to sell a negro Boy Jacob on a credit of
nine months by giving notice agreeable to law of time and place-

(p-390) MARTIN THOMAS   )
                VS   ) Sci Fa
        THE HEIRS AT LAW OF PHILIP JOHNSON DECD)

This day came into court the plaintiff by his attorney and thereupon the defendants being solemnly called came not but made default-

Therefore it is considered by the court that the Pla ntiff recover of the Defendants William Nelson and his wife Mary Bernard Reynolds and his wife Lucy Milly Stephens Jamex Shackleford and his wife Sally Henry Hodges and his wife Nancy Robert Goodlow and his wife Agnes Jonathan Johnson Robert G. Johnson John Johnson Whitfield Killebrew & his wife Fanny George W. Killebrew the sum of one hundred andTwenty nine dollars & ten cents, Debt & damages and also the further sum of Twenty one dollars and ninety four cents the costs on the Sciere facias and the costs in this behalf expended to be levied of the lands and Tenements whichwere of Philip Johnson deceased at the time of his death and which have come to them by descent from said Philip Johnson as his heirs at law if so much there can be found if not then the costs to be levied ot their own proper goods and chattles-

ELI LOCKERT VS THE HEIRS AT LAW OF PHILIP JOHNSON DECD	Sci Fa This day came into court the plff, by his attorney

and thereupon the Defendants being solemnly called came not but made default Therefore it is considered by the court that the Plaintiff recover of the Defendants william Nelson and his wife Mary Bernard Reynolds and his wife Lucy Milly Stephens James Shackleford and his wife Sally Henry Hodges & his wife (p-391) Nancy Robert Goodlow and his wife Agnes Jonathan Johnson Robert G. Johnson John Johnson Whitfield Killebrew and his wife Fanny and George W. Killebrew the sum of one hundred and Eighteen dollars and sixteen cents Debt and the further sum of Five dollars and Twenty cents damages sustained by reason of the detention of said Debt and the costs in this behalf expended to be levied of the Goods and Tenements which were of Philip Johnson decd. at the time of his death and which come to them by descent from the said Philip Johnson as his heirs at law if so much there can be found if not then the costs to be levied their own proper goods and chattles-

JOHN ALLENSWORTH & VS JAMES MILLER THE HEIRS AT LAW OF PHILIP JOHNSON DECD	This day came into court the Plaintiff by their attorney and thereupon the Defendants being solemnly called came not but made default-

Therefore it is considered by the court that the Plaintiffs recover of the Defendants William Nelson and his wife Mary Bernard Reynolds and wife Lucy Milly Stephens James Shackleford and his wife Sally Henry Hodges and his wife Nancy Robert Goodlow and his wife Agnes Jonathan Johnson Robert G. Johnson John Johnson Whitfield Killebrew and his wife Fanny & George W. Killebrew the sum of one hundred and sixty six dollars and seventy seven cents Debt and the further sum of seven dollars and fifty cents damages sustained by reason of the detention of said debt besides the costs in this behalf expended to be levied of the land and Tenements which were (p-392) of Philip Johnson deceased at the time of his death and which came to them by decent from the said Philip Johnson as his heirs at law if so much therecan be found if not then the costs to be levied of their own goods and chattles-

Solomon HUNT)
VS) Covenant Broken
WILLIAM HUNT) This day came the party by his attorney and says
he will no further prosecute his said suit but
dismisses the samde-

Therefore it is considered by the court that said suit stand dismissed
and that the Defendant be hence fully discharged and recover of the Plaintiff the costs in this behalf expended-

THOMAS SMITH)
VS) Soi fa
ELI LOCKERT) This day came the Plaintiff by his attorney and says
he will no further prosecute his said Sciere facias
but dismisses the same whereupon the Defendant came and assumes the one
half of the costs-

Therefore it is considered by the court (p-393) that said Sciere
Facias be dismissed and that the Defendant be hence discharged and recover
of the Plaintiff the one half of the costs in this behalf expended-

HENRY W. SMITH)
VS) Case
JOHN WILLIAMS) This day came the Plaintiff by his attorney and
says he will no further prosecute his said suit
but dismisses the same

Therefore it is considered by the court that said suit be dismissed
and that the Defendant go hence without day and recover of the Plaintiff
the costs in this behalf expended-

ROBERT G JOHNSON ADMR.)
VS)
CHARLES BAILEY &) Debt
HENRY SMALL) This day came into court Charles Bailey
) and Henry Small and acknowledges themselves
indebted to the Plaintiff in the sum of
one hundred and seventy six dollars and Eighty six cents including Interest
to the third Monday in October next-

Therefore it is considered by the court that the said Plaintiff recover of the Defendants the aforesaid sum of one hundred and seventy
six dollars and Eighty two cents the Debt and damages so confessed as
aforesaid and the costs in this behalf expended - and the Plaintiff stays
Execution untill October court next-

STERLING NEBLETT ADMR)
VS) Debt
JOHN P EPPS) This day came into court John P Epps and
acknowledges bound and indebted to Sterling
Neblett admr in the sum of one hundred and six dollars (p-394)
and five cents Debt-

Therefore it is considered by the court that the said Sterling Neblett
Administrator as aforesaid recover of the Defendant the sum of one hundred
and six dollars and five cents so confessed as aforesaid, and the costs
in this behalf expended and the Plff. stays execution 3 months-

WILLIAM WHITEHEAD)
VS) Trespass
DAVID DAVIS?) This day came the Defendants by their attorney
HEZEKIAH DAVIS &) and the Plaintiff William Whitehead being solemnly
JOHN DAVIS) called to come into court and prosecute his
said suit failed so to do - It is therefore
considered by the court that the Defendants go hence without day and recover
of the Plaintiff the costs in this behalf expended-

JAMES BLANKS ASSEE)
VS) Debt
MOSES COLLIER) This day came the parties by their attornies
and thereupon (p-395) this cause is con-
tinued by consent of Parties & leave given to take the deposition of Ingram
Blanks by giving Ten days notice thereof-

CHARLES P ROBERTSON)
VS) Case
RALPH CUSHMAN) This day came the parties by their attornies
and by consent of parties this cause is
Transferred to the Circuit Court for Trial to be had thereon-

REDDING LAWRANCE)
VS) Case
SAM'L B. VANCE) This day came the parties by their attorneys and
thereupon this cause is refered to the award of
James Reasons and Edward S. Walton and their award to be final and the
Judgment of this court-

ROBERT CLARK)
VS) Appeal
Samuel C HAWKINS) This day came the parties by their attorneys and
the matters arrising on the face of said appeal
being fully heard and understood by the court and for reasons appearing
to the court it is considered by the court that said appeal and all the
matters arising thereon be dismissed that the Judgment below be in all
things appealed and that the appeller recover of the appellant the sum of
fourteen dollars debt the amount of the Judgment before the Justices of
the together with his costs about his suit in this behalf expended-

DORREL Y HARRIS & WIFE)
VS) Petition
HAYDON E WELLS GUARDIAN) This day came the Plaintiffs by their attorney
and being dissatisfied with the Judgment of
this cause preys an appeal to the Circuit Court of (p-396) Montgomery
County and having entered into Bond and security satisfactory to the Court
and the same is allowed-

NEEDHAM B FARRIER)
VS) Case
RICE COLEMAN)

This day came the Defendant Rice Coleman into open court and prays an appeal to the Circuit Court of Mongtomery County from the Judgment of this cause and having entered into Bond and security satisfactory to the court and the same is allowed-

JAMES R MCMEANS FOR THE BENEFIT OF)
D. ANDERSON)
          VS) Debt
SAMUEL CHAPMAN) This day came the parties by their
                           attornies and thereupon came a
Jury of good and lawful men to wit Sam'l Grant William Jackson James W. Carney Hyram Lankford Thimas Wyatte Willie Parker John Pollard Dennis Daugherty Bingham Trice John Edward Nathan Vick & Joshua Weakley who being duly elected tried and sworn the truth to speak upon the issue joined upon their oaths do say that they find the issue infavour of the Plaintiff that the Defendant doth owe to the Plaintiff the sum of one hundred dollars the Debt in the declaration mentioned and the further sum of Twenty four dollars damages sustained by reason of the Detention of said Debt-

Therefore it is considered by the court that the Plaintiff recover of the Defendant the sum of one hundred and Twenty four dollars the Debt and damages so assessed by the Jury in form aforesaid besides his costs about his suit in this behalf expended-

(p-397) Ordered by the court that the fine assessed by the court on the 21st Instant against Sam'l Lynes for contempt shown to this court be set aside and that the said Lynes pay the cost that has accrued &c-

JOHN BRODIE)
    VS)
P. H. DARBY &) This day came the Defendants by their attorneys
WILLOBY WILLIAMS) and prays an appeal to the Circuit Court of Mont-
                  gomery County in the nature of a Writ of Error
from the Judgt. of this cause and thereupon the Defendants by attorney entered into Bond and security satisfactory to the court and the same is allowed-

Court adjourned untill Tomorrow morning 9 O'clock 23rd Jany. 1824
                          Sterling Neblett
                          A.M. Rogers
                          Stephen Cooke

The Worshipful court of Montgomery County have met according to adjournment January 24th 1824 - Present
                          A.M. Rogers   )
                          Sterling Neblett) Esquires
                          Thomas W. Atkinson)Justices

On motion ordered by the court that Joseph Shamwell be appointed Guardian to John Olvin & Thomas Blakeney heirs of Harriet Blakney and the said Joseph Shamwell came into court and entered into Bond and security and qualified agreeable to law-

On motion ordered by the court that Alexander M. Rogers Charles Bailey Joshua P Vaughn and Thomas Smith or any three of them be appointed commissioners to settle with Stephen Cooke and Mary Duff admrs of Barny Duff and report to next Court-

(p-398) WILLIAM PEAY)
        VS)
    STEPHEN PETTUS)   Motion

This day came into court William Peay by attorney and moved the court for a judgment against Stephen Pettus and thereupon it appearing to the court that on the 14th of January 1822 the said William Peay executed his joint obligation with sd. Pettus to Elizabeth Robbins administrator of the estate of John Robbins decd and it appearing to the court that William Peay was only security to sd Pettus and it appearing to the court that at the January term of the County court for Montgomery County 1824 sd Elizabeth obtained a judgment against the sd. William Peay on sd. obligation for the sum of two hundred & thirteen dollars debt & damages besides the further sum of eight dollars costs of suit-

It is therefore considered by the court that the sd. William Peay recover of the sd. Stephen Pettus the said sum of two hundred twenty one dollars debt besides his costs about this motion in this behalf expended

ANTHONY W VANLEER)
       VS)
PETER MARTIN ADMINISTRATOR OF THE ESTATE OF JOSEPH HESLIP DECD)

This day came into court Anthony W. Vanleer by attorney and moved the court for a judgment against sd. Peter Martin administrator as aforesaid-

Whereupon it appearing to the satisfaction of the court that at the August term of the Circuit Court for the County of Montgomery 1823 on the 25th day of sd. month Joseph Woolfolk (p-399) obtained a judgment at law against sd. Anthony W. Vanleer for the sum of one hundred & thirty three dollars ninety seven cents debt and costs of suit and it further appearing to the court that sd. judgment was obtained on an obligation in which sd. Anthony W. Vanleer was security for sd. Haslip in his lifetime It is therefore considered by the court that the plaintiff Anthony W. Vanleer recover of the sd. Peter Martin administrator of the estate of Joseph Heslip Decd. sd. sum of one hundred & fifty eight dollars Debt costs & damages aforesaid to be levied of the goods & chattles which were of the sd. Joseph in his lifetime and which have come to the hands of said administrator to be administered if so much thereof can be found if not then the costs to be levied of the proper goods & chattles lands & tenements of sd. Peter Martin -

SALLY STALY)
     VS)
ANDREW SMITH)   Case

This day came into court the Plaintiff by attorney & moved the court for an appeal to the Circuit Court in the case & the same is allowed-

Elizabeth Robbins)
     vs   )   This day came William Peay one of the Defendants in
Thomas Watson,)   this case and prays an appeal to the Circuit Court
Wm. Peay &)   of Montgomery County in the nature of a writ of
Stephen Pettus)   Error and having entered into Bond and Security
                          satisfactory to the Court and agreeable to law, the
same is allowed.

(P400)

Robert W. Clark)
     vs   )   For reasons appearing to this Court from the
Samuel C. Hawkins)   affidavit of said Defendant It is considered
                          by this Court that the Judgment of this Court of
his Town dismissing the appeal in this cause & entered in favor of said
Plaintiff against said defendant be set aside that the Plaintiffs motion to
dismiss the same be overruled and that this cause be continued & stand
for trial next Court.

Wallace L. Williams Assnee)
     vs   )   This day came the parties by their
William S. White & John Haville)   Attornies and it appearing to the
                                     Court that the Judgment entered in
his cause at a previous day of the term of this Court suonerucus because
here are demurrers in the Pleadings in this cause yet undetermined. It is
considered the same be anullity and thereupon all and singular the matters
of law arrising on plaintiffs demurrer to Defendants plea being argued &
by the Court understood Because it seems to the Court that that said pleas
are insufficient in law, it is considered by the Court that said demurrer
be sustained, and that the Plaintiff recover against said defendants the
sum of three hundred & twelve dollars the debt in the declaration mentioned
as also the further sum of fourteen dollars & four cents damages by the
Jury in this cause assessed & his costs about his suit in this behalf
expended &c. Whereupon the defendants being dissatisfied with the
Judgment of the Court rendered in this cause pray an appeal in the nature
of a writ of Error & having given bond &c the same is allowed to the
Circuit Court

(P401)

On motion ordered by the Court that James Brame be permitted to keep
a house of Intertainment at his dwelling house in Montgomery County for
the Twelve months immediately preceedings this time, whereupon the said
Jas. Brame came into Court and entered into Bond and security satisfactory
to the Court and qualified agreeable to law.

On motion ordered by the Court that Alexander M. Rogers and Sterling
Hoblett, Charles Bailey and Stephen Cock or any two of them be appointed
commissioners to settle with Elias F. Pope Guardian for Drew Smith and make
report to this Court during this term.

The Commissioners appointed at this Term to settle with Elias F. Pope
Guardian of Drew Smith make their report to this Court and on motion
ordered to be Recorded.

On motion ordered by the Court that the following hands work under John
Hedlock overseer of the road from Peter Holts ferry to Peter P. Roberts's
To wit Peter P. Roberts and hands John James John Hail, William Hail, &

James Howel.

Francis Baker & Joseph Howel Administrators of the Estate of Stephen G. Jones returned into Court an Inventory of the Estate of said Decd and on motion ordered to be Recorded.

On motion ordered by the Court that John Smith be appointed Overseer of the Road from Jerry Browns to Thomas Smith's and that the said work under him that worked under Jacob Walker former overseer.

On motion ordered by the Court that Stephen Cook and Bright Herring be appointed commissioners to settle with Sarah Bird as Guardian (P402) of John Bird, also to make a division between her and her ward of the property and make report to the next Term of this Court.

This day came into Court Francis Baker the Executor of Nancy Radford and produced to the Court the last will & Testament of Nancy Radford Decd. which was proven by the oaths of Gladwell Killebrew & Elizabeth Davis the subscribing witnesses thereto and on motion ordered to be Recorded- And the said Francis Baker Executor as aforesaid came into Court and entered into Bond and security satisfactory to the Court and qualified agreeable to law.

An Indenture between George C. Morris and David Laird for an apprentice to the Tailoring business for his son George C. Morris, was produced in open court, and the Execution thereof duly proven by the oaths of Philander McB. Priestly and Robert Philips the subscribing witnesses thereto and on motion ordered to be Recorded.

On motion ordered by the Court that John Rock be permitted to keep a ferry across Cumberland River at Vicks old ferry and the said John came into Court and entered into Bond and security satisfactory to the Court, and the same is allowed.

On motion ordered by the Court that Richard Bagwell be permitted to keep a ferry across Red River at its mouth and the said Richard entered into Bond and security as ferryman aforesaid, satisfactory to the Court and the same is allowed.

On motion ordered by the Court that John Cawlishaw be permitted to keep ferry across   (P403)   Cumberland River opposite the Town of Clarksville and the said John Cawlishaw came into Court and entered into Bond and security satisfactory to the Court, and the same is allowed.

Ross Jones administrator of the Estate of Joseph Gaus, returns into Court the account of Sales of said deceased and on motion ordered to be Recorded.

Francis Baker & Joseph Howel Administrators of the Estate of Stephen G. Jones Decd. returns into Court the account of Sales of said deceased, and on motion ordered to be Recorded.

A Bill of Sale from Hugh Campbell and his wife Elizabeth Campbell to Stephen Contrell for negro Girl Emaline was produced in open Court and (p-404) On motion ~~of~~ ordered by the court that David McMannus be appointed Guardian to Tobias Blackney whereupon the said David came into court and entered into Bond and security-satisfactory to the court ~~the~~ and qualified accordingly-

This day came into Court Isaac Dennison who had been appointed entry Taker for Montgomery County and entered into Bond and security with James Elder Joel C. Rice and Cave Johnson which was approved of by the court and took the oath prescribed by law as Entry taken aforesaid and the same is ordered to be Recorded-

On motion ordered by the court that John H. Poston be allowed the sum of Twenty dollars for his services as commissioner settling with the county Trustees and that the County Trustee pay the same out of any monies in his hands not otherwise appropriated-

the Execution thereof duly proven by the oath of Isaac Dennison a subscribing witnesses thereto and on motion ordered to be recorded-

An Indenture between Sterling Neblett Esqr and James N. Smith for an
orphan child Mary Cato was this day signed by the said parties for the
purposes therein mentioned and it is ordered that the same be recorded-

On motion ordered by the court that Robert Hester Joseph Shamwell and Ed.
Hancock be appointed commissioners to lay off the one years provisions for
the widow of Stephen G. Jones Decd. at this Term-

The commissioners appointed at this Term to lay off one years provision
for the widow of Stephen G. Jones Decd. make their report and on motion
ordered to be Recorded-

On motion ordered by the court that James Trotter be appointed overseer
of the Road in place of James Brame and that the same hands work ~~Andress~~
under him that worked under the said James Brame-

The commissioners appointed at the last Term of this court to settle
with Henry Small late a Trustee of this County make their report to this
Term and on motion ordered to be Recorded-

On motion ordered by the court that John Williford be permitted to keep a
house of Entertainment at his dwelling house in this county and the said
John Williford came into court and entered into Bond and security satis-
facotyr to (p-405) the court and qualified agreeable to law-

The administrators of the Estate of George S. Mallory Decd. returns into
court the accounty of sales of said Estate and on motion ordered to be Re-
corded-

On motion ordered by the court that Thos Carraway Stephen Mallory & Joseph
Mallory be appointed the commissioners to lay off one years provisions
for Polly Gee out of the Estate of her deceased Husband Joseph Gee and
make report to the next Term of this court-

On motion ordered by the court that Washington lee be appointed overseer
of the road from Clarksville by James Hamiltons old ferry leading on so
as to intersect the Hopkinsville road at James Trice's and that John P
Poston's hands Mrs. Spead's hands Abram Brantley's hands work on said road
under said Washington lee-

Ordered by the court that A. M. Rogers & Thomas W. Atkinason be appointed
a committee to take the privy examination of Mrs. Sidney Searcy wife of
Robert Searcy relative to her signing a Deed of Conveyance from Robert
Searcy to Moses and John Steele for Two hundred and Twenty five acres of
land on the South side of Cumberland River opposite the Town of Clarksville
and make report to the next Term of this Court-

On motion ordered by the court that Charles ~~Dixon~~ Bailey be permitted to
keep a house of Entertainment at his dwelling house in this County and the
said Bailey came into Court and entered into Bond and security and
qualified accordingly-

(p-406) On motion ordered by the court that Cave Johnson be allowed the sum of fifty dollars for his ex-officio services for the year immediately proceeding this time and that the County Trustee pay the same out of any monies in his hands not otherwise appropriated-

STATE)
VS)
MAJOR BARBEE, JOSEPH BARBEE & ELISHA WILLIS)   Upon motion and it appearing to the court that
Major Barbee had been charged as the Father of a Bastard child begotten upon the Body of Polly Chumney and had been ordered at the April Term 1820 of the County Court of Montgomery to pay annually for the maintenance of the same the sum of Twelve dollars and it further appearing to the court that said child was yet living and that the said Major Barbee had neglected to comply with the order of said court relative thereto - It is therefore ordered by the court that the said Major Barbee and also against Joseph Barbee and Elisha Willis his securities for the faithful performance of the same and that they pay the costs in this behalf expended-

A deed of conveyance from Hugh McClure to James Elder for Two hundred and sixty six acres of land was produced in open court and the Execution thereof duly acknowledged by the said Hugh McClure to be his act and Deed for the purposes therein mentioned and on motion ordered be to be certified for Registration-

(p-407)   A Deed of conveyance from James Elder to Hugh McClure for one hundred and seventy two acres of land was produced in open court and the execution thereof duly acknowledged by the said James Elder to be his act and deed for the purposes therein mentioned and on motion ordered to be certified for Registration -

A Deed of conveyance from Hugh McClure to James Elder for one hundred and forty acres of land was produced in open court and the execution thereof duly acknowledged by the said James Elder to be his act and deed for the purposes therein mentioned and on motion ordered to be certified for Registration -

A Deed of conveyance from Hugh McClure to James Elder for one hundred and forty acres of land was produced in open court and the execution thereof acknowledged by the said Hugh McClure to be his act and deed for the purposes therein mentioned and on motion ordered to be certified for Registration -

A Deed of conveyance from Hugh McClure to James Elder for two lots in the town of Clarksville number thirty three and thirty four was produced in open court and the Execution thereof duly acknowledged by the said Hugh McClure to be his act and deed for the purposes therein mentioned and on motion ordered be certified for Registration-

A Deed of conveyance from James Elder to Hugh McClure for lott number nineteen in the town of Clarksville was produced in open court and the execution thereof duly acknowledged by the said James Elder to be his act and deed for the purposes therein mentioned and on motion ordered to br certified for Registration-

(p-408)   A Deed of conveyance from Cornelius Crusman to John H Poston for Town Lotts in the Town of Clarksville Nos. 102 & 104 was produced in open court and the Execution thereof duly acknowledged by the said Cornelius Crusman to be his act and Deed for the purposes therein mentioned and on motion ordered to be Certified for Registration -

A Deed of conveyance from Jacob H. Fort to John H. Poston for //// Town Lotts in the town of Clarksville Nos. 62 & 64 was produced in open court and the Execution thereof duly proven by the oaths of Sam'l Lynes and G.W. Garth the subscribing witnesses thereto and on motion ordered to be certified for //// Registration-

A Deed of conveyance from Hugh McClure to James Elder for Lotts No.s. 33 & 34 in the Town of Clarksville was produced in open court and the Execution thereof duly acknowledged by the said Hugh McClure to be his act and Deed for the purposes therein mentioned and on motion ordered to be certified for Registration-

A Deed of Conveyance from James Elder to Hugh McClure for Lotts in the Town of Clarksville Nos. 52 & 54 was produced in open court and the Execution thereof duly acknowledged by the said James Elder to be his act and Deed for the purposes therein mentioned and on motion ordered to be certified for ////// Registration-

A Deed of conv yance from Valentine Meriwether to Henry W Meriwether for the one half of 280 acres of land was produced in open court and the Execution thereof duly acknowledged by the said Valentine Meriwether to be his act and Deed for the purposes therein mentioned & on motion ordered to be certified for Registration-

(p-409)   A Deed of Conveyance from Jesse Blackfan William Sheppard & Egbert H Sheppard by their attorney in fact Frederick W Huling to Hugh McClure for Eighty five acres of land was produced in open court and the Execution thereof duly acknowledged by the said Frederick W. Huling as attorney aforesaid to be his act and deed for the purposes therein mentioned and on motion ordered to be certified for Registration-

A Deed of conveyance from Jessee Blackfan William Sheppard & Egbert H. Sheppard by their attorney in fact Frederick W. Huling to Sheppard / Trice for Eighty acres of land was produced in open court and the Execution thereof duly acknowledged by the said Fred W. Huling attorney as aforesaid to be his act and Deed for the purposes therein mentioned and on motion ordered to be certified for Registration-

A Deed of conveyance from John Gibson of Scott County Kentucky to William Gibson of //////// Montgomery County for two hundred and thirteen acres of land was produced in open court and the Execution thereof duly proven by the oaths of John B Rice & Cornelius Crusman the subscribing witnesses thereto and on motion ordered to be certified for Registration-

A Deed of Conveyance from William L Williams to Jam s Barret and Cave Johnson for one hundred and ninety nine acres of land was produced in open court and the execution thereof duly acknowledged by the said William L Williams to be his act and Deed for the purposes therein mentioned and on motion ordered to be certified for Registration-

A Deed of conveyance from //y/y/ Payton R Buckley & his wife Zebeah Buckley John Mallory (p-410) and Lucy Mallory to Hugh McClure for two /X hundred and Eighty acres of land was produced in open courtand the Execution thereof duly acknowledged by Payton R Buckley and John Mallory two of the Grantors in said Deed and the Execution of said Deed as to Lucy Mallory one of said Grantors was proven by the oaths of Thomas W Atkinson and John Long subscribing witnesses thereto and it is //p// ordered by the court that Sterling Neblett and Stephen Cock Esquires Justices of this court to take the **privy** examination of Zebeah Buckley relative to the execution of said deed and she having been duly examined by the said Sterling Neblett and Stephen Cock members of this court seperate and apart from her Husband and upon such privy examination she having acknowledged that she executed the same freely and voluntarily and without the constraint and compulsion of her husband it is therefore ordered by the court that said Deed be certified for Registration—

RICHARD C GREGORY ⎫   Debt
     VS   ⎬
THE ADMINISTRATRIX OF SAM'L CREATH DECD⎭   This day came into court Frederick W. Huling to whom by consent of said parties and by the order of the County Court of Montgomery of this Term /of/ to settle all matters in litigation between said parties in this suit exhibits his award as follows to wit— That the Plaintiff recover of said Defendants administratrix the sum of Two hundred and seventy five dollars with Interest thereon from the 6th of September 1821 untill paid as also the sum of Twenty two dollars and Twenty six cents costs of former suit and /other/ of this /cost/ suit—

    Therefore it is considered by the court (p-411) that the Plaintiff recover of the Administratrix of Sam'l Creath deceased the sum of Three hundred and thirty seven dollars and ninety seven cents the amt of Debt and damages together with the costs on former suit as also the Record upon which this suit was founded & the costs in this behalf expended—

WILLIAM L WILLIAMS   ⎫
     VS   ⎬   Debt
WILLIAM S WHITE & JOHN NEVELL⎭   This day came into court Hugh F Bell by his attorney William A Cook and prays an appeal from the Judgment of this cause to Circuit Court of Montgomery County in the nature of a writ of Error and having entered into Bond and security satisfactory to the court the same is allowed—

On motion ordered by the court that C.H.P.Marr Peter N. Marr & George W.L Marr be permitted to give in their list of Taxable property for the year 1823 and that the same be annexed to the last years Tax list—

On motion ordered by the court that Sterling Neblett Stephen Cock & Isaac Dennison or any two of them be appointed Commissioners to settle with Alexander M Rogers Guardian of Elizabeth Waller and make return to the next Term of this court—

On motion ordered by the court that William Haynes be appointed overseer of the road leading from Clarksville to the forks of the road beyond John Kezee's in the place of John Cawlishaw and that the same hands work under him that worked under the said Cawlishaw—

On motion ordered by the court that the following hands that worked on the Road leading by Mrs. Nelsons be taken off of said Road and put on the Road from H.W.Merriwether's ferry to Thomas Cherry's old place on the Russelville (p-412) road- To wit Elisha R. Oldham & hands John Chipman Chapman Osman Thomas Dunbar's hands Judy Sim's hands William Hust and Richard Hust to work under Henry W Meriwether overseer of said Road-

The court proceeded to the appointment of jurors to attend the next County Court at April Term & the following jurors were appointed viz Randolph Ramey and Benjamin Orgain Senr. Jacob Foust Philip Crotzer Abraham Brantly Shepherd Trice Mark Booth Samuel Ryburn James Stuart James Brown Stephen W Carney Samuel Daniel Ludlowick Brodie John Bowery William Blair Elisha Willis John Smith Benjamin W Trotter John Wyatt John Russell Macajah Baggot Andrew Haile Samuel Edmondson Needham Whitfield Lee Trice and Thomas Orgain & Joseph J Harris constables were appointed to attend the next County Court-

On motion ordered by the court that the County Trustee receive the one half of the appraised value of two strays a Bay filly taken up by William O Robbins 10th September 1822 appraised to $22.50 and a sorrel Horse taken up by Hugh Blackney 12th Septr. 1822 appraised to $35.00 and that said Robbins and Blackney be subject to the payment of only the one half of said appraisment-

On motion ordered by the court that Jonathan Johnson be entitled to Twenty four dollars and seventy five cents the costs of a suit in the Circuit Court Madison against Philip Johnson who was only the security for said Philip and that the Clerk of the County Court of pleas and quarter sessions add to the costs in the (p-413) Execution Jonathan Johnson against the Heirs at law of said Philip Johnson Decd. for the aforesaid sum of Twenty four dollars and seventy five cents-

Court adjourned untill monday morning 9 O'clock-
A.M. Rogers
Thos. Smith
Isaac Dennison

The Worshipful court of Montgomery County have met agreeable to adjournment-

Present A.M. Rogers)
Thos. Smith) Esquires
Isaac Dennison) Justices

On motion ordered by the court that A. M. Rogers & Sterling Neblett Esqrs. be appointed commissioners to settle with Haydon E. Wells Guardian of Sam'l Peoples and make report to the next Term of this court-

On motion ordered by the court that Cornelisu Crusman be allowed the sum of fifty dollars for his Exofficio services for the year 1823 and that the county Trustee pay the same out of any monies in his hands not otherwise appropriated-

NOBLE OSBURN)
     VS   )   Debt
MATHEW D SIMMONS)   This day came into court the Defendant and
                              prays an appeal to the Circuit Court of Montgomery
County and having entered into Bond and security satisfactory to the
court and the same is allowed-

The executors of Peter H. Cole Decd. returns into court and Inventory of
the Estate of //// said Estate and on motion ordered to be Recorded-

(p-414) John Breathet)
         VS   )
THE EXIS OF SAM'L VANCE DECD)   This day came the parties by their attornies
                             and by consent of parties leave is given
to both parties to take ////// depositions by giving ten days notice
within the state and the Logan County Dy. and twenty days notice if taken
out of the state-

ROBERT G JOHNSON & A V HAMPTON)
         VS   )   Debt
WHITFIELD KILLEBREW & WM. KILLEBREW)   This day came into court the
                             Plaintiffs by their attorneys
and says that he will no further prosecute his their said suit but dismisses the same and the Defendants came into court in proper person and
assumes the costs inthis behalf expended-
    Therefore it is considered by the court that said suit stand dis-
missed and that the Plaintiff recover of the Defendants the costs in
this behalf Expended-
    On motion ordered by the court that the order made on saturday taking
hands from William Nelson's Road and putting them on Meriwether Road be
rescinded and that said road stand as they are now-

Court adjourned untill court in course-

                        A M. Rogers
                        Thos. Smith
                        Francis Baker

                    END

www.ingramcontent.com/pod-product-compliance
Lightning Source LLC
Chambersburg PA
CBHW082352270326
41935CB00013B/1601